History
of
Marshall County
West Virginia

Scott Powell

HERITAGE BOOKS
2015

HERITAGE BOOKS
AN IMPRINT OF HERITAGE BOOKS, INC.

Books, CDs, and more—Worldwide

For our listing of thousands of titles see our website
at
www.HeritageBooks.com

A Facsimile Reprint
Published 2015 by
HERITAGE BOOKS, INC.
Publishing Division
5810 Ruatan Street
Berwyn Heights, Md. 20740

Originally published 1925

— Publisher's Notice —
In reprints such as this, it is often not possible to remove blemishes from the original. We feel the contents of this book warrant its reissue despite these blemishes and hope you will agree and read it with pleasure.

International Standard Book Numbers
Paperbound: 978-0-7884-0920-2
Clothbound: 978-0-7884-6259-7

SCOTT POWELL.

AUTHORITIES CONSULTED

Early History and Indian Wars in Northwestern Virginia—De Hass.

Chronicals of Border Warfare—Withers.

Our Western Border—McKnight.

Annals of the West—Albaugh.

Records of Marshall County Court.

Roster of Soldiers of the Civil War—T. S. Bonar.

Report of Adjutant General of West Virginia.

War Work of Marshall County (World War)—R. J. Smith.

Miscellaneous Papers.

HISTORY OF MARSHALL COUNTY, W. VA.

The author of this book commenced work on it when he was in his seventy-first year of age and labored under many difficulties to complete it. It was not one of his projects but that of Walter R. A. Morris, a very bright, energetic young lawyer. He came to him in the summer of 1918 and requested him to write a history of Marshall County. Mr. Morris stated that he thought it one of the needs of the people and would be of educational value. He would render aid in preparing the work; attend to publishing the book when prepared for the printer, and put it on the market when ready and see that it was properly distributed as the author was unwilling to undertake such arduous labors as would be required for that part of the work. With the assurance of Mr. Morris he commenced work immediately. And having some material suitable for the work he commenced within ten days from their conversation on the first pages of this history. He worked diligently and by the end of the year, 1918, had much of the material gathered and many sheets of typewritten copy lay on his desk.

During the prevalence of Spanish Influenza, Mr. Morris was one of its victims. The author thought for a time to abandon the work, but concluded to go on with it; complete his part as contemplated.

The work was chiefly done in evenings after a day's regular work had been completed, till the advance of the season and short days compelled him to give up the work other than gather material. His wife proposed a plan which would permit him to continue the work. She prepared a stand for the typewriter which could be placed under a light near the winter fire where he could work with all comfort and convenience of warm weather, till the return of spring permitted him to return to his former place of work.

Day by day the work went on through winter and spring till the Fourth of July, 1919, the last pages of the history were written. Since that date some matter has been added and in 1923, the history was brought up-to-date, making it cover the history of Marshall County from the first settlement in it till the close of 1923.

The sheets were temporarily bound in 1920 and exhibited at a "Homecoming" at which some citizens examined it and concluded it would interest people and ought to be published and put on the market that people might have opportunity to add it to their home libraries.

The matter was taken up by different organizations and

since October, 1920, there has been much talk of having it published.

No less than five times in the past four years have representatives of different organizations assured the author that they were going to have the history published but the matter of publishing it remained a matter of uncertainty, till the early days of autumn of 1924, when Rev. J. M. Rine, an ex-county superintendent of schools and a veteran teacher of the county, took up the matter and decided to fill the place left vacant by the death of Walter Morris and soon arranged to have the work published and put on the market and to him and his unbounded energy rests the credit of having it published after four years of disappointments to the writer.

HISTORY OF MARSHALL COUNTY, W. VA.

EARLY SETTLEMENT ON BIG WHEELING CREEK, THE FLATS OF GRAVE CREEK AND AT McMECHEN

THE first settlement in what is now Marshall County, West Virginia, was made in the District of West Augusta, Virginia. The country was then a wilderness covered with a growth of heavy timber which is only found where there is a soil of great fertility and a bountiful rainfall. The great abundance of game of all kinds common to this latitude in North America, especially deer and the common black bear, made it a paradise for hunters and also very attractive to those in search of homes for themselves and families, who looked with bright hopes of peace and plenty after the forest had been fallen and cleared away and in its place fields of golden grain, green pastures and beautiful meadows.

The first white man known to have trod upon the virgin soil of this county was Christopher Gist, then in the employ of the Ohio Company, who crossed the Allegheny Mountains in autumn of 1751 to examine land lying between the Great Kanawha and Monongahela rivers. The company had received a grant of five hundred thousand acres of land from the king of Great Britain conditioned upon the company making settlement and certain improvements upon the land and locating one hundred families upon its grant within seven years.

The company made a settlement west of the mountains near the Youghiogheny river in autumn of 1753, and started work early in 1754 to erect a fort at the forks of the Ohio, the key to the West. The fort was captured by the French in April while it was not more than half completed. The settlement made the previous autumn by eleven families and known as the Gist Settlement, was broken up by the French on the fifth of July, the day after the surrender of Fort Necessity.

The capture of the half finished fort was the beginning of the war known in America as the French and Indian War and in Europe as the Seven Years' War. The war did not close until 1763 and conditions had so changed that the Ohio Company did not make further efforts to make settlements and improvements as contemplated by the board of directors. The fact is that the early movements of that company led to the first conflicts of that long and bloody war for the possession of the Ohio Valley.

Ohio County was created by an act of the General Assembly of Virginia in 1776, and the boundaries as designated by the act, was a line commencing at the Ohio River at the mouth of Cross Creek and following the creek to its source and from thence to the top of a ridge or water shed dividing the waters flowing into the Monongahela River from the streams that flow into the Ohio. It followed this ridge to the southern boundary of the District of West Augusta and west on that line to the Ohio River and up it to the starting place, including an area of one thousand four hundred and thirty-two square miles. It was the first county in Virginia organized west of the Allegheny Mountains.

Much of the early history of Marshall County is so closely connected with and interwoven into that of Ohio County, of which it was formerly a part, that it is inseparable. There were few, if any, important events in the early settlement and Indian wars in this section of the Ohio Valley, in which the settlers did not participate. They were usually among the first into the field of action and among the last to leave it; and among the daring scouts and warriors known in border warfare, none were superior to those of what is now Marshall County.

The first settlement made within the limits of this county was made in what is now Sand Hill District, in connection with the settlement at the mouth of Wheeling Creek where the flourishing city of Wheeling now stands.

A writer of early history stated that an amusing incident led to the first settlement made in the county. Dr. De Hass in speaking of it, said, Trivial in its character but important in its result.

The account of the settlement, as given by some of the writers of early history, is that in 1769, Ebenezer Zane left his home on the South Branch of the Potomac, crossed the mountains and reached the Ohio River just above the mouth of Wheeling Creek. Being much pleased with the country he thought to settle there. On his return home he spoke of the country in such glowing terms that he induced a number of farmers of like spirit to join him in seeking homes on the banks of the Ohio River or near them. In the spring of 1770, Ebenezer Zane and his brothers, Silas, Jonathan and Andrew, with John Wetzel, Mercer, Bonnett and some others, whose names are not given, left their homes on the South Branch of the Potomac, crossed the mountains and arrived at Redstone on the east side of the Monongahela River where they thought it best to leave their families until homes were provided for them in the contemplated new settlement. They left Redstone and crossed over the water shed or divide and reached the headwaters of Little Wheeling Creek near Catfish Camp, now Washington, Pennsylvania, and followed the creek, knowing that it would flow into a larger stream. They rode through an unbroken forest and when a short distance from the forks of Wheeling Creek, the saddle girth of John Wetzel, who was some distance ahead of the others of the party, broke and he dismounted to repair it. While he was engaged in making the repairs Silas Zane came along and passed on down the creek. By the time Wetzel had the girth mended ready to mount his horse, the other members of the party arrived and all proceeded down the creek to the forks. Here Silas Zane commenced marking trees with his tomahawk. He took up what was called at that day a tomahawk claim of four hundred acres.

Ebenezer Zane and the other members of the party, except Wetzel, started down the creek towards the river. Wetzel thought that they had gone up the creek and decided that he would beat them to the river and get the choice of the river bottom land and went several miles before he discovered that he was going up the creek and not down it. It appears that he had noticed the water rippling over the stones in the bed of the creek and mistook the direction it was flowing. He found some fine bottom land above the forks of the creek and took up and improved a claim.

Mercer and Bonnett took up claims about eight miles above the forks of the creek near Wetzel and made improvements. It appears clear that none of the party except Ebenezer Zane and his brothers took up any river bottom land.

Several years later Jacob Earliwine and Frederick Sivert settled on ridges not far from Big Wheeling Creek, and Adam Grandstaff settled on a ridge some two or three miles from the forks of the creek. It is very difficult to give a correct account of this settlement and many other events in early settlement of this country as others, as there is such a disagreement of dates and particulars by different authors of pioneer history. It is not uncommon to find instances in which statements of events do not harmonize, or in other words, writers contradict their own statements.

All writers of early border history agree that John Wetzel was the first to take up a claim on Big Wheeling Creek above the forks and that the others named joined him as stated above.

SETTLEMENT AT THE FLATS OF GRAVE CREEK

THREE brothers, Joseph, Samuel and James Tomlinson, arrived at the Flats of Grave Creek about the year 1771 and took up land and made the first improvements where Moundsville now stands. Joseph Tomlinson, in a statement relative to the settlement at Grave Creek and Round Bottom, said that he and his brothers came to the Ohio River in search of homes for his father's family in March about the year 1771. They built a cabin about three hundred yards north of the mound and spent the summer on the Ohio River. The cabin they built was the first ever erected in the Flats of Grave Creek. They took up a fine tract of land at Grave Creek and also some valuable hill land. They also took a claim on the upper end of Round Bottom the same spring but lost it later.

After building the cabin, Joseph went down the river to examine the country. He found Colonel Crawford at the mouth of the Little Kanawha River with a surveying party, engaged in surveying land. Mr. Tomlinson entered the service of Colonel Crawford and remained with him some time. The surveying party ascended the river and when it reached Round Bottom, Crawford ordered a survey of the river front although Mr. Tomlinson protested against it as he and his brothers had taken up a claim on it.

In autumn they returned to their homes east of the mountains and the following spring Joseph Tomlinson, Jr., and his wife, nee Elizabeth Harkness, his father and mother and two brothers, left the old home east of the mountains for their new homes the young man had provided for them in the Ohio Valley. This was the first settlement at Grave Creek. They remained at the Flats of Grave Creek until death removed them from earth, except for a few years they were compelled to leave on account of Indians and seek safety elsewhere. While the brothers were east of the mountains preparing to remove to their new homes, a man by the name of Con O'Niel remained and took care of the improvement for which he received one hundred acres of land. O'Niel, in addition to the one hundred acres, took up a claim on a ridge between Big Grave Creek and Middle Grave Creek, all of which was fine land.

There is a tradition that O'Neil killed a great many wild turkeys while taking care of the improvement and put the feathers in a corner of the cabin and when the families arrived in the spring Mrs. Joseph Tomlinson, Jr., filled a bed tick which she had used as a saddle cloth for her saddle, upon which she had ridden across the mountains, with the feathers, making the first feather bed in the Flats of Grave Creek. It was said that O'Niel was the only white man in what is now Marshall County that winter and only one was in what is now Ohio County.

At the breaking out of war with the Indians in 1777, the settlers at Grave Creek left for places of greater safety. Joseph Tomlinson, Sr., and wife and Isaac Williams and wife went to Redstone and resided there several years. Others of the settlers are thought to have gone to Wheeling. Little is known of them during the war with the Indians which lasted from 1777 till 1795.

Joseph Tomlinson and Colonel Beeler, of Beeler Station, are said to have made a trip to Philadelphia in the winter of 1780, with a petition to the Continental Congress, then in session there, requesting that it take some action for the protection of the frontier settlements.

Samuel Tomlinson was at Fort Henry and participated in the bloody conflict which occurred near it on the morning of September 1, 1777. He was one of the party who discovered the Indians that waylaid the path leading from the fort. He and two other men escaped and one of the party was killed.

At the breaking out of Dunmore's War, the cabin of Joseph Tomlinson was fortified by erecting pickets around it for refuge for the settlers. When notice was sent to the settlers of the intended invasion of Northwestern Virginia by Indians, in August, 1777, it was thought the fort was not of sufficient strength to withstand an attack by a large force of Indians, and the garrison being weak, it was thought best to abandon it, and tradition says that the fort was abandoned on the 17th of August and soon after the settlers left that it was burned by Indians, who were thought to have been closely watching the movements of the settlers.

The Tomlinson family returned to Grave Creek about the spring of 1785 and in the spring of 1786, Isaac Williams and wife removed to a tract of land belonging to his wife, which land was situated opposite the mouth of the Muskingum River, where they remained until their death.

Previous to the breaking out of Dunmore's War, Mrs. Rebecca Martin kept house for her brothers Samuel and James Tomlinson in a cabin near the mouth of Big Grave Creek and was there alone for weeks while her brothers were away hunting, trapping or taking up and improving land. The two brothers gave her four hundred acres of fine river bottom land on the Ohio River opposite the mouth of the Muskingum River for keeping house for them. Her brothers took up several tracts of land and made the usual improvements of the day upon them. They were usually occupied in taking up and improving land in the summer and in the winter engaged in hunting and trapping. Samuel and James spent the winter of 1773 trapping on the Great Kanawha River.

When the Tomlinson family returned from Redstone, and elsewhere, to their improvements at Grave Creek, a blockhouse or fort was erected which afforded the settlers protection. After they returned to their improvement, in or about the year 1785, they never left it again on account of danger from the Indians.

Notwithstanding the bloody war with the Indians from the year 1777 till 1795, settlers arrived almost every year and took up and improved land along the streams of water or on ridges near the Ohio River.

Soon after the Tomlinson family arrived others found their way to the country drained by the three Grave Creeks. Stephan Parr settled near Little Grave Creek and his land adjoined that of the Tomlinson brothers. A run and a point bears the name of Mr. Parr.

Harry Clark settled between Little Grave Creek and Jim's Run about the year 1773. He did not like the bottom land as he feared that fever and ague would be prevalent on the bottoms while the hills would be comparatively free from it. He participated in the stirring events of the Indian War. He erected a block-house where the village of Sherrard now stands soon after the siege of Fort Henry in September, 1782.

Nathan Masters was one of the early settlers on the waters of Big Grave Creek. He settled some distance from the mouth. He was a great hunter and frequented some springs on Roberts Ridge where bears came to wallow in the cool water about the springs, and from the number of bears that were found about the springs wallowing in the water the place was called, and has ever since been known, as Bear Wallow.

Roberts, Freeland and Riggs are names that were once familiar among the names of early settlers on the hills south of the Flats of Grave Creek. They came in an early day and many of them were often engaged in skirmishes with Indians.

Settlement at McMechen

WILLIAM McMECHEN was the first settler on a bottom about five miles below Wheeling, which bears his name, and on which the city of McMechen now stands. He came from the South Branch of the Potomac River about the year 1773, and took up a tomahawk claim to a large tract of fine bottom land. His wife, nee Sidney Johnson, came with him and was the first white woman to make her home on that bottom. The land of Mr. McMechen, known as McMechen's Bottom, extended down to the Narrows above the Flats of Grave Creek, and it was on this land that Captain William Foreman and a number of his men were murdered by a party of Indians under Half King, a Wyandot chief, on the 27th of September, 1777.

Mr. and Mrs. McMechen were among the many early settlers who endured the horrors of Indian war from 1777 until after the Battle of Fallen Timber in August, 1794, and the treaty at Greenville a year later. They had many unpleasant experiences with Indians. On one of their forays into Northwestern Virginia, they stole all Mr. McMechen's horses. He started in pursuit of them on foot and followed them almost to the Great Lakes but failed to overtake them and recover his horses. When he arrived home he found that his wife and family were gone. They had concluded that from his prolonged absence that he had been slain or captured by Indians, and Mrs. McMechen, with their children and negro servants and property, had removed to Red Stone Old Fort for safety. They remained there several years and then returned to the bottom and settled there permanently.

FREDERICK SIVERT, one of the early settlers in Sand Hill District. was born in Hesse Casel, Germany, and came to America in the early part of the Revolutionary War. He was a Hessian soldier in the service of Great Britain and was captured by Americans under General Washington on the twenty-sixth of December, 1776, at Trenton, N. J. While he was held a prisoner of war, he learned of the German citizens the real condition of the country and cause of the war and then enlisted in the Continental Army and fought to the close of the war for the independence of the colonies.

After the close of the war he married an American girl by the name of Martha Curtis and removed to the wilds of Northwestern Virginia and settled near Big Wheeling Creek and became identified in the development of the country and changing it from forest to field.

NATHANIEL PARR KILLS TWO INDIANS

The first blood said to have been shed in making a settlement at the Flats of Grave Creek was that of two Indians killed by Nathaniel Parr. A few years after the Parr family settled on the hill back of the Flats, the oldest son, Nathaniel, went out one afternoon to hunt and late in the evening he saw a deer drinking from a pool of water in Little Grave Creek, which he shot, dressed and hung up out of reach of wolves and went home intending to return and get it the next morning. Five Indians came along early in the morning and found the deer hanging where left and knowing that some one would be after it, lay in ambush to await the arrival, and when young Parr attempted to take the deer down, they fired at him, one of the bullets striking him and breaking a hip. He was by a large tree against which he leaned, resting on one foot, and quickly raised his gun and shot one of the Indians. Quickly he reloaded his gun and shot another of them. His strength giving away he fell to the ground by a pile of small stone with which he made a vigorous defense against the attack of the other three, who attempted to attack him with their tomahawks. They were young Indians and appeared cowardly and the fact that he struck them a number of times with stones, and kept up such a fusilade of stones they withdrew and carried the two dead companions with them. After the first fire they did not attempt to use their guns and it was thought that they had no more ammunition. The three were seen later in the day. Parr was made a cripple for life by the encounter.

INDIANS ATTACK ADAM ROWE'S FAMILY

In November, 1776, Adam Rowe started with his family from the waters of Buffalo Creek in what is now part of Washington County, Pennsylvania, with his wife and four sons, for Kentucky, leaving a married daughter behind. They traveled down on the southeast side of the Ohio River and reached a point near the mouth of Grave Creek where they were attacked by Indians. Mrs. Rowe and the oldest son were killed on the spot. Jacob, a ten-year-old boy, escaped by running into a thicket of willows, pursued by an Indian, who had his youngest brother, Robert, on his back. Jacob did not leave his hiding place until late in the day when he was sure no Indians were near. He started to return to his old home but night soon overtook him and he found a bed at the roots of a fallen tree where he spent the night in the leaves that had gathered in a hollow place by the roots of the tree. Late the next evening he reached the home of his married sister. His father and the remaining son reached their former home on Buffalo Creek and remained there some time and then emigrated to Kentucky. Jacob remained on Buffalo Creek and later became identified in the war with the Indians and was one of the three daring men who saved a number of women from the tomahawk at Miller's Block-house near his old home, several years later.

Nothing was ever heard of Robert and it was thought that he was also killed by the Indians.

EVENTS OF 1777

Indian Hostilities—Alarm Spread—Settlement Abandoned—
Whites Prepare for Defense—Indians Attack Fort
Henry—Massacre at McMechen's Bottom
of Captain Foreman and Twenty-
One Men

Early in the spring of 1777, the bloody year of the three sevens, as the old settlers properly named that year, roving bands of Indians made their appearance on the south side of the Ohio River and commenced depredations in many places.

HISTORY OF MARSHALL COUNTY, W. VA.

The first depredations in what is now Marshall County was that of stealing horses and killing some colts and cattle.

Morgan Jones, in a letter to his parents at Jacob's Creek in Pennsylvania, gives an account of conditions at the Flats of Grave Creek in the early part of that year. He stated that on the previous Saturday, Indians had killed two of his horses, two belonging to Joseph Tomlinson, took two horses belonging to John Harris, one belonging to Samuel Harris, one from Zephiniah Blackford, and shot four cattle of Mr. Rogers, and two of Yates Cornwell. Some young colts were also stolen by them. He said that some of the cattle came home with arrows sticking in their sides. The alarm soon spread and men gathered to the number of twenty-three. Eight were left to protect the settlement and fifteen started in pursuit of the Indians. They followed the trail to Fish Creek and crossed the river near the mouth of the creek and went down on the north side to the mouth of Sunfish Creek and followed the trail up that stream some distance until the camp of the Indians was discovered. Preparations were made for an attack upon the Indians when by an accident John McClean's gun went off giving the alarm. The Indians returned the fire but were driven from the camp. The whites took position on a hillside near the camp when two more fires were discovered. After considering the matter and viewing the situation, it was thought best to retreat, which was done. After going down the creek towards the river some distance the company received a small reinforcement that was following them with all possible speed. They returned and followed the trail a short distance but the Indians were then two days ahead and they abandoned the pursuit and returned home as it was deemed inexpedient to pursue the Indians further.

Two canoe loads started to cross the river at the mouth of Sunfish, but as they approached the south shore they were fired upon by Indians from that side of the river. The men laid down in the canoes except two who were paddling them. They made for the north side of the river with great haste. A great many shots were fired by both whites and Indians. He said that Indian bullets fell as thick as hail. They went up the river and crossed it a short distance below the mouth of Fish Creek and hastened home. A trail was found soon after crossing the river and when they arrived at the fort at Grave Creek, they found some men who had been at the mouth of the Little Kanawha River had passed up and they were the men whose trail they had seen. The men were at the fort when they arrived. A large camp of Indians were discovered not far below the mouth of Fish Creek.

The summer passed by with no invasion by the Indians other than by small scalping parties and people did not all abandon their homes and go into forts for safety. Scouting parties were kept watching the usual paths of Indians and covered the country generally. About the first of August, General Hand was informed by friendly Indians that the hostile Indians contemplated an attack upon Wheeling. White Eyes, a Delaware, and a friend to the whites, told General Hand that the hostile Indians intended to take Wheeling home. This information created a general alarm. On the second of August General Hand wrote to David Shepherd, lieutenant of Ohio County, informing him of the threatened invasion, ordering him to abandon his fort at the forks of Wheeling Creek, about six miles from the river, and rally all the militia between the Monongahela and Ohio Rivers at Fort Henry. Colonel Shepherd proceeded to carry the orders out as given him and collected nine companies at Wheeling. The alarm became general and not without cause and people retired into forts as soon as they were warned of their danger.

The fort at Wheeling had been erected by the Colonial authority of Virginia in 1774 and named Fort Fincastle, but the name had been changed to Fort Henry in honor of Patrick Henry, Governor of Virginia. It was supplied with arms and ammunition by the authorities of Virginia but not with a garrison of regular soldiers at this time, but left to be defended by settlers who might seek safety within its walls except militia, as ordered by the commander of the Middle Department of the West with his headquarters at Fort Pitt. Fort Henry was considered Indian-proof and as no Indians appeared, vigilance was somewhat relaxed, and the nine companies of militia were allowed to return home and by the last of August there were only two companies at the fort and they were local men commanded by Captain Samuel Mason and Captain Joseph Ogle.

Scouting parties had been kept out watching the Indian trails or war paths by which they would most likely approach Wheeling.

On the last day of August, Captain Ogle and a party of twelve men who had been out several days watching the paths, arrived at the fort and reported they had found no signs of Indians and were assured that there was no immediate danger. With this assurance the inhabitants of the village remained in their cabins. The Indians had evidently suspected that the whites were watching for them and had carefully avoided the usual paths and had eluded the vigilance of the scouts. In the course of the night an army of Indians of between three hundred and four hundred warriors, under command of a white man, arrived at Wheeling and lay in ambush. They possibly thought that the whites were expecting them and were prepared to receive them as there were lights burning in the fort, and thought that their only chance of success was in an ambuscade, which was successfully accomplished.

INDIANS ATTACK FORT HENRY

EARLY in the morning of September 1st, Andrew Zane, John Boyd, Samuel Tomlinson and a negro went out from the fort to catch a horse for Dr. James McMechen, who intended to start east that day on a trip to some of the older settlements, or to the east of the mountains, on business. The men had gone but a short distance when Indians fired upon them and killed Boyd, but the other three escaped and returned to the fort and reported that they had seen six Indians. Andrew Zane is said to have saved his life by jumping from a cliff about seventy feet high. A heavy fog hung over the bottom and it was impossible to see any distance, hence the Indians in the cornfield were not seen.

The companies of Captains Samuel Mason and Joseph Ogle had occupied the fort the preceding night. Captain Mason, with fourteen men, went from the fort to dislodge the Indians. They had not advanced far from the fort when they came in view of the six Indians. Moving briskly forward they soon found themselves surrounded by a body of Indians that had been concealed and now showed themselves when the whites were within their lines. Mason saw the impossibility of maintaining a conflict with such superior numbers, ordered a retreat but it was too late. They were intercepted by Indians on all sides and but few escaped. Captain Mason and his sergeant succeeded in passing the front lines but were observed and pursued by Indians and fired at as they began to ascend the hill. The sergeant was so badly wounded that he fell and was unable to rise again. Seeing his captain pass without a gun and so crippled that he could move but slowly, and being pursued, he handed him his gun and quietly met his fate, the tomahawk. Mason, who had received two wounds, was so weak from the loss of blood and faint from fatigue, that he had almost given up all hopes of escape, again exerted his utmost power to reach the fort. He was aware that an Indian was near him and expected any moment that a tomahawk would end his days. He thought of this and exerted himself and recollected that his gun was loaded; he wheeled about to fire at his pursuer, but found him so close that he could not bring his gun to bear on him. Having the advantage of the ground he pushed the Indian with his hand from him. The Indian had his tomahawk raised to strike a blow when pushed backward and it descended to the earth with great force, and before he could regain his footing and again strike with his tomahawk, Mason turned about and shot him dead. He was unable to proceed but a few paces further but found a large fallen tree beside which he concealed himself and remained while the Indians remained about the fort.

Captain Ogle hearing the firing of the guns, shrieks of the men and yells of the Indians, went out with twelve men to reinforce them. The men being some distance in advance of Captain Ogle the Indians enclosed them leaving him outside the circle. He concealed himself in some bushes and briars until night enabled him to return to the fort.

The number of men killed that morning is a matter of uncertainty. Some writers say that out of twenty-six men lead out by Captains Mason and Ogle, only three escaped death and two of them were badly wounded.

R. G. Thwaits gives the loss of the whites at fifteen killed and nine wounded, and the loss of the Indians, one killed and five wounded.

While the terrible massacre was taking place in the cornfield, the inhabitants of the village fled from their cabins to the fort and prepared for its defense. Many fled with nothing but their clothes and some of them with only their night clothes, leaving everything behind in their cabins. They saw that the forces of Captains Mason and Ogle had been cut to pieces and that there was no chance for an open conflict with the Indians. So quickly had all this happened that the gates of the fort were scarcely closed till the Indians appeared before it. The white leader of the Indians appeared at a window of a house near the fort and told the inmates of it that he had come with a large army to conduct the inhabitants along the frontier to Detroit, such as would accept the terms offered by Governor Hamilton. The terms were that they renounce the cause of the colonies and espouse the cause of Great Briton. He read Governor Hamilton's proclamation and then informed them that he would give them fifteen minutes to consider his proposition. It was all the time the inmates needed. Colonel Zane informed him that they had consulted their wives and children and that they had decided that they would perish in defending themselves rather than place themselves under the protection of a savage army with him at the head of it. He then told them of the size of the army and of the uselessness of their resistance. A shot from the fort fired at him put an end to his harangue. He withdrew from the window and commenced an attack upon the fort.

There were but thirty-three men in the fort according to Withers' account, but they were determined to hold it or die in its defence. Almost every man was for a time a host in himself, so determined were they to defend the fort; and the women were not behind the men in their resolution to hold it, and two of them Mrs. Betsey Wheat and a Mrs. Glum did duty as soldiers; took guns and places with the men in the the defence. Others not so resolute and expert in the use of arms cooled the guns and loaded them for the men and prepared food and carried it to the heroic defenders and rendered valuable aid, while others more timid moulded bullets for the guns. Each one had some particular duty to perform and performed it promptly. There were no wringing of hands and wailing but a cool deliberate determined resolution to fight it out to an end and die in defense of the fort rather than surrender it.

Most of the writers of early history say that the Indians attacked the fort and for twenty-three hours there was great activity in the fort and a heavy fire was kept up by the Indians against it.

Thwaits contradicts the statement and says that the Indians satisfied with their success in the ambuscade only threw up some blinds and earthworks, scalped the dead, killed all the stock within their reach, burned the houses and retired across the Ohio the following night and disappeared.

There is no event in history recorded in which there are more conflicting accounts, than the attack upon Fort Henry on the morning of September the first, 1777, and at the present day it is impossible to give what might be termed a correct account of it. All that can be done is to give the different accounts of it and submit the matter to careful readers and let them decide which account appears to them most plausible.

Withers says that after the attack was made upon Wheeling the alarm reached Shepherd's Fort at the forks of Wheeling Creek, six miles distant, and a messenger was sent from there to Holliday's Fort with intelligence and the apprehension that if speedy relief was not afforded the garrison, Fort Henry must fall. There was no thought of gathering a force sufficient to defeat the Indians in an open battle and all that could be done or expected, was to get a small force into the fort to reinforce the garrison. Colonel Sweringen left Holliday's Fort in a large canoe with fourteen volunteers for the relief of the fort. The men paddled industriously to reach Wheeling in time to render service to the besieged. It was deemed hazardous but they thought only of relieving the fort and saving the lives of the inmates. The night was dark and a heavy fog hung over the river, making it difficult to guide the canoe, hence they frequently ran into the river banks. Finally they ceased rowing and let it drift lest they might pass Wheeling and fail to return before daylight. They landed some distance above the fort which they located by lights of the burning cabins and decided to reconnoiter and examine the situation before attempting to gain admission to the fort. It was a matter of uncertainty to them whether or not the fort was in ruins. Three of the party, Colonel Swearingen, Captain Bilderbock and William Bosher volunteered to proceed cautiously and ascertain the situation and report to the others. When they arrived near the fort it was a question to them whether the Indians had abandoned the attack or only lying in ambush in the cornfield awaiting the approach of a relief party to fall upon it. Fearing an ambuscade they thought it best not to give a signal to the men but to return by a circuitous route to them and avoid the cornfield in returning, and bring their companions to the fort.

It was not known that Indians were not concealed in the corn near the fort and to ascertain whether or not, two men were requested to go out from the fort and examine the cornfield. Two vigilant scouts left the fort and examined the cornfield carefully and returned to the fort without seeing any indications of the presence of Indians. Upon their return to the fort twenty men under the guidance of Colonel Zane marched around the cornfield and approached nearer than the two men, and became assured that the Indians had really withdrawn from the field. About this time Major Samuel McCullough arrived with forty-five men from Short Creek and they all proceeded to view the battlefield. Here they found twenty-three of the men who went out with Captains Mason and Ogle, most of them had been killed with tomahawks and scalping knives. About three hundred head of cattle, hogs and horses had been wantonly killed by the Indians and all the cabins with their contents, which the Indians could not conveniently carry off with them, were burned. It was a long time before the inhabitants of Wheeling regained the comforts of which that night's work of the Indians deprived them. No one was killed during the siege and only one man was slightly wounded.

The abandonment of the homes in the village and leaving everything in them and rushing to the fort will be best understood when it is remembered that the inhabitants depended upon the scouts to give them timely warning of danger so they could remove their effects into the fort and save them from destruction. They knew nothing of the presence of the enemy until the four men were attacked as they went through the cornfield for the horse and the entire time spent in the affray was of short duration and occurred between daylight and sunrise, hence no time to remove anything and they were fortunate to escape with their lives.

McKNIGHT, in OUR WESTERN BORDER, gives a somewhat different account in some particulars. He says, Early on the morning of September the first, a white man and a negro went out to catch a horse and had not advanced far before they were fired upon by a party of six Indians in ambush. Boyd was killed but the negro was permitted to return. Captain Samuel Mason, who the preceding evening brought his company to the fort, sallied out with fourteen men to shake up the impudent murderers. He soon routed up the six Indians and fired upon them. On the crack of their rifles the entire army arose and with blood-curdling yells rushed upon the little band. Mason at once ordered a retreat, cutting his own way through the Indians' lines, but most of his gallant command were hacked to pieces. Only two escaped by hiding beneath brush and fallen timber. William Shepherd, son of Colonel David Shepherd, commandant of the fort, reached Indian Spring where the Wheeling market house now stands, when his foot caught in a grapevine, he fell and was immediately dispatched with a war-club. A heavy fog hung over the bottom at this time and those inside of the fort could neither see the effect of the conflict nor surmise the number of the foe. Captain Joseph Ogle, with a dozen scouts, sallied out to the relief of the men and covered their retreat. The Indians attacked them and all but Captain Joseph Ogle, Sergeant Jacob Ogle, Martin Wetzel and one or two others were killed. Captain Ogle escaped by hiding in some high weeds in a fence corner. While there, two warriors sat on the fence, one of whom was severely wounded and cried piteously with pain. Ogle saw the blood streaming down his leg and feared that they would discover him and kept his finger on the trigger of his gun so he could fire instantly, but they moved off without noticing him. Scarcely had the groans of the wounded and dying ceased when the Indians appeared flourishing the bloody scalps and demanding the surrender of the fort. They advanced in two divisions headed with drum and fife and flying British colors; the right wing being distributed among the cabins on the bluff behind the fort and the left under cover of the river bank and close to the fort. The leader shouted aloud Hamilton's proclamation and offered protection in case of surrender and indiscriminate massacre if not. The garrison only numbered ten or twelve men and boys. Colonel Shepherd replied, "Sir, We have consulted our wives and children and all have resolved to perish at our posts rather than place ourselves under the protection of such savages with you at their head." The leader attempted to reply but a shot from the fort put a stop to further words. A rush was now made by a large body of Indians who tried to force the gates open and try the strength of the pickets by their united effort. Failing to make any impression, and suffering from the fire of the garrison, they withdrew a few yards and opened a general fire upon the port holes. An unintermittent fire was kept up during most of the day and part of the night but without any effect. About noon a temporary withdrawal took place and the garrison prepared for renewed resistance. To each man was assigned a post. Of the women, some run bullets, others got ammunition ready, others cooled and cleaned guns, loaded them and handed them to the men, and two of the women took their places at port holes and sent death messengers towards the dusky warriors. About three o'clock in the afternoon the Indians renewed the attack with redoubled fury. One-half of their number distributed themselves among the cabins and behind fallen trees, while the other half advanced along the base of the hill south of the fort and commenced a vigorous fire. This was to draw the defenders to that quarter while a rush was made from the other side and an attempt made to force an entrance into the fort with heavy timbers. Their effort failed and many a dusky warrior paid the penalty of his rashness with his life. Several similar attempts were made during the afternoon but all failed. Just before the savages retired, Bazel Duke, son-in-law of Colonel Shepherd, who had been stationed at Beech Bottom block-house, rode rapidly up to the fort and had almost gained entrance when he was shot dead in full view of the garrison he so gallantly attempted to aid. About nine o'clock that night the Indians reappeared and opened fire on the fort, making night hideous with their yells. All the lights in the fort had been carefully extinguished, giving the inmates the advantage of the light on the outside. They could see the Indians and themselves unseen, thus giving the garrison an opportunity to get many a good shot at stalwart warriors that caused them to lay down their arms forever. Repeated efforts were made to storm the fort during the night as well as to set it on fire. All efforts failed. Each attempt gave the sharp-shooters an opportunity to get in their work. Becoming discouraged in their efforts to capture the fort they killed all the stock that they could and set most of the buildings on fire and were preparing for one mort last and final effort when a relief party from Holliday's Fort arrived under command of Colonel Andrew Swearingen, landed under the river bank and secretly entered the fort.

Shortly after their arrival, Major Samuel McCullough, with forty mounted men from Short Creek, arrived and made an impetuous rush for the gates of the fort, which were joyfully thrown open to admit them. All succeeded in entering safely except Major McCullough, who delayed until every man in his party entered the fort. He was surrounded by Indians and compelled to fly for his life. Being mounted on a spirited horse, he galloped for the hill at full speed, followed by yelling Indians. He ascended the hill and reached a point where he thought he had left his pursuers so far behind him that he was safe, when he encountered a considerable body of Indians who had been on a plundering expedition among the settlements. In an instant he comprehended his danger. With foes in front and behind and spreading out on the slope of the hill, escape seemed impossible. He saw only one opportunity to escape death at the hands of the Indians and that was a desperate leap down a steep hill towards Wheeling Creek. Death among the rocks was preferable to torture by Indians. They were closing in on him. With a steady nerve, he adjusted the rein of his bridle and with his left hand he firmly gripped it and with his right he held his trusty rifle and urged his horse over the precipice towards Wheeling Creek. A crash, a crackling of limbs, a tumbling of loose stones and down the horse and rider went toward the creek. The astonished Indians looked over the precipice and to their surprise saw horse and rider cross the creek that flowed at the foot of the precipice and cross a peninsula at a rapid rate, the horse with head up and the gallant rider sitting straight in the saddle as if nothing had happened out of the ordinary. It was over three hundred feet from the top of the ridge to the bottom and it seemed that a stronger hand than that of man had guided the horse in that fearful leap.

ABRAHAM ROGERS, a participant in the defense of Fort Henry in 1777, gave an account of it which was published in a Wellsburg paper in 1833, which is given below:

The fort was situated on the higher bank or bluff and covered between one-half and three-fourths of an acre of land and was enclosed by a stockade eight feet high. The garrison at the time of the attack did not exceed fifteen, including all who were able to bear arms, several of whom were between twelve and eighteen years of age. The number of women and children were not known, as little account was taken of them.

The first intimation the commandant of the fort, Colonel Shepherd, had of the approach of an enemy, was received from Captain Ogle, who with Abraham Rogers, Robert Lemon and two others who had just arrived from Beech Bottom fort, on the Ohio River, twelve miles above Wheeling. Captain Ogle had, on his approach to Wheeling, observed below that place the appearance of smoke in the atmosphere which he rightly conjectured was caused by the burning of the Grave Creek fort by hostile Indians, and upon his arrival he immediately communicated his suspicion to Colonel Shepherd, but it was too late in the evening to reconnoiter. At a very early hour the next morning, September the first, the commandant of the fort sent two of his men in a canoe down the river to ascertain the cause of the smoke, and whether any Indians were in the neighborhood. The two men were murdered by the Indians on their return to the mouth of Wheeling Creek, it was thought, a few hundred yards below the fort. In the meantime an Irish servant and a negro had been sent out to reconnoiter in the immediate vicinity. The Irishman was decoyed, seized and killed by the Indians but the negro was permitted to escape, who on his return to the fort gave the first alarm of the actual approach of Indians. Captain Ogle, on receipt of the intelligence, accompanied by fifteen or sixteen of the garrison, leaving but twelve or thirteen in the fort, immediately proceeded towards the mouth of the creek in pursuit of the Indians. They were lying in ambush and permitted Captain Ogle and his devoted followers to advance almost to the creek, when a brisk and deadly fire was opened upon them. They fought bravely, desperately, but were overpowered by numbers of the enemy, and all except the Captain and two others were killed and scalped. Upon hearing the firing at the creek, Biggs, Rogers and Lemon left the fort to join their comrades and met the enemy who, with yells, were advancing towards the fort. The three men were fired upon and compelled to return. On their arrival at the gate of the fort, so near were the Indians, that it was not without the most imminent danger that it was opened for their admission. A general attack was immediately made upon the fort by the whole body of Indians, consisting of about five hundred men commanded by the infamous Simon Girty.

The assault was from the east side under cover of a paled garden and a few half-faced cabins within forty or fifty yards of the fort, of which they took possession, and from whence a brisk fire was kept up until a late hour at night. During the engagement the Indians sustained a great injury from the bursting of a maple log, which they had bored like a cannon and charged to fire upon the fort.

The little garrison of twelve sustained this protracted siege from about seven o'clock in the morning till ten or eleven o'clock at night, when the savages were finally repulsed and obliged to retreat without having killed or wounded a single individual in the fort. The loss on part of the Indians was variously estimated at from twenty to one hundred, and the conjecture of the number killed could only be formed from the great amount of blood which was observable for many days after the battle as their dead were principally carried off or concealed. The day was fair and most of the gunners were called sharp-shooters, all of whom had a number of fine shots. It is therefore not improbable that some thirty or forty of the enemy were killed and perhaps many more, for there was a continual firing during the whole time of the engagement.

Every man did his duty and was entitled to an equal amount of praise. The women rendered valuable service, some running bullets, cutting patches, cooling and loading guns for the men. Mrs. Ebenezer Zane rendered valuable service in this way. The Spartan band of patriots had not time to take any sustenance from Sunday, the last day of August, until the second day of September, after the Indians had abandoned the siege and crossed the Ohio.

Writers of early history disagree as to the number of defenders of Fort Henry at the time of the attack on September the first, 1777. It is evident that some of them are mistaken in the number. There are a number of names that are prominent in border history, who escaped that terrible massacre and there are many reasons to believe that they were among the defenders of the fort on that occasion. The names of Ebenezer Zane, Samuel Tomlinson, Andrew Zane, Martin Wetzel, Silas Zane, David Shepherd, Jonathan Zane, Dr. James McMechen, Abraham Rogers, Joseph Biggs, Robert Lemon, John Lynn and John Caldwell, beyond doubt belong to the list of defenders of the fort. There are reasons to believe that the names of William McMechen, James Tomlinson, Joseph Tomlinson and some others belong to the list also. It is generally stated that there were twenty-five or thirty cabins above the mouth of the creek about the fort and besides the inmates of the cabins, there were people from outlying settlements, who had taken refuge in the fort when the alarm was given in the early part of August by General Hand. Traditional history clearly indicates that several persons from the Flats of Grave Creek were at Wheeling at the time and had been there about two weeks before the attack. Some have estimated the number of defendants as high as forty-two and it seems reasonable that the number was not much over-estimated. There being no written records of any consequence concerning the events about Wheeling at the time, it is difficult to determine just what did occur. Good authority gives the arrival of Major McCullough after the Indians had left, and if that be the case, the famous leap for life occurred at another time and under different circumstances. It is possible that tradition and poor memories are the cause of much of the conflict in historical statements.

MASSACRE OF CAPTAIN FOREMAN AND TWENTY-ONE MEN

The ambuscade and massacre in the cornfield near Fort Henry on the morning of September the first, 1777, was followed by another about four weeks later at the foot of McMechen's Bottom, a few miles below Wheeling, in which twenty-two men were killed, one captured and several wounded by Indians.

Early in September a company of militia arrived from Hampshire County, Virginia, under command of Captain William Foreman, to join the forces under General Hand in an expedition against the Indians, which had been contemplated. Scouting parties had been kept out to watch the paths of the Indians from the first alarm and were kept in the forest after the attack, watching every part of the country then inhabited as they were suspicious that Indians would appear again somewhere that autumn. On September the twenty-fifth, Captain Foreman, with twenty-four men, Captain Ogle, with ten men, and John Lynn, with nine men, were sent by Colonel Shepherd on a scouting expedition to Captina. The party arrived at the Flats of Grave Creek, twelve miles below Wheeling, and halted. The settlement had been abandoned in August when General Hand sent out the first alarm. The party found no canoes in which to cross the river and encamped for the night. Captain Foreman was in command of the party of scouts. He was a brave man but had no knowledge of Indian warfare and did not care to be advised by those who had. His men built a large fire and lay down about it for the night, although John Lynn, one of the most reliable scouts in the Middle Department of the West, cautioned Foreman of the danger of it. Lynn with his men went some distance from the fire and lay down in the darkness of the forest to sleep. Late in the after part of the night Lynn, being awake, heard a noise at the river, which he said sounded like launching a raft in the river somewhere near the mouth of Little Grave Creek, but on the opposite side of the river, and related the incident to Captain Foreman in the morning, but the Captain paid no attention to it. Lynn felt assured that Indians were lurking somewhere near and had been watching the movements of the party of scouts under Foreman, although he had seen nothing to clearly indicate their presence in the neighborhood, and spoke of his suspicion that it was possible that they were lurking somewhere near, while at the camp on Monday morning. Sounds to a man like him meant a great deal, while to other and untrained ears, they meant nothing at all. Being unable to cross the river for want of canoes, Captain Foreman decided to abandon the expedition and return to Wheeling.

The entire party marched up the trail towards Wheeling until it reached a point near the foot of the Narrows about two miles above the mouth of Little Grave Creek when it halted and a controversy took place regarding the route from there to Wheeling. Lynn again called attention to the danger of lurking Indians and the danger of an attack by them. He insisted that the party return to Wheeling by taking the route over the hill and avoid the bottom, giving as a reason that he believed that there were Indians near and that they had watched the party from the opposite side of the river and that the noise which he heard in the night was made by launching a raft to cross the river and if that be the case, that they would most likely attack them somewhere along the bottom. Foreman did not understand the danger or was unwilling to heed the advice of a backwoodsman, a scout and hunter, and insisted on following the trail along the bottom near the river. There was quite a long controversy over the matter and John Harkness, a relative of the Tomlinson family, and one of the party, said that at times it ran high, but Foreman would not heed the advice of Lynn and take the route over the hill. Foreman and Ogle started up along the trail and Lynn and his scouts took the route over the hill or rather along the side of it, and followed along the side of the hill facing the river.

Captain Foreman and Captain Ogle followed the path that lead up the river bottom without anything occurring to attract their attention until they reached a point where the bottom begins to widen, when one of the men picked up an Indian ornament in the path. Immediately the men gathered about him to examine the ornament and while their attention was attracted by it two lines of Indians, one concealed under the river bank and the other in a sink at the foot of the hill, hidden from view by bushes and weeds, fired upon them and kept up the firing several minutes. Captain Foreman and twenty-one of his men were killed and one captured and several wounded. Among the slain were two sons of Captain Foreman. The men fled for their lives and several sought safety by ascending the hill. Robert Harkness caught hold of a sapling to aid him in getting up the hill when the bark was knocked into his face by a bullet from the gun of an Indian fired at him. John Collins was shot in the thigh, breaking the bone. What the result might have been had not Lynn and his scouts rushed down the hillside yelling and firing their guns, is difficult to conjecture. They frightened the Indians with their noise and they evidently thought that it was a reinforcement coming to the relief of the party which they had attacked, and which caused them to give up pursuit and hasten from the scene of the conflict, and possibly saved the lives of several men.

Lynn and his men aided in caring for the wounded. They took Collins to a spring over the hill a short distance and threw their provisions together for him and provided the best they could for his comfort until he could be removed to Wheeling. Some accounts say that he was removed to Wheeling on the following day and others say that it was two days later.

R. G. Thwait says that Colonel David Shepherd went down from Wheeling on the fourth day after the occurrence with a force of considerable size after a reinforcement had arrived from Fort Pitt, buried the dead and took care of Collins. The dead were all buried in one grave at the head of the Narrows where they fell.

In the year 1835, money was raised by a Light Horse Company at Elizabethtown, now Moundsville, and a stone was placed at the grave of the heroes. The stone was hard sandstone common in the section of the country and on it was inscribed:

THIS

HUMBLE STONE

IS ERECTED

TO THE MEMORY

OF

CAPTAIN FOREMAN

AND

TWENTY-ONE OF HIS MEN

WHO WERE SLAIN BY A BAND OF

RUTHLESS SAVAGES, THE ALLIES OF A

CIVILIZED NATION OF EUROPE

ON THE 26th OF SEPTEMBER, 1777.

"So sleep the brave who sunk to rest
    By all their country's wishes bless'd."

The stone stood there forty years and was then removed by order of the county court of Marshall County and placed in Mount Rose Cemetery just north of the city limits of Mounds-

ville. The following was inscribed on the stone when removed:
"This monument was originally erected above the Narrows on the Ohio River four miles above Moundsville, on the grounds where the fatal action occurred, with the remains of Capt. Foreman and his fallen men placed here June 1, 1875, by Capt. P. B. Catlett under orders of the county court of Marshall County."

REPORT OF
LIEUTENANT MILLER AND ENSIGN WILSON

"A list of the effects lost, by sundry soldiers of Captain William Foreman's company of Hampshire county volunteers, appraised by Lieutenant Anthony Miller and Ensign David Wilson, officers of said company, being duly qualified for that purpose.

		£	s.	d.
1	Captain William Foreman: rifle-gun, £11, 5s; shot pouch and horn, 10s; pocket compass, 5s; a blanket, £1, 17s, 6d............	15	17	6
2	Edward Peterson: A rifle-gun, £11, 5s; shot pouch and horn, 10s; blanket, 30s............	13	5	0
3	Benjamin Powell: A rifle-gun, £12, 10s; a blanket, £1, 17s, 6d; shot pouch and horn, 12s, 6d	12	5	0
4	Hambleton Foreman: A rifle-gun, £11, 5s; a blanket, 30s; shot pouch and horn, 10s.......	13	5	0
5	James Greene: A rifle-gun, £10; a blanket, 37s, 6d.	11	17	6
6	John Wilson: A rifle-gun, £10; shot pouch and horn, 7s, 6d; blanket, 22s, 9d...........	11	10	0
7	Jacob Pew: A rifle-gun, £8, 15s; a shot pouch and horn, 7s, 6d; blanket, 18s, 9d...........	10	3	9
8	Isaac Harris: A rifle-gun, £12, 10s; shot pouch and horn, 10s; blanket, 37s, 9d..............	14	17	6
9	Robert M'Grew: blanket, 22s. 6d.............	1	2	6
10	Elisha Shriver: A blanket, 22s. 6d............	1	2	6
11	Henry Risera: A blanket, 37s. 6d............	1	17	6
12	Bartholomew Viney: A blanket, 22s. 6d.....	1	2	6
13	Anthony Miller: A blanket, 22s. 6d.........	1	2	6
14	John Vincent: A blanket, 30s..............	1	10	0
15	Solomon Jones: A blanket, 30s..............	1	10	0
16	William Ingle: A blanket, 22s. 6d..........	1	2	6
17	Nathan Foreman: A blanket, 22s. 6d........	1	2	6
18	Abraham Powell: A blanket, 37s. 6d.........	1	17	6

19	Samuel Lowery: A blanket, 30s............	1	10	0
20	Samuel Johnson: A rifle-gun, £7. 10s.; shot pouch and horn, 10s.; a blanket, 22s, 6d......	9	2	6

We the subscribers, do certify that the within specified appraisments are just and true to the best of our judgements; and that the several articles were lost in the late unhappy defeat near McMechen's Narrows on the 27th of September, 1777, as witness our hands, this third of October, 1777.

(Signed) Anthony Miller, Lieutenant.
David Wilson, Ensign.
Sworn before me, David Shepherd."

NOTE.—The date on the last line on page 32 and on the stone are both incorrect and should be the 26th and 27th of September, as the above report clearly indicates.

INDIANS ATTACK FORT HENRY

Fort Henry was erected in 1774 and was considered a very strong fortification of the kind. It was said to be Indian-proof. Within the enclosure was a good well of water for the use of the garrison. A small cannon had recently been added to the armament of the fort. Some men were bathing near the site of the old French fort at the forks of the Ohio and found some cannon which the French had spiked and thrown into the river when they abandoned the fort in November, 1758. The spikes were drilled out of the vents and the cannon again brought into use, one of which was sent to Wheeling for the defense of Fort Henry. It was placed in position on the top of the storehouse, one of the buildings in the fort. A supply of grape-shot and balls was provided that it might be of service in case of an attack.

There is no account of any repairs being made to the fort in preparing to repel an attack, notwithstanding the fort had been erected eight years. There is much disagreement as to who was commandant at Fort Henry at the time of attack in 1782. Some authorities say that Colonel Ebenezer Zane was the commandant and other equally as reliable say that Captain Boggs was in charge of the fort at the time as the regular commanding officer.

For some time John Lynn, one of the most vigilant scouts in the Upper Ohio Valley, was engaged in watching the war paths of the Indians on the northwest side of the Ohio River, and on Wednesday afternoon, September the eleventh, about three o'clock, he discovered a large body of Indians marching very rapidly towards Wheeling. He hastened to warn the people of their danger in time for them to retire into the fort.

He swam the river and reached Wheeling only a few hours in advance of the enemy. The inhabitants of the village, not already in the fort, hurried into it and hasty preparations were made for a vigorous defense of the fort. Colonel Zane and a few others retired into his house. The Indians had burned his house in 1777 when they attacked the fort and he erected another much stronger and better arranged for defense. It was built like a block-house with loop-holes for guns and stood about sixty yards from the fort. He had decided not to abandon his home to be again destroyed by Indians. When the alarm was given, he retired into his house determined to defend it and render aid to the fort at the same time. In it were Colonel Zane and wife, Andrew Scott, George Greer, Mollie Scott and it is thought that Miss Elizabeth Zane was also in the house, but it is questioned whether or not such was the case. In a kitchen adjoining the residence, was an old negro, generally known by the name of Dady Sam, and his wife Kate.

In the fort there were not more than twenty efficient men for its defense against three hundred warriors.

Soon after the arrival of John Lynn, Captain Boggs left the fort to spread the alarm and solicit aid. Colonel David Shepherd was absent on some business relative to the military affairs. The attacking party consisted of forty British soldiers commanded by Captain Pratt, and two hundred and sixty Indians, said by many, to have been commanded by George Girty, appeared a few hours after the arrival of John Lynn. They quickly formed their lines about the fort and demanded the surrender of the garrison which was promptly refused. Several shots were fired at the colors by order of Silas Zane who had been selected to command the fort in the absence of Captain Boggs. The Indians opened fire upon the fort and rushed upon it with great impetuosity and were greeted with a well directed volley of bullets from the garrison and from Colonel Zane's house, which drove them back in confusion. They rallied and attacked it again and were again repulsed. Both the house and fort were well supplied with guns and many of the women rendered effective service in moulding bullets, cleaning guns and loading them for the men who fired them rapidly at the attacking party, and it also led the enemy to believe that the garrison was much stronger than it really was. The cannon attracted their attention and they called to the garrison to fire it, saying that it was a wooden gun. When a proper opportunity arrived a man by the name of Tate fired a load of grape-shot into their ranks which changed their tune and caused them to set up a yell of rage. Captain Pratt ordered them to stand back, swearing that there was no wood about it. He had heard cannon before and knew by the sound just what it was. The attacking party now drew back toward the hills and kept up a constant fire until about dark, when they withdrew for a short time, leaving the garrison undisturbed. Soon after firing ceased a canoe loaded with cannon balls, in charge of Daniel Sullivan and two men, arrived at Wheeling on their way to the Falls of the Ohio, and the three men made a rush for the fort and succeeded in entering it at the rear gate, but did not escape the attention of the Indians. They fired upon them and wounded Sullivan slightly in a foot. The garrison got no rest that night. A party of Indians in the loft of a cabin near the fort kept up a terrible noise by their yelling and dancing until the cannon quieted them. At first grape-shot was tried but it failed to dislodge them or quiet them and a ball was fired into the cabin. It cut a joist and let the crowd of yelling Indians down much to their discomfiture. The cannon was fired sixteen times during the night with more or less effect each time.

The enemy suffered severely from the fire from Colonel Zane's residence and they thought to set it on fire and drive the inmates from it. An Indian crept along towards it cautiously with a firebrand in his hand and every now and then he would wave it in the air to freshen the flames. When he arrived near the kitchen he raised up and waved it to and fro to rekindle the flames, when the quick eye of the old negro, Dady Sam, caught sight of the Indian and quickly seized his gun and fired at the Indian. The warrior uttered a piercing yell, let the firebrand fall, and went away limping. Several similar attempts were made that night but through the vigilance of the old negro, whose keen eye caught sight of every warrior before he got near the kitchen with his firebrand.

About midnight the enemy again assaulted the fort and attempted to carry it by storm. The pickets resisted the battering and they failed to make a breach in the stockade and a well directed fire from the garrison and Colonel Zane's residence drove them back. Two other attempts were made that night to effect an entrance into the fort by storm and massacre the garrison but the fire of the defenders each time repulsed the enemy with loss. When the sun appeared the next morning the enemy were about the fort but did not renew the attack. It was evident that they had not abandoned the siege. About eight o'clock a man was observed creeping quietly towards the fort. A man by the name of House seized a gun and fired at him, wounding him severely. He was a negro who had been with the Indians as a prisoner and was trying to escape from them. He was admitted into the fort and his wound dressed, but he was closely guarded lest he might be a spy. He gave the inmates of the fort all the information he possessed concerning the size and intentions of the attacking party.

The Indians in the meantime contemplated greater efforts to take the fort by storm. They had found the canoe loaded with cannon balls and were preparing to use them in the reduction of the fort. They procured a log, split it open and cut out the center to suit the size of the cannon balls and with some chains found in Reikart's blacksmith shop, bound the log together, imagining that they had a cannon. They charged it with powder and a ball was taken from the canoe and placed in the cannon and they then pointed their wooden gun towards the fort and announced that their artillery had arrived. They believed that they had a death-dealing instrument of war, and so it was. An Indian applied a firebrand to it. An explosion followed, scattering splinters and destruction in every direction. Several of the Indains were killed and a number were wounded by the explosion of their cannon which they expected would batter down the pickets of the fort. When they recovered from the shock, they were furious with madness of despair and in their rage assaulted the fort with more desperation than before. The inmates of the fort received them with coolness and determination and kept up such a deadly fire that they were compelled to retire again. This was very fortunate for the garrison. The powder in the fort was becoming exhausted and it was feared that if the firing was continued that the supply of powder would be consumed and in such an event there was great danger from an assault. It was known that there was a supply of powder in Colonel Zane's residence and it was decided to make an attempt to get a keg of it. It was now a question to decide who would go after the powder. It was an enterprise full of danger. Several volunteered to engage in the hazardous enterprise. Elizabeth Zane, a sister of Silas Zane, proffered her service. She was young, active and very courageous. She insisted that the garrison was weak at best and not a man could be spared and that the loss of a woman would not be so much felt as that of a man. No argument could deter her from the undertaking. At length it was agreed that she might make an attempt to secure a supply of powder for the garrison. She arranged her clothes to suit the occasion and when the gate was opened she bounded out like a frightened deer. She was confident of success. The Indians in amazement beheld her. They exclaimed, a squaw, a squaw, but made no attempt to interrupt her progress. She arrived at her brother's residence which was opened to receive her. She told her errand and quickly a table cloth was fastened about her waist and a keg of powder emptied into it. She again ventured out. The Indians were not so passive this time and fired at her but the bullets flew harmlessly by knocking dirt into her face. She reached the gate of the fort which was opened for her and she entered it safely.

She had recently arrived from Philadelphia where she had been attending school and was not accustomed to the excitement of the frontier.

The Indians continued the siege and kept up firing all day without intermission, from behind logs, stumps, trees and anything within gunshot of the fort that would screen them. About ten o'clock that night there was another attempt to storm the fort and force their way into it. They received a well directed fire from the fort and also from Colonel Zane's house, which compelled them again to retire out of range of the rifles of the besieged, with the loss of a number of warriors. They now abandoned the siege. The next morning they commenced burning the cabins and killing the stock, the only injury they could inflict. Soon a long peculiar yell by an Indian was heard. He had been watching for the approach of relief and was giving warning of the approach of succor for the fort. Soon after the yells had ceased, the Indians moved rapidly to the river, crossed it and encamped at Indian Spring, a few miles from the river on the northwest side. In less than an hour after they disappeared, Captain Boggs, Captain Swearingen and Williamson arrived with ninety-five mounted men for the relief of the fort. Colonel Zane, in a report, stated that the loss of the enemy was not ascertained, but the loss of the whites was none. One man was slightly wounded.

MURDER OF THE MARTIN FAMILY

A band of roving Indians attacked the family of a settler by the name of Martin in the summer of 1789, and murdered every member of it. Martin had taken up a claim near Wheeling and had made an improvement and was living on it with his family, thinking there was no immediate danger when attacked, of which no account is given, as no one was left to relate the incident. It was soon learned that the family had been murdered and a party of about a dozen men left Fort Henry under the command of a man by the name of Howser to investigate the rumor of the murder and attempt to overtake and chastise the murderers. In their search, they traveled eight or ten miles in a southerly direction and found no trace of them and were about to retrace their steps when they saw an Indian girl descending a hill toward them. They made signs of peace and she approached within a few rods of them when she drew a piece of paper from her bosom and threw it towards them and with the fleetness of a deer fled in the direction from whence she came.

Howser picked up the note which read: "Make your escape; Indians are pursuing you." They started for Baker's Station as fast as they could run but did not reach it until they were attacked by Indians who had been pursuing them. The men treed and returned the fire and drove the enemy from their position and put them to flight without loss to the whites. They arrived at the station and related the circumstance and later it was learned that the note had been written by a white man by the name of Watson who was with the Indians and it was delivered by a daughter of a Delaware chief who was friendly to the whites.

There appears to have been two parties of Indians and while the whites were following in the direction one party had taken the other party was following the whites and overtook and attacked them. From tracks about the premises, it was thought that the party that murdered the Martin family consisted of five Indians.

Murder of the Tush Family.

A band of roving Indians attacked the family of George Tush at the mouth of Bruce's Run in what is now Sand Hill District, wounded Tush, murdered two children in the evening and his wife soon after leaving the scene of the attack.

Tush had settled there some years before and had made some improvements and as there had been no Indians in the neighborhood for some time it was thought that there was no danger and he and the family were engaged in the usual farm work, when on a September evening, in 1794, as he was feeding some hogs in a pen, the stillness of the evening was broken by the ring of three rifles, and Tush rushed past the cabin door and fled into the forest in agony and excitement. One of the bullets struck him across the breast, cutting deeply into it and carrying away part of the bone and lodging in his shoulder, causing great pain.

The Indians entered the cabin and in their usual brutal manner seized the youngest child by the heels, dashed it against the wall and left it for dead. Three others were tomahawked, scalped and left for dead. After plundering the house and taking what they could carry, they started for the river with Mrs. Tush a prisoner. Her strength was evidently not sufficient to enable her to travel as rapidly as the Indians and she was tomahawked about two miles from the cabin. Her bleached remains were found by her husband more than a year after the murder while he was hunting.

Tush, in a crazed condition from the pain, passed the cabin and reached the home of Jacob Wetzel late in the night, very weak from pain and loss of blood and badly crippled from a fall over a cliff of rocks while in the woods. He and Wetzel visited the scene of the murder the next morning and found the infant alive and also one of the children that had been tomahawked and scalped, both of whom recovered. The little fellow had been struck with the pipe end of the tomahawk and stunned and while he lay as quiet as death, was scalped and the scalp carried away as a trophy by the Indians.

Indians Murder Adam Grandstaff

One of the early settlers of what is now Sand Hill District, was a man by the name of Adam Grandstaff. He settled some time near that of Wetzel, Bonnett and Earliwine. His improvement was some distance from the creek and was about three miles from Shepherd's Fort, which was on Little Wheeling Creek near the Monument Bridge.

After Indian hostilities commenced he removed his family to a fort, and after Shepherd's Fort was rebuilt, he removed his family to it, but went almost every day to his farm and spent the day at work. One day in March, 1787, he went to work in the morning as usual, clearing the land and preparing to plant a spring crop.

There had not been any Indians seen in the neighborhood nor signs of them, yet most of the settlers were very careful and gave much attention to safety as well as to work. He went to his work that morning alone as was his custom, and spent the day at work and was returning home in the evening when he was shot and scalped by Indians who evidently had been watching for him.

The shot was heard and his failure to arrive at the fort at the usual time, caused a fear that he had been murdered. A search was made and his body was found where he had been shot and scalped as he was returning home and was not more than a mile from the fort.

Murder of the Bevans Children.

Harry Clark was one of the early settlers in what is now Union District. His farm was on the ridge back of the upper end of the Grave Creek Narrows. In time of danger he removed his family to Wheeling, and was one of the defenders

HISTORY OF MARSHALL COUNTY, W. VA. 37

of the fort in the attack commenced on the eleventh of September, 1782.

A few years after this siege there was quite a large settlement on the ridge between Big Wheeling Creek and the waters of Little Grave Creek. It was thought advisable to build a block-house on that ridge and provide a place of safety nearer their homes than Wheeling. A block-house was erected on a ridge near the site of the Pleasant Hill church at the village of Sherrard. The fortification was called Clark's Blockhouse in honor of the promoter. It consisted of four cabins arranged that when enclosed with pickets twelve feet high, was quite strong.

In time of danger the settlers of the neighborhood gathered at the block-house. There were few summers for some years that depredations committed by Indians did not cause the settlers to seek the protection of the little fortification.

In the year 1787, Indians were quite bad, as there were an unusual number of small scalping parties prowling through the forest committing depredations upon the settlers.

A family by the name of Bevans had settled on the ridge about a mile from the fort. The family consisted of the parents, two sons and two daughters. One of the daughters was married to a man by the name of James Anderson, who was at the fort that summer with the Bevans family.

One day that summer the two girls and the two boys of that family went to their farm to pull flax. As there had been no signs of Indians for some time they never thought of danger. They reached the field and were sitting on the fence looking at the flax when they were startled by the report of rifles and John, the oldest boy, was shot through the body. He started for the block-house as fast as he could run with an Indian after him. He kept ahead of the Indian until within sight of it when he fell dead. The Indian had given up pursuit when he saw him fall, but he proceeded to tomahawk and scalp him.

Cornelius, the younger boy, ran in a different direction and in going down a hill he jumped over the trunk of a fallen tree and hid in the brush of the top of it and escaped. The two girls were tomahawked and scalped at the place where they were attacked. They were buried in one grave where they fell.

One account states that James Anderson, the husband of one of the murdered girls, was murdered at the same time, having accompanied his wife to assist in the work, but it is a matter of uncertainty as there are conflicting statements concerning the attack upon the children at the field.

Indians Attack Hunters.

Frederick, John and Martin Crow and a young man by the name of Davis, left their homes on the waters of Wheeling Creek and went to Fishing Creek, in what is now Wetzel County, in August, 1789, to hunt. The first preparation was to make a hut or hunter's camp which was made like the old-time house as was usually found in sugar camps. They were made open at the front and sloped to the rear and were generally covered with bark.

The second day they started out to hunt and late in the afternoon Frederick and Martin were returning to the camp together and had almost reached it when they were fired upon by Indians who were concealed in the rear of the camp. The Indians had evidently found the camp and had concealed themselves to await the arrival of the hunters.

Frederick received a flesh wound in the left breast and under the arm, while a bullet carried away part of one of Martin's ears. The two brothers ran off at the top of their speed and in the chase Martin appeared to have changed his course and escaped the Indians, while they followed Frederick as fast as they could, expecting to overtake him. They had fired the loads from their guns when they shot at them near the camp and had no opportunity to reload them yet.

Frederick came to the creek and without a moment of hesitation, jumped down the bank and waded the creek which was waist deep, and reached the south bank where he hesitated a moment. The Indians reached the bank where he had jumped down but showed no inclination to cross, but one threw his tomahawk which came unpleasantly near Frederick. He lost no time in getting up the bank and started up the creek as fast as he could run. His wound was bleeding freely all the time, but he snatched sasafras leaves from the bushes which grew abundantly in the woods and chewed quite a wad into mucilage which he pressed into the wound and stopped the flow of blood. He started up the creek at full speed and the Indians followed up on the north bank expecting to intercept him at a sharp bend where the bank is close to the creek.

Once he looked back and by doing so probably saved his life. An Indian who had reloaded his gun had raised it to his shoulder to shoot at him. He threw himself upon the ground and the bullet went whistling harmlessly by. Then he jumped to his feet and started for a final race. Darkness settled down upon the primeval forest and he left the path and escaped in the darkness.

The hunters had agreed that in case of separation that

they would imitate the hooting of the owl or the howling of a wolf as signals by which they would make their whereabouts known to each other. By use of these signals Frederick and Martin Crow and Davis got together in the night and left for home, having failed to find John Crow.

A number of men started from Wheeling Creek as soon as the three hunters arrived home, for Fishing Creek, to ascertain what had become of John Crow. They found him the third day after the attack upon the camp a short distance from it, dead and scalped.

It was thought that he heard the firing at the camp and came to see what caused it, and in case of danger, to aid the other three, and was killed a short distance from it. It is said that five bullet holes were found in his breast in a space that could be covered with an ordinary sized hand. One writer stated that nine bullet holes were found in him. He was buried the same day he was found. His grave was dug in the creek bottom with knives, sticks and tomahawks. A tree was cut down and puncheon were split from it to make a coffin, at least what had to be used as such. There was one puncheon for each side, one for the bottom, and one for the lid, while short pieces sufficed for ends.

He was buried under a tree and hsi name and the date of his death were carved upon the tree.

Murder of the Crow Girls.

Among the many bloody murders committed by Indians none were more revolting than the murder of the Crow girls.

The father of the girls settled on the south branch of Wheeling Creek about one and one-half miles from the mouth of it, or where it empties into Big Wheeling Creek. This branch is frequently called Dunkard Creek, but is better known as Crow's Creek. The improvement was made in a wide bottom on the north side of the creek.

The story generally related is given in connection with events in the history of Marshall County, as part of the farm is in the county but the residence was in Pennsylvania, only a short distance from the dividing line between the two states.

Three of the family were tomahawked and two were shot. Four of the family were killed by Indians. The murder of the three girls, probably, occurred in May, 1785. That year was noted for the murders committed by roving bands of Indians generally called scalping parties.

In the evening the four sisters started to take a walk up the creek and walked along the bank of the beautiful stream, enjoying the scenery until they reached a point near the mouth of Stone Coal Run, about a mile from home. They turned about to return home when two Indians and a white renegade sprang from behind a rock where they had been concealed, and took them prisoners. They threatened them with instant death if they made any noise. They took the girls a short distance up the hill from the path along the bank and made them sit down on a log. They questioned them as to the number of men at the different places of safety, and the general conditions of the settlement.

A consultation was held in which the conversation was carried on in the Indian tongue, but the girls soon became aware that there was a strong disposition to murder them. They held the girls by the wrists all the time to prevent them attempting to escape.

The names of the girls as given were Elizabeth, Susan, Catharine and Christina. Christina was the only one who escaped and she lived to be quite old and it was she that related the sad story of the murder of the three innocent girls.

She became aware that death was decided as their fate and was resolved to improve the first opportunity to attempt to escape. She said that a big Indian began to tomahawk her sister Susan and struck at her with a tomahawk. She dodged and it struck her on the neck, severing the jugular vein. The blood spurted and the Indian holding her sprang to one side and she gave her arm a twist with all her might and in doing so broke his grasp upon her wrist and freed her from him and she started up the hill as rapidly as she could run, pulling herself up by bushes and in doing so, dodged from side to side and escaped a bullet fired at her by an Indian, although it passed through her hair and grazed the skin. She said that the Indian could have caught and killed her but if he had attempted to do so he would have been compelled to release her sister and give her an opportunity to escape. She ran in an opposite direction to that of her home and in doing so escaped. One of the Indians ran around the hill to intercept her if she came down the hill but he failed to find her and passed around below where she was hid in a cluster of bushes. After the Indians had disappeared some time she left her hiding place and ran home as fast as she could run.

By the time she reached home it was late in the evening and it appears that no one went to the scene of the murder until the next morning. One account states that the family went to Findley's Block-house that evening and with the first rays of light the next morning a number of settlers were ready to start in pursuit of the murderers. They found two of the girls dead and one, Elizabeth, yet alive but mortally wounded and scalped. She was kindly cared for by loving friends and parents but expired the third evening after the murder of her two sisters. She was conscious and had sufficient vitality to relate the story of the murder.

They were buried on the farm near the residence and a cedar tree was planted by the grave and it may be seen to this date, marking the resting place of the three girls.

It is said that Christina grew up to womanhood but never forgot the appearance of the savages, red and white, who murdered her sisters. A number of years after the horrid murder, a number of neighbors of their father were gathered at his improvement participating in an old-time log rolling. Mrs. Crow and Christina were preparing dinner and the men were slowly wending their way to the house for the midday meal, when an Indian and a white man rode up to the house and asked Mrs. Crow for a drink of milk. She started to get it and Christina, who was putting the dinner on the table, heard the voices and ran to the door and looked at them and said to her mother, "Don't give them any for they are two of the men who murdered my sisters." They sprang upon their horses and rode off. The men gathered around the table and the matter was mentioned and the girl said that she was positive that they were two of the men who had murdered her sisters.

Her father and a man by the name of Dickerson left the table and held a conversation for some time, after which they started in pursuit of them. They took the trail which went up the creek. They took to the ridges to save time, and being well acquainted with the country, thought to intercept them at some point in advance. They rode rapidly over the ridges and late in the afternoon passed over the dividing ridge and started down Dunkard Creek toward the Monongahela River. They struck the trail where they expected to find it and followed it until darkness prevented them from following it farther that night.

They encamped for the night and with the first rays of light, they were again in the saddle and in pursuit of the murderers. They went back to the place where they had last clearly seen the trail and there started upon it and soon found where they had encamped for the night the coals from their fire were still smoldering when they reached it. They followed the trail down towards the river quite a distance and then returned home. They gave out no statement on their return as to whether or not they overtook the men and it is said that they were rather reticent about their success in the pursuit, but would remark, "They will do no more harm in this neighborhood."

One writer of the story stated that in arranging for the pursuit, Dickinson was to shoot the white man, who appears to have been known to them by the name of Spicer, and Mr. Crow was to take care of the Indian. It is generally thought that they overtook them and meted out justice as would have been upheld by any jury composed of settlers at that day.

Death of Hugh Cameron.

Captain Boggs settled near the river at the mouth of a run that bears his name, at an early date. He made improvements there and in time of danger removed his family to Wheeling to Fort Henry, and when it was thought safe to venture out from the fort returned to the farm and worked on it.

In the spring of 1782, Indians appeared early and commenced their usual depredations on the south side of the Ohio River.

Boggs had two men in his employ, one of whose name was Hugh Cameron. Early in February of that year Captain Boggs removed his family to the fort, but continued to work on his improvement. Bright, warm weather in February started sugar water to run; they opened a sugar camp and tapped a number of trees and commenced making sugar. The two young men remained at the camp at night to attend to the boiling of water. Mr. Boggs requested them to be cautious and give attention to safety, more especially at night. He cautioned them that under no circumstances were both to sleep at the same time; but one of them to keep awake and on a careful watch for danger, lest Indians might be prowling in the forest and see the fire and attack them. There had been no indications of the presence of Indians so far and as no depredations had been committed the young men did not heed the warning given them. One night while both were asleep Indians attacked them and killed Cameron. The other young man escaped in the darkness and reached Wheeling safely.

Some years afterwards the remains of Cameron were found near the mouth of Boggs Run but the head was not there. It was found soon after almost a mile up the run where it was thought to have been carried by wild animals and was recognized by a peculiar tooth.

John Neiswanger Killed by Indians.

In the summer of 1783, John Neiswanger, a noted hunter

and Indian scout of the Upper Ohio Valley, was killed at the mouth of Little Grave Creek by a party of Indians.

He was engaged much of his time, from the breaking out of the war until the time of his death, as a scout, and his efficiency as such saved the life of many a settler by his timely warning of the presence of Indians in the neighborhood. He would dress in the costume of an Indian and penterate into their country and, knowing their habits, would lay in concealment and watch their movements, and with a fleetness creditable to a deer, would hasten to the settlement and spread the alarm.

He and Joseph Heffler left Fort Henry on a scout down the Ohio River to gather information of the movements of the Indians along the river front. They reached the mouth of Little Grave Creek and ran their canoe into it to spend the night. A party of Indians who had been watching their movements in the night, made a furious attack upon them, killing Neiswanger. Heffler escaped. In attempting to capture Heffler, the canoe got loose and drifted from the creek, thus preventing the Indians from getting the much-prized scalp of Neiswanger. The canoe drifted upon the head of Captina Island, where it was found some months after with the dead body of the scout and his gun in it.

Neiswanger came to the waters of Wheeling Creek about the year 1776 and took up a tract of four hundred acres of land on Middle Wheeling Creek, deadened the trees on a few acres and built a cabin, but later found it unsafe to remain on that spot as it was quite a distance from any of the few forts or block-houses; so he moved to the other side of his claim and built a cave under a shelving rock in a small stream. He dug out and walled a room, making a fortified cave under the cataract where the family went in case of alarm. At a time of great danger he took his family to Shepherd's Fort or to Fort Henry. His death was a great loss, as men of his type were very essential to the safety of the infant settlements in that section of the country.

William McIntosh Decoyed and Killed by Indians.

In the early days of the settlement of this country the whites and Indians were in the habit of imitating birds and animals for various purposes. When they were scattered in time of danger they used certain sounds made by birds or animals to give their whereabouts to each other and by doing so gather their scattered force together. The turkey call was often used in daytime for the same purpose. Its imitation was so complete that even turkeys were decoyed by hunters of both races, and at times they decoyed each other.

A case of the latter occurred at the Flats of Grave Creek in the days of Indian depredations. A man by the name of William McIntosh, with a wife and one child, was at the Tomlinson fort. He, like most others, was fond of turkey. He and others frequently heard a turkey gobbling on the north side of the river opposite the mouth of Little Grave Creek. McIntosh spoke of crossing the river and bringing the turkey over and having a roast. He was warned by hunters who suspected that the gobbling was done by an Indian. He thought that he knew a turkey when he heard it, and accordingly, one morning he took his gun and dog and crossed the river near the mouth of Little Grave Creek, thinking that he would bring the turkey home with him.

After almost two days' absence, some men crossed the river to ascertain what had become of him and found him about ten steps from the river, dead and scalped, where he had been shot by an Indian who had spent some time gobbling to decoy some settler that he might murder him. His faithful dog was lying by the side of his master keeping watch over the dead body.

His body was brought back to the Flats of Grave Creek and buried.

Robert Carpenter Escapes from Indians.

A young man by the name of Robert Carpenter, a nephew of Joseph Tomlinson, had a close call in hunting some horses in the Flats of Grave Creek in the days of Indian hostilities. He was after some horses near the Big Creek and went too near a party of Indians who were trying to catch the same horses. They fired at him and a shot struck him in the shoulder, breaking the bone. The Indians captured him. After trying in vain to catch the horses they concluded that Carpenter could catch them as they knew him and would not be so shy of him. They released him and told him to catch them. He started to run in the direction of a house but was soon recaptured by the Indians. After trying some time to catch the horses, Carpenter told them that if they would let him he would catch the horses and go with them to their towns. They threatened him with all kinds of horrid deaths if he tried to escape. After some time they saw they could not catch any of the horses, they released Carpenter, who was determined to effect his escape. He had been impeded in the first attempt to escape by having on a pair of old shoes. This time he walked gently, driving the horses in a direction suiting his purpose and at the same time loosening his shoes. After proceeding about two hundred yards, he kicked the shoes off and grasped his wounded arm and summoned all his strength for a final run for liberty. With the start he had and free from his shoes he went through the woods with a speed that would have been creditable to a frightened deer, and soon reached the residence of a settler by the name of Nathan Masters. With a poultice of slippery elm bark and the usual frontier treatments, Carpenter soon recovered from the wound.

COLONEL BEELER

The story below, giving the experience of one of the early settlers of Marshall County, was written by an unknown writer and the story was about the experience of Colonel Beeler, and the title of it was, ABOUT COLONEL BEELER AND THE MOHAWK TRIBES.

When Colonel Beeler emigrated to this section (Cameron) he located a great deal of land, the greater part of which was about the fort. The entire neighborhood where Cameron now stands, was a wide scope of country extending to the forks of Fish creek, also was owned by him at that early day. Shortly after his coming to this point, in company with other men, they were permanently located at the fort. A great many Indians from the Shawnee and Mohawk tribes, who were stationed about Wheeling and the Flats of Grave Creek, came to prowl about the fort to annoy Colonel Beeler in every conceivable way they could, and if possible, drive him from the dominions, which they claimed the "Great Spirit" had bequeathed unto them.

Beeler's Station at that time, was indeed a situation of sadness. The sun rose in the morning and as its glittering beams gleamed down upon the earth, through the heavy timber that then clothed the hills and vales of Virginia, its dawning influence came in contact with the solitary fort, standing in the midst of a desolate wilderness. Evening came and the inmates of Beeler's fort looked with eyes expressive of the saddest reluctance to see the sun sink down in the west. The curtains of darkness is drawn over creation and darkness settles around and envelopes the fort.

The women and children of this secluded structure shudder with awe to think of the monotony of the night, and truly the nights were terrible. The valley of Grave creek sloped off to the west, the dark valley of Wolf Run stretches far to the north, in the darkness and stillness of the night, birds of evil omen flew from one valley to the other, and as they passed over the fort they flapped their wings and uttered their unearthly shrieks. In the deep valleys and ravines, on all sides the howls of the wolf, the fierce shriek of the panther, and the yell of the wild cat could be distinctly heard. The harsh-toned voice of the terrible red man could be heard on every hill top as they echoed and re-echoed their answers to each other. These were the agencies and elements that surrounded Beeler's Station in the night during the primeval ages of Virginia.

During the summer of 1780 it is said that Colonel Beeler became discouraged, and I presume it was no wonder; for where is the man of this day and date that could have faced what Colonel Beeler did and live? New obstacles were constantly being conceived and brought into existence day after day to barricade his pathway, to frustrate and hinder him from accomplishing the great designs he had undertaken. His enemies were numerous, and they were so terribly disfigured with evil designs, that the lives of Colonel Beeler and his family were constantly endangered whenever they went outside the fort. Under these terrible circumstances for Colonel Beeler to establish a colony in the neighborhood presupposes to him the idea that he must have additional aid. Accordingly, in the dead of winter, 1780, he accompanied by Mr. Tomlinson of the fort at Moundsville, and Ryerson of Ryerson's Station, Pa. walked over the mountains through deep snow, in the dead of winter, through Pennsylvania to the city of Philadelphia. He there laid his complaint to the chief officers of that state regarding his sad situation in the wilds of Virginia. He requested them to send him assistance. They were moved by his story and agreed to furnish him the desired aid. So in the spring of 1781, fifty-three men under the command of Captain Jerremiah Long, arrived at Beeler's fort.

They assumed the name of "six months men," and the duty was to guard the different forts which were then located at different points in this country, and to pilot and protect men who wished to go from one station to another. Braver and nobler men never lived than were these who composed Captain Long's company. They were all in the prime of manhood, except Captain Long, who was a tolerably old man. They stayed in the wilds of Virginia for a number of years, and the greatest respect was manifested towards them by those early settlers whom they protected. And the services which these six months men rendered were the very instrumentalities which enabled the frontiersmen to colonize this neighborhood and bring about settlements of civilized people.

During the year 1782 spies were appointed by the different parties throughout the country. Thomas Younken was appointed a spy at Beeler's Station. Martin Wetzal was appointed by the people at Wetzal's fort to act as a spy in conjunction with the spy for Beeler's Station. These two men were not only acquainted with the Indians and their language, but also understood thoroughly their customs and plans of warfare. The energy, bravery and perseverance these two men possessed did not only secure for them the positions of spies, but won for them destinies which will live as history bears record of the great deeds and daring feats performed by these heroes of an early frontier. Their history is one repeated scene of combat, blood-shed and massacre with Indians, and that degree of success which attended them on all occasions and under all circumstances, has gone far towards characterizing them as among the bravest and most daring men that ever walked the face of the earth.

The duty of Younken and Wetzal, when acting as spies for Beeler's Station, was to scout through the woods round about the fort, to ascertain, if possible, the exact strength of the Indian forces, and to determine whether they were making any signs indicative of an attack on the fort.

The year in which Colonel Beeler died is not known, but the spot of ground that now contains his smoldering ashes is only a few rods distant from where his old fort stood. The graves of many others who had undergone the terrible ordeals which surrounded and effected the early settlers of this once distracted neighborhood, can plainly be seen near the fort.

But what a change has taken place in this vicinity since they passed away. One hundred years ago, and the fort could have been seen standing alone in solitude—to-day can be seen two magnificent church-houses, where men, women and children come up each Sabbath to worship—not an imaginary spirit the Indians once did—but to worship the true and living GOD.

THE WETZEL FAMILY

Of the many names of early settlers in the Upper Ohio Valley none is more familiar than WETZEL.

JOHN WETZEL settled on the waters of Big Wheeling Creek in what is now Marshall County at an early day and soon became identified with the stirring events of the times. He was of German descent. It is not known from what colony he came. Some say from Pennsylvania and others from Maryland. He seems to have known the Zane family before he started in search of a home in the Ohio Valley. He had five sons and two daughters. The names of the sons were Martin,

Lewis, Jacob, George and John. The daughters were Susan and Christina.

Wetzel took up a claim about fourteen miles from the mouth of Wheeling Creek and improved it and also took up land elsewhere. When the Indians became hostile a fort was built at the forks of Wheeling Creek on the land of David Shepherd and was known in history as Shepherd's Fort, and was a place of refuge for the settlers at and above the forks of Wheeling Creek in time of danger until abandoned the twenty-seventh of September, 1777, and burned by Indians later. After that they went to Fort Henry at Wheeling until about the year 1785 when Shepherd rebuilt the fort, when they left the fort at Wheeling and returned to the fort at the forks of the creek which was much nearer their improvements and more convenient.

John Wetzel took up a claim on Middle Island Creek and it was on his return from it that he lost his life.

In the summer of 1787, as he and a companion were returning to Wheeling Creek from his improvement on Middle Island Creek, he was killed by Indians. They were paddling up the river on the west side and were nearly opposite Baker's Station when some Indians on the west or Ohio side of the river ordered them to land. This they did not do and the Indians fired upon them and shot Wetzel through the body. Realizing the nature of the wound, he ordered his companion to lay down in the canoe while he plied the paddle and got out of range of the guns of the Indians. They landed at Baker's Station where Wetzel died shortly after landing. He was buried at what has long been known as Grave Yard Run, a short distance below Captina station on the Ohio River Division of the B. & O. Railroad. Until the past few years a grave marker of common sandstone marked the place where the body lay. On it was the simple inscription, J. W., 1787. The stone has been broken and carried away until none of it remains to mark the spot where he was buried. The largest piece of it known is now said to be in a museum at Philadelphia.

JOHN T. WETZEL gave the following account of the Wetzel family, which has been handed down as tradition and adds somewhat to the history of the members and supplies a missing link in the history of the family.

He said that John Wetzel, Sr., lived at Oldtown, Rockingham County, Virginia, at an early day, and that his grandfather, Martin Wetzel, was born there and he thinks some of the other children were born there. From Oldtown he re-

HISTORY OF MARSHALL COUNTY, W. VA.

moved to Pennsylvania and lived for some time not far from Wills Creek, then a frontier settlement and became acquainted with the Zanes, Shepherds and Earliwines and came with them when they came to Wheeling Creek in search of homes in the forest of Northwestern Virginia.

Wetzel and Earliwine settled in what is now Sand Hill District, Marshall County, and Shepherd settled below on another branch of the creek.

The elder Wetzel spent much time in taking up and improving tomahawk claims, other than the one taken up on the waters of Big Wheeling Creek. He took up claims down the river and he was on his way home from working on one of his claims when he was killed.

He had taken up a claim on Middle Island Creek and had been there at work in the summer of 1787 and was returning with his sons, Martin, Lewis and George and a man by the name of Scott. A dog belonging to him was also in the canoe with them. When they reached a point almost opposite Baker's Station in Cresap's Bottom, they were attacked by some Indians concealed on the west side of the river. The elder Wetzel was killed and his son George was shot through the body. The bullet that went through the body of George killed the dog that lay in the canoe. George told the others to lie down in the canoe and he would paddle them out of danger, as he was already fatally wounded. Martin and Scott did as directed but Lewis did not; he loaded his gun and fired at the Indians till out of range of them.

George died that night and was buried on the banks of Grave Yard Run beside his father, both in coffins made of hickory bark. This account was given by Martin Wetzel and preserved traditionally by his descendants and clears the mystery of what became of George, whose name is never mentioned in the many stirring events of the bloody Indian war that broke out in the year 1777 and closed with the Battle of Fallen Timber in 1794.

Lewis.

In June of 1778, Martin Wetzel was out one day hunting and John was on an errand and the rest of the family were at work in a field cultivating corn. Lewis and Jacob were working in a distant part of the field from the others. They were working very quietly and industriously when suddenly the crack of a gun and the yell of Indians broke the stillness of the valley. The bullet struck Lewis in the breast giving him a slight wound. The father, mother and other members of the family in that part of the field hid in a thicket near them and remained there until the Indians had been gone some time. The Indians, with the two boys, started for the river and reached it not far from the mouth of Bogg's Run and crossed to the mouth of McMahon's Creek and camped for the night. The second night they camped at a place called Big Lick in what is now Goshon Township, Belmont County, Ohio. The boys appeared cheerful and the Indians did not take the precaution to tie them or guard them at night. The moon was full and the night was very bright, all lay down and were to all appearances sound asleep. Lewis kept awake and thought that now was their best opportunity to make their escape. He aroused Jacob and they quietly stole away from the camp and sat down on a log a short distance from it to decide what to do. Lewis said, "We can not go home barefooted. You stay and I will go back and get some moccasins." He soon returned with them and said to his brother, "We ought to have a gun. I will go and get one." He soon returned with a gun. When he was at the camp to get the gun one of the Indians raised up on his elbow and muttered, rolled over and lay down. Lewis stood over him with a tomahawk that had dropped from the belt of the Indian, ready to strike if he attempted to arise to his feet, but the Indian lay down and saved his life.

The boys started on the trail back towards the river as rapidly as they could go. The Indians awoke and found that the boys had escaped and started after them. The boys noticed them as they kept a careful wacth on the movement behind them and went into a thicket and remained hid until the Indians had passed. They soon returned and the boys by the same movement hid from them again. The Indians then went back to the camp and got their horses and again started after the boys, and again the boys slipped aside in a thicket and escaped them. The Indians gave up the pursuit and the boys hurried as fast as they could travel and on the next evening reached the Ohio River opposite Zane's Island and constructed a raft and crossed it, and to the surprise of their parents reached home the fourth day after they were captured. It is said that Lewis was fourteen and Jacob twelve. It was their first experience with the Indians.

In the summer of 1780 Indians stole some horses from settlers on the upper waters of Wheeling Creek and a party of whites started in pursuit of them. They passed the Wetzel farm and found Lewis at work cultivating corn and asked him to join them in the pursuit but he refused, stating that his father had gone from home and had requested him to stay at home and cultivate the corn and he did not like to go without his father's permission. They continued their persuasion; he unhitched his father's favorite mare and with his gun joined the party in pursuit of the Indians. The Indians reached the river somewhere near the foot of Boggs Island and crossed it. The whites pursued the trail and soon found them encamped thinking they were out of danger of pursuit. They were lying down near a spring and the horses were hobbled and grazing near them. The Indians, three in number, fled. leaving the horses grazing. The whites decided to take the stolen horses and leave the horses they had rode to graze and rest a while and left three men to bring them when rested. The Indians soon made their appearance between the men and the horses and the white men took to their heels and soon joined those who had started to return.

Now Wetzel's troubles commenced. He said that he had left home without the consent of his father and had brought his favorite mare and she had been left for the Indians to take away. Lewis is said to have both loved and feared his father and it might be added that he was an obedient son. He asked the men to return with him and get the horses. None were willing to return and it is said that he used all manner of persuasion and all kinds of argument but none would agree to return and attempt to get the horses and he finally said that he would go by himself if no one would go with him. He said that he would prefer to go home without his scalp and with the mare than to go with his scalp and without the mare. At last two men most to blame for his leaving home without permission agreed to return with him and get the horses if they had to fight it out with the Indians. They started back to the spring where the horses were and arranged their line of operation.

It was arranged that Wetzel should go first and when they passed three trees all were to tree and open the fight. Wetzel reached his tree and looked around to see if the other two men were at their posts ready for action, but instead of being in line as agreed they were out of gunshot and running at the top of their speed. He was now in a critical situation, three Indians and a boy only sixteen years old, very unequal forces. He took in the situation in a moment and decided that as the odds were against him some strategy must be used or both scalp and mare would be lost.

The Indians were treed and had been since they discovered the approach of the whites. After some hesitation he put his hat on the ramrod of his gun and gradually exposed it as if he was quietly attempting to get sight of the Indians. His scheme succeeded and all three Indians fired and the hat fell riddled. He let the hat fall as if it had been on his head and he had been shot dead. All three Indians threw down their guns and with a yell rushed to the fallen hat thinking to tomahawk and scalp him. Young Wetzel jumped from behind the tree and shot the foremost Indian dead. The other two sure of killing him rushed at him and he started to run with a fleetness of a dear and soon had his gun loaded and wheeled around and one more Indian was killed. The other now sure of the scalp of the boy rushed at him with his tomahawk raised but in a short time the boy wheeled around as he was about to throw it and fired a bullet through him that ended his life and the unequal conflict.

Wetzel scalped the Indians, loaded his gun, got the mare and soon overtook the men who were too cowardly to stand by him when they got him into trouble and danger of his life. This was the first fight he had with Indians and the matter soon brought him into prominence, for his courage and also the fact that he had learned to load a gun while running at full speed, and which proved of great value to him afterwards in many instances when he was pursued by Indians.

The second thrilling encounter Lewis Wetzel had with Indians was in the summer of 1782 when he was eighteen years old. The incident was related by an eye witness, who was himself a participant in the race for life.

Thomas Mills, a straggler from the army of the unfortunate Colonel Crawford, was making his way home near Wheeling, and reached Indian Springs about a mile east of where St. Clairsville, Ohio now stands. His horse was so tired and worn out with the trip from Sandusky Plains that he decided to leave it and make the rest of the way home on foot and after resting he said he would go back and get his horse.

His cousin Joshua Davis, a boy a little past fifteen years old, insisted that he wait till Lewis Wetzel return from a scout and get Wetzel to go with him. To this he consented. Lewis came in that night and when young Davis asked him to go he readily consented to it. Davis now asked permission to go with them but as he had done little scouting, Mills refused to let him go. The boy insisted upon going and finally Wetzel said: "Josh'll make a scout; he's got metal."

All things were arranged to start the following morning. Soon after daylight they crossed the river just below the point of the island and went up the hill and followed the ridges. It was a hot June day ahd near noon they arrived near the spring. Wetzel who was in the lead. turned around and said: "If there are any Indians we had better know it. They will be at the spring at this time of the day or near it." They stopped and Wetzel said that he would go first and Mills after him and Davis behind. They moved cautiously till the first two reached a thicket on a bank just above the spring. The crack of guns and yells of Indians and the scream of Mills broke the stillness of the forest.

Wetzel came back on the trail running at full speed, loading his gun. Davis shot at the first Indian he saw and started back as fast as he could run. Wetzel soon overtook him, running in a long dog-trot, which was his usual gait when pursued by Indians. He said to young Davis: "Don't run. Josh. trot, it'll not tire you so much." The Indians, thought to be fifty or more from the noise they made, were jumping as they ran and yelling at the top of their voices.

After running almost a mile, Wetzel looked back and said: "There's only four Indians after us now; I'll try a pop at the foremost one." He did so and the Indian fell to the ground dead.

Wetzel soon had his gun reloaded and as they made a turn an Indian who had cut across came out beside them. As Wetzel attempted to shoot, the Indian caught hold of the barrel of the gun, but Wetzel was too quick for him and jumped to one side and brought the gun to the breast of the Indian and shot him dead in his tracks.

He said to the boy: "Josh, at the next turn there's a thicket just over the bank; hide in it and the Indians will follow me. I'll meet you at the creek." At the turn the boy jumped over the hill and laid down in the thicket and soon the foremost Indian passed and bang went the gun of Wetzel and another Indian was killed. The other stopped on the bank near the boy and took a look at Wetzel and said, "Whew, no catch him, gun always loaded." He started back as fast as his legs could carry him toward the spring.

The two met at the creek and went leisurely home. A few days later some men went to bury Mills and found that the bullet had broken his ankle.

In the summer of 1786 Indians were troublesome about Wheeling, especially in the Short Creek settlement, and some murders were committed by them. The Indians all seemed to escape. At last the settlers concluded to make up a purse and offer a reward for an Indian scalp. A purse of one hundred dollars was made up and a party of twenty men gathered on the fifth of August at Beech Bottom in command of Major McMahon. They went towards the Muskingum Valley. Five men were detailed as scouts and were sent some distance in advance of the main body. Lewis Wetzel was one of the party. The little army proceeded along their way without anything to interrupt their quiet peaceful march in quest of Indians until it reached the valley.

One day the scouts returned to the main body and informed the men that they had found a camp of Indians containing a large number. A consultation was held and as the number at the camp was reported too large for this force to attack it was decided to retreat.

While the controversy was in progress Lewis Wetzel sat on a log with his gun laying across his knees. When a retreat was ordered Wetzel was asked if he was not going along, to which he answered "No." He said they were out there in search of Indians and now since they had found them he saw no use in leaving without scalps. He said that he would get a scalp or lose his own.

The party started home; Wetzel started in a contrary direction. He saw no signs of Indians that evening but was determined to find a small number of them before he gave up the hunt. The night was cold and it was necessary to have a fire, and he knew such a thing would invite destruction. He built a hut of bark something like a charcoal pit and covered it with dirt and leaves, leaving an airhole here and there in it. He got into it and with his blanket drawn around him, spent the night quite comfortably and said it was as warm as a stove room.

The next day he saw a smoke and found a camp with two blankets and a small kettle, which he knew belonged to two Indians who were hunting. He hid near the camp and spent the day waiting for the Indians to return. About sundown the two Indians arrived at the camp and built up a fire and prepared their supper, after which they amused themselves for some time telling stories and singing songs.

About nine or ten o'clock one of the Indians took a firebrand and wrapped his blanket around himself and left the camp. He evidently intended to watch a deer lick, as deer are not afraid to approach fire.

Wetzel waited impatiently for the Indian to return, but he remained away until the birds began to give notice of the approach of daylight. He stealthily approached the sleeping Indian and with one thrust of his knife stopped the throbbing of the heart of the Indian forever. He took his scalp and started home and arrived one day later than the others of the party. He claimed and received the reward for the taking of an Indian scalp.

Louis Wetzel would take what he called a fall hunt in the Indian country. It was at the season of the year when he could expect to find small parties of Indians hunting. On one of these hunts for Indians, he went into the Muskingum Valley. He spent some time before he found an Indian camp

HISTORY OF MARSHALL COUNTY, W. VA.   55

but finally he discovered a camp of four. He saw that the camp was rather large for one man to attack in daylight but he could not think of leaving and not attacking it, so he awaited until late in the night when the hunters were sound asleep.

Carefully and cautiously he emerged from his hiding place near the camp and with his gun in one hand and tomahawk in the other and his hunting knife between his teeth he approached the sleeping hunters. There they lay in the dim light of the camp fire with their swarthy faces turned up to the sky, some of them sleeping a sleep from which they never awoke.

He set his gun against a tree and with tomahawk in one hand and knife in the other he commenced the work of destruction. One after another sank beneath the hatchet of the infuriated hunter till three lay lifeless near their camp fire. His blows were quick and accompanied with the most furious yells. One jumped to his feet and took to the forest followed by Wetzel. He succeeded in eluding the hunter who scalped the three warriors and returned home with the scalps. When asked what luck he had, he replied. "Not much; I treed four but one got away."

Lewis Wetzel roamed the forest and took many hunts and scouts on the north side of the Ohio River. Returning from one of his trips into the Indian country, he saw an Indian standing with his gun ready to fire. Wetzel jumped behind a tree, the Indian doing the same. They stood there for some time.

Wetzel did not relish the idea of spending the day there awaiting the darkness of night to give him an opportunity to get from behind the tree. He decided to try stratagem, so he placed his bearskin cap on the ramrod of his gun and gently pushed it out from behind the tree as if trying to get sight of the Indian and not expose his body in doing it.

The Indian was caught with the scheme of the hunter and and raised his gun and fired at the cap piercing it with a bullet. He imagined that all he had to do now was to scalp the hunter and make his way home to some of the Indian towns in the interior of what is the State of Ohio. Wetzel, to the surprise of the Indian jumped from behind the tree and shot the Indian. He took his scalp and made his way back to Wheeling Creek.

FORT HARMER was erected by the United States Government in the year 1786 on the point below the mouth of the Muskingum River and garrisoned with regular soldiers; and two years later the first legal settlement was made in what is now the State of Ohio.

Soon after General Harmer took command of the Western

Department he sent notice to the Indians that he desired to make peace with them and issued a proclamation warning the whites to cease hostilities so that a peace could be arranged with the Indians. Notwithstanding his efforts to make peace in the West with the Indians, they continued murdering settlers along the Ohio River and also in interior settlements.

In the year 1789 Lewis Wetzel and Veach Dickerson went on a scout on the Ohio side of the river and reached the Muskingum River near Fort Harmer. They watched a path some time and while there an Indian came down the river towards the fort riding a horse in a gallop. They called to the Indian but he did not halt and it was thought that the noise made by the catter of its hoofs on the ground prevented him from hearing them. When he was almost out of range of their guns both fired at him without any apparent effect as he did not change his speed. They returned home and when asked about their scout and seeing Indians they said that they only saw one Indian and shot at him and thought that they had both missed him. They had not missed him as they thought they had but had shot him through the hips and he died that night at the fort.

General Harmer became much enraged and soon after the death of the Indian, a rumor reached him that Lewis Wetzel had shot the Indian. Soon after he heard this he learned that Wetzel was at the cabin of Hamilton Kerr who had made an improvement on an island above the mouth of the Muskingum River. He sent a file of soldiers to the island in the night and arrested Wetzel on the charge of murdering the Indian. He placed Wetzel in chains and in close confinement. Wetzel did not deny shooting the Indian. He proposed to General Harmer that he give him a tomahawk and let him and the Indians fight it out but the General would not listen to any proposition as he was determined to maintain the dignity of his high position.

Soon the colse confinement began to seriously effect Wetzel who had been accustomed all his life to freedom in the open air. He told General Harmer that he could not stand such close confinement and an officer was instructed to take the hunter out each day for exercise. His shackels were removed but his handcuffs remained on him. He would run and jump and caper like a young colt that had been confined in a stable for some time and then turned loose in a pasture. He soon regained his usual vigor.

One day he was taken out for exercises as usual. He would run quite a distance, whirl around and return until he felt his usual strength return when he made up his mind to make a run for liberty or death. He got some distance before

HISTORY OF MARSHALL COUNTY, W. VA. 57

the guards suspected an attempt to escape. They fired their guns at him but missed him. He had entered the forest and knowing the country, he made for a thicket about two miles from the fort. He reached the thicket and found a tree that had fallen across a log under which he squeezed himself and was concealed from view by underbrush so completely that it would be very difficult to find him without very close inspection.

Soldiers and Indians were started in pursuit of Wetzel and passed through the thicket and two of the Indians stood on the log for some time. Wetzel said that his heart beat so violently that he was afraid that they would hear it. They soon left the thicket and Wetzel was alone in the forest. While he lay under the log he could hear the soldiers and Indians yelling as they searched the forest for him. Late in the afternoon the search was abandoned and the soldiers and Indians returned to the fort. Wetzel crawled from his hiding place when he was satisfied that there were none of his pursuers near him.

The thicket was on the Muskingum River and by a circuitous route he reached the Ohio River about three miles below the fort knowing that they would watch for him wherever they knew of a canoe. He knew a friend by the name of Isaac Wiseman who had made an improvement on the Virginia side and he reached the river opposite it. He saw Wiseman in a canoe fishing on the Virginia shore. He was afraid to make a noise and being handcuffed he could not make a raft nor cold he safely attempt to swim the river, although he was an expert swimmer. He waved his hat but Wiseman did not see him. He made a splash in the water which caused Wiseman to look towards him and he waved his hat and in a short time he was safely landed on the Virginia shore.

With a file and hammer in the hands of his friend the handcuffs were removed and he was again free. He was furnished with a gun, blanket and other equipments by his friends and was ready for other adventures. Wiseman was not in a hurry to tell of his part in the escape of Wetzel until after General Harmer had returned to Philadelphia after an inglorious defeat by Indians.

General Harmer heard that Wetzel was at Mingo Bottom and sent Captain Kingsberry with a squad of soldiers with orders to bring him back dead or alive.

He proceeded to Mingo Bottom but it happened that the day he was due to arrive there most of the settlers of that section were at a shooting match at the bottom, Wetzel among them. When they heard of the intentions of the Captain they decided to waylay him and his soldiers and make targets of them. Major McMahon requested them to do nothing until he could see Kingsberry and return to them. He told the Captain that it was absurd to arrest a man for killing an Indian when they were killing whites almost every day. Further, it would be impossible to take Wetzel from that community and stated that an attempt to take him would result in the death of every man in the squad. The Captain, knowing what was the best course to pursue, quietly withdrew and returned to Fort Harmer without Wetzel.

Wetzel thought now that it was at an end and continued to roam up and down the Ohio River. Soon after this he met Captain Kingsberry at Fort Randolph but they passed and each man went his way. In the meantime General Harmer removed his headquarters from Fort Harmer to Fort Washington where Cincinnati now stands.

He offered a large reward for Wetzel, dead or alive. One day Wetzel was sitting in a tavern door at Maysville, not thinking of any danger. Lieutenant Lawler landed with what was usually called a Kentucky boat, with a load of soldiers for Fort Washington and seeing Wetzel, returned to the boat and with a file of soldiers, returned to the tavern and arrested him and pushed off from the shore and landed him that night at the fort where he was again placed in irons.

It was well for Lieutenant Lawler that he made the speed he did for if the settlers had got word of the act in time there is no doubt that he would have received a different kind of reward than that offered by General Harmer.

The news spread like wild-fire and the anger soon reached a white heat, so indignant were the settlers. Petitions were sent to General Harmer from the settlements along the Ohio River asking for the release of Wetzel. All the leading citizens asked for his release but he paid no attention to their petitions. Seeing that petitions were of no avail they started a different kind of movement. They started to gather a sufficient force of men to release him if they had to kill General Harmer and all the troops at the fort. This decided the case as the General saw that the settlers were all in sympathy with Wetzel and determined that he should be released and very wisely set him at liberty to molest him no further.

About the year 1790, or a year later, Lewis Wetzel arrived from a stroll in Kentucky and was hunting on the waters of Wheeling Creek and met a young man who lived on the branch of Wheeling Creek formerly called Dunkard, but is known at present as Crow's Creek, the south fork of Wheeling Creek.

HISTORY OF MARSHALL COUNTY, W. VA. 59

The young man and Wetzel were acquainted and it has been stated that they were cousins. The young friend invited him to go home with him and visit the family, which invitation he accepted. They started up the creek towards the young man's home hunting; they traveled along; being in no hurry, they prolonged the journey some time, not thinking of harm to any one or need of haste in getting to the end of their journey. When they arrived at the home of his friend Wetzel found, instead of a family ready to greet him kindly, that Indians had been there and murdered the family and burned the house. Wetzel examined the trail and found that the party consisted of three Indians and a white man and further examination revealed the fact that five persons left the cabin and from the tracks it was decided that a young woman the family had reared was one of the number and was a prisoner in the hands of the Indians and white renegade. The rest of the family had been murdered and their bodies burned in the cabin which was now burned to the ground. No time was to be lost if anything was to be done towards the rescue of the young woman. The matter was left to Wetzel to direct and lead a rescuing party. Wetzel said that they would attempt to overtake them before they reached the Ohio River. It was late in the day and movements must be made quickly as they had considerable start of them and were well on their way to the river. Caution had been taken to conceal their trail but the quick eye of the hunter soon detected it.

They followed the trail like a hound follows that of a deer or fox until Wetzel was satisfied at about the point at which the party would reach the river. He then changed his plan and took the most direct route to the river at the point at which he was sure they would reach it to cross. He was sure they would reach the river at the mouth of Bip Captina and for that point he directed their course. They followed their course with the object of overtaking them before they reached the river and to that end hurried as rapidly as possible, taking the shortest routes in all cases and avoided long winding paths around knowls by going over them and thus gaining time. They found a deer path in the direction they wished to go and followed it till late in the night, only stopping a short time for supper, after which they resumed their pursuit. About midnight a heavy cloud overcast the sky and they were for the time compelled to give up the pursuit and lay down to await the coming light of day. With the first light of morning they were again in pursuit of the murderers at their utmost speed. The knowledge Wetzel had of the country enabled them to save distance and the desire to avenge the murder of the family animated them and the young man was very anxious to rescue the young woman. In the afternoon they left the ridge and traversed a small valley where it appeared that man had never trod. They crossed a small stream and on the margin of it they detected the impression of a heel of a shoe that was identical with the one they found at the cabin and which had left it with the three Indians and the white man. The freshness of the track was sufficient to satisfy Wetzel that they were gaining on them. Late in the evening they reached the river at Hog Run, nearly opposite the mouth of Big Captina and found that the murderers with their captive had reached the river first and were now on the Ohio side of it. Wetzel was not in the least discouraged but confident of overtaking them and rescuing the captive. They went a short distance down the river and swam it. By the time the pursuers were ready to start in pursuit of the murderers on the west side of the river darkness had settled down over the forest but they were ready for a night's travel. They were not destined to such hardship, as they found them encamped only a short distance from the river.

The Indians and white renegade were lying near the fire and the young woman securely bound and tied to a small tree. She was moaning and bewailing her misfortune, not thinking that friends were close at hand. The young man was in favor of attacking the camp immediately, but Wetzel would not listen to it, but said, "Wait till daylight." All night long they heard the girl moaning, not thinking that daybreak would end her captivity.

The first streaks of gray dawn in the east found Wetzel and the young man ready for action. Wetzel desired daylight that he might the better do the work he so much desired, kill all of the four murderers. He wanted to give no opportunity for any of them to escape. The Indians and white man arose and were standing about the fire when the stillness of the morning was broken by the report of two rifles and the white man and one Indian were shot dead. The two remaining Indians ran into the forest to ascertain the strength of the attacking party, closely followed by Wetzel. He failed to draw their fire so he fired his gun at random and succeeded in getting them after him. They dropped their guns and with their tomahawks took after the hunter. This was their last race, as Wetzel had the game just as he wanted it. He soon had his gun loaded and one of the Indians was shot dead but the other pursued Wetzel vainly thinking to kill him and get his scalp, but soon the mysterious gun was loaded and the last Indian was killed and with the other two, scalped.

The young man sprang to the captive and cut the cords binding her as soon as the first two fatal shots were fired, leaving Wetzel to deal with the two Indians much to the delight of the hunter who had taken the choice of the Indians leaving the young man to shoot the white renegade.

Once when Lewis Wetzel was scouting near Fort Henry a stormy night overtook him near a deserted cabin. He concluded to spend the night in the cabin, and gathered some clapboards and made a place on the joist to sleep and had not been there long until six Indians entered it and prepared to spend the night. They built a fire, cooked their supper and lay down and went to sleep.

When they entered Wetzel grasped his hunting knife and determined that if he was found by them that he would attempt to escape by jumping into their midst and fighting his way to the outside of the cabin to freedom.

The Indians were soon sound asleep, not even dreaming that a white man was so near them. Wetzel quietly descended and left the cabin and hid behind a log to await developments. Morning came and one of the Indians arose and walked to the door and stretched himself and gave a hearty yawn, taking in a full breath of inspiring air, not thinking it would be the last for him. Bang, went the gun of the hunter and the Indian fell dead at the door. Wetzel started in a run and was soon out of the reach of the Indians in the cabin.

A turkey was often heard on the side of the hill across the creek from the village of Wheeling and it finally attracted the attention of Lewis Wetzel. One morning he started out and reached a point near a cave concealed by vines and bushes, suspecting that an Indian was concealed in it, as the gobbling had been heard at that place on several occasions. He awaited the appearance of day thinking that he would at least see what was there. Soon after daylight, when birds of all kinds were greeting the morning with songs, the turkey commenced gobbling. Wetzel saw the head of a warrior as he gradually arose from the cave and gobbled, thinking to attract the attention of some one from the village, whom he would shoot and scalp. Wetzel prepared to greet him when again he appeared. Soon the head appeared and the usual gobbling sound was made, the last for him. He would look around to see if any one was approaching, gobble and drop back into the cave. This time when his head appeared Wetzel fired his never-failing rifle and down dropped the head with a bullet hole in it that forever put a quietus on that Indian. Wetzel added one more scalp to the number that he had already taken.

Lewis Wetzel was born in Old Town, Rockingham County,

Virginia, in 1764, and brought by his parents to the wilderness in the district of West Augusta when about six years of age. He grew up to manhood in what is now Marshall County, where the howl of the wolf, the scream of the panther and blood-curdling yell of the Indian became familiar sounds to him.

The surroundings and necessities of the day made him one of the greatest scouts and hunters of the day. He could travel the forest and no Indian could long follow his trail. He was of a mild disposition and was kind-hearted except for his hatred for Indians, which was said to have been caused by the death of members of the family and friends by the hands of the Indians.

He had long black hair and it has been stated that when combed out to its full length it reached almost to his heels.

It has been stated that he cut a notch in his gun stock each time he killed an Indian and that seventy-eight notches were cut in the stock, indicating that he had killed that number of Indians.

He died in the summer of 1808 at the home of a cousin by the name of Goodrich about eight miles back from Natchez, Mississippi, at the age of forty-four.

Martin.

MARTIN WETZEL, the oldest of the Wetzel brothers, was one of the most efficient scouts in the Upper Ohio Valley and spent much time during the long and bloody Indian war in that capacity and rendered much service by so doing.

Once he was surprised and captured by one of the roving bands of Indians that were such a menace to the settlers, and taken to their town in the northern part of what is now the state of Ohio.

His genial disposition soon made him a favorite with his captors. Both old and young soon learned to like him as he would engage in all the frolic and fun with the Indians and take part in all their amusements. He danced with the young Indians and made himself so agreeable that he became to them an Indian by adopting himself to the surroundings. They soon learned to regard him as an Indian and appeared to have great confidence in him.

He was permitted to hunt around in the forest near the town and was so successful a hunter as to win their admiration. A successful hunter is highly honored by Indians and he soon proved himself worthy of this high honor.

While he was daily becoming more favorably regarded by his captors he was not losing any of his desire for his old

HISTORY OF MARSHALL COUNTY, W. VA. 63

haunts among the hills of Virginia. After spending almost a year with them and proving himself a hunter of the highest type for a young man it was his good fortune to be permitted to accompany three braves on a fall hunt on the headwaters of the Sandusky River. He had, by this time, so gained their confidence that he was without restraint.

When they arrived where they intended to hunt, a place was selected for a camp and Martin went to work to arrange it that they might have a pleasant camp for a resting place at night. When the hunt began Martin was always first to return to the camp in the evening and arrange for the night. He would gather wood, build a fire and prepare supper and do all the work, which was very pleasing to his companions, as Indian hunters are not noted for industry aside from the pursuit of game.

Soon he began to plan for escape. He was now away from all Indians except the three hunters and the only trouble was to get away from them.

After everything was settled down to everyday hunting, he made up his mind that he would make his escape from them. One morning he concluded to set to work with his scheme to get away from them. The hunters scattered about in different directions to cover as much ground as possible and this gave Martin an opportunity to carry out his scheme. He followed one Indian till late in the day when he shot him and hid his body in a hole made by a tree being torn out by the roots by a storm. He covered the body carefully with leaves and brush and in due time was at the camp and as usual had everything in order when the two hunters arrived. He asked about the other Indian and appeared very anxious about his safety and was assured by the other two that he would turn up all right in time. He might have gone farther than he intended and concluded to remain in the woods all night rather than walk so far after dark, or he might have wounded a deer and pursued it till too late to return, and as he was a good hunter he would return in due time. The Indians appeared to think it a matter of no importance, so he said no more about it. After supper they lay down, but Martin did not sleep that night. He had started and there was no way out but to go ahead and kill the other two and make his escape. He first thought of falling on them with his tomahawk and end the matter but concluded to take a more cautious course if it took a little longer. He decided upon a plan for the next day and put it into effect as contemplated.

The next morning he arose and prepared breakfast and was as pleasant as usual and soon the three were ready for their day's hunt. Martin resolved to complete the work undertaken and make his escape. He followed one of the Indians with the intention of killing him before returning to the camp. All day long he followed as a dog follows the trail of a deer and late in the afternoon he managed to meet him and engage him in conversation and getting his attention turned to something that caused him to turn his head, when with one stroke of his tomahawk he laid the Indian dead on the ground. He hid his body in a hole after scalping him and returned to the camp and awaited the return of the remaining Indian. Every preparation was made for the usual evening in the camp. The fire was built and wood gathered as usual so that nothing appeared out of the ordinary everyday life in the camp. He started supper and was doing his usual work when the last Indian arrived with a heavy load of game on his back. Martin, in his usual pleasant manner, approached the Indian to assist him in unloading his load and as he stooped down to give Martin a better opportunity to get hold of the load, he struck the hunter with his tomahawk and laid the last Indian dead on the ground. This completed the work so far as disposing of the three hunters was concerned. He was in no danger of pursuit. He selected what he wanted from the camp and with a good supply of provision, he started for Wheeling, where he arrived safely in due time.

John.

Early in the spring of 1786, or a year later, settlers had left their homes and gathered at Shepherd's Fort for protection against the Indians. Two boys left the fort early one morning to hunt horses. They were John Wetzel and Frederick Earliwine. The former was about seventeen years old and the latter several years younger. John Wetzel was much interested in the hunt as one of the animals wanted was a mare belonging to his sister and she had given a colt to him for caring for its mother.

The boys had not gone far when they heard the tinkle of a bell and they hastened to the spot thinking they would soon have the horses and be on their way home. The horses were in a thicket and the boys went into it to get them but to their surprise they saw four Indians. They tried to run and make their escape by flight but the Indians were too quick for them and fired at them and a bullet struck Wetzel's arm and confused him and he was captured. He seemed to see the situation clearly and when in their hands he became very cheerful and talked with them freely, but the younger boy cried and made so much noise that they tomahawked him.

HISTORY OF MARSHALL COUNTY, W. VA. 65

About noon they reached the Flats of Grave Creek. When they reached the mouth of Big Grave Creek they took a canoe from its hiding place and the Indians shot a hog that was roaming in the woods and placed it, their prisoner and guns in it and were ready to start across the river when the Indians were attacked by three white men and three of the Indians killed and the prisoner rescued.

Three men, Isaac Williams, Hamilton Kerr and a German by the name of Jacob, had gone down from Fort Henry that morning to look after some stock belonging to Isaac Williams, and when at the mouth of Little Grave Creek they heard the shot that killed the hog and Williams said that a Kentucky boat (an emigrant boat) had landed and were killing his hogs and they started in a run to get there before they got away with the hog. Kerr being the younger and swifter on foot, reached the bank of the creek a short distance in advance of the others, and to his surprise saw a canoe containing three Indians in the creek near the mouth of it. He shot the one in the stern as he dipped the paddle into the water to start the canoe out into the river from the shore. He fell into the water and at that moment Williams arrived and shot one standing in the bow, leaving one sitting in the center of the canoe. Jacob came rushing up and Kerr gave him his empty gun and took his gun and shot the Indian in the center of the canoe. In a moment their guns were reloaded and as the canoe drifted out with the current a man was seen lying in the bottom of it, a gun was raised when he called out, "Don't shoot, I am a white man." The last Indian was still clinging to the side of the canoe and he was told to loosen him. He answered that he could not as his arm was broken. The canoe drifted to some rocks just below the mouth of the creek and Wetzel waded to the shore but did not or could not draw the canoe to shore with him.

The white men did not cross the creek as it was too deep to wade without going up it quite a distance to find a shallow place and it was permitted to drift down the river.

The fourth Indian who was swimming the horses across the river had so far escaped their attention but was seen and one of the men shot at him. He was nearly half way across the river but the bullet splashed water on him. He saw the situation and slipped from the horse he was on and swam to the canoe that was floating down the river and paddled it to the north bank of the river and taking a rifle from it, he uttered a yell of defiance, mounted a horse and disappeared in the forest. Without the gun he would have had a good opportunity to have suffered hunger before reaching the Indian towns on the Muskingum River.

He shoved the canoe out into the river and it drifted more than two hundred miles with the three rifles and dead hog in it. It was found near Maysville, Kentucky.

In the year 1792, Indians became very troublesome in the Upper Ohio Valley, especially between Wheeling and Mingo Bottom. Numerous murders were committed and several families carried into captivity and many horses were stolen by them.

After one of their forays into the settlement in which a number of valuable horses were stolen, it was determined to pursue them and to make an attempt to recapture the horses and administer some punishment if possible.

A company consisting of John Wetzel, William McCullough, Joseph Hedges, Kinzie Dickerson, Thomas Biggs and William Lynn, with John Wetzel for leader, undertook the hazardous enterprise.

They crossed the Ohio River near where Steubenville now stands and proceeded in a northerly direction till they reached the old trail leading from Fort Pitt to Sandusky. They followed this trail past Fort Laurens till they reached an Indian town on Mohican Creek; there they saw the horses they were after. They lay hid all day and at night they got the horses and started home. They decided not to take the back trail as they feared pursuit, but turned to the southward and followed less traveled trails and crossed the Tuscarawas River at what is now Newcomerstown and reached Wills Creek, a branch of the Muskingum River near where Cambridge now stands.

The party reached this point in the evening of the second day after recapturing their horses. One of the men having been attacked with a sever cramp colic, they went into camp, as he could travel no farther at the time. A guard was detailed to watch the back trail as they were not certain that Indians had not followed them.

Late in the night the guard went to a brook near the camp and found muddy streaks in the water. He immediately returned to the camp and informed Wetzel of it. He was of the opinion that Indians were near but Wetzel said that raccoons or muskrats might have been wading in the water and caused the muddy streaks in it. Raccoons often travel along in the water in small streams in quest of crawfish which they eat and this was the reason Wetzel gave for the streaks in the muddy water. The guard was less vigilant after that and in less than an hour a volley was fired into the camp from behind the bank of the brook and the sick man was riddled with bullets.

The surprise was complete and the men ran from the camp without guns or blankets. In the attack three men were killed. They were Joseph Biggs, Thomas Hedges and William Lynn. The others made their way to Fort Henry suffering from fatigue and hunger.

Captain John McCullough, with a small force of men from the settlement at Wheeling, went to the scene of the disaster and buried the dead a few days later.

The Indians were a party of Munceys with some of the Moravians who had escaped murder ten years before and had joined the hostile Indians. They had been on an unsuccessful foray against settlements on the south side of the Ohio River and had accidentally stumbled upon the camp.

Not long after the return of the ill-fated expedition after stolen horses, John Wetzel and Veach Dickerson started on an expediiton into the Indian country near the head of Sandusky River. They started with the avowed purpose of bringing a prisoner home with them. They were dressed in Indian attire, not omitting the usual paint, and as they could speak Indian language to some extent they felt certain of some success. They reached an Indian town and found a path that appeared to be traveled considerably, and they concealed themselves near it awaiting for Indians to appear. A number of them passed during the day but in too large parties for them to attack. Late in the evening they saw two walking leisurely, talking and laughing, and thought that this was their opportunity. They approached the Indians who never suspected them and walked up to the Indians and spoke in very good language and with one stroke of his tomahawk Wetzel killed one of them, and at the same time Dickerson grabbed the other and threw him to the ground. After securely tying the Indian and scalping the dead one, they started homeward. They did not travel long on the war path toward Wheeling Creek but left it and followed devious courses, keeping on hard ground to make as few tracks as possible in order to avoid pursuit. They made fairly good headway until they crossed the Muskingum River, when the Indian began to give them trouble. They tried to pursuade him to go with them, promising him kind treatment, but to no purpose. He had decided to go no further and they tried the effect of a good hickory but it was of no use as he had resolved to go no further. He said that he would rather die there than to be taken to the settlement south of the Ohio River and there be tortured for the amusement of a large number of people. It was in vain that they insisted that he would not be hurt. He bowed his head and said that they might tomahawk him at any time as he would go no further. They tomahawked him and took his scalp and proceeded home somewhat disappointed as they were very anxious to return with a prisoner.

Jacob.

Jacob Wetzel was not behind any of his brothers in any daring deeds and was always ready for any hazardous enterprise or undertaking that any one might suggest.

Once when he was in Kentucky, he and Simon Kenton decided to take a fall hunt near the mouth of the Kentucky River. They started at an early date in the hunting season for the hilly country that they might have as much of the season to hunt as possible. The region was near the Ohio River and consequently not far from Indian towns in the western part of what is now the state of Ohio.

They deemed it advisable to ascertain if there were any Indians there before they began to hunt and discovered signs of their presence and later saw smoke and heard guns in the direction of the smoke. They quietly approached the smoke till they discovered the camp. They lay hid near it the greater part of the day awaiting the return of the hunters, and late in the evening five Indians arrived at the camp and prepared their suppers and spent the evening hours, as was the custom of both whites and Indians, in telling stories and singing songs, not for a moment suspecting that two of the most daring of the Long Knives were near them.

Quietly and patiently did the two hunters await the approach of day for their attack upon the camp. Daylight came and the two hunters were behind a log ready for the opportune time for an attack. The Indians arose. The two fired, each at a man and two Indians dropped dead. Wetzel had a double barrel rifle and a moment later one more was pierced with a bullet and lay dead on the ground, leaving only two of the hunters. They started to the woods followed by the white hunters, yelling like demons, close behind them, but did not follow far before they overtook them and killed and scalped them, completing the destruction of the entire camp of hunters.

In October, 1790, Jacob Wetzel was at Fort Washington where Cincinnati now stands, and engaged in his usual occupation—hunting. The country was covered with a dense forest of beech and maple trees with an undergrowth of spice wood and grape vines, making a remarkably fine hiding place for lurking Indians as well as an excellent resort for deer.

One day Wetzel went out to hunt as usual accompanied by his hunting dog. The success of the day compelled him to

HISTORY OF MARSHALL COUNTY, W. VA. 69

return to the fort for a horse upon which to carry his game as it was too heavy a load for him to carry. While on his way he sat down on a log to rest with his dog lying at his feet. While resting there he heard a rattle of leaves which caused the dog to growl. He silenced the dog which seemed conscious of danger. He sprang behind a tree and looked in the direction the dog's attention had been attracted and saw an Indian a short distance from him partly concealed by the trunk of a tree. The Indian had his gun in his hands ready for any emergency and appeared to be looking for danger, probably having heard the low growl of the dog. The dog now saw the Indian and barked aloud, giving notice of the presence of Wetzel. Both now raised their guns and fired at each other at the same time. The Indians' gun fell from his hands, the bullet from Wetzel's gun had struck his left arm and broke it at the elbow, while Wetzel was uninjured by the bullet fired by the Indian. Wetzel now rushed upon the Indian with his knife. The Indian warded off the thrust with such skill and force that he knocked the knife out of Wetzel's hand and threw it thirty feet from him. Wetzel attacked the Indian although his adversary had his knife in his right hand. He caught him about the body encircling the right arm while the Indian still held his knife in his right hand. They engaged in a doubtful struggle apparently with equal chances. The Indian struggled to get his right arm from the grasp of Wetzel while the latter was endeavoring to prevent him. In their struggle their feet became interlocked and both fell to the ground, the Indian being uppermost, which released his right arm from Wetzel's grasp. He was intending to use the knife while Wetzel was forcing him over on his right side to prevent him from using it. The Indian, with a yell, and an exertion of all his strength, turned Wetzel under him and was about to plunge the knife into him when the dog, which so far had only been a silent spectator, sprang upon the Indian, seized him by the throat with such force that the Indian dropped the knife from his hand. Wetzel now threw the Indian from him and before he had time to recover from the attack of the dog, he seized his knife and firmly planted his foot on the breast of the prostrate body of the Indian and plunged the knife to the hilt into the body of the Indian. He gave a shudder and lay still in death at the foot of the white hunter. Wetzel got his gun and that of the Indian and started for the fort and had not gone far when he heard the whoop of several Indians. He ran to the river and found a canoe on the beach near the water and was soon out of reach of danger of the Indians. The Indian he had killed was one of their bravest chiefs.

The Baker Family

Of the early settlers in Marshall County the Baker family is one that is worthy of mention. Henry Baker lived for more than one-half of a century in the lower end of Round Bottom. Colonel Samuel P. Baker, his son, gave the following account of the early history of the Baker family:

He said that his grandfather, John Baker, settled on Dunkard Creek in Green County, Pennsylvania, about the year 1767, and lived there a number of years near Indians, who then lived in that section of the country and were very friendly with the whites. At the breaking out of Dunmore's War in 1774, his grandfather removed his family to Redstone Old Fort, now Brownsville, and remained there some time after the war was over. Later he removed his family to Catfish Camp where Washington, Pennsylvania, now stands.

In the spring of 1781 reports were circulated that Indians were preparing for early and active operations on the south side of the Ohio River, and it was rumored that a large body had crossed the river near Holliday's Cove. Three young men were started to Fort Henry at Wheeling to inform the settlers of their danger. They were Henry Baker (eighteen years old), Henry Yoho, and a man by the name of Stalnater. Only one of them reached the fort.

They rode along without seeing any indications of Indians until they reached the narrows on Wheeling Creek near the old Woods residence, when they ran into a number of Indians in ambush awaiting them. Stalnater shot the Indian nearest him and was in turn shot by the Indians. A bullet struck Yoho's horse, causing it to fall to its knees, but it quickly arose and in its fright started in the direction of the fort at the top of its speed and reached the fort and saved the life of its rider.

A bullet struck Baker's horse which ran about one hundred yards and fell dead. It fell on Baker's leg and it was with some difficulty that he freed himself from the dead horse. Seeing his danger he abandoned his gun and started for the fort in full speed but ran only a short distance when he met an Indian with a tomahawk in one hand and a pistol in the other. He saw he had no chance to escape and when the Indian called to him in good English, "You are a prisoner," he stopped. He was taken back to the other Indians, and a brother of the warrior killed by Stalnater, wanted to kill him but was prevented by the chief.

With their prisoner they started for the river. They crossed the hill and went out the ridge that runs just on the top of the hill along the Narrows and descended the hill at

Kate's Rock where they found a number of Indians in canoes as if they were awaiting the arrival of the party.

They embarked in canoes and descended the river a short distance and left the canoes and went around the fort at the Flats of Grave Creek, keeping along the foot of the hill and crossing Big Grave Creek not far below the mouth of Middle Grave Creek, and from there they went over the hill and arrived at the river at the lower end of Round Bottom. The party crossed the river and encamped on the north side opposite the head of Captina Island.

Early the following morning they started and for three days and nights they made no halt. They did not rest until they arrived at Chillicothe, having evidently been in fear of pursuit. After that they were in no hurry. They killed deer and had plenty to eat. When they arrived at Sandusky three hundred Indians had just arrived from a foray against settlements in Kentucky with nine prisoners. The nine young men taken by them were burned at the stake after running the gauntlets. One was burned each day.

All this time Baker was reminded frequently that his turn was coming after the nine were burned. On the morning of the tenth day Baker was taken to the place where they had burned the other prisoners and compelled to run the gauntlet which he did with little difficulty. It so enraged a warrior that he knocked Baker down after he had reached the council house in safety. Baker fought them and delayed them some time and seeing a man riding toward them in the uniform of a British officer he ran to meet him and asked him to save his life if it was possible.

The man was no other than the notorius Simon Girty. Girty talked with the Indians two hours or more, arguing with them and finally induced them not to burn him. Girty evidently had motives other than that of humanity, as he took Baker out from the Indians and questioned him about the conditions at Wheeling and many other places, especially the former place. Baker afterwards believed that Girty contemplated an attack upon Fort Henry. He was taken to Detroit and in a short time was released. He hired with a trader and remained with him some time.

He and three Virginians concluded to return and started for Wheeling. They got lost and wandered about for three weeks before they reached the Ohio River, where Bridgeport has since been built. Some men were making sugar on that side of the river and when they saw the four men approaching in Indian dress they mistook them for Indians and crossed over to the island and watched them. After some time Baker and his companions made the men understand who they were and the men crossed back and brought them over in a canoe.

While Henry was away his father moved to the lower end of Round Bottom. He learned where the family had gone and he went to it. He remained in the Round Bottom until his death, except the time spent at Tomlinsons' Fort. He died in 1848.

Another account of the Baker family says that Captain John Baker was born in Prussia and came to America about 1760. He arrived at Philadelphia and five years later married Elizabeth Sullivan of that city, and from there the young people removed to the Shenandoah Valley in Virginia, where they lived two years and from there they removed to the waters of Dunkard Creek now in Green County, Pennsylvania, in the year 1767, and remained there seven years. At the time they lived on that creek there were a number of Indians residing on it and they and the whites were very friendly. At the breaking out of Dunmore's War he removed his family to Redstone Old Fort, now Brownsville. The American revolution breaking out soon after the close of Dunmore's War, Indian hostilities soon followed the breaking out of the war. He remained at the fort a number of years, and was in the service of the Colony of Virginia much of the time during the war, but there is little record of him.

He went from Redstone to Catfish Camp in 1781, where he remained a short time and then removed to Round Bottom and in 1784 Captain Baker built a block-house near the upper end of Cresap's Bottom. The place was generally known by the name of Baker's Station.

While two of the Wetzel's were at Baker's Station in 1787, they and Captain Baker noticed some Indians on the opposite shore walking about leisurely. Baker, getting an opportunity, shot at one of them and killed him. The others ran away as if badly frightened, leaving the dead Indian where he fell. They did it evidently to deceive the whites as it was proved later by their actions. Baker and the two Wetzels crossed over the river and were viewing the dead Indian when several shots were fired and Baker fell, mortally wounded. The Wetzels treed and commenced a fight and some other men crossed the river and reinforced them and drove the Indians off and recovered the body of Baker. He had crawled a short distance from where he fell and was alive when recovered, but died soon after arriving at the station. He was buried on a flat near a stream called Grave Yard Run at the upper end of Cresap's Bottom.

Baker's Station soon became a rendezvous for scouts as it was at one of the crossings of the Indians on a war path from the Muskingum River into the interior of Virginia. They traveled up Wills Creek from the Muskingum River and crossed a divide and went down Big Captina to the Ohio River and up Fish Creek or broke up into small parties of marauders and visited the various settlements committing all kinds of depredations.

The Baker family appears to have resided in the blockhouse and it never had a regular garrison. Hunters and scouts were so frequently at it that it was seldom without a fairly good force, in case of attack, to have defended it against a large force of Indians. In time of danger scouts gave much attention to the war path down Big Captina and among others who frequented the place were the Wetzel brothers. It was a custom to send scouts to the west side frequently to look for indications of the presence of Indians. Indians were frequently seen on the west or Ohio side of the river and frequent shots were exchanged.

Martin Baker gave a very interesting account of an engagement between fourteen whites and a number of Shawnee Indians at the mouth of Cat's Run, some distance up the creek from the river.

Martin said that one morning in May, 1794, four scouts, Adam Miller, John Daniel, Isaac McCown and John Shopton, crossed from the station to look for indications of Indians. Miller and Daniel went up the river and the other two went down it.

McCown and Shopton soon discovered signs that indicated to them that Indians were near them and attempted to make their escape by immediate flight. McCown started for the canoe and was shot and wounded. He ran to the river, jumped over the bank and ran into the water but was pursued by Indians who overtook him and killed and scalped him. Shopton escaped by running to the river and swimming it.

The two who went up the river soon encountered Indians. Miller was killed and Daniel was wounded in an arm and sought safety by flight. After running about three miles up the creek he was overtaken by Indians, taken prisoner and kept by them till after the treaty at Greenville in 1795, when he was released.

There were about fifty men at the station and a call to arms was beat and volunteers called for to cross the river and attack the Indians. There seemed to be a hesitancy and no one seemed anxious to cross the river and engage the enemy, and getting volunteers was slow work.

John Baker, for a wonder, seemed to hesitate until his sister May Jane remarked that she would not be a coward. That was sufficient. He joined the other thirteen. Captain

Adam Enoch commanded the force. One of the volunteers was Duncan McArthur, who was many years later elected Governor of Ohio. They crossed from the station and followed the trail of the Indians up the creek to the mouth of Cat's Run when they were fired upon by Indians who were concealed on a hillside above them but they were too high and the bullets went whistling over the heads of the whites. The whites treed and the battle began. Captain Enoch and a man by the name of Hoffman were killed by some Indians who attacked them from the rear. After the death of Enoch young McArthur took command of the small force and commenced a retreat. They had not retreated far when John Baker was shot through the hips and being in the rear it was impossible to get him and carry him from the field.

From what was afterwards seen it was thought that Baker knowing that he would be killed, determined to sell his life at as high a rate as possible. He got into a hollow place with a large rock at his back so they could not get at him from behind. Soon after he fell two shots in quick succession were fired and it was thought that he killed an Indian and was in turn killed by another. When whites visited the ground the second day after the battle they found the bodies of the men killed horribly mutilated.

They were taken to the Virginia shore and buried on the bank of Grave Yard Run, where John Baker and John Wetzel had been buried some years before. They were buried in coffins made of hickory bark.

The Indians had gone up the creek, after killing the scouts, some distance, and returned to the mouth of Cat's Run and there lay in ambush for the whites who started in pursuit of them.

Some years afterwards some whites visited the spot and found seven skeletons in the rocks where it was thought that the Indians had hid their dead.

There is a tradition among the Baker family that Henry and his sister Kate were taken prisoner by Indians while at work near the station and taken to an Indian camp back of Round Bottom. Henry was compelled to gather wood which he thought was intended to burn him but in this he was mistaken. While gathering wood and carrying it to the camp he picked up a knife some warrior had dropped. He concealed it in his clothes and worked on quietly. The Indians had some whiskey and at night indulged in it quite freely and lay down, many of them, in an intoxicated condition. The two prisoners had been tied securely, so thought by the Indians, but with the knife hid in his clothes, Henry was not long in cutting the thongs when he thought the Indians asleep, and soon he and

Kate were free. They started but had not gone far when the Indians discovered that the prisoners had escaped, and began scouring the woods in search of them.

They saw that they were cut off from the station and also from the fort at the Flats of Grave Creek, with Indians in the woods yelling blood curdling yells. A party soon got directly after them and they ran through the woods in a direction from either of the places of safety mentioned, and as they ran along a path, they came to a log that lay directly across it. They started to run around it but found that it was hollow and one crawled into it from each end. The pursuers jumped the log and ran in the direction they had been running and after the Indians were a safe distance from them they left their hiding place and started for the river and reached it at Kate's Rock and swam to the Ohio side and went down it to the mouth of Big Captina and swam it again and arrived at their home none the worse by having one more experience with Indians.

Of the Baker family, three were killed by Indians. The father, his son John and daughter Margaret were killed by them but no account of the death of Margaret is given.

ISAAC WILLIAMS.

ISAAC WILLIAMS, the hunter, scout, and one of the early settlers of the Ohio Valley, was born in Chester County, Pennsylvania, in the year 1737. Soon after his birth they removed to Winchester, Virginia, then a frontier settlement. While Isaac was young his father died and his mother married a man by the name of Buckley.

Isaac, in his youth, took to the forest as a young duck does to water, and he did not abandon the pursuit of hunting and trapping and taking up land until he had passed the prime of life. At the breaking out of the French and Indian War in 1755, he was employed by the colonial government of Virginia as a scout and spy. He was then only eighteen years old, yet he was one of the best scouts of the day. He served in that capacity under General Braddock and was with him when his army was almost annihilated near the head of the Ohio River. He served in the campaign against the French and Indians in 1758 under General Forbes, and was with the army when it captured Fort Duquesne at the forks of the Ohio. He was one of the guards that convoyed the first train of supplies and provisions to Fort Pitt for the garrison after the French had been driven out from the Key to the West. The road followed, or rather the path, followed by the pack train was through a country covered with thickets and in many places it followed ravines where Indians had the best of opportunities to attack the convoy. The supplies were then, and for many years after, carried on pack-horses. Isaac Williams was a scout and spy in the service of Lord Dunmore of Virginia in the campaign against the Indians in 1774.

After the peace made with the Indians by Colonel Bouquet in 1765, settlers from the east of the mountains began to settle on and along the waters of the Monongahela River. It is said that he was with Ebenezer and Jonathan Zane when they visited the country about the waters of Wheeling Creek previous to settling there.

In the fall of 1767 he and two companions visited the regions of the Ohio River and spent some time trapping and started for their homes on the east side of the mountains late in December, and while passing through the glade country in the mountains one of the terrible snow storms that are common in the mountains overtook them and they came near losing their lives in the snow. It fell to a depth of more than five feet and for weeks they had to subsist upon the skins and pelts they carried with them. They singed the fur from the pelts in the fire and then boiled them in water made by melting snow, and subsisted upon this unpalatable food but it was that or death for the snow was too deep to hunt. One of the men sickened and died from exposure and bad and insufficient food. The weather became extremely cold and the other companion of Williams suffered from the cold and his feet were so badly frozen that his toes came off and he lay there two months before he was able to travel.

All the long and trying winter of storms and starvation, Williams exerted himself to obtain fuel and cared for his unfortunate companion. It was with the greatest difficulty that the dead man was buried beneath the snow. Williams would not leave the disabled man and make his way to a settlement lest the wild beasts would devour the man or he would die before he could hope to return. At last he recovered sufficiently to start home and with the greatest exertions they reached a settlement in a terribly reduced condition from the effect of exposure and starvation. Williams was so reduced that it required several months for him to regain his former strength.

In 1768 his parents removed to the waters of the Monongahela River under his guidance. They settled not far from Redstone Old Fort. His parents remained there and he continued in his favorite pursuit, hunting and trapping. He located some land on Buffalo Creek near where Bethany now stands.

He was one of the venturesome trappers and it is said that he, at the early date of 1770 descended the Ohio and ascended the Mississippi River as far as the mouth of the Missouri River and spent one winter trapping on a branch of it, returning in the spring with a valuable lot of furs.

He took up claims under what was known as tomahawk rights and made what was called a tomahawk improvement on the claim. The claims were often sold at a price amounting to less than ten cents per acre.

In the spring of 1775 he married Mrs. Rebecca Martin, widow of John Martin, a trader among the Indians, who was killed by Shawnee Indians on the Big Hockhocking River in 1770. Mrs. Martin's maiden name was Rebecca Tomlinson and a sister of the Tomlinson brothers who made the first settlement at the Flats of Grave Creek.

In the latter part of the summer of the bloody year of the three sevens, as the old settlers called the year of 1777, he and his wife, with her parents, removed to Redstone, now Brownsville, Pennsylvania, and remained there until about the year 1785, or perhaps a year later, and then returned to their former home at Grave Creek, and it is said that the following year they removed to Wheeling to Fort Henry as it was not deemed safe to remain at their improvement at Grave Creek as there were many Indians prowling through the country and committing many depredations.

It was while his family was at Wheeling that he and Hamilton Kerr and Jacob, a German, came down to Grave Creek to visit his home and notice conditions that they were attracted to the mouth of Big Grave Creek by a shot fired by an Indian which killed one of William's hogs and resulted in the death of three Indians and the rescue of John Wetzel from captivity.

After Fort Harmer was built at the mouth of the Big Muskingum River and garrisoned with soldiers, he decided to remove his family to a tract of land belonging to his wife, on the east side of the Ohio River opposite the fort.

In the spring of 1787 he removed to the land, having previously visited it and erected a cabin. Considerable land had been cleared but it was then grown up with saplings and bushes but it was not long until he had quite a nice farm cleared and in cultivation. He gave up his favorite pursuit of hunting and trapping and spent the remainder of his life improving and cultivating the farm and enjoying the home life of peaceful pursuits. Their only child, a daughter, married a man by the name of Henderson, and died at the age of twenty leaving no issue. Mr. Williams died September the twentieth, 1820, at the age of eighty-three, respected by all who knew him. The city of Williamstown commemorates his name.

It is said that one year he raised quite a large and fine crop of well matured corn, while the crop was generally a very poor one and of very poor quality, the result of which was that good corn commanded an unusually high price, and he was offered some very high figures for what he had to spare from his abundance, but he refused to accept it, and gave as a reason that he did not intend to profit by the misfortune of his neighbors, showing that he was entirely devoid of any selfishness. He died beloved by his many neighbors who loved him for his many manly qualities.

REBECCA WILLIAMS.

Mrs. Rebecca Williams, nee Rebecca Tomlinson, daughter of Joseph Tomilson, Sr., and sister of Samuel, James and Joseph, the three brothers who made the first settlement at the Flats of Grave Creek, one of the most beautiful spots in the Ohio Valley, reflects honor on womanhood.

She was born at Wills Creek, Maryland, in the year 1754, and was a widow at the age of seventeen. She married John Martin while very young. Martin was a trader among the Indians and was on the Big Hockhocking with a man by the name of Harkness and two men from Pennsylvania in the year 1770, when they were attacked by Shawnee Indians. Martin and Harkness were killed by them while the two men from Pennsylvania were spared. The recollection the Indians had of William Penn saved their lives, so great was the respect for the memory of Penn and the Quakers.

When her parents and brothers removed to the Flats of Grave Creek she came with them and it is said that she was housekeeper for her brothers, Samuel and James, until she married Isaac Williams in 1775. While keeping house for her brothers she was often alone for weeks at a time while they were hunting and taking up claims. For keeping house for them they gave her four hundred acres of fine river bottom land opposite the mouth of the Big Muskingum River, where she spent many days of her useful life. Williamstown now stands on part of the tract of land.

In the summer of 1774, while her home was near the mouth of Big Grave Creek, an Indian entered the cabin one morning while she was blowing some coals to kindle a fire. She heard his steps as he entered the cabin and looked up and saw the warrior shake his tomahawk at her to keep silent. She apparently paid no attention to him and made no noise. He looked around the room for some time as if looking for something, when he took Samuel's gun from the hooks above the fireplace and went out of the cabin and left. She left the cabin and hid in a cornfield until her brother returned home a few hours later.

The same spring she visited her sister, Mrs. Baker, at Baker's Bottom, opposite Yellow Creek, not long after the murder of Logan's family. When the time came for her to return home after her visit, she stepped lightly into a canoe one afternoon, took up the paddle and started for Grave Creek. She paddled along till darkness settled down on the beautiful waters of the Ohio, when she paddled to the shore and tied her canoe to a willow and jumped to the shore and lay down in a thicket to await until the moon arose and cast her light over the slumbering waters, which would give here notice to resume her journey. The water being shallow at the shore she had to wade some distance to get her canoe clear of the shore, when the moon arose, so she could resume her journey. When she had cleared the shore and was about to step into the canoe her naked foot came in contact with the body of a dead Indian. She stepped into the canoe, took up the paddle and at an early hour the next day arrived home, having paddled the canoe about fifty miles from the middle of the afternoon of the previous day. In speaking of the Indian, she merely remarked that she was glad it was not alive.

Mrs. Williams was one of the women of the day who aided in fighting the great battles which were common to the early settlers. During the long and bloody war commencing in 1777 and not ending until the victory of General Wayne at Fallen Timber in August, 1794, women shared equally in the hardships with the men. In all the sieges of the different forts they did their part as well as the men. They engaged in moulding bullets, cooling and loading guns for the men and in not a few cases did they load them and shoot at the enemy with telling effect. Others were equally useful in caring for wounded and among those expert in caring for wounded, Mrs. Williams could be consistently numbered. One case is mentioned in history when she and Mrs. Ebenezer Zane saved the life of a wounded man who was thought to have been beyond the reach of medical skill.

While Mrs. Williams and her husband were at Fort Henry after they had returned from Redstone to their former home in the Flats of Grave Creek, on account of the presence of Indians, four men from the fort were up the river fishing one night; one of the party, Thomas Mills, was riddled with bullets. He was standing in front of the canoe holding a torch while two men were spearing fish and the other man was paddling the canoe. They were about a mile above Wheeling when some Indians fired at them, or rather at Mills, and fourteen bullets struck him. It was thought the amputation of a lower limb was absolutely necessary. There was no surgeon at hand nor within fifty miles of Wheeling at the time. One arm was also broken besides a number of flesh wounds.

Mrs. Zane and Mrs. Williams went to work and fairly encased him in poultices of slippery elm bark, which were frequently removed and the patient given a bath of hot towels just wrung out of hot water and the poultices renewed. Mills' life was not only saved but both his arm and leg, through the skill and persistency in the work. A physician afterwards, in speaking of the case, said that if Mills had been in the regular service he would most likely lost both of the limbs if not his life, and spoke very highly of the success of the two ladies.

Their treatment of gunshot wounds and similar injuries were to give the wounds frequent towel baths with hot water to reduce the temperature and apply poultices of slippery elm bark or jimson and change them frequently and keep them damp at all times to prevent irritation and keep the wounds clean so that nature could get in its work.

After ten years of exciting scenes of Indian war and almost thirty years of wild and exciting border life her husband thought that they would seek quietness from bloodshed and strife. They settled on her land opposite Fort Harmer and spent many years there surrounded by friends whom they drew to them by their amiable qualities and died surrounded by loving friends.

WAR PATHS.

THERE were two Indian trails or war paths through what is now Marshall County. One was a trail from the Delaware towns on the Muskingum River below the forks, and towns to the west of them inhabited by other tribes. The trail was up Will's Creek from the Muskingum River to a point not far from where Barnsville, Ohio, now stands. From there it crossed a dividing ridge to the headwaters of Big Captina Creek and followed it to the Ohio River. It crossed the river at the head of Cresap's Bottom and went around the foot of the hill on the east side of the river to Fish Creek, more than a mile from the river. It followed up the creek to the upper waters and crossed a ridge dividing the waters that flow into the Ohio River from the streams that flow into the Monongahela River to Dunkard Creek and followed it down to the Monongahela River or diverged from it as their destination might require.

A war path from Indian towns in the upper part of the

Muskingum Valley or the Tuscarawas Valley and towns to the northwest, was up Stillwater Creek from the river and across ridges to the headwaters of Indian Wheeling Creek or to McMahon's Creek and down one or the other of these creeks to the Ohio River. The trail crossed the river about the mouth of Bogg's Run and up it and across a ridge to Big Wheeling Creek above the forks. From the headwaters of it to the waters of Ten Mile Creek and down it toward the Monongahela River.

These paths were the usual ones followed by Indians in their expeditions against settlements on Wheeling Creek and south of there and also into the interior settlements of Pennsylvania or northwestern Virginia.

Scouts watched these trails in the war with Indians commencing in 1777, the bloody year of the three sevens. Indians did not always follow these paths closely but deviated from them as their plan of attack might require.

It was from watching this war path that scouts returned on the last day of August, 1777, and reported to the commandant at Fort Henry that no signs of Indians had been discovered and that there was no immediate danger from them and the residents of the village of Wheeling, with a feeling of security, rested in their homes that night to be aroused early the next morning by a terrible conflict and massacre in a cornfield near the village. Indians had avoided the usual paths and eluded the scouts that they might surprise the fort. Quite well did they succeed as they drew most of the men from the fort and killed many of them in a conflict in a cornfield near it.

JOHN LYNN, one of the best scouts in the Upper Ohio Valley, was watching this path in September, 1782, when he saw a large body of Indians and British soldiers marching hurriedly towards the river to attack Fort Henry. He reached Wheeling a few hours before the enemy and gave the alarm. Residents of the village retired into the fort and prepared to defend it and when the enemy arrived they were prepared to give them a warm reception and greet them with showers of bullets, causing the loss of many warriors and the defeat of the attacking party.

FORTS.

Beeler Station.

BEELER STATION, sometimes called Beeler's Fort, stood on a ridge between Middle Grave Creek and Wolf Run. No description of the fort or station is given nor is the date of the erection of it mentioned. It was probably a block-house surrounded by pickets and erected some time after 1782. There is nothing mentioned in history concerning it that is of historical importance, but a very amusing account of Colonel Beeler's hardships is given on page forty-five of this book.

Old settlers gave an account of a family by the name of Blue, living on the end of a ridge some distance from Beeler Station, being murdered by Indians.

Signs of Indians had been found in the neighborhood and settlers warned of their danger. All removed into the fort except Blue, who insisted that there was no immediate danger and remained at his improvement. The family was attacked a day or two later and every member murdered.

Baker Station.

BAKER STATION was erected about the year 1784 at the upper end of Cresap's Bottom, not far from Grave Yard Run. It consisted of a block-house surrounded by pickets and was erected by the joint labor of the settlers of the neighborhood. John Baker resided in it as proprietor. It afforded protection to the settlers of Cresap's Bottom and those of the lower end of Round Bottom.

It was in the line of a war path of Indians and it soon became a rendezvous for scouts who were on the watch for Indians. Many scouts gathered there at times of danger and crossed the river every morning and watched the trail which came down Big Captina Creek. Four scouts crossed from the station one morning and were attacked by Indians; two of them were killed, one wounded and captured and one escaped without injury.

It was from Baker Station that a number of men crossed the river and encountered Indians and fought what is known in history as the Battle of Captina, in which several were killed. Among the number was one of John Baker's sons.

John Baker, for whom the station was named, was killed by Indians opposite the station. John Wetzel and his son George were shot near the opposite shore from the station. Both died the evening of the day they were shot and were buried on the banks of Grave Yard Run near the grave of John Baker. Several were killed near there on the opposite side of the river and were buried on the banks of a run which from the graves was properly named GRAVE YARD RUN.

There were a number of encounters with Indians not far from this station, which are given in the early history and settlement of this county and found in the forepart of this work.

Fort Clark.

FORT CLARK stood where the village of Sherrard now

HISTORY OF MARSHALL COUNTY, W. VA.   83

stands. It was named in honor of the promoter, Harry Clark, and was erected but few years after the attack upon Fort Henry in 1782. The fort was of the class known as a station. It consisted of four cabins at four corners with the intervening sides closed with high pickets. While not a strong fortification it afforded protection to the settlers on the ridges between Little Grave Creek and Wheeling Creek.

It was very inconvenient for the settlers to remove their families to Fort Henry at Wheeling whenever there was an alarm of Indians in the neighborhood, and to avoid that trouble the settlers erected the fort so they could retire into it in a short time after Indians appeared in the settlement, or it was thought best to retire into a fort. They could go from this fort to their farms and continue their work all the summer by proper precaution and better provide for their families, by being near their improvements.

Three members of a family by the name of Bevans were killed near this fort, and some say another person was killed at the same time, but it is not certain that the fourth person was killed.

Fort Tomlinson.

FORT TOMLINSON was at the Flats of Grave Creek and the first fortification stood near the site of the high school building in Moundsville.

The first fort was a cabin surrounded by high pickets and was thought to have been Joseph Tomlinson's residence fortified for protection against Indians. The stockade was erected in the spring of 1774, when war with the Indians seemed inevitable. It was again used as a place of safety in 1777, but was abandoned on the seventeenth of August of that year and burned by Indians soon after abandoned.

A new fort was built about 1785 by the settlers and their families were brought back to the Flats of Grave Creek from the different forts or settlements to which they had been taken in August, 1777, when it was learned that a large body of Indians contemplated an attack upon Fort Henry. They never left their homes after that on account of Indians though they frequently removed into the fort. The location of the second is not definitely known nor is it known what kind of a fort was erected, but it is generally thought that it was a blockhouse surrounded by pickets.

Settlers from the upper end of Round Bottom depended upon this fort for safety in time of danger from Indians. While little is given in history concerning the fort it is of historical value as there were a number of encounters with Indians not far from it and which are given in this work.

Some writers of early history say that two other forts were erected in the county. One of the forts, they say, was on Big Wheeling Creek and one was at the mouth of Fish Creek, but nothing has been found to corroborate the statement, hence it is fairly safe to say no such forts were erected.

PIONEER LIFE.

GENERAL WAYNE gave the Indians a severe chastisement at the battle of Fallen Timber in August, 1794, and at the treaty at Greenville the following year they promised to cease hostilities and live in peace with the whites. They were thoroughly frightened and many of them were wise enough to flee the wrath of the old general whom they said never slept and who promised to give them a worse thrashing the next time they commenced scalping settlers. He told them that it would make no difference if he was dead as he would come out of his grave and give them a thrashing that would make most of them permanently good.

Peace brought great joy to the hardy settlers and their families. Captives were released and the living members of many families were once more united. They could now go to their homes in the forest and remain there without fear of painted redskins murdering them or carrying them into captivity. Many had spent, for years, much time in forts and block-houses. Children had grown up and knew little or nothing but life in some stockade or to remain in their cabin home in dread of Indians.

Now children could, for once in their lives, play in the woods in summer and not fear the painted savage. They had lived in dread of the scalping knife and subsisted upon venison and hominy, and not all the time had plenty of that. Now peace had come and with industry they were to have plenty.

While the hunter and scout had been fighting the Indians and providing for his family as best he could, living in hopes of better days, the brethren on the east side of the mountains had not been idle. They had fought a successful war against the mother country and gained independence. They had solved the problem of self-government and had a written constitution and had successfully started a government under which they would secure untold blessings. When the old hunter and warriors of the frontier returned to their cabins in the forest they had brighter prospects than they had ever anticipated. They lived in a government for the people, of the people, by the people. They had liberty. Nothing was sweeter to them than the word LIBERTY. The sky was brighter and the air more balmy. There was to be no more war-whoop of the Indian; the smoke of the burning cabin of the settlers was no more to be seen. Sounds were to be heard and smoke to be seen, but the smoke was that from burning logs in the clearing and the sound that of the ax of the settler as he felled the trees and cut them so they could be piled in heaps and burned as he cleared the land to cultivate. He now engaged in removing the forest and preparing the soil for cultivation.

It might well be said, "All work at our house." Father worked also. He was the leader of the work. He and the larger boys cut down the trees and cut them into logs so they could be handled, and the children gathered the brush and piled it up and spent many pleasant evenings burning it. The rifle was hung up in the cabin for future hunting and the tomahawk and scalping knife were made implements of industry, no more to be used as weapons of war. They were now at work to make pleasant homes. Early and late the sound of the ax could be heard as they labored to remove the forest to convert the ground into fields. The smoke of the burning log heaps started on its way toward the sky; they were happy and contented with their lot. It was not a life of ease but of contentment and neighborly feelings which leveled many bumps and removed many difficulties. They were ready to enter upon the full enjoyment of life and of the many good things that go with a life of industry and good fellowship.

The little spots of cleared land soon grew to be large tracts with fences and fields. Trees were cut down and all things made ready for a log-rolling, not a political one.

The hardy settlers and their grown sons gathered at the neighbors' clearing at an early hour and the work and fun commenced. It was fun because they enjoyed it. The day was spent in piling the logs into heaps ready to burn. Night came and the work for the day ended. As night, sabel goddess, dropped her curtain o'er a slumbering world, the old folks began to leave for their homes while girls who had remained at home began to arrive.

A log-rolling without a dance was not thought of; it was out of reason. At an early hour the sound of the fiddle was heard and the dance commenced. There was not much time wasted and the dance went merrily on and often continued till daylight as many of the roads were not adapted to night traveling as there were yet many wild animals that no one cared to meet after night and would avoid them in the day.

There was often a scarcity of chairs and the beds around

the cabin walls were utilized for seats and were generally taken up and then all were not seated. Boys were not expected to get up and offer their seats to girls but were expected to offer her a seat on his lap and it was not expected to be refused but the offer accepted.

Young men were not accustomed to make unbecoming remarks about young women and start slanderous reports, as is often the case in the days of greater refinement, or if he did, her big brother or someone else would call on him and generally after an interview the face of the slanderer would have somewhat the appearance of having encountered something out of everyday life. Many amusing incidents are related concerning the social gatherings of the pioneer days in this country. One of the amusing incidents is said to have occurred at a back-woods wedding. Many of the guests were young and bashful. The amusement of this occasion was an old-time play party, or what was frequently termed, a kissing party. The young men (boys they were called at that date) were rather shy of the bride and this matter did not escape the notice of the young and gallant groom who was very proud of his wife. After a few instances in which some of them should have kissed the bride but failed to do so, the irate husband became very angry at the slight and could stand it no longer and as the party progressed the matter became worse instead of better and the boys became more shy. He stopped the play and loosening his garments to give his arms more freedom he interrupted the hilarity by calling out, "Say, the next cuss that refuses to kiss my wife when her turn comes will be thrashed out of his hide. I'll stand this no longer. She isn't to be slighted by any cuss here." That ended it; she was soon as popular as the other girls and the proud husband as well pleased with the young men as a boy with red-topped boots.

Life was not all fun. They had really very hard work of the hardest kind. They were free to plant and enjoy the fruits of their labor. Orchards were planted, meadows were sown, the forest disappeared and fruitful fields took the place thereof. Bears and wolves were numerous and destructive to sheep and hogs and the hunter found opportunity to exercise his skill in the use of the old rifle in getting rid of them.

County courts offered bounty for scalps of wolves or their heads. Some counties offered larger bounties than others and there was due attention given to the county in which higher bounty was offered and county lines were a matter of some interest to the hunter in catching and killing wolves and it has been stated that wolves when caught near a county line were taken across it and killed in the one offering the higher bounty. For many years Ohio county offered fifteen shillings for the scalp or head of an old wolf and half that amount for a young one. Among the names of persons from Grave Creek receiving bounties for wolf scalps were Nathan Masters, Robert Carpenter and Mrs. Elizabeth Tomlinson.

The famous Wolf Spring, on the banks of Parr's Run, received its name from the catching of a wolf near it, by a man by the name of Abijah McClean. Wolf trapping was interesting from a financial standpoint and at the same time afforded the hunter and trapper no little amusement.

People endeavored to meet as often as possible and hunting parties were common and much benefit was derived from hunting as wild game afforded no small gain in the matter of supplying the table with meat.

Selfishness was not so common in the pioneer days as at a later period and the early settler came as near obeying the commandment, "Love thy neighbor as thyself," as is done at the present day. They helped each other in almost all kinds of work. If a settler was sick and could not gather his harvest the neighbors were not backward in lending a helping hand and joined together and gathered it for him. The log-rolling, grubbing, corn-husking and many other things of the kind afforded opportunity for gatherings and all were attended with social features.

Education was not neglected. The log schoolhouses appeared whenever there were enough families within a radius of four miles or about that, a schoolhouse was erected and a teacher employed and a school opened and the usual three months of school was taught in the winter and some very good work was done both by teachers and pupils and a foundation laid for future generations and better schools.

It will be seen that the work of clearing the forest away and converting the ground upon which it stood into fields was not the work of a few months but that of many years of hard work and many privations, yet these hardy people, full of industry and determination to succeed, have cleared it up and left it for future generations to cultivate the fertile soil and enjoy the prosperity in their happy homes.

ROADS.

THE first roads in country were horse paths, more commonly called bridal paths. In making these roads logs and bushes were removed so people could ride through the forest and where the timber was considerably scattered and the woods open, trees were blazed on two sides so that persons not familiar with these trails could find the way without difficulty. All the merchandise for many years after the first settlements were made, was carried on pack-horses. Thirty years after the first settlements were made in Marshall County not a wagon road had been made in it.

In the year 1800 the county court of Ohio County ordered a road opened down the river to Middle Island Creek, but it was not done for several years after ordered.

Between that date and 1810 a road was located from Wheeling to the Flats of Grave Creek. It was surveyed by A. McMahon. A road was located to Fish Creek soon after under the directions of Morgan Jones, one of the early settlers at Grave Creek and a pioneer surveyor.

In the year 1811 a road was ordered by the county court of Ohio County, opened from Parr's Point to the Pennsylvania line and was continued to Waynesburgh in that state and became the Waynesburg Pike, a famous drove road about the middle of the last century. Drove stands along this road were at one time numerous. These drove stands consisted of the usual wayside tavern of the day with ample stock yards and pasture fields to accommodate large droves of cattle, horses, sheep and hogs. Much of the surplus corn grown along this road was fed to stock in the fall, especially to hogs.

Large droves of stock of all kinds were driven from the country west of the Ohio River to Baltimore over this road. Frequently droves of mules from western Kentucky were taken across part of Indiana, Ohio and struck the drove road at Moundsville and followed it to Baltimore, which was at that date the great stock market of the United States.

The writer of this article saw many droves of mules from Kentucky on this road en route to the east.

It is safe to say that more of the western stock was ferried across the Ohio River at Moundsville than at any other ferry on that river. A steam ferry boat would freuqently run as rapidly as it could be handled from early in the morning until near midnight to clear the road on the Ohio side of the river of stock. The drove road from the ferry landing on the Ohio side of the river has been filled, at times, with droves of cattle to the village of Businessburg on Pipe Creek, a distance of more than five miles.

After the Baltimore and Ohio Railroad was completed to the Ohio River on the last days of 1852, it began to carry stock and by the close of the Civil War, droves ceased to travel the old drove road and the drove stands became a thing of the past.

Much stock was shipped over this road for many years to

HISTORY OF MARSHALL COUNTY, W. VA.   89

Baltimore, the principal stcok market for a number of years after the war, but the great packing houses in Chicago and other western cities cut off the western shippers and soon after that the packing industries at Wheeling purchased the stock from this section and it is probable that at the present day a hog from Marshall County never enjoys a ride in the old-time stock cars to some city.

In years long gone by, farmers in settlements remote from rivers or railroads, paid much attention to stock raising of all kinds. The land being fresh and fertile, large crops of corn were raised and fed to hogs in the fall and they were driven to market, giving very good returns to farmers for their work. Farmers in those sections would remark that the distance to market was too great to haul grain but it was not to drive it to market in beef and pork. Today the few hogs that are raised for market are hauled there in wagons; soon they will be taken there in automobile trucks.

Roads were hard to make and in opening them at an early date crossing streams was a matter not to be overlooked. In crossing large streams the location of a ferry was one of the important matters to consider and in crossing small streams such as creeks and runs, a shallow place or ford, was one of the important matters to take into consideration in locating roads. Bridges were few and, it may be added, far between.

About the year 1840 the county court of Marshall County passed an order to build a bridge over Big Grave Creek at the mouth of it, which has ever since been known as Lindsey's Bridge. It was a wooden structure; iron or steel bridges at that date were unknown. It was not until the year 1882 that an iron bridge was erected in this county by the order of the county court. Three iron bridges were erected that year by the order of the county court consisting of W. J. Burley, J. W. Bonar and J. H. Baird. One was over Big Grave Creek to replace a wooden bridge, one at Hornbrook's Mill, now Graysville, over Fish Creek, and one over Big Wheeling Creek below Birch Run. The bridges were erected at a cost of fifteen thousand dollars each.

Many citizens thought that the county would be ruined by the recklessness of the county court in expending public money. They thought and expressed their thought, that it was too much to build three bridges at that price at one time; one at a time would be far better. One each year would not be too heavy on the taxpayers, but three was entirely too heavy a burden for them to bear. A few appeared to look upon such extravagance in improvements about the same as a Kansas farmer did a visitation of grasshoppers. Those so seriously affected soon recovered from their shock and the improvement continued and steel bridges span the creeks in many places and even large runs are bridged today. Many miles of county roads have been macadamized or paved with brick of late years and the work of improving county roads is yet in its infancy.

RAILROADS

THERE are three lines of railroads in the county. Two are steam roads and one electric railway.

The Baltimore and Ohio Railroad, the first to reach the Ohio River, laid the last rails that closed the last gap in the road on the twenty-fourth day of December 1852 just east of the village of Roseby Rock, completing the line from Baltimore to Wheeling.

It has about thirty-six miles of main line in the county, and aided materially in developing the county as it passes through a fertile section of the Ohio Valley and brought the people in closer communication with the cities on the Ohio River with which they did most of their business.

The Ohio River Railroad was completed in 1884 and commenced operations early that year. It has about twenty-eight miles of main line in the county and passes through the fertile river bottoms.

An electric railway connects Moundsville with Wheeling and intermediate towns. It was commenced in 1895 and in 1896, was in operation to the northern part of Moundsville.

It was first known as the "Benwood and Southern Electric Railway" and was a Marshall County enterprise but later purchased by a company that had acquired the electric roads in Wheeling and those that centered in Wheeling and for a number of years it has been known as the Moundsville Division of the Wheeling Traction lines.

It is a first class road and furnishes transportation for passengers and also freight. It is in line with the other improvements of the day of which Marshall County is struggling to get to the front as in all other matters of interest and importance in the developments of the present century.

CONTEST FOR POSSESSION OF ROUND BOTTOM

ONE of the many suits at law for the possession of land in the Ohio Valley was that for the possession of Round Bottom.

The first settlement made in it was made in connection with the settlement in the Flats of Grave Creek by Joseph, James and Samuel Tomlinson; they were followed by Michael

Cresap about two years after they had made the first improvement in it. Tomlinson brothers made their improvement in the upper end and the Cresap improvement was made about the middle of the bottom.

A slight dispute arose between the Tomlinson brothers and the heirs of Michael Cresap but it was soon adjusted to the satisfaction of both parties and for years after that they thought that they were the owners of that fine bottom but were destined to be disappointed and to lose the land.

Joseph Tomlinson in a sworn statement of his knowledge of the settlement of Round Bottom, gave quite an interesting story of early life in the west.

He stated that he and two brothers, Samuel and James, arrived at the Flats of Grave Creek in March about the year 1770 or 1771, in search of a home for their father's family. They were much pleased with the land about the flats and took up some land there and went down to Round Bottom where they found that no claim had been taken up and they made an improvement at the upper end of the bottom.

From there Joseph Tomlinson went down the river to examine land and fell in with Colonel Crawford who was surveying some military lands between the Little Kanawha and Big Sandy rivers. He engaged with Colonel Crawford as a hand and continued until the surveying was completed.

The work being completed, the surveying party returned back up the river, and in July reached Round Bottom. Before they reached the bottom Mr. Tomlinson learned that it was the intention of Colonel Crawford to make a survey of Round Bottom and he objected to any survey being made as he and his brothers were interested in it as they had taken up a claim and intended to make improvements immediately. Colonel Crawford stated that Colonel Washington had requested him to make a private survey of the bottom and that it would be reported as such and he would not be injured by the survey being made, pledging his word to the same.

Mr. Tomlinson still objected to the survey but it was made. He went along as a spectator and saw the lines run along the river and no more. It stopped at that and there was no other survey made by Colonel Crawford from that time until he was brought by David Rogers to that section of the country in 1775, to survey some military land for him on the Ohio River near the Flats of Grave Creek and at Fish Creek.

Mr. Tomlinson stated that in the year 1772, Michael Cresap of Old Town, sent fourteen men to make improvements in Round Bottom and they made two improvements on the banks of the river about the middle of the bottom but did not fence them. From there they went down the river to make improvements on other land claimed by Mr. Cresap.

In the spring Mr. Cresap sent Francis Purcell and family to Round Bottom to make improvements and take care of his interest. Mr. Purcell cleared six acres of land, fenced it, built a cabin and raised a crop of corn on the ground. He remained there until the spring of 1774, when the breaking out of Dunmore's War, drove the settlers from this section to Old Fort Redstone on the Monongahela River.

In February 1775, the Tomlinson family returned to the Flats of Grave Creek and from that time, Joseph Tomlinson, said he never was away except occasionally for a short time on business or when Indians compelled settlers to leave their homes for a time, but in every case he returned as soon as possible. He stated that his brother James spent the first three years after their arrival on the Ohio River on Round Bottom and that he had frequent intercourse with Mr. Purcell. His brother was only three and one-half miles from his home on Grave Creek.

Michael Cresap died in 1775 and some time after his death there was a dispute about the land, and appears that the Cresap heirs wanted to hold the entire bottom. Mrs. Cresap was notified to be present or send a representative to meet Mr. Tomlinson at a meeting of the commissioners that the General Assembly of Virginia would send out to adjust claims. They were to meet at the Morgan settlement, near where Morgantown now stands. This meeting was held in the year 1779, and a nephew of Mrs. Cresap was there and he and Mr. Tomlinson agreed to divide the bottom as nearly equal as possible without regard to improvements, by a line from the river to the hill. The commissioners ordered the clerk to make a note of the agreement and so state the same on their certificates, which was done and the matter was thought to be adjusted for all time.

The Cresap heirs were to take the lower end and the Tomlinson brothers were to take the upper end. Each party now considered that the matter has been adjusted satisfactorily, were free to make such improvements as they desired and circumstances would permit.

Mr. Tomlinson stated that no other survey of land was made by Colonel Crawford, after he came to the Ohio River, as he kept a careful watch on every survey, being afraid some one would make a survey of it and give them trouble. They rested a number of years believing that they had a clear title to the land they claimed in Round Bottom.

On the eighth of August 1798, Archibald McClean purchased from General Washington all of that tract of land and received a deed for it. The tract purchased by Mr. McClean was to contain 587 acres be the quantity more or less for $5,870, making the price ten dollars per acre.

From old letters, some of which are yet in the possession of descendants of Mr. McClean, and court records, it appears there were two conditions in the proposition of General Washington to Mr. McClean in the negotiation for the sale of the land. General Washington offered to sell him 587 acres, be the quantity more or less, for $5,870 or he would have the land resurveyed and Mr. McClean abide by the survey and pay for the land found to be contained in it. Mr. McClean chose the first proposition and closed the deal. By a careful survey some years after it was found that the tract contained 1293 acres.

That fall and the following spring Mr. McClean sent tenants to the land to clear it and make improvements and then found that others claimed the land which he had bought and paid for. He leased a large tract in the lower end to Jonathan Roberts who proceeded to improve it.

A suit was soon started and was many years in court before it was settled and when concluded and a decision was rendered it confirmed the claim of General Washington and confirmed the title of Mr. McClean to the land.

Michael Cresap, Jr., son of Michael Cresap who caused the first improvement to be made in Round Bottom in Cresap's name, in a bill of complaint in a chancery case against Archibald McClean and Jonathan Roberts, stated that his father died in 1775 and that in his will he bequeathed Round Bottom to the three daughters, Mary, Elizabeth and Sarah, who were minors at the time of the death of their father. He stated that one Luther Martin married Mary and in the year 1781 he got a certificate of right of settlement and had a survey made in 1784 and the same year the plot and certificate of the survey were returned to the Register's office and in July, 1785, General Washington entered a caveat which was dismissed in 1787 and a grant was issued to Luther Martin and his wife and her two sisters, Elizabeth and Sarah Cresap.

In the final disposition of the estate of his father, he acquired the land of the said Luther Martin and the two Misses Cresap. He stated that he was in peaceful possession of the land for a long time until Archibald McClean came to the place with a deed from General Washington. He made the charge of fraud on the part of General Washington in getting the title to the land. He seemed to think that he obtained the field notes of a private survey and made a plat which covered 587 acres and sold the tract to Mr. McClean. He stated that the tract contained 1293 acres. A suit was started in the early part of the last century and was carried through the various courts and was not decided until the twenty-eighth of April, 1834.

The case was decided in the Supreme Court of Appeals in the city of Richmond on the above date and in favor of the claim of General Washington. This decision made the claim of Mr. McClean valid.

Mr. McClean, in his answer to the bill of complaint filed by Mr. Cresap, stated the two conditions offered him in the purchase of the land and he chose the first and took the land at the price and knew nothing of any one making any claim to the land until after he came into the neighborhood of it. At the time he made the purchase he had no reasons to suspect that any claim existed accept that of General Washington.

He stated that Washington received his patent for the Round Bottom on the thirtieth of October, 1785, and the land contained in the boundaries of the tract was 1293 acres, and as for the surplus land it was a matter between the Commonwealth of Virginia and the patentee. Washington had been granted the land contained within the boundaries which he had purchased and he had a right to all found therein. The survey upon which the patent was issued to General Washington, was founded upon a military warrant and made before an act was passed appropriating any land to actual settlers.

The case was in court many years and was fought with determination by both sides. The courts were supposed to settle questions of the validity of claims of parties to disputes and it appears that the higher courts only confirmed the decision of the lower courts. It was only one of the many suits that grew out of the peculiar manner in which land was taken up by settlers and others at an early day in the regions of the Ohio Valley on the east and south side of the Ohio River. Washington was one of the soldiers of the French and Indian war and a grant of two hundred thousand acres of land in the western part of Virginia was appropriated and granted them for service rendered in that war, and it appears that the claim to Round Bottom grew out of that grant. It has often been stated that nearly all the early surveys contained more land than the amount reported in the survey.

WASHINGTON'S LETTER TO COL. McCLEAN

Mount Vernon, Va., August 2, 1798.

Sir:

The annual meeting of the Potomack Company requires my attention in Alexandria today. It will be held, I presume at Gadsby's; if so, I shall be there from ten o'clock until three—also shall be ready to see you at any hour between the earliest and the later.

Enclosed is the Patent for the 587 acre tract (with plat thereof on the back); and a memorandum of my understanding of our agreement; by which the writings are to be drawn.

Mr. Keith has usually done this kind of business for me, and I presume would draw the writing between us as accurately as any other, but it is indifferent to me who the draughtsman is, if professional, and can be correct.

The lease as proposed is prepared to an absolute sale. The usual covenants to enforce building, planting orchard, making meadows-re-enter in case of non-performance, it must be inserted, for although the privilege of becoming the purchaser in fee in seven years is greater, it is no less incumbent on me to attend to the property while the right remains unalienated. To render it unnecessary hereafter to see that these covenants are complied with and to avoid difficulties in securing the Renter, were my inducements for suggesting the alternative or final bargain on the terms proposed in the mem, but I repeat, that I am equally ready to execute the mem.

I am Sir,   Y's Very H'bly Serv.,
MR. ARCH McCLEAN.   GEO. WASHINGTON.

ELIZABETHTOWN

The first house built in what is now Moundsville, was built by Joseph Tomlinson about the year 1771. It was the ordinary log cabin of the early settlers and stood near where the high school building now stands.

In the year 1798 Mr. Tomlinson laid out a tract into town lots and named the town Elizabethtown in honor of his wife.

The lots were on First, Second and Third streets. They were numbered commencing at the corner of what is now Tomlinson avenue and First street, and numbered eastward. Tomlinson avenue, then called Wheeling street, was on the west side and Washington avenue, was on the east side of the town as far as streets were concerned. What is now Morton avenue and Baker avenue were then alleys, hence their narrowness. Lots were laid out on the east side of Washington avenue between Second and First streets and were bounded on the east by a county road; the lots between Second and Third streets on the same side of Washington avenue were bounded by farm land. No lots were laid out on the north side of First street.

Most of the lots were sixty feet wide and two hundred and forty feet long. A few lots were one hundred and twenty feet square.

The first lot sold was to Andrew Rogers. The deed was dated November 15, 1799. It was one of the square lots and brought eight dollars. Joseph Riggs purchased two lots the same year at the same price. His lots were the long ones. James O'Niel and William Ward, each purchased a lot in the year 1800. The latter paid eight dollars and the former paid eleven dollars.

The town grew very slowly and in 1815, there were not one hundred houses in the town and they were generally one story log houses and small at that. The total population was not three hundred persons.

The first store in Elizabethtown was opened in the year 1815 by James Nixon. It would not compare with some of the fine stores of today. Two years later Thomas List opened a second store. He was the first postmaster and the first postoffice was called Grave Creek. It was in Ohio county, Virginia.

Wheeling was the county seat and court being held there many people attended court and that gave Wheeling a better opportunity for a trade center. Trade was not very extensive.

For many years after the first settlements were made the trading was done at Hagerstown, Maryland. The products for exchange were principally pelts, skins and ginseng, which were exchanged for salt and various articles of use to the settlers. The goods were carried on pack-horses.

The only occupations open to residents of Elizabethtown, except to a few mechanics, were clearing land and cultivating crops of various kinds in summer and clearing land and hunting in winter. The ginseng was generally gathered by children in the summer and no small amount of it was gathered as the woods abounded with it and it was in demand and sold readily.

Mr. Tomlinson died in 1825, and five years later his widow had a tract of land added to the town already laid out. The line started at the corner of what is now Third street and Baker avenue and ran down in line with the east side of the avenue to what is now Seventh street and west on the south side of it to the extension of Wheeling street, now Tomlinson avenue, and down on the east side of it to what is now Tenth street and west with the south line of it to the Ohio River. The ground between the line mentioned and Little Grave Creek was laid out into lots.

About the time Joseph Tomlinson laid out the first town lots he started a ferry at the mouth of Little Grave Creek and the first ferryman was a man by the name of Catlett and was the father of Peter B. Catlett, who removed the monument erected to the memory of Captain William Foreman and his men murdered by Indians at the head of the Narrows.

When steamboats began to plow the waters of the beautiful Ohio River, a wharf or steamboat landing was made a short distance below the mouth of Little Grave Creek.

SCENE ON THE OHIO RIVER

All the town at the Flats of Grave Creek was at that time above the reach of high water.

The town was incorporated by an act of the General Assembly of Virginia on the seventeenth day of February, 1830. The act of incorporation gave the town authority over the strip between what is now First street and Parrs Run. The incorporation of Elizabethtown placed the government in the hands of twelve trustees to be elected by the voters on the second Monday of May of each year. The trustees were to choose one of their number president. The power vested in them was about the same as that of the mayor and council at present. The first trustees were elected on the second Monday in May, 1830, and were Thomas H. List, S. P. Baker, Dr. Thomas McCormack, Joseph McClean, James McKean, David Nace, J. B. Roberts, Walter Gray, John Jefferson, Sr., Thomas Nichols, Benjamin Cockayne, B. W. Price. Thomas H. List was chosen president.

This act was amended in the year 1832, taking in the addition made by Mrs. Elizabeth Tomlinson. It also provided that in case of a failure to elect trustees as specified by the act of incorporation, the old trustees should continue in office until their successors were elected and qualified.

Simeon Purdy purchased a tract of land near the river and in the year 1831 had part of it laid out in lots with streets and alleys and in the year 1832, had a town incorporated. The provisions for the government of the town were similar to that of Elizabethtown and the new town in the Flats of Grave Creek was named Moundsville to commemorate the famous mound.

A number of new business houses were built near the river and a wharf was made near the central part of the river front. The towns were now called the Upper and the Lower town, having reference to the one farthest up the river and at the same time to the one farthest up from the river or vice versa.

The two towns with the usual privileges existed until 1865, when it was thought best to consolidate them into one town, and by an act of the legislature of WEST VIRGINIA in the year 1865, the two towns were consolidated into one and named MOUNDSVILLE. A new order of affairs were now introduced; the trustees were a thing of the past, and the officers in the new town under the act of incorporation, were very much the same as they are at the present day.

Robert McConnell was the first mayor of Moundsville and H. W. Hunter was the first city clerk and treasurer. Mr. Hunter served a number of years in the official capacity above named.

The first industries were distillery, flouring mills and tanneries. Later the town grew to considerable size and of late years a number of additions have been added to it until it is a city of considerable size. It might be called a city of magnificent distances, if distance is considered, as it has over thirty miles of streets within the corporation.

It has a sanitary sewer system giving the city a good sanitary drainage and a surface drainage sewer system which gives it such drainage that no water is permitted to collect and remain in pools, but is quickly carried away. The sanitary sewer is twenty-three miles in length and the surface drainage sewers are several miles in length. The surface drainage sewer installed by F. B. Sweeten & Son is three miles in length but there are several sewers which were installed by the city at divers times not counted as their length is uncertain and some of them are connected with private sanitary sewers.

There are over eight miles of paved streets in the city at present. It has several large industries and four large coal mines in or near it.

The census of 1920 reported a population of 10,669.

First ward 3,387
Second ward 2,873
Third ward 2,591

Fourth ward 1,718

DISCONTENT

DISSATISFACTION developed in Northwestern Virginia at an early date and about 1830, citizens began to desire a separation from the Commonwealth of Virginia. It was, perhaps, because of the distance to the seat of government of the state and the inconvenience in getting to it; and the fact that all state institutions were east of the mountains. While this feeling ceased to be voiced, it did not cease to exist, and eventually resulted in a separation and a new state being made of the territory west of the Allegheny mountains with a few counties east of them, thirty-three years later.

A clipping from the "Wheeling Gazette," of November 10, 1830, gives a clear view of the situation and an idea of the feeling at that date:

At a numerous and respectable meeting of the citizens of Elizabethtown and its vicinity held on the 13th, inst. to take into consideration the propriety of petitioning the Legislature of Virginia to cede that portion of her jurisdiction comprised in a line due West from the South West corner of the State of Maryland to the Ohio river, including the territory North of said West line, to the State of Maryland—John Jefferson was called to the Chair and Walter Gray was appointed Secretary.

The following resolution was unanimously adopted.

Resolved, That the meeting approve the proceedings of our fellow citizens held at the Court House at Wheeling on the 1st, inst., relative to the proposed cession of a part of the territory of this State to Maryland, including all that portion of the territory North of a West line from the South West corner of said State to the Ohio river.

Resolved, That this meeting appoint a committee of five persons to ascertain by correspondence and otherwise, the feelings and disposition of the inhabitants included with the above described limits, relative to the proposed cessation.

Resolved, That this meeting appoint Messrs. John McCullock, Samuel Howard, Daniel Terrell, Timothy Mayhall, and James Green, as a committee to carry the above proceedings into effect.

Resolved, That the proceedings of this meeting be published in the Compiler and Gazette at Wheeling; the Wellsburg Gazette and the Clarksburg Enquirer.

Resolved, That this meeting adjourn to meet at this place the second Monday in January, 1831.

JOHN JEFFERSON, Chairman.
WALTER GRAY, Secretary.

The citizens in the lower part of Ohio County became dissatisfied with the county court of the county and of the location of the county seat, as it was far from being centrally located. There seems to have been general dissatisfaction, and it is probable that there was cause for it. Records show that in the selection of officials, either by election or appointment that official honors were not equally distributed. Of the residents of that part of the county now comprising Marshall County, two men were elected members of the General Assembly of the State.

William McMechen, the first settler in McMechen's Bottom, in which Benwood and McMechen now stand, was elected a member of the House of Delegates and attended the annual session of the General Assembly which convened January 30, 1788, and was elected to the same office and attended the session which convened at Richmond, October 17, 1791.

John Parriott, a resident of the Flats of Grave Creek was elected to the House of Delegates at an annual election held on the fourth Thursday of May, 1827, and was reelected to the same office on each of the following seven years, making eight years of successive service in the General Assembly.

Blair Moran, a resident of the lower part of the county was appointed sheriff of Ohio County in the early part of 1835, and by the act of separation of the county, was made sheriff of both counties for the official year for which he was appointed.

A memorial to the legislature of Virginia covers the ground and sets forth the several grievances of the citizens and of the unfair course pursued by the county court in regard to an effort to locate the seat of justice in a more central location. The result of the course taken by the county court resulted in an act of the General Assembly cutting off the lower part of the county and making a new county of the territory cut off and locating the county seat in a very convenient location for the new county.

MEMORIAL

To The Honorable Senate and House of Delegates

of

VIRGINIA

In General Assembly Met

THE memorial of the undersigned inhabitants of Ohio county respectfully represents, that on the 8th day of December, 1832, an act was passed for appointing commissioners to fix on a site for a court-house and other public buildings for said county and requiring the county court thereof, at their first term after said commissioners shall have determined on the spot, or as soon thereafter as practicable, to appoint commissioners to contract for the erection of said buildings, and to appropriate money for carrying the same into effect; that five commissioners chosen by the legislature in conformity with said act, met at Wheeling according to its provisions on the 15th day of May in 1833, and having proceeded thence to examine the county with a view to the object of their appointment, made choice of Elizabethtown and there laid out ground for said purpose; and the proprietors of the lots thus selected have since made a donation of and conveyed them to the justices of the county and their successors in office agreeable to the requirement of the aforesaid act. But the court (obviously under an improper bias for the wishes and interest of Wheeling) have pertinaciously refused or evaded a compliance with the law, in wholly omitting to make the required appropriation, and in choosing commissioners with the design that they should not—and unquestionable reasons to know they would not act. Thus has the authority of the legislature been set at defiance and a law of the state defeated by the magistrates of the county. And as if this manifest spirit of insubordination and total disregard of legislative injunctions were not sufficiently disrespectful, what was the astonishment of your memorialists, to find set up at the door of their court-house a notice that a petition or petitions would be presented to your honorable body at their present session, praying a repeal of the very law which had been violated (by the movers themselves probably of these petitions) and a revocation of the decision of the commissioners, with sundry other matters tending to evince that rather than submit to the arbitrement of disinterested men selected by the grand inquest of the state, the authors of these proceedings would sever the county and throw the administration of its internal concerns into disorder and confusion. They ask of the legitimate power of the commonwealth, not merely a silent approbation of their disobedience but a reward for their contumacy.

Of what use is arbitration, if the parties disputant are not bound by the judgment of the arbitrators? If the party dissatisfied, shall be at liberty to reject the award with impunity?

A reasonable hope was indulged that when this vexatious and long protracted strife about the location of the court house was brought to the test of impartial enquiry and decision of competent and disinterested judges, it would forever be laid at rest by the acquiescense of the parties. But this reasonable hope has been frustrated, and the citizens of the county again involved in all the bitterness of party collision by the determination of one side not to abide by the issue thus fairly obtained.

And what is the ground assumed for this virtual nullification of the law—this illegal resistance of the act of the commissioners which has again embroiled brethren of the same county in the evils of an acrimonious controversy for their local rights, of uncertain continuance, unless brought to a close by the intervention of your honorable body? Has any acknowledged principle of justice been infringed? any just claims of Wheeling sacrificed? or has the voice of the people been sported by the commissioners in the fulfillment of the trust confided to them? On this last point let the late election testify. It will not be questioned that the strength of the county was put forth on that occasion; or that the entire vote was concentrated upon the sole object of the removal of the seat of justice to the Flats of Grave Creek.

Every political feeling—every private prejudice was utterly merged in that single consideration. Yet what was the result of the animated contest, and by many hundred votes the largest ever taken in the county. Out of more than 1600 votes given, the parties came out strikingly near equality in numbers; and though the Wheeling candidate was returned by an extremely meagre majority, the investigation of contested votes which has been since instituted, the report of which will be laid before the house of delegates, will, memorialists confidently believe prove that even that majority was not merited.

In this trial, the three lower precincts, with trifling of one or two persons, gave a consolidated vote in favor of the location at Elizabethtown. The two upper precincts polled a respectable majority for the same interests, leaving the opposite side, in the whole county, exclusively of the Wheeling district, less than 140 votes. And even the extreme upper end, and most of the remote corners of the county, sanctioned by merely a moiety, the removal of the seat of justice to the place designated by the commissioners; thus evincing that distance is not the sole object to its continuance in Wheeling, and that the tenderness expressed by the latter for the hardships to which the people of that section would be subjected by having the courts established at Grave Creek, is altogether gratuitous and not felt by themselves.

Much dissatisfaction has arisen from the belief, prevalent in the country, that the internal economy of the county—the disbursement of its funds, and the distribution of improvements, the appointment and recommendation to office, etc. the town of Wheeling and the county court of Ohio are synonimous terms. And the unworthy intrigues which have been practiced by that body on special occasions, by convening early in the day, which the facility of collecting magistrates of the town enabled them to do; transacting the business designed and adjourning before the magistrates from the country can arrive, gave weight to the opinion, and strengthen the desire to separate their "local habitation".

That the citizens of Wheeling and its immediate vicinity should have felt themselves impelled, in this struggle to bring their whole force into the field, was naturally to be expected; and had they confined themselves to their legitimate resources, no complaint would have been heard. But when, besides intimidating persons dependent in their pecuniary circumstances on the monied aristocracy of the town, from voting agreeable to their sentiments, it was known that they unscrupulously introduced to the husting and received the votes if not of "foreign mercenaries" at least of men alien to the suffrage of the state, it was deemed by the opponents of a duty they owed to themselves, to justice and purity of elections to institute a scrutiny at the polls. Of the propriety of adopting this course your honorable body will be better able to judge when the matter shall have been fully sifted by that branch to which it has been appropriately committed.

It is alleged in favor of retaining the county seat at Wheeling that the main part of the judicial business originates in that town and in the northern section of the county. We are aware of no reason why the farmers of Short Creek should be more involved in law suits, or more inclined to litigation than their neighbors of the South; but if it be so, we must deem it a misfortune; and if this litigious disposition is encouraged by the proximity of the courts their removal would doubtless be a blessing. Nevertheless if the fact be as stated, we are not conscious of its resting on any natural or abiding cause; and in the fluctuations and vicissitudes of time, the reverse of the present may be the posture of affairs at no very remote period. And this will appear more probable from a view of the comparatively stationary population of the North and the rapid increase of the southern portion, especially since the confidence given to land titles by the late law passed for that purpose. And even this growing settlement of the lower end, would no doubt be still accelerated were a few monopolizing landholders of the North to remove the barriers by opening their immense tracts to the purchase of actual settlers at fair prices. However, the best evidence of public feeling on this disputed subject is the sense of the people, and that has been recently expressed at the election.

Elizabethtown, seated on the elegant extensive Flats of Grave Creek, with a population of about 800, commanding from the higher parts a handsome view of the Ohio river and extending along its margin, surrounded by a fertile hill country capable of sustaining a dense population and ready to pour in its abundant products by the numerous avenues which descend along the converging ridges, etc. to beauty adding salubrity of situation, is a flourishing and rapidly increasing town and bids fair at no remote period to be a place of commercial and domestic enterprise.

The judicial business of town and country conjoined is even now unwieldly. The accumulation of suits on the docket has already become too burdensome for continuance. The sessions are protracted from six to eight weeks, and suitors and witnesses from a distance are sometimes detained on expenses ten or twelve days before they can get a hearing. This state of things imperiously demands alteration and renders at no distant period a separation of the legal business of the town and country indispensable and inevitable. Wheeling then must have her borough courts whether the other be removed or not. Yet has she employed her ingenuity and illegal power for retaining within her borders in the face of a plain statute the courts of the county, notwithstanding more than four-fifths of the territory lies south of the town, and an equal proportion of the qualified voters of the county have declared in favor of the selected site selected by the commissioners. Should Wheeling succeed against law and these evidences of equity and popular will, the southern part of the county will be left void of redress. And the people, who have long felt and complained of the grievance under which they labored from the unequal distance of the judiciary of the county, and who, confiding in the stability of their legislature, thought themselves on the point of relief, would have the mortification to find themselves thrust back upon the evils from which they fondly believed they had emerged, and doomed to endure them in hopeless perpetuity.

To the sum of these wrongs (could their occurrence be supposed to lie within the sphere of probability) must be added the flagrant injury and injustice which would be inflicted on those individuals who, trusting to the good faith of the legislation of the state, have made investments in real estate at enhanced prices in the vicinity of the contemplated courthouse, some of whom have perhaps expended nearly their all in those purchases and improvements and who, should they be disappointed in their expectations must consequently sink. But we will not harbor a sentiment so abhorrent to our feelings or derogatory to the character of the representatives of the "Ancient Dominion."

The location which shall now be established will be permanent and forbids the idea of future change to accommodate itself, at successive intervals to the varying circumstances of the people, and consequently ought to be prospective in its view.

Your memorialists owe perhaps an apology to your honorable body for the length of this communication. But they wish to present a comprehensive view of the subject the better to enable you to judge of the merits of their case.

And now, relying with perfect confidence on the justice and rectitude of the high tribunal to which they appeal, your memorialists most respectfully solicit your honorable body to take such measures as in your judgement shall seem meet to vindicate the sanctity of your laws against the infraction of bold invaders and carry into effect the act passed on the 8th day of December, 1832 for the appointment of commissioners to fix on a site for the court-house of the county.

MARSHALL COUNTY

This county was created by an act of the General Assembly of Virginia of the twelfth of March 1835, which cut two hundred and forty square miles from the lower part of Ohio County. The Act read: "That all that part of the county of Ohio south of a line beginning on the Ohio river at a stone to be fixed on the bank of said river one-half mile above the mouth of Boggs Run thence a direct line to the northern boundary of the town of West Union, and thence to the Pennsylvania line, shall form one distinct county to be called and known by the name of Marshall County." It was named in honor of John Marshall, Chief Justice of the United States.

JOHN MARSHALL

The county courts of Virginia composed of justices of the peace, were vested with authority not exercised by such courts at the present day. They appointed all county and district officers or recommended persons of its selection to be appointed by the Governor.

The term of office of justices of the peace appears to have been for life or good behavior and that without remuneration and each county should have at least twelve justices of the peace commissioned in it as soon as it was possible to have that number appointed and commissioned after a new county was formed, and four of the number constituted a legal quorum for the transaction of business. The law required the court to recommend three of its members annually to the governor for appointment for county sheriff whose term of office was one year and he could not serve more than two consecutive terms. The court recommended three of the senior members of it for such appointment as it was considered a method of remunerating them for their services as justices.

In June after the act was passed creating the new county, the justices of the peace within the limits thereof, convened and proceeded to organize civil government for the county and get it into operation.

The only county officer in the county at the time was Blair Moran, Sheriff of Ohio County, who by the act of separation, was made sheriff of Marshall County until the first of June 1836 (until a sheriff could be regularly recommended and commissioned by the Governor of the Commonwealth.

It will be interesting to notice the language in which the proceedings are recorded and notice the many changes made in the years passed since that date and also the changes made in the several offices and no less important matter, that of remuneration for official service.

THE COUNTY COURT ELECTS AN ATTORNEY FOR THE COMMONWEALTH AND A CLERK FOR THE COURT—OTHER MATTERS

June 18, 1835.

Marshall County, to-wit;

In pursuance of an Act of the Assembly passed March 12, 1835, forming Marshall County out of the lower part of Ohio County; Jacob Burley, Benjamin McMechen, John Parriott, Samuel Howard and Zadock Masters, gentlemen, met at the Brick School house in Elizabethtown in said county and produced Commissions from the Governor of the Commonwealth commissioning them Justices of the Peace for said county and having severally taken the oath to support the Constitution of the United States, the oath of fidelity to the Commonwealth, the oath against duelling and the oath of office as prescribed by law to be taken by Justices of the Peace in this

Commonwealth (a certificate whereof under the hand and seal of A. Wood, Esq., of Ohio County is on file in this office) took their seats upon the bench and proclamation being made by the sheriff as the manner is, the court proceeded viva voce to the election of an attorney for the Commonwealth for this county; whereupon Jacob Burley, Benjamin McMechen, Samuel Howard and John Parriott, Zadock Masters having voted for Elbert H. Caldwell, Esq., he was declared duly appointed Commonwealth attorney for this county and thereupon said Caldwell came into court and took the several oaths as prescribed by law to be taken by him as such and the oath of a practicing Attorney of the court.

The court proceeded to elect a clerk for this county; whereupon ballotting for the same stood thus:

First, For James Burley, candidate, Jacob Burley, Samuel Howard.

First, For Jas. D. Morris, candidate, John Parriott.

First, For Hiram McMechen, candidate, Benjamin McMechen and Zadock Masters.

Second, For James Burley, candidate, Jacob Burley and Samuel Howard.

Second, For James D. Morris, candidate, John Parriott.

Second, For Hiram McMechen, candidate, Benjamin McMechen and Zadock Masters.

Third, For James Burley, candidate, Jacob Burley and Samuel Howard.

Third, For James D. Morris, candidate, John Parriott, Benjamin McMechen and Zadock Masters; whereupon it appearing that James D. Morris had a majority of the votes of all the Justices in Commission in the county, he was declared elected clerk of this court and thereupon the said James D. Morris with John Parriott, Wm. McConnell, Z. Masters and Benjamin Cockayne his securities entered into and acknowledged a Bond in the penalty of Three Thousand dollars and the said James D. Morris took the oath of fidelity to the Commonwealth, the oath to support the Constitution of the United States, the oath to suppress duelling and the oath of office.

Moses C. Good, William McConnell, Zachariah Jacob, John McFarren, Francis C. Campbell, Lewis Steenrod, Morgan Nelson, Isaac Hoge, Jr., James A. Clark, J. Y. Armstrong, Esq., who have been duly licensed to practice the law in the Commonwealth, on their motion, have leave to practice in the court in this county and thereupon they took the oath prescribed by law.

Ordered that this court meet after dinner at four o'clock at Mrs. Susan Parriott's, in Moundsville and that that be the place for holding the courts of this county in the future until the public buildings shall be erected.

Walter Grey, gentleman foreman, Jesse Burch, John Criswell, John Riggs, Vincent Cockayne, John Ward, Samuel Burris, John Barto, John Huggans, James Dunlap, Reuben Roberts, Edward Gregg, James Riggs, John Taylor, Zachariah Wayman, John Anderson, William McFarland, Benjamin Cockayne, Samuel Venus, William Woodburn and John Brown were sworn a grand jury for the body of this county and were adjourned over until tomorrow morning at nine o'clock.

On the petition of Samuel Cockayne who produced the sheriff's receipt for the taxes imposed by law and entered into Bond with good security in the sum of $150 conditioned as the law directs, a license is granted him to keep an ordinary at his house in this county until the next May term of this court, the court being of the opinion that he is a man of honesty. probity and good demeanor, not addicted to gaming or drunkenness.

Benjamin Harvey having produced the sheriff's receipt for the taxes imposed by law, permission is granted him to keep private entertainment at his house in this county.

The last will and testament of Margaret Cauglin, deceased, is produced in court and proved by the oath of John Parriott, William Vansyoc and Alexander McDonald the subscribing witnesses thereto and thereupon the said will is ordered to be recorded.

The court being of the opinion that John Parriott is a discreet person he having given bond with security in the penalty of Fifteen Hundred dollars conditioned as the law directs and taken the oath of fidelity to the Commonwealth, doth authorize said Parriott to celebrate the rite of marriage in this county.

Ordered that court adjourn till tomorrow morning at nine o'clock.   B. McMECHEN.

Grand Jury Returns Indictments

On June the nineteenth the grand jury convened pursuant to its adjournment, as recorded, and received its instructions from the Attorney for the Commonwealth and retired to a room to take up its work.

Late in the day four indictments were reported, all true bills, of which they were for assault and battery. The grand jury having completed its work was discharged.

The court ordered the sheriff to subpoena all the persons indicted to appear at the next quarterly term of court to answer to the indictments.

The records of the court shows that they appeared as

cited and were represented by attorneys and were given a trial before a jury as in the Circuit Court at the present day.

Recommendation for Coroner

June 19, 1835.

The court doth recommend to the executive Richard Morton and William Woodburn to be commissioned to execute the office of coroner within this county upon which recommendation stood thus:

For Richard Morton—Benjamin McMechen, John Parriott, Samuel Howard, Jacob Burley and Z. Masters.

For William Woodburn—Benjamin McMechen, John Parriott, Samuel Howard, Jacob Burley and Z. Masters.

Under the date of July 25, 1835, the following appears on the records:

RICHARD MORTON this day produced to the court a commission under the hand of the Governor and of the seal of the Commonwealth appointing him to execute the office of coroner within this county during good behavior, and thereupon the said Richard Morton took the several oaths required by law and Simeon B. Purdy, Samuel Dorsey and Walter Gray his securities entered into a bond in the penalty of $3000 conditioned as the law directs, which bond was acknowledged by the several obligors therein named and ordered to be recorded.

Saturday, June 20, 1835.

Present: Jacob Burley, John Parriott, Zadock Masters and Samuel Howard.

Ordered that the sheriff summons the justices of the county to appear here on the first day of the next July Term of this Court for the purpose of making recommendations of other persons to be appointed and commissioned Justices for this County.

Jacob Lewis who was on yesterday appointed one of the overseers of the poor for this county came into court and was duly qualified as such by taking the several oaths prescribed by law.

Odered that the $200 laid in the levy of this year for the improvement of the navigation of Fish Creek be paid to the future order of this court.

Ordered that Samuel Howard, Esq. and Joseph McClean, Jr. be and are hereby appointed Commissioners to examine the improvement made by Jacob Burley, Esq. in the navigation of Fish Creek and make a report thereof to the October Term of this Court.

Present: John Parriott, Z. Masters, Jacob Burley, and

Samuel Howard, gentlemen. The court proceeded to lay the county levy for the year 1835, which is as follows:

To E. H. Caldwell, attorney for the Commonwealth, for public services............................$	50.00
To James D. Morris, clerk of this court, for public services	110.00
To Blair Moran, sheriff...............................	90.00
To James D. Morris, clerk of this court, for books and stationery	90.00
To Joseph McClean for running the line between Marshall and Ohio counties subject to the order of this court	45.00
To George Corrathers, jailor.........................	12.00
To For the improvement of the navigation of Fish Creek	200.00
To B. Moran, sheriff commission.....................	35.00
	$572.00

It appearing to the satisfaction of the court by the return of the Commissioner of the revenue that there are thirteen hundred and five titheables in this county, it is ordered that the sheriff collect off of each titheable in this county the sum of forty-eight cents as a county tax for the year eighteen hundred and thirty-five.

Ordered that Henry Ewing be appointed surveyor of the road leading from Robert Martin's Mill on Stulls run through the lands of the heirs of Robert Woods, deceased, Robert Martin, Willis Rush, William Scott, John Null, Skelton Standiford, Henry Ewing and that the usual titheables do work thereon under him.

Ordered that court adjourn until court in case.

JACOB BURLEY.

County Surveyor and Commissioner of the Revenue and Justices

On July the twenty-third the County Court recommended or appointed officers to be commissioned as the following records indicate:

Present: Jacob Burley, John Parriott, Zadock Masters, Benjamin McMechen, Samuel Howard and Thos. Buchannan, gentlemen.

A majority of the acting Justices of this county being present and deeming it expedient it is ordered that Lewis Bonnett, Charles P. Wells, William McFarland, Thomas H. List, John T. McCreary and Robert McConahey, gentlemen, be recommended to the executive of the Commonwealth as fit and proper persons to be commissioned Justices of the Peace for said county.

The County Court proceeded to recommend the executive a County Surveyor for this county, whereupon the vote stood thus:

First, For Jesse Burch—Jacob Burley and Samuel Howard.
First, For Joseph Wilson—John Parriott.
First, For Joseph McClean—Benjamin McMechen, Z. Masters and Thomas Buchanan.
Second, For Jesse Burch—Jacob Burley and Samuel Howard and John Parriott.
Second, For Joseph McClean—B. McMechen, Z. Masters and Thos. Buchanan. Whereupon it appearing that neither Joseph McClean nor Jesse Burch had a majority of the votes of all the Justices present; the sheriff of Ohio County, who is sheriff of this county by the act of Assembly forming this county, was called to give the casting vote; the said sheriff came into court and voting for Joseph McClean, the court doth recommend to the executive Joseph McClean as a fit and proper person to be commissioned to execute the office of County Surveyor within this county.

Friday, August 21, 1835.

Present: Z. Masters, Benjamin McMechen, Samuel Howard, John Parriott and Jacob Burley, Gentlemen Justices.

Ordered that the overseers of the poor bind out according to law to John Barto (Cooper), Samuel Henderson, a poor orphan son of—until he attains the age of twenty-one.

Ordered that the article of agreement entered into by Thomas H. List and Simeon B. Purdy and Joseph McClean of a commission with Joseph McClean, Jr., for the erection of a jail for said county, is approved by this court and that the same be recorded.

Ordered that the sheriff summon the justices of this county to attend on the first day of the next term for the purpose of appointing a commissioner of revenue for this court and for other purposes.

The court set the following rates and prices to be paid at all ordinaries within this county for liquor, diet, lodging, provender, stabling, fodder and pasturage, to-wit:

  For a quart of Mederia wine...............$1.00
  For a quart of Sherry wine.................. 1.00
  For a quart of other wine................... 1.00
  For a half pint of imported spirits.......... .25
  For a half-pint country gin.................. .25
  For a half-pint whiskey .... .12½
  For a half-pint peach or apple brandy or
    cherry bounce .... .12½

Dinner .... .25
Breakfast or supper...................... .25
Horse at hay per night................... .12½
Gallon of oats........................... .12½
Horse pasture per night.................. .12½
Lodging .... .12½

Ordered that the sheriff deliver to the surveyors of roads in this county the copies of orders handed him by the clerk of this court which shall be a sufficient execution of the same.

Ordered the court adjourn till court in course.

JOHN PARRIOTT.

Under the date of September 24, 1835, the following proceedings of the county court are found recorded:

Simeon B. Purdy, Thomas H. List, Francis Kelley, and William McFarland, gentlemen who have been appointed justices of the peace for the County of Marshall by commissions under the hand of Littleton W. Tazwell, Governor of the Commonwealth, with the seal of the Commonwealth thereto affixed, this day appeared in court and took the oath of fidelity to the Commonwealth, with the several oaths of office, the oath prescribed by an act entitled an act to suppress duelling, and the oath to support the constitution of the United States.

The county court proceeded to the appointment of the commissioner of the revenue for this county, whereupon the vote stood thus:

For Christopher Parriott, candidate—John Parriott, Simeon B. Purdy, Samuel Howard, Jacob Burley and Francis Kelley.

For Michael Dunn, candidate—Thomas H. List, Thos. Buchanan, Z. Masters, Benjamin McMechen and William McFarland, and it appearing that neither Christopher Parriott nor Michael Dunn had a majority of the votes of all the justices present the sheriff of Ohio County, who is sheriff of this county, by the act forming this county, was called to give the casting vote, and the said sheriff came into court and voting for Christopher Parriott, the court doth appoint him, the said Christopher Parriott, to execute the office of commissioner of the revenue for this county.

Deputy Sheriffs and Election Commissioners.

Under date of September 25, 1835.

Robert Shoemaker and Jacob Jefferson are by Blair Moran, sheriff of this county, appointed deputy sheriffs during pleasure and the court being of the opinion that the said Robert Shoemaker and Jacob Jefferson are men of honesty, probity and good demeanor. They took the several oaths prescribed by law.

The court appointed the following persons as commissioners to superintend the election to be held for a senator to fill a vacancy occurred by the death of Col. Jno. McCoy, to be held in this county at the several precincts ...... day of October court, viz.: at Elizabethtown, James C. Bonar, Joseph McClean, Jr., John Riggs, Simeon Purdy and Walter Gray; at Fish Creek, C. P. Wells, Nicholas Wykart, Timothy Mayhall, and Joseph Alexander; at Howard, Jesse Burch, John Wilson and Edward Dowler; at Buchanan, James Ewing, John B. West, and Levi Bonnett.

Committee Reports on Navigation of Fish Creek.

Friday, October 23, 1835.

James Bohanan, Jesse Burch and Samuel Howard reported to court in words following: In pursuance to an order of the court to us directed to examine the improvement made by Jacob Burley, Esq., in the navigation of Fish Creek from the forks of said creek to the mouth of the same, are of the opinion that the improvement made therein agrees with an article signed by Joshua Garner and Samuel Howard, commissinoers appointed by the court of Ohio County for this purpose, and Jacob Burley.

Given under our hands this 19th day of October, 1835.

        James Bohanan (Seal.)
        Jesse Burch (Seal.)
        S. Howard (Seal.)

Thursday, 19th of November, 1835.

Samuel Howard, John Parriott and Zadock Masters are by this court recommended to the Governor as fit persons to execute the office of sheriff for the ensuing year, to which recommendation the vote stood thus:

For Samuel Howard—Z. Masters, Jacob Burley, Thomas Buchanan, John Parriott, James McConaghy, Thos. H. List, and Francis Kelley.

For John Parriott—Z. Masters, Jacob Burley, Thomas Buchanan, James McConaghy, Thos. H. List, Samuel Howard and Francis Kelley.

For Zadock Masters—Jacob Burley, Thomas Buchanan, John Parriott, James McConaghy, Thomas H. List, Samuel Howard and Francis Kelley.

Commissioner of Revenue Gives Bond.

Christopher Parriott, who was appointed commissioner of the revenue for the county, this day entered into bond with Samuel Howard and John Parriott, his securities, which bond is in the words: Know all men by these presents, that we,

Christopher Parriott, Samuel Howard and John Parriott, are held and firmly bound unto Littleton W. Tazwell, Esq., Governor and Chief Magistrate of the Commonwealth of Virginia, in the just and full sum of one thousand dollars to be paid to the said Governor and his successors for the use of the said Commonwealth; for the payment whereof well and truly to be made, we bind ourselves and each of our heirs, executors and administrators jointly and severally firmly by these presents, sealed with our seals and dated the 19th day of November, 1835.

The conditions of the above obligation is such that whereas the court of Marshall County have appointed the above bound Christopher Parriott commissioner of the revenue for said county for the term of one year; now, if said Christopher Parriott shall faithfully perform the duties of said office during the said term then the above obligation to be void, otherwise to remain in full force and virtue.

                           C. C. Parriott (Seal.)
                           S. Howard (Seal.)
                           John Parriott (Seal.)

Which bond was acknowledged by the said commission and his securities and it is ordered that the clerk transmit a copy of said bond to the Auditor of Public Accounts.

Surveyor Gives Bond.

January 11, 1836.

Joseph McClean produced a commission under the hand of the Governor and the seal of the Commonwealth appointing him surveyor of this county for the term of seven years from this day; and thereupon the said Joseph McClean took the several oaths required by law and with Horatio J. McClean and James Burley, his securities, entered into and acknowledged a bond and penalty directed by said commission and conditioned as the law directs.

Morgan Jones is, by Joseph McClean, surveyor of this county, appointed his deputy during pleasure, and he took the several oaths required by law.

Sheriff Gives Bond.

March 24, 1836.

SAMUEL HOWARD, gentleman, this day produced to the court a commission under the hands of the Governor of the Commonwealth with the seal of the Commonwealth thereto affixed, whereby he is commissioned to execute the office of sheriff of this county until the first quarterly term of this court for the year 1837. And thereupon the said Samuel Howard together with James Burley, Joseph Alexander and

Joseph McClean, his securities, entered into and acknowledged three several bonds in the penalty of $30,000 each, conditioned according to law, which bond is ordered to be recorded, and the said Samuel Howard took the oath of fidelity to the Commonwealth, the oath prescribed by the act entitled, an act to suppress duelling, the oath to support the constitution of the United States and the oath of office.

James Burley and Joshua Burley are, by Samuel Howard, sheriff of this county, appointed deputy sheriffs during pleasure and the court being of the opinion that the said James Burley and Joshua Burley are men of honesty, probity and good demeanor and they severally took the several oaths prescribed by law.

March 26, 1836.

Jesse V. Hughes and James Dunlap are, by Samuel Howard, sheriff of this county, appointed deputy sheriffs during pleasure and the court being of the opinion that the said Jesse V. Hughes and James Dunlap are men of honesty, probity and good demeanor, they severally took the several oaths prescribed by law.

Saturday, April 23, 1836.

Present: Wm. McFarland, Zadock Masters, Simeon B. Purdy, and John Parriott, Geneltmen Justices, etc.

Samuel Howard is, by Samuel Howard, Sr., gentleman sheriff of this county, appointed his deputy sheriff during pleasure and the court being of the opinion that the said Samuel Howard is a man of honesty, probity and good demeanor, he took the several oaths prescribed by law.

Ordered that court adjourn till court in course.

WM. McFARLAND.

Other appointments made to fill the many official positions in the county for the several purposes were:

School Commissinoers, term of office, one year—Walter Gray, Timothy Mayhall, Nathaniel Shepherd, Jacob Burley, Mordacai Bane, Wm. B. Buchanan and George Dowler.

Constables; term of service, two years—Joshua Burley, John Dickey, Robert Shoemaker, Jesse V. Hughes, Samuel Gatts, Benjamin Blodget, James Dunlap and Samuel Howard. Several of these were later appointed deputy sheriffs.

Road Supervisors; term of office, one year—Henry Parsons, Henry Campbell, Edward Gregg, James Ramsey, Bennett Logsdon, David Lutes, Reason B. Howard, Thomas Howard, John Ward, Robert Patterson, Wm. O. Powell, Samuel Venus, Richard Rulong, John Barto, Joseph Magers, Joshua Garner, Job Smith, Andrew Jenny, David Wells, Miner

HISTORY OF MARSHALL COUNTY, W. VA. 117

Burge, James Standiford, John Reed, David Rush, Edward Dowler, John Gray, Silas Price, Benjamin S. Gregg, John Minson, Thomas Pollock, Wm. Vanscyoc, John Rine, Michael Dowler, Samuel Dorsey, Philip Jones, Robert Davis, Abraham Earliwine, David Anguish, Samuel Smith, Thomas Coffield, William Hull, Abraham Covolt, Joseph Loudenslager, Jacob Crow, William Williams, Jonathan Roberts, Thomas Clegg, Benjamin Harvey, Joseph Montgomery, Isaac Hubbs, Micajah Doty, Lazarus Ryan, Jacob Grandstaff, John Scott, Harvey Bowers, Benjamin Shepherd, Joseph White, Alexander Caldwell, Wm. Holliday, Robert Cecil, Bonham Martin, Peter Orum and Daniel Gorby.

At a regular session of the county court in the year 1837, the county was divided into three districts for convenience of constables, as is stated in the language of the records, and as follows:

First District—All north of Wheeling Creek.

Second District—Beginning at the Ohio River at the county line between Ohio and Marshall, then down said river to the mouth of Hog Run and up said run to Nathan Masters' farm, thence with the dividing ridge to Pennsylvania line and with said line to Wheeling Creek, and thence down said creek to the county line and thence with it to the beginning.

Third District—Beginning at Hog Run, thence down the river to the Tyler County line and thence east with said line to the Pennsylvania line, and thence north to the dividing ridge, thence with it to Masters' farm and down Hog Run to the river where it started.

At a regular session of the county court in February, 1842, at which session there were present the following Justices of the Peace: Walter Gray, Jos. Junkins, William McFarland, Benjamin McMechen, John Parriott, Jas. Alexander, John Criswell, James C. Bonar, Robert McConaughey and Thomas Brown, the following action was taken and is here given in the exact words as recorded:

A majority of the magistrates being present the following resolution was adopted and ordered to be entered upon the Order Book of this court:

> "Resolved that in the opinion of this court no license ought to be granted at the next May term for the retail of spiritous liquors within the limits of said country."

NEW STATE.

First Constitution.

WEST VIRGINIA was admitted into the Union as a state on the twentieth day of June, 1863. Its constitution differed from that under which the people had lived and it was necessary that laws be made to conform to the new constitution that the new system of government might go into effect as soon as possible.

The Legislature convened on the morning of Statehood and remained in session until the eleventh of December following.

The constitution provided for a township system for county government. The county court consisted of the justices of the peace of the county, held its last session on the nineteenth of June, 1863, the day previous to the admission of the state into the Union.

Article VII, Sections 1 and 2 read:

> 1. Every county shall be divided into not less than three nor more than ten townships, laid off as compactly as practicable, with reference to natural boundaries, and containing as nearly as practicable, an equal number of white population, but not less than four hundred. Each township shall be designated, "the township of.................., in the county of ....," by which name it may be sued.
>
> 2. The voters of each township, assembled, in stated or special township meeting, shall transact all such business relating exclusively to their township as is herein, or may be required by law or authorized. They shall annually elect a supervisor, clerk of the township, surveyor of roads for each precinct in their township, overseer of the poor, and such other officers as may be directed by law.
>
> They shall also every four years, elect one justice of the peace; and if the white population of their township exceeds twelve hundred in number, may elect an additional justice; and every two years, shall elect as many constables as justices.
>
> The supervisor, or in his absence, a voter, chosen by those present, shall preside at all township meetings and elections and the clerk shall act as clerk thereof.

That the counties of the state might be divided into townships as required by the constitution of the state, the Legislature passed an act on the thirty-first of July, 1863, appointing persons and directing how the work should be done. It read:

> The persons named in the schedue of this act, being one for each magisterial distrct, in each county of the state, a majority of whom may act, are hereby appointed commissioners to divide their respective counties into townships, in accordance with the provisions of the first section of the seventh article of the constitution; and shall as soon as practical, first being dully sworn, proceed to make such divisions. When a city or incorporated town necessarily constitutes a part of two or more townships, and is divded into wards, the boundaries of such townships within such city or town, shall, if practicable, be so located that parts of the same ward are not thrown into different townships.

The act provided—That commissioners for each county shall employe a competent surveyor who shall attend them when required and shall run and mark such lines as they may designate.

The commissioners appointed for Marshall County were: John Winters, Jeremiah Jones, Wm. McFarland, Sr., Alex Kemple, G. W. Evans, Wm. Stewart, John Burley and John Alley.

The commissioners employed Michael Dowler as their surveyor and divided the county into nine townships, viz.: CAMERON, CLAY, FRANKLIN, LIBERTY, MEADE, SAND HILL, UNION, WEBSTER and WASHINGTON.

The first township election was held on the fourteenth of January, 1864, and was called by the supervisors by authority given then at a township meeting. It was for the purpose of filling the township offices that the work might be started at as early a date as possible.

The supervisors met on the twenty-sixth of January of the same year, as provided by law, to canvass the returns of the township election held on the above date. After the first township election they were held annually on the fourth Thursday of April.

The term of office of the first officers elected at the township election was provided in a special act regulating the term of office and read as follows:

> The term of office of the officers elected at the first township election, if the same are held before the time for holding the state and county elections in the present year, shall commence on and include the tenth day after the respective elections, but shall continue and be computed as if the same had begun on twentieth day of June in the past year. But if the time of holding the first election occurs after the said state and county elections, and before or at the time appointed for hold-

ing the annual township election in the year one thousand eight hundred and sixty-four, the term of office shall be computed as if the same began on the twentieth of the next June.

Elizabethtown, January 26, 1864.

In pursuance of an act of the Legislature, passed March 2, 1863, entitled, an act defining in part the powers and duties and regulating the proceedings of the Board of Supervisors of the several counties of the state, the Board of Supervisors of the County of Marshall, this day assembled at Elizabethtown in the court-house of said county and after taking the required oath, organized by electing W. H. H. Showacre, president, and John M. Turner, clerk.

Resolved, That we proceed to examine the poll books of the different townships, which we found to result as follows:

UNION TOWNSHIP.

Henry Keltz, Supervisor; Wm. D. Campbell, Township Clerk; Robert Morgan, Overseer of the Poor; John Allen, Township Treasurer; Thomas Dowler and John R. Moore, Inspectors of Elections; Hiram McMechen and Alexander Kimple, Justices of the Peace; Peter O. Criswell, Constable; John Talbert and C. J. Bartlebaugh, 88 votes each—tie.

CLAY TOWNSHIP.

Samuel Riggs, Supervisor; William Dobbs, Township Clerk; John Arnold, Overseer of the Poor; Miles Bonar, Township Treasurer; Joseph Wallace, Inspector of Elections; William Collins and G. W. Evans, 26 votes each, tie; Inspector of Electiins, Samuel Wykart, and J. W. Ney, Justices of the Peace; Robert G. St. Clair and William Francis, Constables.

WASHINGTON TOWNSHIP.

Jeremiah Jones, Supervisor; G. S. McFadden, Township Clerk; John Kyle, Overseer of the Poor; John Riggs, Township Treasurer; Jacob F. Cox and B. W. Price, Inspectors of Elections; Joseph Turner and Wm. Blake, Justices of the Peace; Nicholas Zediker and Stephen S. Bloyd, Constables.

WEBSTER TOWNSHIP.

Noah Hadsall, Supervisor; John K. Francis, Township Clerk; Labon Riggs, Overseer of the Poor; Mahlon Riggs, Township Treasurer; David Jones and William Conner, Inspectors of Elections; James Pritchell and James Allison, Justices of the Peace; James Cooper and Benedict McMillen, Constables.

SAND HILL TOWNSHIP.

John Mooney, Supervisor; Charles Jones, Township Clerk; John Winters, Overseer of the Poor; James Jamison, Township

HISTORY OF MARSHALL COUNTY, W. VA.

Treasurer; John Wherry and Albert Davis, Inspectors of Elections; James Smith, Justice of the Peace, and Joseph Marsh, Constable.

FRANKLIN TOWNSHIP.

James Rine, Supervisor; George Rine, Township Clerk; David Lutes, Overseer of the Poor; John Hornbrook, Township Treasurer; Henry Miller and D. B. Smith, Inspectors of Elections; Samuel Wilson and C. M. Williams, Justices of the Peace; O. G. Mason and John Rankan, Constables.

LIBERTY TOWNSHIP.

Thomas Howard, Supervisor; Thomas Butler, Township Clerk; Richard Criswell, Overseer of the Poor; Brice Howard, Township Treasurer; Samuel Reed and Henry Grindell, Inspectors of Elections; J. B. Lydick, Justice of the Jeace, and Joseph Geho, Constable.

CAMERON TOWNSHIP.

W. H. H. Showacre, Supervisor; W. T. Head, Township Clerk; Thomas Allen, Overseer of the Poor; William Hosack, Township Treasurer; Adam Earliwine and William McConaughey, Inspectors of Elections; J. B. Hager and J. H. Dickey, Justices of the Peace; Wm. Fry and Joseph Wilson, Constables.

MEADE TOWNSHIP.

David Anguish, Supervisor; Peter Koltz, Township Clerk; David McDowell, Overseer of the Poor; J. W. Richmond, Township Treasurer; Nathan Shepherd and James Richey, Inspectors of Elections; John Richmond, Justice of the Peace, and Joseph Corbut, Constable.

Resolved, That we do hereby declare N. K. Shattock elected to the office of County Treasurer.

On motion of Mr. Hadsall:

Resolved, That we decide the cases in which it is a tie, who shall be elected.

Result as follows: In Clay Township, William Collins, Inspector of Elections; in Union Township, C. J. Bartlebaugh, Constable.

On motion, adjourned till tomorrow morning at 9 o'clock.

Present: W. H. H. Showacre, President; Jeremiah Jones, Henry Keltz, John Mooney, Samuel Riggs, Noah Hadsall and David Anguish.

W. H. H. SHOWACRE,
President.

JOHN M. TURNER,
Clerk.

January 27, 1864.

Journal of yesterday read and approved.

Be it ordained by the Supervisors of the County of Marshall

1. That the assessors do list all dogs in accordance with an act of the Legislature of the state, passed October 20, 1863, entitled, an act defining in part the powers and duties of the several counties of the state.

On motion of Jeremiah Jones:

Resolved, That the clerk of the Board of Supervisors be and is hereby authorized to furnish the Justices with necessary dockets where the old dockets can not be procured.

On motion of Mr. Riggs:

Resolved, That the President of this board be and is hereby authorized to ascertain from the Legislature now in session when the term of the office of Supervisors-elect expires.

On motion of Mr. Riggs:

Resolved, That we do hereby declare the persons named in the journal of yesterday elected to the offices therein named.

Be it ordained, by the Supervisors of the County of Marshall:

1. That the following townships shall compose and be known as the first and upper assessor's district, viz., Union, Sand Hill, Washington and Webster.

2. Be it further ordained that the following townships shall compose and be known as second, lower assessor's district, viz., Clay, Franklin, Cameron, Meade and Liberty.

On motion:

Resolved, That the Justices in each township hand over to the Supervisors-elect the books belonging to the state.

On motion:

Resolved, That the clerk of this board furnish himself at his own expense with the necessary book or books, in which to keep the records of his office, the same to be refunded from the county treasury.

On motion of Mr. Riggs:

Resolved, That the clerk of this board ascertain whether W. E. Parriott, who was elected assessor in the second and lower assessor's district, has vacated the office by not qualifying and giving bond.

Present: W. H. H. Showacre, President; Jeremiah Jones, Henry Keltz, John Mooney, Samuel Riggs, Noah Hadsall and David Anguish, members.

JOHN M. TURNER, Clerk.

W. H. H. SHOWACRE, President.

HISTORY OF MARSHALL COUNTY, W. VA.

February 20, 1864.

At a special meeting of the Board of Supervisors of the County of Marshall, held at the court-house of said county on the 20th day of February, 1864.

Present: W. H. H. Showacre, President; Henry Keltz, James Rine, Thomas Howard, Samuel Riggs, Noah Hadsall, Jeremiah Jones and John Mooney, members.

The resignation of J. W. Ney, Justice of the Peace of Clay Township, handed in and accepted.

The resignation of Robert G. St. Clair, Constable of Clay Township, handed in and accepted.

Be it ordained by the Supervisors of Marshall County:

1. That the sum of thirty thousand dollars be and is hereby appropriated for the purpose of paying bounty to persons volunteering in the service of the United States.

2. That each person so volunteering and is accepted in the service of the United States shall receive from this county a bounty of three hundred dollars.

Provided, that the number so volunteering shall exceed one hundred men.

3. That to carry out the above, a loan shall be negotiated by commissioners appointed to negotiate such loan of thirty thousand dollars.

4. That Henry Keltz, Jackson Reed and George Edwards are hereby appointed said commissioners with power to negotiate such loan upon the bonds of Marshall County, which amount shall bear interest of six per centum. They shall borrow said loan from the citizens of Marshall County, but if they fail to negotiate the amount from citizens, they are authorized to borrow such sums as are needed from bank or banks on credit as aforesaid.

5. That said commissioners are authorized to pay said bounty of three hundred dollars, to accepted and mustered recruits, credited to Marshall County, who have entered between the 4th day of February and the 1st day of March, 1864.

6. That the said commissioners are authorized to pay said bounty in full to the volunteers who may have been mustered into the United States service. The said volunteer presenting his certificate of enlistment and credit to said county.

7. That the former proceedings of the commissioners to pay accepted recruits be and is hereby legalized.

8. The said commissioners shall adopt as guide in paying said bounty, the Provost Marshall mustering roll and pay from it to those persons who have first entitled and have been credited to this county between the times aforesaid.

Be it ordained by the supervisors of the County of Marshall, 1. That the sum of five thousand dollars be and are hereby appropriated for the relief and support of the wives and families of private soldiers in the service of the United States.

2. That N. K. Shattuck be and is hereby appointed commissioner to negotiate a loan of five thousand dollars to be appropriated as follows:

1. To the wives of non-commissioned officers, musicians and privates, two dollars per month.

2. To widows of non-commissioned officers, musicians and privates who have died in the service of the United States, two dollars per month.

3. To the widowed mothers of non-commissioned officers, musicians and privates who was her only support, two dollars per month.

4. To each child of non-commissioned officer, musician and private under twelve years of age, two dollars per month.

5. That the persons receiving the above donation must be a resident of Marshall County.

6. Provided that the families of those persons who have received the County Bounty of three hundred dollars, and the families of those persons who enlisted for the term of six months, shall not be entitled to receive the benefit of the foregoing appropriation.

7. That the property of private soldiers, who are now, or who have been or may hereafter enter the service of the United States, shall be exempt from taxes to pay the bounty and relief fund.

8. That each supervisor shall appoint some suitable person or persons in his township to distribute the same as prescribed to each person who is entitled to the benefits of the above appropriation. Provided, that in case the supervisor fails to appoint or can not find a suitable person to serve as distributing officer, he, the supervisor, shall act himself.

9. The distributing officer shall render a just and true account of all money paid out by him, to the supervisor of his township, the supervisor shall render the same to the board of this county.

10. That deserters' families shall not receive the benefits of this donation.

11. That each supervisor shall draw from the treasurer such sums as will be sufficient to pay the families of his township, he shall draw upon the treasurer but once a month.

On motion of Mr. Riggs:

Resolved, That twenty thousand dollars of the bounty money be levied for the first year, also that the five thousand dollars appropriated for relief and support of soldiers' wives and families be levied for the first year.

2. That the remaining ten thousand dollars of the bounty money be levied for the second year.

On motion of Mr. Jones:

Resolved, That Joseph Turner be and is hereby authroized to furnish the county jail with a stove and some bed clothes, same to be levied for.

Resolved, That the commsisioners appointed negotiate for the money and pay the same as they have been doing.

On motion:

Resolved, That George Edwards be and is hereby requested to furnish all stamps that may be necessary for use of the county bonds. The same to be levied for.

A list of orders given members of the Board of Supervisors on County Treasurer:

Noah Hadsall, $88.00, Webster Township.
Jeremiah Jones, $91.00, Washington Township.
Samuel Riggs, $150.00, Clay Township.
Henry Keltz, $87.00, Union Township.
James Rine, $47.00, Franklin Township.
Thomas Howard, $50.00, Liberty Township.
John Mooney, $40.00, Sand Hill Township.
W. H. H. Showacre, $75.00, Cameron Township.

On motion of Mr. Riggs:

Resolved, That the above amounts be and are hereby appropriated to the township therein named.

Be it ordained by the Supervisors of the County of Marshall, that N. K. Shattuck be allowed (for his service of negotiating for and distributing the foregoing five thousand dollars) one dollar on every hundred dollars.

On motion:

Resolved, That the clerk of the Board be and is hereby instructed to notify the assessors to designate the property of private soldiers from the property of citizens.

Be it ordained by the Supervisors of the County of Marshall:

1. That Jeremiah Jones, Samuel Riggs, George Edwards and John M. Turner be and are hereby appointed to examine the books and ascertain what claims this county has against this state.

2. That they report the same to the Adjutant General of this state.

On motion the Board adjourned.

W. H. H. SHOWACRE,
JOHN M. TURNER, President.
    Clerk.

Moundsville, May 10, 1864.

In compliance with law the following members of the Board of Supervisors assembled at the Court House on the twelfth day after the annual township election for the purpose of examining the returns and declaring the results thereof and for other business, viz., W. H. H. Showacre, President; Jeremiah Jones, Samuel Riggs, Noah Hadsall, Thomas Howard, David Anguish, James Rine, John Mooney and Henry Keltz.

After examining the returns of the late election the following persons were declared elected, viz.:

UNION TOWNSHIP.

Henry Keltz, Supervisor; W. D. Campbell, Clerk; Robert Morgan, Overseer of the Poor; John Allen Treasurer; Thomas Dowler and James McCombs, Inspectors of Elections; for School Commissioners, John Pedley received 99 votes; Dr. McCoy, 99 votes, and Thomas Morgan, 95 votes.

WASHINGTON TOWNSHIP.

Jeremiah Jones, Supervisor; G. C. McFadden, Clerk; John Kyle, Overseer of the Poor; Jacom Hammond, Treasurer; Jacob T. Cox and George McC. Jones, Inspectors of Elections; Robert Tomlinson, Constable; School Commissioners, Reuben Zink, Wm. White and George Edwards.

CLAY TOWNSHIP.

Samuel Riggs, Supervisor; Wm. Dobbs, Clerk; John Gorrell, Overseer of the Poor; Miles Bonar, Treasurre; Jacob Bowers and William Collins, Inspectors of Elections; Wm. Riggs, Jesse Bonar and Wm. Varley, School Commissioners.

FRANKLIN TOWNSHIP.

James Rine, Supervisor; George Rine, Clerk; Peter Yoho, Overseer of the Poor; H. B. Yoho, Treasurer; D. B. Smith and Henry Miller, Inspectors of Elections; A. W. Wilson, Constable; School Commissioners, John Hornbrook, G. W. McKimmey and Thomas Ruckman.

MEADE TOWNSHIP.

David Auguish, Supervisor; Peter Keltz, Clerk; David McDowell, Overseer of the Poor; J. F. Kelley and Jacob Bowers, Inspectors of Elections; N. Shepherd, J. W. Richmond and Jackson Travis, School Commissioners.

CAMERON TOWNSHIP.

W. H. H. Showacre, Supervisor; W. H. Bassett, Clerk; Thomas Allen, Overseer of the Poor; W. Hosack, Treasurer; F. W. Reynolds and M. Crow, Inspectors of Elections; J. H. Pipes, J. W. Phillips and George Hubbs, School Commissioners.

HISTORY OF MARSHALL COUNTY, W. VA.

WEBSTER TOWNSHIP.

Noah Hadsall, Supervisor; John K. Francis, Clerk; Labon Riggs, Overseer of the Poor; Mahlon Riggs, Treasurer; David Jones and Wm. Conner, Inspectors of Elections; Wm. Keyser, Wm. McCreary and Eli Salter, School Commissioners.

SAND HILL TOWNSHIP.

John Mooney, Supervisor; J. W. Winters, Clerk; John Winters, Overseer of the Poor; James Jemmison, Treasurer; N. Davis and Wm. Luke, Inspectors of Elections; John Ritchey, A. R. Kimmins and Daniel Dague, School Commissioners.

Resolved, That the persons named in the foregoing are hereby declared elected to the offices affixed to their names.

Resolved, That Wm. J. Alexander is hereby declared elected to the office of County Superintendent of Free Schools.

Resolved, That all persons who take out license to sell at retail spirituous liquors are hereby required to give the bond authorized by law for the sum of seven hundred and fifty dollars and persons who take out license to sell at retail native wine, porter, ale, beer, give bond in the sum of seven hundred and fifty dollars.

Resolved, That the following persons are hereby authorized to take out license as follows:

Jacob Burr, to sell at retail, spirituous liquors.

A. P. Smith, to sell at retail, spirituous liquors.

Daniel Buzzard, to sell at retail, spirituous liquors.

Mary Burr, to sell at retail native wine, porter, ale, beet, etc.

James Cunningham, to sell at retail spirituous liquors.

John Miller, to sell at retail native wine, porter, ale, beer, etc.

Thomas Fox, to sell at retail spirituous liquors.

Elijah Hubbs, to sell at retail spirituous liquors and keep hotel.

John Higgins, to sell at retail spirituous liquors.

Samuel Hagerman, to sell at retail native wine, porter, ale, beer, etc.

Joseph Turner, to keep hotel or tavern.

Adjourned till tomorrow morning at 9 o'clock.

JOHN M. TURNER,
Clerk.

Moundsville, August 19, 1864.

The following members of the Board of Supervisors assembled this morning, viz., W. H. H. Showacre, President; Jeremiah Jones, Thomas Howard, Henry Keltz, Samuel Riggs, David Anguish, Noah Hadsall, James Rine and John Mooney.

Resolved, That the place of voting in Union Township, known as Chestnut Grove, is hereby changed to Sherrard.

Mr. Hadsall moved to tax the first dog 25 cents; the second, 50 cents; and the third, 75 cents, and so on in that proportion.

Mr. Riggs moved that the clerks of the townships issue license to persons to keep dogs, but if the clerk's office should be vacant in any township, the supervisor shall issue said tax.

Resolved, That the license to persons to keep dogs commence this day and expire of the 20th day of June.

Resolved, That ten cents be allowed to township clerks or to supervisors for each license issued to keep dogs.

George Edwards, Esq., made the following report of loans negotiated and received by himself and Messrs. Reed and Keltz:

1864.

February—
- 22—Wm. Collins, due November 15, 1865............$ 600.00
- 22—Mrs. R. J. Alexander, same.................... 300.00
- 22—Dennis Dorsey, same......................... 2,000.00
- 22—Levi Cunningham, due one year from date.... 2,400.00
- 23—Wm. Holliday, due one year from date........ 100.00
- 23—Wm. Holliday, Jr., due November 15, 1865.... 200.00
- 23—Elisha Lindsey, due two years from date...... 1,600.00
- 23—S. L. Bloyd, due December 15, 1865.......... 300.00
- 23—John Brown, due two years from date......... 500.00
- 23—Alfred Riggs, due one year from date......... 33.00
- 23—Geo. Edwards, due nine months from date.... 500.00
- 23—John Kyle, due one year from date........... 150.00
- 24—J. W. Probasco, due one year from date....... 660.00
- 25—Margaret Ray, due one year from date........ 200.00
- 26—John R. Morris, due two years from date...... 1,000.00
- 23—Elisha Lindsey, due two years from date...... 200.00
- 29—John S. Cunningham, due one year from date... 200.00

March—
- 2—Wm. Collins, due two years from date........ 300.00
- 8—Ruth McMillan, due one year from date....... 250.00
- 21—Wm. Holliday, Jr., due one year from date..... 500.00

February—
- 24—John Kyle, due oen year from date........... 600.00
- 24—John Reese, due two years from date......... 700.00
- 25—Jacob Hammond, due one year from date...... 300.00
- 27—Eliza Rulong, due one year from date........ 200.00

March—
- 12—Benjamin Hill, due one year from date........ 1,000.00
- 29—J. C. Reed, due one year from date.......... 2,100.00
- 29—Thomas Dorsey, due one year from date...... 250.00

29—W. H. Dunlap, due one year from date........ 200.00
30—James M. Wilkinson, due two years from date.. 250.00
30—James A. Dilley, due two years from date.... 250.00
30—James McGill, due one year from date.'....... 400.00
April—
1—James Dolen, due two years from date........ 200.00
4—John W. Magers, due one year from date....... 200.00
9—Elza Lutes, due one year from date........... 1,175.00
15—Elisha Lindsey, due two years from date...... 1,500.00
May—
10—Thomas Riggs, due ten months from date..... 800.00
10—George Hubbs, two bonds.................... 446.00
13—First Nat'l Bank of Wheeling, 7 months...... 2,705.00
February—
22—F. W. Brown, due December 15, 1864.......... 300.00
23—Alfred Riggs, due one year from date.......... 300.00
23—Alfred Glass, due two years from date......... 300.00

$30,619.00

Mr. Edwards' report continued, money paid out.

1864.

February—
22—Francis Bird ....$ 300.00
22—F. M. Brown 300.00
22—G. A. Dowler 300.00
23—Morris Rulong 300.00
23—Joseph Wallace 300.00
23—John Clegg 300.00
23—Alfred R. Riggs 300.00
23—James M. Cox................................ 300.00
23—W. A. Beagle 300.00
23—George O. Grimes 300.00
23—David A. Sibert 300.00
23—Joseph Montgomery 300.00
23—M. H. Holliday 300.00
23—Henry Andrew 300.00
23—Samuel Leach 300.00
23—John Roney 300.00
23—Henry Chase 300.00
23—Roseby Bird 300.00
23—John Bird 300.00
23—Benj. Barcus 300.00
23—Peter O. Criswell 300.00
23—Andrew McCartney 300.00
23—A. G. Leonard 300.00
23—Robert Welch 300.00

23—C. O. Chase	300.00
23—Alfred Glass	300.00
23—W. W. Roberts	300.00
23—Wm. Black	300.00
23—Wm. Riggle	300.00
23—John McGlumphy	300.00
23—Gideon Kent	300.00
23—Francis McGlumphy	300.00
23—Samuel Wykart	300.00
23—Harrison Allen	300.00
23—Joseph Stilwell	300.00
23—John Logsdon	300.00
23—Timothy Stilwell	300.00
24—John Ray	300.00
24—Wm. Auten	300.00
24—John Davis	300.00
24—Isaac D. Riggs	300.00
24—Samuel W. Peters	300.00
24—Wm. Foreman	300.00
24—Ira Kidder	300.00
24—Wm. H. Shimp	300.00
24—Wm. Chase	300.00
25—John A. Miller	300.00
25—Adam Emery	300.00
29—Wm. E. Abott	300.00
29—E. J. Bloomfield	300.00
29—Joshua Colton	300.00

March—

25—Elias W. Gray	300.00
25—John S. Turner	300.00
25—Abraham Keyser	300.00
25—Amos Murrell	300.00
25—J. B. Nuss	300.00
26—J. W. Redman	300.00
26—Lewis H. Smith	300.00
26—Lewis A. Deitz	300.00
26—Richard Rine	300.00
26—Henry Rifle	300.00
26—Jacob Whitlatch	300.00
26—Wm. Gullentine	300.00
26—Wm. H. Daugherty	300.00
28—A. J. Lightner	300.00
28—J. L. Powers	300.00
28—Wm. Wright	300.00
28—W. S. Purdy	300.00
28—Wm. McGill	300.00

28—W. H. Dunlap		300.00
28—J. B. Gorby		300.00
28—Beeler Mannnig		300.00
28—James Dilley		300.00
29—James Dowler		300.00
29—Samuel F. Carney		300.00
30—James M. Wilkinson		300.00
29—Joseph Wayt		300.00

April—

2—John C. Nuss		300.00
4—John T. Johnson		300.00
5—John E. Powell		300.00
27—Pierson Knight		300.00
27—Ira W. Johnson		300.00
29—C. H. Remmick		300.00

May—

12—John Wingrove		300.00
12—Thurman Hall		300.00
20—George W. Widows		300.00
23—John Montgomery		300.00
24—John Simmons		300.00

June—

14—Alexander Whipkey		300.00
14—Silas Simmons		300.00
14—James Howard		300.00
14—Charles Riley		300.00
14—Wm. P. Harris		300.00
14—Henry C. Easton		300.00
14—Leonard Dilley		300.00
14—D. Clifford Burley		300.00
14—John Blake		300.00
16—John McCombs		300.00

July—

14—Robert Gray		300.00
14—I. D. Pratt		300.00
14—John Cunningham		300.00
14—G. W. Vance		300.00
Stamps for bonds		19.00

$30,619.00

Resolved, That $576.25 be levied to defray the expenses of the election heretofore held and for dividing the county into townships.

Resolved, That a committee of three be appointed to settle with the treasurer, whereupon Messrs. Riggs, Mooney and Anguish were appointed such committee.

Mr. Hadsall moved that a committee be appointed to settle with the sheriff and that George Edwards, Esq., be politely requested to assist said committee, whereupon Messrs, Hadsall, Riggs and Howard were appointed such committee.

Resolved, That we pay no persons for work after night to ascertain the results of any past elections.

Adjourned till tomorrow morning.

W. H. SHOWACRE, President.

JOHN M. TURNER, Clerk.

GEORGE EDWARDS, HENRY KELTZ and JACKSON REED, Commissioners to negotiate a second loan to pay bounty, reported in detail to the Board of Supervisors on the twenty-first of December, 1864, the amount of money they had borrowed on bonds of Marshall County and the disbursement thereof.

1864—

Aug. 19	Walter Evans, one year from date	$ 300.00
Aug. 20	James A. Blake, two years from date	840.00
Aug. 22	First Nat'l Bank, one year from date	10,000.00
Aug. 22	Merchants & Mechanics Bank, same	15,000.00
Aug. 23	Martin Davidson, one year from date	300.00
Aug. 24	Richard Allen, two years from date	1,300.00
Aug. 26	Levi Cunningham, 16 months from date	1,100.00
Aug. 29	Stephan L. Bloyd, one year from date	500.00
Aug. 29	Robert Blake, one year from date	500.00
Aug. 29	John Reed, one year from date	300.00
Aug. 31	Margaret Davidson, one year from date	200.00
Sept. 1	John R. Morrow, one year, $8,000 net	7,520.00
Sept. 1	V. Arnold, one year from date	500.00
Sept. 1	Wm. Collins, one year from date	580.00
Sept. 1	Samuel Riggs, one year from date	740.00
Sept. 1	Samuel Dorsey, Sr., one year from date	3,000.00
Sept. 3	L. Burley, one year from date	300.00
Sept. 3	George Potts, one year from date	200.00
Sept. 12	Samuel Gray, one year from date	200.00
Sept. 21	Lemuel Riggs, one year from date	200.00
Sept. 21	Philip Jones, one year from date	800.00
Sept. 28	John W. Magers, one year from date	100.00
Oct. 1	Joseph Hammond, one year from date	1,300.00
		$46,280.00

1864	To whom paid	enlistment	Amount
1—Aug. 23	Isaac Dowler	for 1 year	$310.00

HISTORY OF MARSHALL COUNTY, W. VA. 133

2—Aug. 24	Moses Land ....for 1 year	310.00
3—Aug. 24	Wm. G. Thomas ....for 1 year	310.00
4—Aug. 24	John F. Temple ....for 1 year	310.00
5—Aug. 24	David S. Helmick ....for 1 year	310.00
6—Aug. 24	Francis M. Burnes ....for 1 year	310.00
7—Aug. 24	Calvin McKiny ....for 1 year	310.00
8—Aug. 24	Newton M. Hurbly ....for 1 year	310.00
9—Aug. 24	John A. Loyd ....for 1 year	310.00
10—Aug. 24	Nathaniel D. Helmick......for 1 year	310.00
11—Aug. 24	Samuel A. Reese ....for 1 year	310.00
12—Aug. 24	Thomas A. Hartley........for 1 year	310.00
13—Aug. 24	Amos B. Vincent ....for 1 year	310.00
14—Aug. 24	Stewart E. Hartley ....for 1 year	310.00
15—Aug. 24	Thomas B. Harbison ......for 1 year	310.00
16—Aug. 24	Samuel S. Davis ....for 1 year	310.00
17—Aug. 24	John J. Standiford ....for 1 year	310.00
18—Aug. 18	Lloyd Orum ....for 1 year	310.00
19—Aug. 24	James Henry ....for 1 year	310.00
20—Aug. 24	David Magers ....for 1 year	310.00
21—Aug. 24	Wm. Mason ....for 1 year	310.00
22—Aug. 24	Aquilla Gilbert ....for 1 year	310.00
23—Aug. 24	David Heston ....for 1 year	310.00
24—Aug. 24	John Clemens ....for 1 year	310.00
25—Aug. 24	Joshua Layman ....for 1 year	310.00
26—Aug. 22	Martin Davidson ....for 1 year	310.00
27—Sept. 6	Thomas M. Radcliff ....for 3 years	310.00
28—Sept. 6	George W. Echols ....for 1 year	310.00
29—Sept. 3	Hiram Doyle ....for 1 year	310.00
30—Sept. 3	John W. Criswell..........for 1 year	310.00
31—Sept. 3	Wm. F. Head ....for 1 year	310.00
32—Sept. 3	Rufus S. Purdy ....for 1 year	310.00
33—Sept. 3	Corbly H. Bowen ....for 1 year	310.00
34—Sept. 3	George W. Potts ....for 1 year	310.00
35—Sept. 3	John Duncan ....for 1 year	310.00
36—Sept. 3	David McCracken ....for 1 year	310.00
37—Sept. 3	Zebadee Shook ....for 1 year	310.00
38—Sept. 3	John M. Fordice ....for 1 year	310.00
39—Sept. 3	Mathias B. Ross ....for 1 year	310.00
40—Sept. 3	Wm. J. Clouston ....for 1 year	310.00
41—Sept. 3	W. L. Pierce ....for 1 year	310.00
42—Sept. 3	John G. Ayers ....for 1 year	320.00
43—Sept. 3	Elias Lemasters ....for 1 year	310.00
44—Sept. 3	Stewart F. Earliwine ......for 1 year	320.00
45—Sept. 3	Joseph W. Bonar ....for 1 year	320.00
46—Sept. 3	David B. Johnson ....for 1 year	320.00
47—Sept. 3	Hamilton C. Harris ....for 1 year	320.00
48—Sept. 3	John Curtis ....for 1 year	320.00

49—Sept.	3	John Fitzgerald ....for 1 year	320.00
50—Sept.	3	Samuel E. Gatts ....for 1 year	320.00
51—Sept.	3	Charles Keller ....for 1 year	320.00
52—Sept.	3	John A. Harris ....for 1 year	320.00
53—Sept.	3	Samuel Gray ....for 1 year	320.00
54—Sept.	3	Henry Parkinson ....for 1 year	320.00
55—Sept.	3	A. O. Baker ....for 1 year	320.00
56—Sept.	3	John Stricklin ....for 1 year	320.00
57—Sept.	3	Ebenezer Earliwine ....for 1 year	320.00
58—Sept.	3	Jacob Harris ....for 1 year	320.00
59—Sept.	3	James P. Stewart ....for 1 year	320.00
60—Sept.	3	Thomas Moore ....for 1 year	320.00
61—Sept.	3	Joseph Venus ....for 1 year	320.00
62—Sept.	3	Barney Sibert ....for 1 year	320.00
63—Sept.	3	Warren Sockman ....for 1 year	320.00
64—Sept.	3	Wm. T. Morris ....for 1 year	320.00
65—Sept.	3	John W. Bush ....for 1 year	320.00
66—Sept.	3	Lindsey Burley ....for 1 year	320.00
67—Sept.	3	Hyden Burley ....for 1 year	320.00
68—Sept.	3	W. R. Coe ....for 1 year	320.00
69—Sept.	3	David Founds ....for 1 year	320.00
70—Sept.	3	Joseph R. Ross ....for 1 year	320.00
71—Sept.	3	James M. Baker ....for 1 year	320.00
72—Sept.	3	Wm. Ross ....for 1 year	320.00
73—Sept.	3	James C. Bonar ....for 1 year	320.00
74—Sept.	3	James Parkinson ....for 1 year	320.00
75—Sept.	3	W. B. Hicks ....for 1 year	320.00
76—Sept.	3	Taylor Richmond ....for 1 year	320.00
77—Sept.	3	J. P. Harris ....for 1 year	320.00
78—Sept.	3	Franklin Johnson ....for 1 year	320.00
79—Sept.	3	John W. Grimes ....for 1 year	320.00
80—Sept.	3	Anthony W. Talbert ......for 1 year	320.00
81—Sept.	3	John W. Wable ....for 1 year	320.00
82—Sept.	3	Silas W. Gatts ....for 1 year	320.00
83—Sept.	3	Samuel A. Parriott ....for 1 year	320.00
84—Sept.	3	Lewis Reynolds ....for 1 year	320.00
85—Sept.	3	George W. Griffith ....for 1 year	320.00
86—Sept.	3	George W. Hubbs ....for 1 year	320.00
87—Sept.	3	Franklin W. Williamson ...for 1 year	320.00
88—Sept.	3	Jack Robinson ....for 1 year	320.00
89—Sept.	3	Elias E. Riggs ....for 1 year	320.00
90—Sept.	3	Samuel B. Manning ....for 1 year	320.00
91—Sept.	3	Amos Chambers ....for 1 year	320.00
92—Sept.	3	Thomas D. Welch ....for 1 year	320.00
93—Sept.	3	Franklin B. Blue ....for 1 year	310.00
94—Sept.	3	John R. Blackburn ....for 1 year	320.00
95—Sept.	3	Charles D. Moore ....for 1 year	310.00

HISTORY OF MARSHALL COUNTY, W. VA. 135

96—Sept.	3	Wm. Myers	for 1 year	310.00
97—Sept.	3	Samuel Gray	for 1 year	320.00
98—Sept.	3	Thomas H. Williams	for 1 year	310.00
99—Sept.	3	George Bowler	for 1 year	310.00
100–Sept.	3	Eli Chambers	for 1 year	310.00
101–Sept.	3	James E. Chambers	for 1 year	310.00
102–Sept.	3	Joseph Earliwine	for 1 year	310.00
103–Sept.	3	John T. Ott	for 1 year	310.00
104–Sept.	3	Wm. B. Dunlap	for 1 year	310.00
105–Sept.	3	Presley M. Burley	for 1 year	310.00
106–Sept.	3	Thomas Butler	for 1 year	310.00
107–Sept.	3	Isaac Ernest	for 1 year	310.00
108–Sept.	3	Robert H. Daugherty	for 1 year	310.00
109–Sept.	3	Peter Ernest	for 1 year	310.00
110–Sept.	3	John W. Daugherty	for 1 year	310.00
111–Sept.	3	Salem L. Pyles	for 1 year	310.00
112–Sept.	3	Jacob Geho	for 1 year	310.00
113–Sept.	3	John R. Robinson	for 1 year	310.00
114–Sept.	3	Joseph Wright	for 1 year	310.00
115–Sept.	3	Elijah Miller	for 1 year	310.00
116–Sept.	3	Joseph H. Wilson	for 1 year	310.00
117–Sept.	3	John S. McDonald	for 1 year	320.00
118–Sept.	3	Edward J. Lewis.........	for 1 year	320.00
119–Sept.	3	John Barns	for 1 year	300.00
120–Sept.	3	Henry C. Pitcher	for 1 year	300.00
121–Sept.	3	Wm. Crawford	for 1 year	300.00
122–Sept.	3	Jacob Moore	for 1 year	310.00
123–Sept.	3	W. E. Layman	for 1 year	310.00
124–Sept.	3	Penny Baily	for 1 year	310.00
125–Sept.	3	Samuel Gray	for 1 year	310.00
126–Sept.	3	John Baker	for 1 year	310.00
127–Sept.	3	Levi Gallaher	for 1 year	320.00
128–Sept.	3	Wm. Reynolds, Jr.	for 1 year	320.00
129–Sept.	3	John W. Harris	for 1 year	320.00
130–Sept.	3	John G. Hartzell	for 1 year	320.00
131–Sept.	3	Isaac D. Lemasters	for 1 year	320.00
132–Sept.	3	John Marple	for 1 year	320.00
133–Sept.	3	Amos Cornell	for 1 year	320.00
134.Sept.	3	Theodore Buzzard	for 1 year	320.00
135–Sept.	3	Wm. Carney	for 1 year	320.00

$42,450.00

Paid recruiting officers, etc............ 3,830.00

$46,280.00

February 10, 1865.

Pursuant to adjournment the following members of the Board of Supervisors assembled this morning, viz., W. H. H. Showacre, President; James Rine, Jeremiah Jones, Noah Hadsall, Thomas Howard, Samuel Riggs, Henry Keltz and David Anguish.

Mr. Jones reported that he had paid soldiers' wives and families $31.06, which report was accepted and the amount ordered to be credited to his account.

On motion of Mr. Jones:

Resolved, That we pay three hundred ($300.00) dollars bounty to those who have enlisted since the first day of February, 1885, who have received no bounty but from whom we have received credit.

Be it ordained by the Supervisors of the County of Marshall:

1. That a sufficient sum of money be levied upon the taxable property of said county to pay three hundred ($300.00) dollars to those who volunteered in the service of the United States and was credited to Marshall County, subsequent to the first day of February, 1864, to fill the quoto of men under the call of the President of the United States for 500,000 men, who did not receive the bounty offered.

The said bounty to be paid to the volunteer or his heirs upon presenting his certificate of muster and credit to W. H. H. Showacre, properly certified to by the Provost Marshall, when he enlisted and was mustered in. The said bounty to be paid in county bonds due in three years after date with interest thereon at the rate of six per centum.

Be it ordained by the Supervisors of the County of Marshall, that a bounty of four hundred ($400.00) dollars be paid to each acceptable recruit to fill the quoto of the county under the call of the President for 300,000 men. The conditions upon which volunteers shall receive said bounty is that they credit themselves to the several sub-districts its due proportion of said recruits. Also that the sum of ten dollars be paid any man who will furnish an acceptable recruit who will credit himself to said sub-district.

Resolved, That we have two hundred blank bonds printed.

Mr. Rine asked and obtained leave of absence.

On motion of Mr. Keltz:

Resolved, That we have one hundred bills or posters printed.

Messrs. Jones and Hadsall asked and obtained leave of absence.

Resolved, That Henry Keltz and George Edwards are

HISTORY OF MARSHALL COUNTY, W. VA.

hereby appointed commissioners to negotiate loans to pay soldiers bounty.

Resolved, That we have our ordinances making appropriations published in the Wheeling Intelligencer.

Approved,

JOHN M. TURNER,
Clerk.

W. H. H. SHOWACRE,
President.

George Edwards and Henry Keltz reported to the Board of Supervisors on the 24th of July, in full, of the loan on county bonds and the disbursement of the funds borrowed for bounty for the call of 1865.

February—

13—Joseph Griffith, one year from date............$	300.00
13—Merchants & Mechanics Bank, thirty days days after date, $5,000 discount net...............	4,972.50
15—Margaret Davidson, one year from date.......	1,000.00
15—John Allen, one year from date...............	600.00
15—Elizabeth Allen, one year from date..........	250.00
15—Daniel McConnell, one year from date........	200.00
15—Wm. Finsley, one year from date.............	175.00
15—John Dunson, one year from date............	200.00
15—George Kemple, one year from date..........	500.00
15—George Cooper, one year from date...........	400.00
15—James Standiford, one year from date........	1,600.00
15—Joseph Pedley, one year from date............	1,000.00
15—Northwestern Bank, one year from date......	10,000.00
15—First Nat'l Bank, $10,600, net discount........	9,964.00
15—George Richea, one year from date...........	1,200.00
15—Alexander McCombs, one year from date.....	300.00
15—Amos Harris, one year from date............	300.00
15—Lucy Harris, one year from date	200.00
16—Dennis Dorsey, one year from date...........	2,500.00
16—J. J. Sommerville, one year from date	400.00
16—W. H. Marple, one year from date............	400.00
17—Cynthia Masters, one year from date.........	90.00
17—Samuel Riggs, one year from date............	530.00
17—Alexander Q. Whittaker, one year from date..	400.00
18—Thomas Howard, one year from date.........	200.00
18—Joseph Kimmons, one year from date.........	400.00
18—E. B. Francis, one year from date............	600.00
18—James Stewart, one year from date...........	500.00
18—John Cunningham, one year from date........	200.00
18—Wm. Holliday, one year from date............	300.00
18—R. C. Holliday, one year from date...........	400.00
18—Wm. Burgess, one year from date............	500.00
18—Richard Allen, one year from date...........	700.00

18—Jesse J. Gorby, one year from date		200.00
20—F. A. Cummins, one year from date		200.00
20—Edward Dowler, one year from date		400.00
20—Richard Allen, one year from date		900.00
20—Michael Dowler, one year from date		400.00
21—W. P. Jones, one year from date		500.00
21—Elias Stilwell, one year from date		400.00
21—Catherine Dorsey, one year from date		200.00
21—James C. Foster, one year from date		500.00
21—A. O. Bradshaw, one year from date		200.00
21—Anthony Johnson, one year from date		500.00
21—Thomas Howard, one year from date		510.00
21—Elias R. Harris, one year from date		500.00
21—J. W. Bonar, one year from date		400.00
22—Samuel Riggs, one year from date		1,000.00
22—Silas Hughes, one year from date		400.00
22—Samuel Dorsey, Jr., one year from date		400.00
22—Wm. Dobbs, one year from date		400.00
22—Wm. Ewing, one year from date		400.00
22—George W. Hall, one year from date		400.00
23—David A. Brantner, one year from date		400.00
23—David Wells, one year from date		500.00
23—Philip Cunningham, one year from date		500.00
25—Joseph Zink, one year from date		550.00
25—Joseph Marsh, one year from date		886.00
25—John Kyle, one year from date		350.00
25—Wm. Bellville, one year from date		500.00
27—Ruth McMillan, one year from date		200.00
21—Samuel Dorsey, one year from date		400.00
22—Alfred R. Riggs, one year from date		353.00
27—Thomas Riggs, one year from date		1,080.00
23—J. J. Cunningham, one year from date		212.00

March—

1—Jeremiah Jones, one year from date		400.00
1—Elijah Hubbs, one year from date		200.00
4—John Crow, one year from date		588.00
4—Philip Crow, one year from date		1,000.00
6—Jonathan W. Roberts, one year from date		400.00
8—Ruth McMillan, one year from date		250.00

February—

22—Fred M. Brown, one year from date		318.00
20—Mrs. R. J. Alexander, one year from date		318.00
17—Joseph Turner, one year from date		175.00

March—

20—Stephan L. Bloyd, one year from date		200.00
7—Jacob Hammond, one year from date		600.00

24—Matilda Hill, one year from date	600.00
7—James C. Foster, one year from date	500.00
7—I. West, one year from date	400.00
February—	
16—Merchants & Mechanics Bank, $10,000 discount net	9,964.00
May—	
16—Wm. Collins, one year from date	600.00
February—	
25—John P. Hornbrook, one year from date	400.00
22—Frederick Dague, one year from date	400.00
April—	
11—Frank Harris, one year from date	250.00
11—John W. Magers, one year from date	200.00
March—	
22—John R. Grandstaff, one year from date	250.00
Subscribed by citizens	11,904.50
	$86,340.00

June 24, 1865.

Paid to the Merchants & Mechanics Bank	$5,000.00
1—James L. Gamble, sub	400.00
2—J. W. Glendenning, sub	400.00
3—W. L. Edwards, sub	400.00
4—George A. Porter, sub	400.00
5—Elias Stilwell	500.00
6—John H. Cummins	500.00
7—Noble F. Cummins	500.00
8—James R. Cummons	500.00
9—W. P. Jones	500.00
10—John W. Berry	500.00
11—Joseph Zink	500.00
12—Robert Butler	500.00
13—James C. Foster	500.00
14—Alfred Brogher	530.00
15—Richard Chaddock	500.00
16—Jacob Quigley	500.00
17—Humphrey Stricklin	500.00
18—John McMullen	500.00
19—A. O. Bradshaw	500.00
20—Benj. F. Pierson	500.00
21—James Stealey	500.00
22—Thomas Howard	510.00
23—Richard M. Johnson, sub	400.00
24—Wm. H. Lydick	400.00
25—Fred Burkhart	500.00

26—Samuel D. Brown		500.00
27—John A. Spadden		500.00
28—David Kershner		530.00
29—Joseph Marple		510.00
30—E. R. Harris		500.00
31—Andrew Newland		500.00
32—John Cartright, sub		400.00
33—Isaac West		500.00
34—David Wells		500.00
35—David A. Brantner		500.00
36—John C. Harris		500.00
37—Wm. Jefferson		500.00
38—Samuel W. Wilson		500.00
39—Elijah Harris		500.00
40—George Whitlatch		500.00
41—Elijah Burge		500.00
42—John S. Rine		500.00
43—Alexander Morrow		500.00
44—Wm. S. Gatts		500.00
45—John P. Allen		500.00
46—Leonard B. Harris		500.00
47—Benj. F. Ford		500.00
48—John Wolfe		500.00
49—George C. Harris		500.00
50—Robt. A. Parriott		500.00
51—John Rutan		500.00
52—James D. Yoho		500.00
53—Samuel W. Wilson		500.00
54—Jobe Bowen		500.00
55—Perry McMahon		500.00
56—George W. Conner		500.00
57—Wm. Ewing		500.00
58—Frederick Dague		500.00
59—Wm. Dague		500.00
60—Charles C. Robison		500.00
61—Samuel Cage		500.00
62—Charles D. Woodburn		500.00
63—Wm. Dobbs		500.00
64—Amos Wilson		500.00
65—Daniel Jones		500.00
66—Philip M. Conner		500.00
67—Wm. L. Conner		500.00
68—Charles White		500.00
69—Samuel Dorsey, Jr.		500.00
70—George M. Jones		500.00
71—Eli Vaughn		500.00
72—G. W. Hall		500.00

HISTORY OF MARSHALL COUNTY, W. VA. 141

73	Timothy Stilwell	500.00
74	Andrew D. Mathews	500.00
75	Alexander Law	510.00
76	John H. Moon, sub	400.00
77	Edward Dowler	500.00
78	John A. Goodman	520.00
79	John C. Jackson	520.00
80	Charles Wilber	500.00
81	Wm. Burgess	510.00
82	Ford Hess, sub	400.00
83	Jesse J. Gorby	500.00
84	Alpheus Pearson	500.00
85	Nicholas Pearson	500.00
86	Francis Montgomery	500.00
87	Joseph Kimmons	500.00
88	Jacob Strober	500.00
89	George Kemple	510.00
90	George T. Cooper, sub	400.00
91	Wm. C. Lord	510.00
92	Alexander McCombs	510.00
93	Richard Gosney	500.00
94	Wm. Swigger	510.00
95	F. A. Cummins	500.00
96	Wm. Rodocker	500.00
97	Wm. A. Knox	500.00
98	Thomas Logsdon	500.00
99	Alfred Fletcher	500.00
100	Thomas J. Price	500.00
101	J. J. Sommerville	500.00
102	Wm. Marple	500.00
103	Asa Wood	500.00
104	Sanford Wood	500.00
105	Wm. Butler	500.00
106	Silas Hughes	500.00
107	Wm. Bonnett	500.00
108	Wm. V. Fish	500.00
109	Joseph Simmons	500.00
110	J. W. Bonar	500.00
111	George Richards	500.00
112	Wm. E. Knapp	500.00
113	Eli Huggins	500.00
114	John Barnes	500.00
115	Joel L. Olney	500.00
116	Anthony Johnson	500.00
117	Elijah Hubbs	500.00
118	Philip Cunningham	500.00
119	Wm. Parks	500.00

120—John G. Shaw		500.00
121—George W. Wolfe		520.00
122—Henry W. Welling		500.00
123—Robert H. Davis		500.00
124—Clark Connelly		500.00
125—Benj. Winesberry		500.00
126—Peter E. Willard		500.00
127—Jacob W. Ogle		500.00
128—Samuel D. Hughes		500.00
129—Charles Turner		500.00
130—W. H. Enix		500.00
131—George Sprague		520.00
132—Joseph M. Smith		500.00
133—David Nelson		500.00
134—Edward Williams		500.00
135—Wm. Buchanan		500.00
136—Peter Orum		500.00
137—James W. Logsdon		500.00
138—Robert Denoon		500.00
139—George Nichols		500.00
140—Thomas Rigby		510.00
141—John Brown		500.00
142—Wm. Otter		500.00
143—Oliver Grimes, sub		400.00
144—Leonard Pickett, sub		400.00
145—John W. Vernon		500.00
146—Samuel Rudle, sub		400.00
147—James Young		
148—J. J. Harkins		
149—Hesikiah Hiley		
150—Robt. S. Pickett		
151—John Hayhurst		
152—James Holt		
153—Samuel Sanders		
154—W. W. Capto		
155—Michael Montgomery		
156—Jesse J. Bogard		
157—George W. Jones		
158—Eli C. Morris		
159—David P. Harst		
160—John B. Aston		
161—W. M. Johnson		
162—John W. Radabaugh		
163—Robt. F. Mullinox		
164—Jesse Dancer		
165—Benj. F. Shuttleworth		
166—Wm. F. Young		

HISTORY OF MARSHALL COUNTY, W. VA. 143

The last twenty were recruited at Grafton.

Capt. Criswell, for 30 recruits	300.00
T. J. Garvin, for 2 recruits	20.00
J. M. Turner, for 3 recruits	30.00
S. S. Fleming, for 1 recruit	10.00
James McCombs, for 1 recruit	10.00
Christian Poly, for 3 recruits	30.00
J. Newland, for 1 recruit	10.00
James Venaman, for 1 recruit	10.00
Joe Smith, for 1 recruit	10.00
John S. Moody, for service	50.00
H. Keltz and Wm. Varley, hotel bill	30.00
W. H. Marple, one recruit	10.00
Geo. Edwards, stamps, expressage, telegraphing	36.30
Hotel bill	22.00
Lieut. F. Harris, for 25 recruits	250.00
Richard Chaddock, recruit fee	10.00
David Brantner, recruit fee	10.00
May 13—First National Bank on bond due Aug. 21, 1865	1,000.00
Error	30.00
Bank note returned, not current	5.00
	$87,158.80

On the twentieth of June, 1865, Samuel Riggs reported to the Board of Supervisors the bounties he had paid to soldiers in county bonds in accordance with resolutions adopted by the Board. The report was:

1865.

May 13—James Giles, one bond due in three years....$	300.00
May 13—Wm. Graham, one bond due in three years..	300.00
May 13—George McIntire, one bond due in three years	300.00
May 13—Charles W. Biddle, one bond due in three years	300.00
May 13—John R. Grandstaff, one bond due in three years	300.00
May 13—Thomas G. Hammond, one bond due in three years	300.00

May 13—John Ray, one bond due in three years..... 300.00
May 13—Jacob Standiford, one bond due in three years 300.00
May 13—Thomas B. Clark, one bond due in three years 300.00
May 13—James F. Richmond, one bond due in three years 300.00
May 13—John Sivert, one bond due in three years... 300.00
May 13—Joseph Shepherd, one bond due in three years 300.00
May 13—Stephen Morris, one bond due in three years, 300.00
May 13—James Kelley, one bond due in three years.. 300.00

$4,200.00

SECOND CONSTITUTION.

The constitution adopted in 1872, made considerable change in the county court and the legislature provided by legislation for the change so made.

ARTICLE VIII.

23. There shall be in each county of the state a county court which shall be composed of a president and two justices of the peace, except when, by the constitution, the presence of a greater number is required. It shall hold six sessions during the year, at times to be prescribed by law; two of which shall be limited to matters connected with police and fiscal affairs of the county; the other four shall be held for trials of causes, and the transaction of all other business within the general jurisdiction of the court, except an assessment or levy on property of the county. In all cases where a levy of the county is laid a majority of the justices elected in the county, shall be necessary to constitute a quorum for the transaction of that business.

24. The president of the court shall be elected by the voters of the county, and shall hold his office for the term of four years. It shall be his duty to attend each term of court and shall receive for such service four dollars for every day he shall preside in court, to be paid from the county treasury. He shall also perform such other duties and receive such compensation therefor as may be prescribed by law; except that he shall not be authorized to try causes out of court. When for any cause he is unable to attend as president of the court, any justice may be added to the court to make the court, who, in conjunction with the other two, may designate one of their own number to preside in his absence.

25. Each county shall be laid off into districts not less in number than three, nor more than ten, as nearly equal as may be in territory and population. In each district there shall be elected by the voters thereof, one, and not more than two justices of the peace who shall reside in their respective districts, and hold their offices for the term of four years.

The present subdivisions of the counties by townships shall constitute such districts until changed by the court constituted of a majority of the justices of the county.

26. The justices of the peace shall be classified by law, for the performance of their duties in court; they shall receive a compensation of three dollars per day, for their services in court, to be paid out of the county treasury, and may receive

fees for other official duties, to be prescribed by law, and paid by the parties, for whom the service shall be rendered.

30. The voters of each county shall elect a clerk of the county court, whose term of office shall be six years, and whose duties, compensation and mode of removal shall be prescribed by law.

32. A vacancy in the office of the president of the court shall be filled until the next regular election by justices of the peace, all of whom shall be summoned for that purpose. Vacancies of justices of the peace may be filled until the next regular election by the county court.

January 13, 1873.

This court met this day at the court-house pursuant to law. John H. Dickey, president and justice, presiding. Justices present: Frank McJilton, A. L. Pelley, Wm. Blake, Reuben Zink, George A. Jones, Wm. A. Knox, R. H. Holliday, O. H. Moore, Geo. Hubbs, Hardesty Long, Joshua Goddard, S. Barnhart, Wm. Cecil, L. G. Martin. Absent: Henry Reed, Alfred Turner, H. S. White and Samuel Howard.

The oath of office was administered by the clerk of this court to Wm. Cecil, Esq.

The justices present proceeded to draw lots for the classification and the present justices drew lots for the absent justices, which resulted as follows, to-wit:

Class No. 1	Class No. 2	Class No. 3	Class No. 4
A. L. Pelley	O. A. Moore	R. H. Holliday	Alfred Turner
Henry Reed	Samuel Howard	H. S. White	Joshua Goddard
Class No. 5	Class No. 6	Class No. 7	Class No. 8
Geo. A. Jones	Wm. Blake	L. G. Martin	Geo. Hubbs
S. Barnhart	Reuben Zink	Wm. Cecil	Hardesty Long

Class No. 9
Frank McJilton
Wm. A. Knox

R. C. Holliday, J. L. Parkinson, James D. Morris, J. W. McCarriher, Robert McConnell, J. Alex. Ewing, James D. Ewing, Gentleman Practicing Attorneys, appeared in court and took the oath required by law; thereupon it is ordered that the said gentlemen be admitted to practice their profession of law in this court.

The oath of office was administered by the clerk of this court to J. L. Parkinson, Esq., as Prosecuting Attorney of this county.

Jno. P. Wayman presented to court his official bond as sheriff of this county in the penalty of thirty thousand dollars, bearing date October 18, 1872, with John S. Redd, Amos Dobbs, Samuel Wellman, and Hanson Griswell his sureties and on

HISTORY OF MARSHALL COUNTY, W. VA. 147

which said bond is the following indorsement, to-wit: The within bond is approved and sureties acknowledged signatures and qualified as to sufficiency, T. Melvin Judge, etc.

Thereupon the said bond is approved by the court and ordered to be recorded by the clerk of this court.

Upon the petition of Frank McJilton, Esq., and others, it is ordered that Edward Tracy, Andrew Quigly, T. C. Edwards and Frank McJilton, Esq., be and they are a committee and authorized to make and enforce such regulations in Union District as may be necessary to secure the inhabitants from the contagion of small-pox now prevailing in Benwood in said district and to prevent its spread among the citizens, and the overseer of the poor is directed to afford such relief to any sufferers from said contagion, who may need relief from the county.

Ordered by this court that the following gentlemen be and they are appointed overseers of poor of their respective districts, to-wit:

T. C. Edwards, of Union District;
John Riggs, of Washington District.
Michael Dunn, of Clay District.
John Snedeker, of Webster District.
Geo. W. McKimmie, of Franklin District.
Thomas Allen, of Cameron District.
E. R. Harris, of Liberty District.
Jeremiah Mason, of Meade District.

It is ordered that the May and August terms of this court in each year be set apart for police and fiscal business of this county.

John Healy, Esq., petitioned the court for a correction of an erroneous assessment against him on the land books of the first assessors district of this county in Union District for the year 1872, he being charged with an excess of $900 on lots Nos. 13, 14 and 16 in the town of Benwood and notice being waived by the prosecuting attorney and the error being fully proved by the oath of said John Healy, and upon consideration thereof, it is ordered by court that the assessor make proper correction upon the land book and the sheriff of this county refund the tax so erroneously assessed on said excess and that the clerk of this court certify a copy of this order to the auditor of state. State tax, $1.80; state school tax, 90 cents; hospital tax, 45 cents; township school, $3.60; county tax, $3.60.

John B. Bole, Esq., petitioned the court for a correction of an erroneous assessment against him on the land books of the first assessor's district of this county in Union District for the year 1872, he being charged with an excess of $540 on lot No. 16 in the town of Benwood, and notice being waived by the prosecuting attorney and the error being fully proved by the oath of said John B. Bole, upon consideration whereof, it is ordered by this court that the assessor make proper correction upon the land books and that the sheriff of this county refund the tax so erroneously assessed on said excess, and that the clerk of this court certify a copy of this order to the auditor of state. State tax, $1.08; state school tax, 54 cents; hospital tax, 27 cents; county tax, $2.16; township school tax, $3.76.

Ordered that this court adjourn until tomorrow morning at 9:00 o'clock.

JOHN H. DICKEY,
President Justice.

The last session of the county court, composed of a president and two justices of the peace, was held on the twenty-seventh of December, 1880. Since that court ceased to exist, the county court ceased to try causes, and give its sole attention to county affairs.

An amendment to the constitution was adopted at the general election in November, 1880, replaced the justice court with a county court composed of three commissioners of the county court which elect one of its members president.

The amendment was passed by the Legislature at a regular session which convened at Wheeling on the eighth of January, 1879, and submitted it to the people for ratification or rejection at a regular election in 1880.

The Legislature anticipated the ratification of the amendment by ordering the election fo three commissinoers of the county court in each county at the general election in November, 1880, that the court might meet in January in regular session and take up the county work just where the previous county court had laid it down.

The amendment provided that the term of office of the commissioners of the county court should be for the term of six years, after the first election. At the first election (1880), three commissioners of the county court were elected whose term of office should be one for six years, one for four years, and one for two years, and by drawing lots the commissioners elected should determine the length of term each commissioner of the three should serve.

At the regular election in 1882, a commissioner of the county court was elected and at each regular election thereafter a commissioner of the county court was elected for the full term of six years, unless death of a commissioner or resignation should cause a vacancy, which vacancy shall be filled by appointment made by the court between general elections. At the regular meeting of the county court in January after each general election, the court organizes by electing one of its members president, whose term of office is two years from the first of the year or until his successor is elected.

At the general election in November, 1880, W. J. Burley, of Washington District; J. W. Bonar, of Meade District, and J. H. Baird, of Sand Hill District, were elected commissioners of the county court.

The three commissioners met on the first day of January and determined the term of office each commissioner should serve and organized in compliance with the law. The court is a continuous body and is supposed to have two experienced members at all times. The regular meetings of the county court are the third Tuesday in January, April, July and October, and may meet in special session at such times as the president deems expedient, the other two members of the court concurring.

They shall receive a compensation of two dollars per day for each day they are in session as a court, to be paid from the county fund.

COUNTY COURT OF MARSHALL COUNTY, JANUARY TERM, 1881.

January 1, 1881.

W. J. Burley, J. W. Bonar, J. H. Baird, the commissioners of the county elected at the October election last, this day met at the court-house and said commissioners having taken the oath of office as required by law, proceeded to draw lots for the two, four and six-year terms with the following results:

W. J. Burley drew the two-year term;

J. W. Bonar drew the four-year term;

J. H. Baird drew the six-year term.

The court then proceeded to organize by electing W. J. Burley president for two years from this date.

The bond of J. B. Hicks as sheriff of this county, dated November 8, 1880, with Joshua Burley, Geo. W. Hicks, Lindsey Burley, Henry Parkinson and John A. Hicks as sureties in the penal sum of thirty thousand dollars, conditioned and payable as the law directs, which said bond having been approved by the county court of this county by an order of said court, entered of record on the eighth day of November, 1880, and which said bond was this day presented to this court and ordered to be recorded.

The bond of T. W. Manning, as assessor of the first district dated November 9, 1880, with Samuel Dorsey and Thomas Finn as sureties, in the penal sum of three thousand dollars conditioned and payable as the law directs, which said bond having been approved by the county court of this county on the ninth day of November, 1880, and which said bond was this day presented to this court. The said bond is this day approved by this court and ordered to be recorded.

The bond of J. F. Parsons, as assessor of the second district, dated December 4, 1880, with A. N. Holmes and Thomas Parsons as sureties, in the penal sum of three thousand dollars, conditioned and payable as the law directs and on which said bond is the following indorsements, signed and acknowledged by J. F. Parsons, A. N. Holmes and Thomas Parsons, the sureties, testified as to their sufficiency and this bond is approved by the court and ordered to be recorded.

Ordered that the sheriff of this county pay to Mahlen Riggs out of Webster District Road levy, forty-five (45) dollars in full for salary as Road Surveyor of said road district to date.

It is ordered that J. W. Bonar be directed and authorized to inspect and if necessary to repair the county bridge near Glen Easton.

For satisfactory reasons appearing to the court, it is ordered that W. L. Edwards be and he is declared successor to G. W. Evans, Esq., whose term of office expired December 31, 1880, and it was ordered, Wm. Cook, in whose hands the books of said G. W. Evans, late J. P. of Washington District now is, turn over to said W. L. Edwards, justice-elect of Washington District.

It is ordered by the court that the regular stated meetings of this court hereafter be as follows until changes by law or further order of court:
1. On the third Tuesday in January.
2. On the first Tuesday in May.
3. On the second Tuesday in August.
4. On the second Tuesday in November.

Ordered that this court adjourn until the eighth day of this month.

W. J. BURLEY.

EDUCATION.

The constitution provided for a system of free schools, in which the township was made the unit.

Article X, Section 2 of the constitution read:

> The legislature shall provide, as soon as practicable, for the establishment of a thorough and efficient system of free schools. They shall provide for the support of such schools by appropriating thereto the interest of the invested school fund; the net proceeds of all forfeitures, confiscation and fines accruing to the state under the laws thereof; and by general taxation on persons and property, or otherwise. They shall also provide for raising in each township, by the authority of the people thereof, such proportion of the amount required for the support of free schools therein as shall be prescribed by general law.

Chapter 137 of the acts of the Legislature passed on the tenth of December, 1863, read:

An Act providing for the establishment of free schools:

> 1. In conformity with the provisions of the tenth article of the constitution, a system of free schools is hereby established according to the provisions of this act, in order to provide means of instruction for all of the youth of the state, in such fundamental branches of learning as are indispensible to the proper discharge of their social and civil duties; and for this purpose each and every organized township within the several counties of the state, or which may hereafter be organized within the same is hereby constituted a school district, to be confided to the care and management of a board of education as hereafter constituted; but the city of Wheeling, with parts of townships connected therewith, shall constitute but one school district.

Section two of the same act provides for the election by the voters at the regular annual township election, of three commissioners, of whom the one having the highest number of votes, shall hold his office for the term of three years, and the one having the next highest number of votes shall hold his office for two years, and the one having the next highest number of votes shall hold his office one year, and annually thereafter at the time and place of holding township meetings and elections, and in conformity with the act regulating the same, one commissioner shall be elected who shall hold his office three years; provided, that if at the first any two commissioners shall have an equal number of votes, the persons so elected shall determine by lot the duration of their respective terms of office.

Section 4 reads:

> The commissioners so elected together with the clerk of the township, shall constitute the board of education of their township, and they and their successors in office shall be a body corporate in law under the name and style of THE BOARD OF EDUCATION of the township of .... and as such may purchase, hold and sell or convey real and personal property for the use of education within their district.

Section 6:

The board of education of each school district shall, as soon as practicable after they are duly elected and qualified, and annually thereafter, within ten days after the fourth day of July, take or cause to be taken an enumeration of all the youth between the ages of six and twenty-one, distinguishing between males and females.

Section 7:

The board of education shall take control and management of all the schools within their districts in pursuance of which they shall be in charge with the following powers:

First—They shall establish a sufficient number of free schools for the education and instruction of every individual resident within their district, between the ages of six and twenty-one years, who may apply for admission and instruction, either in person or by parents, guardian, or next friend.

Second—They shall cause suitable lots of ground to be purchased and suitable buildings to be erected, purchased or rented for school houses, and shall supply them with proper fuel and with such furniture and fixtures as are necessary to the comfort, health, good order and progress of the pupils.

Third—They shall have the appointment of all the teachers of the public schools within the district, shall fix the amount of teachers' salaries and may dismiss them at any time for incompetency, cruelty, negligence or immorality.

Section 16:

It shall be the duty of all teachers employed in any public school of the state to inculcate the duty of piety, morality and respect for the law and government of their country; and all teachers, boards of education, and other school officers created by this act, are hereby charged with the duty of providing moral training for the youth of this state, which contribute

HISTORY OF MARSHALL COUNTY, W. VA.

to securing good behavior and virtuous conduct, and furnish the state with exemplary citizens.

The branches in which teachers were examined for certificates were orthography, reading, writing, arithmetic, English grammar and geography. The certificates were valid for one year and the grades were from one to five.

The act required the boards of education to divide the township-districts into subdistricts, each containing not less than forty youths between the ages of six and twenty-one years, except that in the opinion of the board that it is necessary to reduce the number.

The act contemplated a school term of six months.

It provided for a central high school.

It provided that the township levy for teachers' fund shall not exceed ten cents on each one hundred dollars of valuation, and for building fund it shall not exceed five cents on each one hundred dollars of valuation.

It provided for the assessment of one dollar upon each white male and each free colored male inhabitant over twenty-one years of age.

The school year commenced on the first day of September and closed on the last day of the following August.

The township treasurer was the treasurer of the board of education and teachers were paid by orders drawn by the clerk of the township, who was also clerk of the board of education, upon the township treasurer signed by the clerk and president of the board.

The officials who, under this act, divided the township-districts into subdistricts, bought land and had buildings erected for schools, were elected at the first annual township election ever held in the state on the twenty-eighth of April, 1864. They were:

WM. J. ALEXANDER—
    County Superintendent of Free Schools.

CAMERON TOWNSHIP—
    J. N. Pipes, J. M. Phillips and George Hubbs, School Commissioners.
    W. H. Bassett, Clerk.

CLAY TOWNSHIP—
    Wm. Riggs, Jesse Bonar and Wm. Varley, School Commissioners.
    Wm. Dobbs, Clerk.

FRANKLIN TOWNSHIP—
    John Hornbrook, Geo. W. McKimmie and Thos. Ruckman, School Commissioners.
    George Rine, Clerk.

LIBERTY TOWNSHIP—
  J. W. Higgins, John S. McDonald and G. Richter, School Commissioners.
  W. H. Henderson, Clerk.
MEADE TOWNSHIP—
  N. Shepherd, J. W. Richmond and Jackson Travis, School Commissioners.
  Peter Koltz, Clerk.
SAND HILL TOWNSHIP—
  John Ritchey, A. R. Kimmins and Samuel Dague, School Commissioners.
  J. W. Winters, Clerk.
UNION TOWNSHIP—
  Joseph Pedley, Dr. McCoy and Thomas Morgan, School Commissioners.
  W. D. Campbell, Clerk.
WEBSTER TOWNSHIP—
  Wm. Keyser, Wm. McCreary and Eli Salter, School Commissioners.
  John K. Francis, Clerk.
WASHINGTON TOWNSHIP—
  Reuben Zink, Wm. White and George Edwards, School Commissioners.
  G. S. McFadden, Clerk.

These school officers whose duty it was to divide the districts into subdistricts, select sites, purchase land, build or rent houses for school purposes, and provide, in part, for the support of schools in the districts. By autumn of 1866, they had the work so far completed that schools were opened in each subdistrict.

By the time they were completing their work a change in the school law relieved the boards of education from a portion of their duties. They appointed three trustees in each subdistrict whose duty it was to employ teachers, fix salaries to be paid to them and to take care of the school property.

The election of a county superintendent of free schools and township officers at the annual township election, held on the fourth Thursday of April was changed to the fourth Thursday of October and was held at the same time and place and in connection with the annual state and county election, and the spring election ceased to be held.

The term of school was not six months as contemplated, but was about four months, depending upon the salary paid teachers in the districts.

The county superintendents of free schools of Marshall shall County from the first establishment of free schools until

HISTORY OF MARSHALL COUNTY, W. VA. 155

the adoption of a new constitution in the year 1872, were:

Wm. J. Alexander, elected on the fourth Thursday of April, 1864, served one term of two years.

John Lorain, elected the fourth Thursday of April, 1866, and re-elected on the fourth Thursday of October, 1867, served two terms of two years each.

John W. P. Reid was elected on the fourth Thursday of October, 1869, and served one term of two years.

Samuel R. Hanen was elected on the fourth Thursday of October, 1871. He served one year under each constitution, two years, a full term.

The constitution adopted in the year 1872, contained about the same constitutional provisions for free schools as the first, but the Legislature made some changes in the law.

CHAPTER CXXIII.

An Act to amend and re-enact the school law of the state. Passed April 12, 1873.

Be it enacted by the Legislature of West Virginia:

1. That for the purpose of free schools, the several counties of the state shall be divided into school districts and subdistricts, until changed, as hereinafter provided, the townships and districts, as now arranged, shall constitute the districts and subdistricts respectively of the several counties.

2. Each county shall be under control of a county superintendent; each district shall be under the control of a board of education; and each subdistrict under the control of one trustee. The same person shall not be eligible to more than one of these offices at the same time. The board of education shall consist of a president and two commissioners.

An election for these officers shall be held at the school house in each subdistrict from nine o'clock in the morning until six p. m. of the second Friday of August, 1873, and every two years thereafter.

5. Each trustee, and commissioner of the board of education, elected as provided in section second of this chapter shall hold his office for the term of two years commencing the first day of September next after his election.

6. The board of education of the several districts shall hold their first meeting on the first Monday of September. At this meeting they shall determine the number of months the schools shall be held in the district, the number of teachers that may be employed in the several subdistricts and fix the salaries that shall be paid to teachers of the same grade in the several subdistricts, and the trustees of the several subdistricts shall in nowise transcend the salaries so fixed in any contract that they may make with teachers. A quorum of the board of

education shall consist of a majority of the members thereof; and in the absence of the president, one of the members may act as such; but they shall do no official business except when assembled as a board, and by due notice to all the members.

The board of education elected a secretary who was not a member of the board.

The branches taught in the primary schools were orthography, reading, penmanship, English grammar, arithmetic, geography and history and such other branches as the board of education might direct.

Provisions were made for graded and high schools. A county board of examiners, consisting of the county superintendent of free schools and two assistant examiners, who were appointed in August of each year by a majority of the presidents of the boards of education or any three of them which constituted a quorum for such appointment. The board of examiners were required to hold two regular examinations each year and other examinations might be held if deemed expedient.

The examinations were public and a majority of the board of examiners must participate in it.

The certificates were only valid in the county in which they were issued and only valid in it for one year from date. Diplomas granted graduates from normal schools of the state were accepted as a certificate of qualification and of the same grade as a number one grade of county certificate. Certificates granted by the boards of examiners of the several counties were of three grades, one, two and three. Salaries were fixed for teachers according to the grades of certificates.

The annual levy for teachers' funds was limited to fifty cents on each one hundred dollars of valuation, and for building fund, the levy should not exceed forty cents on each one hundred dollars of valuation. The minimum term of school was four months.

The first public examination of teachers was held at the school-house in Moundsville on the nineteenth day of September, 1873, and the board of examiners were S. R. Hanen, County Superintendent of Free Schools, and W. M. Wirt and B. B. Newman, assistant examiners.

There was no change in the school law for your years. It was then changed back to three trustees for each sub-district, who were appointed by the boards of education at a regular meeting held on the first Monday of September, whose term of office was three years, after the first trustees were appointed. At a regular meeting of boards of education of the different districts, held on the first Monday of September in the year 1877, three trustees were appointed for each subdistrict; one was for the full term of three years, one for two years and one for one year; and each year thereafter a trustee was appointed to fill the vacancy caused by the expiration of the term of office of one of the three.

From that date there has been many changes in the school law. The commencing of the school year was soon changed from the first of September to the first of July, and the school election from August to May, and the election for school officers and voting on the proposition to lay levy for school purposes was changed from May to the general election for state and county offices in November, and since 1893, all the elections were held at the same time and place and by the same election officers. It had been originally the purpose of keeping the elections separated to keep all school matters free from politics, but it was deemed expedient to hold all elections at the same time and reduce expenses as much as possible.

The first teachers' institute held in Marshall County was held at Cameron in the winter of 1871. The second session was held in Moundsville in the public school building in October, 1873. After that date they were held annually and became an important factor in education. Teachers held an additional week of institute in connection with the regular institute provided by the state commencing about the year 1892 and continued that work for a number of years, but in time it became like rum and tanzy as a summer drink in New England—a lost art.

A system of grading schools and graduating therefrom was introduced into this county by Prof. A. L. Wade, of Monongalia County, at a session of county institute which he conducted in the winter of 1876, and it was a factor of education of real value and in following years a number of pupils graduated from the district schools.

At a session of county institute held in Moundsville, in the circuit court room in the county court-house, a committee of three, J. T. King, W. B. Mathews and E. C. Rowand, were appointed to prepare and report a system for grading district schools. They prepared one in which the grading was based upon the readers used in the schools and which differed very little from the system prepared by the State Superintendent of Free Schools for the grading of country and village schools a few years later. The institute adopted the one reported by the committee named above on the second day of August, 1888.

The writer of this work has carefully preserved the neat little folder containing the system as reported and has it at this time and keeps it as a souvenir of the enterprise of Marshall County teachers in early days.

There have been so many changes made in the school law that they are hard to follow, and in many instances it seems that school officers and teachers could scarcely keep up with the changes. They were so frequent that it was thought that nothing but the moon and weather changed more frequently.

The following were the superintendents of free schools in Marshall County from the establishing of free schools to this date, giving date of their election and term of office:

Wm. J. Alexander, elected in 1864; served one term of two years.
John Lorain, elected in 1866; served two terms of two years each.
John W. P. Reid, elected in 1869; served one term of two years.
Samuel H. Hanen, elected in 1871; served two terms of two years.
W. M. Wirt, elected in 1875; served two terms of two years each.
David Bonar, elected in 1879; served one term of two years.
John W. P. Reid, elected in 1881; served two terms of two years each.
W. M. Wirt, elected in 1885; served three terms of two years each.
J. M. Rine, elected in 1891; served one term of two years.
J. E. Sivert, elected in 1893; served one term of two years.
W. M. Wirt, elected in 1894; served one term of four years.
W. E. Mason, elected in 1898; served one term of four years.
James D. Parriott, elected in 1902; served one term of four years.
Albert S. Winter, elected in 1906; served one term of four years.
H. W. McDowell, elected in 1910; served two terms of four years.
H. E. Carmichael, elected in 1918; served one term of four years.
J. Sherman Welch, elected in 1922.

Those serving two or more terms were regularly re-elected at a regular election.

Education facilities in Marshall County previous to the admission of West Virginia into the Union, were not to be compared with those of the present day. Education was not neglected as some may think, but was fostered under many difficulties.

The first school-houses were the ordinary log cabin of the day, with a great fireplace in one end, a puncheon floor, seats made by splitting small trees into two parts, hewing the flat sides smooth, at least the large splinters were hewn off, boring four holes, putting in legs, making a bench without a back. A puncheon hewn very smooth and set on pins in the wall, made a writing desk. The room was often lighted by cutting out sections of the logs and covering the openings with

OLD TIME SCHOOL HOUSE AND CHURCH

greased paper. The room was heated by an immense wood fire in the fireplace. There was an abundance of fuel. In many instances it was very convenient as the school-houses were usually built in the woods at the side of a road; and the young men and well grown boys were familiar with the use of the ax, and with the abundance of fuel, there was no danger of suffering from cold. The cracks between the logs were filled with chunks and mortar and a roaring fire in the great fireplace, made the room warm and cheerful when filled with rosy-cheeked boys and girls. The house was well ventilated by the large chimney and there was not the least danger of the impure air of the schoolroom impairing the health and taking the color from their youthful cheeks.

Later a hewed log house with a floor of sawed plank fitted together, a board ceiling, with seats made of boards with backs to them, a board on rests on the wall for a writing desk, a stove for wood or coal stood in the center of the room for heating it, took the place of the round log cabin with its primitive equipments.

Teachers then were not generally so well educated as they are at the present day, although there were many fine scholars among the pioneer teachers and much good work was done by them.

It was not a hardship for the well grown boys and girls to go two, three, and even four miles to school. They were full of life and vigor and in many instances no small effort was required to restrain or control their youthful mischievous inclinations. But few branches were taught in these schools. Spelling was carefully studied and good spelling was a popular accomplishment. There were many good penmen among the pioneer pupils and they all wrote with a quill pen. Three months was the usual term of winter school. That, with one or two months for small children who could not wade through the deep snow and stand the winter storms, were the amount of schools in prosperous settlements.

Some of the counties of Virginia, which are now counties of West Virginia, adopted a system of free school in and for the county, much the same as the present school system. The General Assembly of the Commonwealth of Virginia passed an act providing for a system of free schools in counties by submitting to the legal voters a proposition to adopt the system; and in case two-thirds of the votes cast at an election at which the proposition was submitted, were in favor of the adoption, then the same became effective and officers were elected or appointed much the same as at the present day to carry the system into effect.

Ohio County adopted the system and had free schools in it many years before this county had them.

There were many citizens of Marshall County who were ardent advocates of the adoption of the system and establishing free schools in the county and made it a matter of interest to office-seekers to keep on the safe side of such voters, as there was really a majority in favor of free schools, but the majority was too small to adopt a system. One one occasion a man who had filled an office for many years and was always anxious that his calling on convention days and election on election days be sure, was interrogated as to his views on the matter of adopting the system of free schools as provided by acts of the General Assembly of the state. He knew that it was not a good policy for him to oppose it and was uncertain as to his safety if he was too strong in favor of it, and replied:

"I am in favor of a consistency in the practical utilities of purposes and a strict adherance to the law."

Educational work in early days was not entirely destitute of social features. Spelling schools or spellings, were very common and free for all who wished to participate in them, and spelling matches, in which two or more schools entered into a contest, were very common. There was much interest taken in these contests not only by the young but by the older people, and such gatherings were really social gatherings as much as they were educational gatherings. Literary societies were another feature of educational value. Pupils of the schools were expected to perform certain work in these societies, and they did their part of the work; the main feature, the debate, was left to the older members of the society, many of whom took great interest in the work.

Considerable reading was of necessity done in order to gather facts in support of the sides of the question for debate as well as thought and study in connecting the facts to be presented in the debate, and generally those who took much interest in the work became careful readers and gathered much valuable information. Singing schools were another feature of real interest and improvement in the days gone by many years ago.

It is sometimes said that educational interest today is not equal to the opportunities nor are the opportunities improved at the present time to a greater degree that they were half a century or more ago. Whether this is the case or not it is perfectly safe to say that there is ample room yet for improvement and for an increase of interest in the education of the youth of this fair land of ours. It is certain that some of the purposes of public education have been overlooked or abandoned of late and the public has been deprived of their benefits. A real educational revival, nationwide in extent, would be of great value to America.

A SEMI-CENTENNIAL SURVEY OF SCHOOLS.

A survey of schools in Marshall County in 1923 showed that many changes had been made in schools and school work in the past fifty years.

The county board of examiners that formerly had charge of the work of examining teachers as to their qualifications for teaching, issuing certificates valid only in the county in which issued, and controlling the standard of education in the county, had passed out of existence and the work now in the hands of state authorities, to set the standard of qualifications of teachers, to have examinations held in each county by county boards of examiners, who do not participate in the work further than to see that it is conducted as directed by proper authorities, and return the manuscript to state officials for grading

Certificates are now issued by state authorities and valid in the schools of the state for the grade of work designated by the certificates.

Duties of county superintendents have been enlarged; also his authority has been increased. He is now required to perform duties formerly performed by secretaries of boards of education of districts, which make him financial secretary of the county, and all orders issued by boards of education must be countersigned by him to make them valid.

The school authorities of the state have been greatly enlarged and the number of officials increased, as much work formerly done in counties is now done by state officials.

Besides state superintendent of schools, there is a supervisor of high schools with one assistant; a supervisor of rural schools with two assistants, and a state board of education of which the state superintendent of schools is ex-officio president.

High schools have been established in towns and cities and in some rural districts, especially where consolidated schools have been established.

District superintendents are employed in some rural districts, whose duties are similar to the duties of superintendents of city schools. Many educators in the past quarter of a century have advocated triple supervision, but boards of education have been very slow in adopting it as a general feature of school work.

The number of pupils in rural districts have decreased in the past half century apparently in greater proportions than the decrease in population.

Many schools that formerly had enrolled annually a large number of pupils have so few today that the schools are too small to be interesting. This decrease in the number of pupils in subdistrict schools necessitated a consolidation of several of the former subdistrict schools into one school of modern type.

In a few subdistricts there has been an increase in the number of pupils and two-room school houses have been erected and two teachers employed; also a number of schoolhouses of two rooms have been erected, or a second room added, and two teachers employed with fewer pupils than were formerly taught by one teacher in the same school.

From the beginning of free schools in 1866 to 1873, trustees employed teachers and fixed salaries paid them, and during that period salaries were from thirty-five to forty dollars per month without regard for grade of certificate. Teachers were often scarce and without experience and it was a great work to develop a corps of teachers to fill the schools.

Beginning with the school year of 1873, boards of education fixed salaries of teachers according to grades of certificates and teachers' salaries for that year, for number one certificates ranged at from forty to forty-eight dollars per month and for taking care of school-houses, fifty cents per week was allowed, which added to the salaries as compared to former allowances somewhat increased salaries.

The next year, 1874, cutting of teachers' salaries commenced and continued till one or two districts in Marshall County reduced salaries for number one certificates to twenty-nine dollars per month.

For several years boards of education met in September and appointed trustees and fixed salaries for teachers and did so much cutting that a country newsletter stating that "cutting teachers' salaries and cutting corn was the order of the day" would have been a very correct statement.

This may sound ridiculous, but an examination of records, if school records can be found, would show that in days of business depressions, hard times, no cuts were made in salaries of public officers or functionaries in the county except teachers.

Only twenty-five years ago in some districts teachers with number one certificates were only paid thirty dollars per month, and it was not till two or three years later that boards of education began to increase salaries and then it was only a very small increase.

Today (1923) boards of education are compelled to pay teachers with number one elementary certificates eight-five dollars per month and those having ten years or more experience, an increase of twenty dollars per month, making the salary one hundred five dollars per month.

Fifty years ago the minimum school term was four months; a few districts had five months. A few years later Union District increased the term to seven months and later to ten months. After a number of years it reduced the term of school to nine months and it remains at that and will never be less. Other districts increased the school term at times till now there are eight or nine months of school in every district in Marshall County.

It required years of hard work to secure better conditions and better treatment with better salaries. It is safe to say that the demand for labor in other fields of employment was the most potent factor in bringing about the change of conditions and increase of salaries.

Many teachers spent the best days of their lives in the

work and after they exhausted their strength in attempting to make the schools what they should be, quit the work in disgust, neglected by the people for whom they had labored to benefit. Such was the life of the pioneer teachers.

RURAL CONSOLIDATED SCHOOLS.

There has been considerable activity the past few years in consolidating rural schools in Marshall County and there are several consolidated schools in the county as a result.

Union District consolidated seven subdistricts into one consolidated school at Sherrard and the board of education built an eight-room school-house for the school. Four rooms are for the grade school and four for the high school.

Webster District consolidated five subdistricts into one consolidated school at Pleasant Valley and erected a school-house of three rooms for the school.

Liberty District consolidated two subdistricts into one and erected a two-room school-house at Woodruff for the school.

Washington District this year (1923) consolidated five subdistricts into one and erected a four-room school-house at Limestone for the school.

Meade District this year consolidated two subdistricts into one and erected a modern school-house of two rooms at Nauvoo for the school.

TWO AND THREE-ROOM SCHOOL-HOUSES.
Not Consolidated.

On Boggs Run in Union District is a three-room school-house erected to accommodate the number of pupils in the sub-district. Thirty years ago there was a two-room house for the school and the increase of pupils since required an additional room.

Cameron District has two houses of two rooms each, one at Glen Easton and one at Loudensville.

Clay District has two houses of two rooms each. One at Rosbys' Rock and one at the "Union" school on Robert's Ridge.

Franklin District has two houses of two rooms at Cresaps and Woco, mining villages, in all, six houses of two rooms each and one three-room house of this class.

ONE-ROOM SCHOOL-HOUSES.

Cameron District has eight; Clay District, five; Franklin District, sixteen; Liberty District, fifteen; Meade District,

HISTORY OF MARSHALL COUNTY, W. VA.   165

ten; Sand Hill District, twelve; Union District, one; Washingteon District, two, and Webster District has ten, making in all, seventy-nine school-houses with one room each, six with two rooms each and one school-house of three rooms.

Many improvements have been made in rural schools and school-houses in the past fifty years. New, modern school-houses have replaced those first built. They have comforts and conveniences not thought of half a century ago. Better locations have been selected, with suitable playground; sanitary furniture provided; libraries purchased; many subdistricts consolidated; medcial inspection of pupils introduced; fresh water convenient; means provided to maintain and improve health; arrangements for hot lunches; school term lengthened; salaries increased; annual examinations for graduation from elementary schools. This year eighty-one graduated. Teachers' salaries the past year averaged eight hundred dollars.

URBAN SCHOOLS.
1873.

MOUNDSVILLE, fifty years ago, had one school building for the white pupils with five class rooms and one recitation room.

There was a school for colored children but it was conducted in a building used by colored people for a church.

BENWOOD had a two-room school building, and CAMERON the same.

McMECHEN and GLENDALE were rural subdistrict schools with a one-room school-house of the usual type of that date at each place.

The same schools at this date (1923) are quite different. Moundsville has a high school building and three grade school buildings and a frame school building for the colored school. The teaching force consists of a district superintendent of schools, a principal of the high school, three grade school principals, fifteen high school teachers, fifty-three grade teachers for the white schools and one teacher for the colored school, making the entire teaching force for the year seventy-four.

Benwood has one high school building, two buildings for grade schools, with a teaching force of thirty-three, consisting of a superintendent of Union District, a high school principal, two principals of grade schools, thirteen high school teachers and sixteen grade teachers.

McMechen has a grade school building with a teaching force of a principal and seventeen teachers, making the entire force consist of eighteen.

Cameron has one high school building and one grade school building with a teaching force consisting of a superintendent of Cameron District, ex-officio principal of the high school, seven high school teachers and sixteen grade teachers, making the entire corps of teachers twenty-three in number.

Glendale has two school buildings: one a brick building of six rooms, a frame building of one room and one room in the basement of the brick building, at present used for a class room. The teaching force consists of a principal, who teaches, and seven teachers. It, like McMechen, is only an elementary school.

Fifty years ago the urban teaching force consisted of only ten for schools for whites and one for the colored children, eleven in all. This year they number one hundred and fifty-six; quite an increase.

Fifty years ago there were no high schools, nothing but graded schools with an academic course of study. No social features nor amusements connected with schools. Hard study was a prominent feature of the work and results were in proportion to the labor expended.

Today (1923) high schools have taken the place of the graded schools with extended courses of study. Commercial course with stenography and typewriting; domestic science; manual training; social gatherings under the auspices of school authorities; music on the curriculum of studies; football, baseball and basket ball, part of the school work, with an instructor or "coach" provided by boards of education, have been added to school work within the past quarter of a century, and are now prominent features of school work.

A survey of schools in this county fifty years hence will disclose great changes and teachers will remark of the schools of today, "They were away behind us," as the teachers of today say of the schools and teachers of fifty years ago.

ANNUAL ENUMERATION.
Age from 6 to 20.
1923.
Whites.

	Males	Females	Total
Cameron District	518	519	1037
Clay District	168	146	314
Franklin District	315	281	586
Liberty District	247	219	466
Meade District	227	178	405
Sand Hill District	169	136	305

Union District	1403	1429	2832
Washington District	272	273	545
Webster District	184	167	351
Moundsville Independent District	1454	1429	2883
Total, white	4957	4777	9734

Colored.

Liberty District	1		1
Union District	3	1	4
Moundsville Independent District	17	18	35
Total, colored	21	19	40

Total white and colored in county..................... 9774
Number of pupils enrolled........................... 7198
Average daily attendance 6122
Graduated from elementary schools.................... 81
Graduated from high schools 94

FINANCES.
(1923)

	Estimate	Levy
Cameron District—		
Building and maintenance funds........	$ 11,067	$ 7,254
Teachers funds	39,799	38,108
Clay District—		
Building and maintenance funds........	12,715	8,688
Teachers' funds	9,655	7,924
Franklin District—		
Building and maintenance funds........	11,946	11,108
Teachers' funds	17,923	17,133
Liberty District—		
Building and maintenance funds........	5,704	5,674
Teachers funds	18,488	16,506
Meade District—		
Building and maintenance funds........	10,020	7,510
Teachers' funds	10,981	9,701
Sand Hill District—		
Building and maintenance funds.......	3,870	2,939
Teachers' funds	8,953	7,820
Union District—		
Building and maintenance funds.......	85,845	68,870
Teachers' funds	99,535	94,579
Washington District—		
Building and maintenance funds........	37,472	20,108
Teachers' funds	17,954	14,739

Webster District—
  Building and maintenance funds........ 10,472   6,929
  Teachers' funds 11,798   10,233
Moundsville Independent District—
  Building and maintenance funds........ 55,199   46,774
  Teachers' funds 98,551   87,702

Total for building and maintenance......$244,310 $186,854
Total for teachers' funds................ 333,637 304,445
Paid elementary teachers last year....................$214,688
Paid high school teachers last year................... 79,389
Total expended for schools, same..................... 496,059

MISCELLANEOUS
Teachers (1923)
URBAN SCHOOLS

Number of teachers employed in high schools............ 35
Number of teachers employed in grade schools........... 120
Number of teachers employed in colored school.......... 1
Number of teachers employed in urban schools........... 156

RURAL SCHOOLS

Number of high school teachers employed................ 4
Number of grade school teachers employed............... 104

Total number of teachers employed................. 108
Number of graduates from normal schools teaching this year 93
Number of graduates from normal schools teaching (1873) 4

NOTE.—The distribution of teachers was made upon the understanding of the consolidation of subdistricts into a consolidated school at Limestone. Not having a school-house for this year, schools will be held in four of the five subdistricts; one house was burned, leaving only four houses in the five subdistricts consolidated, making for this year one more teacher in rural schools than given above—one hundred nine.

TEACHERS OF MARSHALL COUNTY
1923
RURAL SCHOOLS
CAMERON DISTRICT
Z. R. Knotts, Superintendent District

Nellie Smith	J. W. Santee	Wm. Carmichael
Dorothy Harris	Elsie Hubbs	Jean Stewart
Blain Hubbs	Irene Best	Okey Stewart
Marjorie Fish	Luella Davis	W. D. Fitzsimmons

HISTORY OF MARSHALL COUNTY, W. VA.

CLAY DISTRICT

M. D. Logsdon	Carrie C. Campbell	J. M. Rine
Neva Smith	Earl Henderson	Virginia Bonar
C. J. Wilson	Blanch Gump	W. B. Wayt

FRANKLIN DISTRIST

Goldie Smith	Berlin O. Smith	M. B. Strawn
Floris Iva Gatts	Orville Baumberger	E. W. Berisford
L. G. Wilson	Twila Friedly	Thomas McHenry
Gilmore Rine	Joseph Wade	Ruth McConnell
Edna M. Walters	Leah Gorby	Forest Flouhouse
Helena Friedly	Sadie Wiley	Beulah Kelley

Leona Gillispie   Bessie Wayne

LIBERTY DISTRICT

Gail Crow	T. D. Emery	Lureta Mackey
Vera Lough	Alice Chaddock	Ray Burch
Archie Yeater	Flo Teagarden	Beulah Emery
Clarence E. Mason	Leah Wood	Virginia Powers
Ruth Todd	Sam. J. Anderson	Ethel Hupp

MEADE DISTRICT

Irene Thompson	Susan Barnum	Geneva B. Young
Thos. B. Bonar	Hattie Bonar Terrill	Ada Ruth Cummins
C. S. Lancaster	Carrie Games	G. F. Mason
	Hildred Mason	

SAND HILL DISTRICT

Foster Rine	Earl Francis	Virginia Loy
Ethyl Junkins	S. R. Lydick	Mary Burke
Flora Richmond	Mabel Orum	William Hazlett
	Ruth Hipsley	

UNION DISTRICT

M. P. Boyles, Superintendent District

Earl C. Blake	Nellie Sonderman	Helen Leeds

Mrs. Bertha Von Philip

WASHINGTON DISTRICT

Carl Crow	S. A. Moore	Tony Jefferson
Beulah Kanner	Adda Baker	Pearl Chambers
Margaret Moorehouse	Ora Dowler	R. W. Kennedy
Opal Deitz	Helen Morningstar	Helen Baker
Marietta Stewart	Leona Holbrook	Alma Riggs

WEBSTER DISTRICT

C. B. Allman	D. Violet Weekley	Ella S. Brown
A. E. Blake	Marie Bungard	Lorena Rinderer
Donald Schultz	Lloyd Bush	Pauline M. Mills
Ethel Hubbs	Wilma Reed	Arthur Crow

CONSOLIDATED

SHERRARD

HIGH SCHOOL

E. Stutzman	Ruth Flota	C. C. Head
	Elvada Marshall	

GRADE SCHOOL

Georgia Hubbs	Virginia Talbott	Mary Caldwell
	Hilda Briemson	

URBAN SCHOOLS

Graded and High

BENWOOD

UNION HIGH SCHOOL

Earl Drummond, Principal

W. W. Swinehart	Chris Sanders	Louis Reidel
J. W. Welch	Helen Graffe	Mabelle Patton
Esther McMillen	Winifred Cruikshank	Lydia Shreffler

GRADE SCHOOL

E. L. Beck, Physical Director

Mrs. Florence Stromberg, Music Director

Virginia Hunter, Art Supervisor

Jessie Hare, Nurse

Anna Neilson, Nurse

C. L. Stricklin	Thelma Smith	Anna Bowman
Mildred Carroll	Minnie Gatho	Mrs. Carrie Hughes
Harry Sonderman	Margaret Bell	Margaret Lukens
Mary Rodgers	Florence McClanahan	E. K. Merinar
Mary Houseman	Elizabeth Schad	Norma Howard
Jessie Belle Rider	Gertrude Jones	Mildred Cusack

HISTORY OF MARSHALL COUNTY, W. VA.

CAMERON
HIGH SCHOOL
Florence Anna Wright, Principal

Edwin Haught	W. Clyde Hertzog	Dessie Cox
Dixie N. Byington	C. S. Gustafson	Eva G. Barnard

GRADE SCHOOL

Dorothy Giles	Sylvia Smith	Dora Hicks
W. H. Foreman	Gladys Summer	Gertrude Keller
Mary Grace Linton	Olive Landfried	Thelma King
Olive Ryner	Lola Matthews	Ethel Corder
Gail Anderson	Blanche Rice	Lucy Rex
Doris Hinerman	Vida Moose	

McMECHEN
GRADE SCHOOL
J. T. King, Principal

Ella Campbell	Amy Woody	Florence Houck
Martha Bode	Mildred Varner	Mary Jenkins
Margaret Miller	Virginia Leach	Mary Morris
Mary Conner	Mildred Woodburn	Veda McCarthy
Irene Rude	Beatrice Gatewood	Carrie Zimmerman
Vera Kiedaisch	Margaret Kerrar	

MOUNDSVILLE
HIGH SCHOOL
John C. Shreve, Superintendent District
D. L. Haught, Principal
Paul R. Ruble, Physical Director
James A. Harvey, Superintendent Manual Art
Annalie Moore, Domestic Science

Harold Rogers	R. G. Stewart	Lawrence Scott
Lillian Smith	Hallie Bonar	Ellen Mattson
Margaret Sigafoose	Dorothy Ketcham	Virginia Patterson
Luke B. Ross		

GRADE SCHOOL
Sarah Porter, Principal First Ward
Alice Sanford, Principal Third Street
Retta Founds, Principal Central Building
Mary Nesbitt, Music Director
Ida Eachus, Art Supervisor

Anna Ewing	Nora Young	Erma Crow
Opal Cherry	Clara Schroder	Gail Francis

HISTORY OF MARSHALL COUNTY, W. VA.

Alice Ewing	Opal Anguish	Ruth Noller
Nanon Hendershot	Nellie Lancaster	Emmie Nesbitt
Edda Martin	Esther Hahn	Edna Harpold
Helen Rogers	Virginia Rafferty	Ruth Hennen
Ethel Travis	Leah Hubbs	Olive Lohr Fisher
Laura St. Clair	Flora Downey	Olive Blair
Charles L. Blake	Cora McConnell	Alma Martin
Ella Freed	Mary McCombs	Gladys Hunter
Alma Glasgow	Catherine Young	Anna Edwards
Margaret Gordon	W. P. Fish	Margaret Kuhn
Anna Dowler	Gladys Gorby	India Evans
Mildred Hankins	Virginia Bottome	William Burley
Nella Meek	Edith Ewing	Martha Gregory
Ocie Dowler	Nellie McDaniel	Evelyn Roberts
Mary Sheets	Gertrude Layfield	Wenona Edwards

COLORED SCHOOL

Mamie Wade West   Mabel Campbell

TEACHERS OF MARSHALL COUNTY

1873

Professor F. H. Crago

Principal Moundsville School

Malcolm Lowery	W. M. Wirt	Mattie Patterson
Samuel Resseger	J. W. Sherrick	W. E. Mason
George Rine	Micajah Rine	Jacob Wichterson
Lizzie Riggs	Mary E. Ruth	W. D. Irwin
J. M. Higgins	Belle Gates	J. F. Quick
Mary E. Hedges	Sidney Hedge	Andrew Hammond
Henrietta M. McKee	George Byrnes	T. J. Pugh
J. M. Adair	Rachel Groves	William McGary
Emma Davis	W. J. Doman	Jacob Perkins
Ella Davis	J. W. Kelley	Cora Myers
W. W. Farrar	A. B. Barnett	Leila Alexander
J. W. Elmsley	R. A. Fisher	W. L. Luke
J. F. Wayman	Ella Harris	Luther Rice
Marie Hoffman	E. M. C. Tracy	I. H. Taylor
W. P. Weekly	Phillip Riley	F. S. Carroll
D. F. Williams	Thomas Riley	William Fowner
Ed. T. Riggs	William McGinty	A. H. McGlenn
Patrick Lavelle	Ezekial Bonar	A. E. Massey
George Parkinson	Phoebe Sinclair	Emma Best
J. A. Blackford	John Booth	A. J. Duff
P. R. Danley	Erastus Hammond	Maggie McGaw
O. W. Crawford	D. S. Hammond	F. V. Yoho

HISTORY OF MARSHALL COUNTY, W. VA.

Isaac Lutes
R. W. Simpson
B. H. Clark
J. F. Parsons
J. W. Yeater
F. J. Keller
John Robinson
Mollie Carman (1)
(1) Later Mrs. F. H. Crago.

M. F. Cox
N. W. Yeater
Phoebe J. Gorby
R. H. Holliday
Ruth Whitney
Ida Wallace
Clara Parkinson
Thomas M. Pedley

Belle M. Steele
W. C. Wallace
Mary Peck
David Bonar
Mary L. Biggs
B. B. Newman
W. S. Powell
F. M. Fisher
Lyda C. Murdy

THE MOUND AT MOUNDSVILLE—Discovered in 1771.

ELECTIONS AND ROSTER OF OFFICERS ELECTED

Previous to the adoption of the constitution of 1850, the right of suffrage was restricted to property owners. The county and district officers were appointed. The governor of the Commonwealth appointed sheriffs, county surveyors of land, coroners and the justices of the peace of the county. The county court, composed of the justices of the peace of the county, recommended three of the justices of the county at a regular session of county court in the month of November or December of each year, as proper persons to discharge the duty of sheriff of the county, to the governor, and he appointed one of the number sheriff whose term of office was one year from the first day of the following July. A sheriff was one from the first day of the following July. A sheriff was generally reappointed once, giving him two terms of office. The county surveyor of lands was also recommended to the governor by the county court, and was appointed to serve a term of seven years, as is indicated by the appointment of Joseph McClean, the first county surveyor of lands in Marshall County, and whose appointment and commission is a matter

HISTORY OF MARSHALL COUNTY, W. VA.

of record in the proceedings of the county court at a regular session held on the eleventh day of January, 1836. He entered upon his duties at that date mentioned, which is so recorded. The office of coroner was also filled by appointment by the governor upon the recommendation of the county court at a regular session. The clerk of the county court, whose term of service was one year, was appointed by the county court. In addition to filling the office of clerk of the county court, he served as clerk of the circuit court, attorney for the Commonwealth, commissioner of the revenue, supervisors of roads, served for the term of one year. Constables were also appointed by the county court, but served for the term of two years.

The principal emoluments of the office of justice of the peace was the appointment to the office of high sheriff of the county. The oldest justices were generally appointed to that office and it was quite often the last of their official service.

Members of the general assembly were elected at the annual election held on the fourth Thursday of May.

The list of officers given below are those elected at the several elections held as directed by law, from the first election in Marshall County, in 1835, to and including the election held under the authority of the "Restored" government of Virginia on the fourth Thursday in May, 1862.
Date

1835—John Parriott, Senate, from a district composed of Brook, Ohio, and Marshall Counties.

1836—John Parriott, Senate, district composed of the same counties.
    Alexander Newman, House of Delegates.

1837—John Parriott, Senate, district composed of the same counties.
    Alexander Newman, House of Delegates.

1838—Elbert H. Caldwell, House of Delegates.

1839—Elbert H. Caldwell, House of Delegates.

1840—Elbert H. Caldwell, House of Delegates.

1841—Alexander Newman, Senate, from district composed of Brook, Ohio, Marshall and Tyler counties.
    Jefferson T. Martin, House of Delegates.

1842—Alexander Newman, Senate, district composed of same counties.
    Jefferson T. Martin, House of Delegates.

1843—Alexander Newman, Senate, district composed of same counties.
    Jefferson T. Martin, House of Delegates.

HISTORY OF MARSHALL COUNTY, W. VA.

1844—Alexander Newman, Senate, same counties in the district.
    John Parriott, House of Delegates.
1845—Alexander Newman, Senate, same counties in the district.
    John Parriott, House of Delegates.
1846—John Parriott, Senate, district composed of Brook, Ohio, Marshall and Tyler Counties.
    .Wylie H. Oldham, House of Delegates.
1847—John Parriott, Senate, district composed of Brook, Ohio, Marshall, Tyler, Doddridge and Wetzel Counties.
    Wylie H. Oldham, House of Delegates.
1848—John Parriott, Senate, district composed of the same counties.
    William P. McDonald, House of Delegates.
1849—John Parriott, Senate, district composed of the same counties.
    Garrison Jones, House of Delegates.
1850—Wellington Jenny, House of Delegates.
1851—Jefferson T. Martin, Senate, district composed of Marshall, Wetzel, Marion and Tyler Counties.

    The new constitution provided for the election of all county and district officers at a biennial election to be held on the fourth Thursday of May. The first election held under it was in 1852.

1852—Jefferson T. Martin, Senate, district composed of same counties.
    Bushrod Price, House of Delegates.
    Enos Howard, Sheriff.
    Wylie H. Oldham, Attorney for the Commonwealth.
    Jackman Cooper, Clerk of the County Court.
    Eli Talbert, County Commissioner of the Revenue.
    Wm. F. Lowery, County Surveyor of Lands.
1854—R. C. Holliday, House of Delegates.
    Enos Howard, Sheriff.
    Eli Talbert, County Commissioner of the Revenue.
1856—Robert Alexander, House of Delegates.
    Jacob Jefferson, Sheriff.
    James M. Hoge, Attorney for the Commonwealth.
    E. H. Caldwell, Clerk of the County Court.
    Eli Talbert, County Commissioner of the Revenue.
1858—James D. Morris, House of Delegates.
    Jackson Reed, Sheriff.
    Joseph Turner, Commissioner of the Revenue for First District.

HISTORY OF MARSHALL COUNTY, W. VA. 177

    Eli Talbert, Commissioner of the Revenue for Second District.
    Michael Dowler, County Surveyor of Lands.

1860—Rembrance Swann, House of Delegates.
    Jackson Reed, Sheriff.
    R. C. Holliday, Attorney for the Commonwealth.
    E. H. Caldwell, Clerk of the County Court.
    Joseph Turner, Commissioner of the Revenue for First District.
    Eli Talbert, Commissioner of the Revenue for Second District.

1862—James Burley, Senate, Second Senatorial District.
    Michael Dunn and Joseph Turner, House of Delegates.
    George Pelley, Commissioner of the Revenue for First District.
    Eli Talbert, Commissioner of the Revenue for Second District.
    A. O. Baker, Sheriff.

    County officers appointed by the governor of the Commonwealth or by the county court; the date of entering upon the discharge of their duties and their official services from 1835 until the close of the year 1852, were:

Blair Moran, appointed Sheriff of Ohio County and made Sheriff of Marshall County also for one year by an act of the general assembly, passed April 12, 1835, creating the county.

Samuel Howard, Sheriff, July 1, 1836, two terms of one year each.

John Parriott, Sheriff, July 1, 1838, two terms of one year each.

Zadock Masters, Sheriff, July 1, 1840, two terms of one year each.

Thomas Buchanan, Sheriff, July 1, 1842, two terms of one year each.

Jacob Burley, Sheriff, July 1, 1844, two terms of one year each.

William McFarland, Sheriff, July 1, 1846, two terms of one year each.

Francis Kelley, Sheriff, July 1, 1848, two terms of one year each.

Simeon Purdy, Sheriff, July 1, 1850, two terms of one year each.

    James D. Morris was appointed clerk of the county court on the eighteenth of June, 1835, and was reappointed to the same each year and served as such and also clerk of the circuit court until a change was made in the constitution of the state, making the county and district officers elective.

    Elbert H. Caldwell was appointed attorney for the Commonwealth on the eighteenth of June, 1835, and served by reappointment, until the last day of December, 1852.

Richard Morton was appointed county coroner in 1835 and served until the last of the year 1852, when a change in the constitution changed the manner of selecting such officials.

Christopher Parriott was appointed commissioner of the revenue for the county in 1835, to serve a term of one year. He was appointed to the same office the three succeeding years, making four years continued service in that office.

James B. Greer was appointed in 1839 and served one term.

Lewis C. Purdy was appointed in 1840 and served one term.

Wm. J. Howard was appointed in 1841 and served one term.

James B. Greer was appointed in 1842 and served one term.

Vanlear Arnold was appointed in 1843 and served one term.

Hiram Orr was appointed in 1844 and served one term.

Simeon B. Purdy was appointed in 1845 and served one term.

Henry Sockman was appointed in 1846 and served one term.

Eli Talbert was appointed in 1847 for the regular term of one year and was reappointed each year for the four years following, after which it was filled by election of such officer at the regular biennial elections held on the fourth Thursday of May.

Joseph McClean was appointed county surveyor of lands by the governor of the Commonwealth in 1835 and gave bond with surety on January 11, 1836, with Morgan Jones as deputy surveyor, as shown in the records of the proceedings of the county court.

John H. Dickey was appointed by the governor of the Commonwealth in 1843 to succeed Mr. McClean, with David Venus as deputy surveyor, and served as such officer until a change in the constitution of Virginia made the several county and district officers elective.

The adoption of a new constitution, the order of things were changed and many improvements were made in the county.

THE first state and county election held under the laws of West Virginia, was on the fourth Thursday of October, 1863.

The regular annual state and county election under the laws of Virginia and of the restored government of Virginia, should have been held on the fourth Thursday in May of the year 1863, but a proclamation by Governor Pierpont, authorized by an act of the General Assembly of the restored government of Virginia, it was postponed until the fourth Thursday of October.

Chapter 42—An Act authorizing the governor to postpone the May election for the year 1863, passed January 30, 1863.
The act read:

1. Be it enacted by the General Assembly, that if the convention and the people of the proposed state of West Virginia shall ratify the change in the constitution proposed by congress, then the governor of this commonwealth shall issue his proclamation, suspending and postponing, until the fourth Thursday of October, within the boundaries of the said proposed state, the election appointed by law to be held on the fourth Thursday of May next; and if the said proposed state shall, within the said period become one of the United States such suspension and postponement shall become perpetual.

2. This act shall be in force from its passage.

Chapter 44—An Act to provide for the election to be held on the fourth Thursday of October in the year eighteen hundred and sixty-three, passed September 24, 1863.
Be it enacted by the Legislature of West Virginia:

1. An election shall be held on the fourth Thursday of October, in the year eighteen hundred and sixty-three, for the election of delegates for the legislature for the several counties and delegate districts; one or more assessors for very county; a senator for each senatorial district; and a representative in the congress of the United States for each congressional district; and fill any vacancies in state or county offices which may have theretofore occurred.

2. If owing to the occupation of any county by persons in rebellion or any other cause, the said election is not held in any county on the day herein appointed, the same shall be held for the county officers and delegates to the legislature, on such day as may be designated by the superintendents appointed by this act to hold the election for the said county, who shall cause notice to be given of the time for holding said election by notice posted at the public places within such county, at least ten days before the day designated.

3. The said election shall be held at the several places of voting established in each county by the laws in force on the nineteenth day of June, eighteen hundred and sixty-three, notwithstanding any act passed at the present session abolishing the former precincts and places for holding elections therein.

4. The persons named in the schedule hereto annexed, being three for each county, shall act as superintendents of said

elections for their respective counties. Any two of the superintendents for a county may act, and they may fill vacancies in their own body; but if there be no superintendents for any county or not more than one willing to act, the sheriff of such county shall appoint the number necessary to fill the vacancies.

5. The superintendents for any county shall, for every place of voting therein, appoint three commissioners, any two of whom may act, and a conductor to superintend and conduct the election at the place for which they were appointed, and shall procure and furnish to them proper ballot-boxes, poll-books and forms.

The superintendents appointed for the election above mentioned for Marshall County were William Blake, J. S. Riggs and W. J. Purdy.

The voting places for Marshall County were: Court-house, Pleasant Hill, Jones' Hotel, Bleak's School-house, Parson's Precinct, Mouth of Fish Creek, Sand Hill, Cross Roads, Smart's School-house, Burley's, Terrell's School-house, Big Run, Fair View, Lynn Camp.

Chapter 100—An Act to regulate elections by the people, passed November 13, 1863.

Be it enacted by the Legislature of West Virginia:

1. There shall be elected on the fourth Thursday of October, in the year eighteen hundred and sixty-four, and on the same day in every year thereafter, delegates for the several delegate districts and counties not included in delegate districts and one senator for every senatorial district; and on the fourth Thursday of October, in the year eighteen hundred and sixty-four, and on the same day in every second year thereafter, a governor, secretary of state, a treasurer, auditor, and attorney general, for the state; a representative in the congress of the United States; for each congressional district, for the term commencing on the fourth of the March next after the election; and a prosecuting attorney, surveyor of lands, recorder, county treasurder, and the number of assessors prescribed by law, for every county.

And on the fourth Thursday of October, in the year eighteen hundred and sixty-six and on the same day in every fourth year thereafter a judge of the supreme court of appeals for the state; and a clerk of the circuit court and a sheriff for every county.

And on the fourth Thursday of October in the year eighteen hundred and sixty-eight and on the same day in every sixth year thereafter, a judge for every circuit court.

The returns of the state and county elections held under the above laws, as returned by the Board of Supervisors of the

HISTORY OF MARSHALL COUNTY, W. VA.

county and the persons elected to the several offices are given as found on the records of the Board of Supervisors.

1863—William Alexander and Michael Dunn, House of Delegates.

1864—Hanson Criswell, Prosecuting Attorney.
   N. K. Shattuck, County Treasurer.
   Walter Evans, Recorder.
   George Pelley, Assessor of First District.
   Eli Talbert, Assessor Second District.
   Michael Dowler, County Surveyor of Lands
   William Alexander and Rev. Thos. H. Trainer, House of Delegates.

1865—James Burley, Senator for Second District.
   Dr. S. B. Stidger, and Rev. Thos. H. Trainer, House of Delegates.

	Votes
1866—Henry Keltz, Sheriff	952
Thomas Finn, Recorder	1607
Walter Evans, Clerk of the Circuit Court	1325
James W. Pipes, County Treasurer	979
Hanson Criswell, Prosecuting Attorney	1308
Michael Dowler, County Surveyor of Lands	1280
Wm. J. Stewart, Assessor, First District	923
Eli Talbert, Assessor, Second District	1454
Dr. Thomas F. Marshman, House of Delegates	1243
S. T. Armstrong, House of Delegates	1259

1867—James Burley, Senator for Second District.
   John Ferguson and S. T. Armstrong, House of Delegates.
   John Lorain, County Superintendent of Free Schools.

1868—Thomas Finn, Recorder.
   Hanson Criswell, Prosecuting Attorney.
   Michael Dowler, County Surveyor of Lands.
   John M. Turner, Assessor of First District.
   John S. McDonald, Assessor of Second District.
   John S. Reynolds and George Edwards, House of Delegates.

1869—John W. P. Reid, County Superintendent of Free Schools.
   *John Arnold, County Surveyor of Lands (to fill vacancy) (?).
   Dr. E. C. Thomas and W. R. Howe, House of Delegates.

---

*Records do not state the cause of the election of Mr. Arnold to the office, but it must have been to fill an unexpired term of one year.

1870—Lindsey T. Gray, Sheriff.
   Thomas Finn, Recorder.
   Walter Evans, Clerk of the Circuit Court.
   John L. Parkinson, Prosecuting Attorney.
   John Armstrong, County Surveyor of Lands.
   Thomas Patton, Assessor of First District.
   Thomas S. Bonar, Assessor of Second District.
   Lewis S. Newman and H. S. White, House of Delegates.
1871—S. R. Hanen, County Superintendent of Free Schools.
   George W. Bier and H. S. White, House of Delegates.
   *Records do not state the cause of the election of Mr. Arnold to the office, but it must have been to fill an unexpired term of one year.

The constitution adopted in the year 1872, made some changes in elections and also of offices, provided for by legislation.

CHAPTER CXVII

An Act making general provisions for elections by the people and providing for filling vacancies. Passed April 11, 1873.

Be it enacted by the Legislature of West Virginia:

1. The general election for state, district, county and county district officers, members of the legislature and congressmen shall be held on the second Tuesday of October.

2. At the said election in 1874, and every two years thereafter, there shall be elected delegates to the lgislature, and one senator for each senatorial district, and a representative in congress of the United States, for the term beginning on the fourth day of March next after the election, for every congressional district, in the year eighteen hundred and seventy-six, and every fourth year thereafter, a governor, a state superintendent of free schools, treasurer, auditor, attorney general for the state, a prosecuting attorney, one or more judges of the supreme court of appeals, a surveyor of lands, sheriff, president of the county court, the number of assessors prescribed by law for each county, constables and justices of the peace as may be prescribed by law for each county district. And in 1878, and every sixth year thereafter, a clerk of the circuit court and a clerk for the county court.

1872—John P. Wayman, Sheriff.
   Thomas Finn, Clerk of the County Court.
   Walter Evans, Clerk of the Circuit Court.
   J. L. Parkinson, Prosecuting Attorney.
   John H. Dickey, President of the County Court.
   John Armstrong, County Surveyor of Lands.
   H. W. Hunter, Assessor of First District.

HISTORY OF MARSHALL COUNTY, W. VA.

W. N. Bonar, Assessor of the Second District.
H. S. White and A. O. Baker, House of Delegates.
1874—H. S. White and Alfred Turner, House of Delegates.
1876—H. W. Hunter, Sheriff.
J. E. Hooton, Prosecuting Attorney.
Wm. Alexander, President of the County Court.
J. C. Wayman, Assessor of the First District.
Jerry Mason, Assessor of the Second District.
G. S. McFadden and W. E. Parriott, House of Delegates. (1)
1878—Thomas Finn, Clerk of the County Court.
A. O. Baker, Clerk of the Circuit Court.
L. S. Newman, Senate, Second District.
A. Alex Ewing and John Nixon, House of Delegates.
1880—J. B. Hicks, Sheriff.
J. E. Hooton, Prosecuting Attorney.
James H. Conner, County Surveyor of Lands.
Thomas W. Manning, Assessor of the First District.
J. F. Parsons, Assessor of the Second District.
W. J. Burley, J. W. Bonar and J. H. Baird, Commissioners of the County Court.
W. D. Wayt and Josiah Sinclair, House of Delegates.
1882—John Nixon and W. S. Simonton, House of Delegates.
(1) Records do not indicate that a County Surveyor of Lands was elected at the regular election of county officers in 1876, but records show that E. H. Criswell was appointed to fill the vacancy on the fifth of January, 1877, to serve till the 31st day of December, 1878. Further indicate that John Armstrong served as Deputy County Surveyor under Mr. Criswell, and it appears that Mr. Armstrong served out the remainder of the regular term of four years.
1884—W. H. H. Showacre, Sheriff.
B. F. Meighen, Prosecuting Attorney.
Thomas Finn, Clerk of the County Court.
A. O. Baker, Clerk of the Circuit Court.
James H. Conner, County Surveyor of Lands.
B. L. Crow, Commissioner of the County Court.
John W. Crow, Assessor of First District.
John F. Young, Assessor of Second District.

---

(1) Records do not indicate that a County Surveyor of Lands was elected at the regular election of county officers in 1876, but records show that E. H. Criswell was appointed to fill the vacancy on the fifth of January, 1877, to serve till the 31st day of December, 1878. Further indicate that John Armstrong served as Deputy County Surveyor under Mr. Criswell, and it appears that Mr. Armstrong served out the remainder of the regular term of four years.

B. W. Price, Senator, Second Senatorial District.
George Edwards and Frank Arnold, House of Delegates.
1886—Josiah Sinclair and J. T. McCombs, House of Delegates.
B. B. McMechen, Commissioner of the County Court.
1888—W. J. Burley, Sheriff.
B. F. Meighen, Prosecuting Attorney.
J. C. Conley, County Surveyor of Lands.
W. H. Hubbs, Commissioner of the County Court.
Joseph Orum, Assessor of First District.
W. L. Manning, Assessor of Second District.
J. T. McCombs and Samuel R. Hanan, House of Delegates.
1890—E. M. Lewis, Clerk of the County Court.
S. W. Kimmins, Clerk of the Circuit Court.
Thomas Anderson, Commissioner of the County Court.
D. A. Dorsey, Senate, Second Senatorial District.
S. R. Hanan and W. M. Miller, House of Delegates.
1892—C. C. Mathews, Sheriff.
Thomas J. Parsons, Prosecuting Attorney.
James H. Conner, County Surveyor of Lands.
S. R. Davis, Commissioner of the County Court.
J. T. Roseberry, Assessor, First District.
J. K. Chase, Assessor, Second District.
E. P. Bowman and G. B. Games, House of Delegates.
1894—W. M. Wirt, Superintendent of Free Schools.
L. L. Stidger, Clerk of the Circuit Court (to fill vacancy).
G. F. Gray, Commissioner of the County Court.
L. B. Purdy and T. C. Pipes, House of Delegates.
1896—J. E. Doyle, Sheriff.
Thomas J. Parsons, Prosecuting Attorney.
E. M. Lewis, Clerk of the County Court.
L. L. Stidger, Clerk of the Circuit Court.
Wilbert Jones, County Surveyor of Lands.
D. F. Geiseler, Commissioner of the County Court.
John T. Roseberry, Assessor, First District.
J. K. Chase, Assessor, Second District.
S. W. Mathews, Senator, Second Senatorial District.
S. R. Hanan and John W. Leach, House of Delegates.
1898—W. E. Mason, Superintendent of Free Schools.
J. M. Dunlevy, Commissioner of the County Court.
John Nixon and Frank Legg, House of Delegates.
1900—S. M. Steele, Sheriff.
Thomas J. Parsons, Prosecuting Attorney.
Wilbert Jones, County Surveyor of Lands.
L. B. Purdy, Commissioner of the County Court.
John T. Roseberry, Assessor, First District.
John Chapman, Assessor, Second District.

HISTORY OF MARSHALL COUNTY, W. VA.

      W. H. Harris and Josiah Sinclair, House of Delegates.
1902—J. K. Chase, Clerk of the County Court.
      C. W. Conner, Clerk of the Circuit Court.
      James D. Parriott, Superintendent of Free Schools.
      Joseph Orum, Commissioner of the County Court.
      W. H. Harris and T. E. Parriott, House of Delegates.
1904—M. A. Dowler, Sheriff.
      A. L. Hooton, Prosecuting Attorney.
      E. P. Bowman, Commissioner of the County Court.
      J. J. Sammons, County Surveyor of Lands.
      H. M. Stewart, Assessor, First District.
      John Chapman, Assessor, Second District.
      Charles McCamic and Josiah Sinclair, House of Delegates.
1906—Albert S. Winter, Superintendent of Free Schools.
      Walter Purdy, Commissioner of the County Court.
      Thomas J. Parsons and Josiah Sinclair, House of Delegates.
1908—J. F. Alley, Sheriff.
      Chas. E. Carrigan, Prosecuting Attorney.
      Victor E. Meyers, Clerk of the Circuit Court.
      J. K. Chase, Clerk of the County Court.
      H. M. Stewart, County Assessor.
      J. J. Sammons, County Surveyor of Lands.
      R. J. Robinson, Commissioner of the County Court.
      H. W. McDowell and Everett F. Moore, House of Delegates.
1910—H. W. McDowell, Superintendent of Free Schools.
      J. E. Chase, Clerk of the County Court (to fill vacancy).
      F. W. Eller, Commissioner of the County Court.
      C. A. Barlow and Everett F. Moore, House of Delegates.
1912—C. E. Hutchinson, Sheriff.
      Jas. D. Parriott, Prosecuting Attorney.
      Wm. Nolty, County Assessor.
      B. B. McMechen, Commissioner of the County Court.
      Robert C. Yoho, County Surveyor of Lands.
      Chas. C. Newman, Judge of First Judicial District.
      Arthur H. Gray and E. M. Hinerman, House of Delegates.
1914—Victor E. Myers, Clerk of the Circuit Court.
      J. E. Chase, Clerk of the County Court.
      H. W. McDowell, Superintendent of Free Schools.
      Martin Brown and E. M. Hinerman, House of Delegates.

                                                                  Votes
1916—W. E. Clayton, Sheriff..........................3894
      Jas. D. Parriott, Prosecuting Attorney............3598
      F. A. McNinch, County Assessor..................3697
      Wm. Kittle, Commissioner of the County Court....3784

　　　　S. Howe Bonar, County Surveyor of Lands........3483
　　　　C. H. Hunter, House of Delegates................3598
　　　　Geo. W. Byrnes, House of Delegates..............3089
1918—H. E. Carmichael, Superintendent of Free Schools.
　　　　R. J. McFadden, Commissioner of the County Court.
　　　　C. H. Hunter, Senator, Second Senatorial District.
　　　　Geo. W. Byrnes and Everett F. Moore, House of Delegates.
1920—John Hazlett, Sheriff.
　　　　J. Lloyd Arnold, Prosecuting Attorney.
　　　　Fred A. McNinch, County Assessor.
　　　　George B. Games, Commissioner of the County Court.
　　　　Francis L. Ferguson, Clerk of the Circuit Court.
　　　　J. E. Chase, Clerk of the County Court.
　　　　S. Howe Bonar, County Surveyor of Lands.
　　　　C. E. Hutchinson and Everett F. Moore, House of Delegates.
1922—O. H. Stewart, Commissioner of the County Court.
　　　　Geo. W. Byrnes and Everett F. Moore, House of Delegates.
　　　　J. Sherman Welch, Superintendent of Free Schools.

HISTORY OF MARSHALL COUNTY, W. VA.

MILITARY RECORD

Roster of Soldiers in War With Great Britain
1812—1815

MUSTER ROLL of a company of VIRGINIA MILITIA under the command of Captain John Bonnett, at Norfolk, in the service of the United States, commanded by Lt. Col. Henry C. Coleman, from the 30th day of May, 1814, when last mustered, to the 28th of June, 1814.

Names	Rank	Date of Appointment or Enlistment
John Bonnett	Captain	April 23, 1814
James Ewing	Lieutenant	April 23, 1814
Pewgrine White	Lieutenant	April 25, 1814
Jacob Keller	Ensign	April 23, 1814
Daniel Wells	Ensign	April 25, 1814
1—Bonce, John	1—Sergeant	April 23, 1814
2—Harding, Vachel	2—Sergeant	April 23, 1814
3—Porter, Jonah	3—Sergeant	April 23, 1814
4—Thomas, Jonathan	4—Sergeant	April 23, 1814
5—Vanscyoc, James	5—Sergeant	April 25, 1814
1—Terrell, Daniel	1—Corporal	April 25, 1814
2—Adams, Thomas	2—Corporal	April 25, 1814
3—Crow, Jacob	3—Corporal	April 25, 1814
4—Bills, William	4—Corporal	April 25, 1814
5—Ogden, Cornelius	5—Corporal	April 25, 1814

PRIVATES

1—Allen, D. Augustus
2—Aihine, James
3—Ankrum, William
4—Ankrum, Aaron
5—Betts, John
6—Biddle, Spencer
7—Baker, John
8—Bell, William
9—Burris, Francis
10—Blodgett, Daniel
11—Bond, John
12—Baker, Benjamin
13—Bogard, John
14—Blake, Isaac
15—Belford
16—Buchanan, John
17—Brown, Isaac
18—Bullman, John
19—Carroll, John
20—Carland, Daniel
21—Craig, David
22—Cox, Joseph
23—Carmichael, John
24—Clegg, Thomas
25—Chanot, Justus
26—Cline, John
27—Day, Daniel
28—Darling, Daniel
29—Daugherty, William
30—Denison, James

31—Darnel, Levi
32—Doty, Chage
33—Neal, Archibald
34—Evans, John
35—Evans, George
36—Edging, Robert
37—Enoch, Bruce
38—Francis, James
39—Fletcher, William
40—Gregg, Levi
41—Given, Neal
42—Gray, James
43—Goodrich, George
44—Grandstaff, Moses
45—Glaspy, John
46—Hicks, G. John
47—Howell, Jonathan
48—Handlan, Richard
49—Jefferson, James
50—Jones, Abraham
51—Hoover, Samuel
52—Kyger, John
53—Kyger, Andrew
54—Kiggins, Thomas
55—Knox, James
56—Lyon, David
57—Lyon, Daniel
58—Lewis, Aaron
59—Martin, Samuel
60—Maly, John
61—McVay, Jacob
62—Martin, Asa
63—Malony, William
64—Medley, David
65—McClelland, William
66—Monis, Morgan
67—Morgan, Uriah
68—McCardle, Horace
69—McHenry, James
70—McCarthy, David
71—Moore, Thomas
72—Moore, Ferdinand
73—Murphy, William
74—Moreland, Nicholas
75—Mavis, Andrew
76—Martin, Alexander
77—Marlin, Elijah
78—Orr, William
79—Owens, John
80—Patterson, David
81—Rice, Jacob
82—Rush, Bethuel
83—Robinson, James
84—Roberts, Levi
85—Riggle, Henry
86—Ryan, Henry
87—Starks, Pardon
88—Stone, John
89—Stone, Joseph
90—Sims, John
91—Smith, William
92—Smith, John
93—Taylor, James
94—Taylor, William
95—Underwood, Isaac
96—Vanscyoc, John
97—Vandevenden, Nicholas
98—Watson, William
99—Weekly, James
100—Ward, Daniel
101—Westbrook, Samuel
102—White, Jacob
103—Winters, John
104—Whitkanac, John
105—Wayman, John
106—Barcly, Robert
107—Burns, James
Fraction, Henry, Servant

Soldier of the United States Army in War With Mexico
1846—1848

Joseph A. Burley   A. R. Davis   Richard Huggins
John Hubbs

CIVIL WAR RECORD

1861—1865

ROSTER of volunteers of the Civil War credited to Marshall County, recorded in the office of the Adjutant General. The following rolls were taken from the records by Thomas S. Bonar and through his courtesy are given in this work.

ROLL of Company F, First West Virginia Volunteer Infantry, enlisted in May, 1861, at Cameron, for three months' service.

1—James F. Donnelly, Captain; mustered in, May 13, 1861; discharged, August 8, 1861.
2—Samuel B. Stidger, 1st lieutenant; mustered in, May 13, 1861; discharged, August 8, 1861.
2—John S. McDonald, 2nd lieutenant; mustered in, May 13, 1861; discharged, August 8, 1861.
4—Jacob B. Hager, 1st sergeant; mustered in, May 13, 1861; discharged, August 8, 1861.
5—Zachariah A. White, sergeant; mustered in, May 13, 1861; discharged, August 8, 1861.
6—Jonathan Elmer Evans, sergeant; mustered in, May 13, 1861; discharged, August 8, 1861.
7—James C. Conley, sergeant; mustered in, May 13, 1861; discharged, August 8, 1861.
8—William F. Jugston, corporal; mustered in, May 13, 1861; discharged, August 8 1861.
9—Wilford Emery, corporal; mustered in, May 13, 1861; discharged, August 8, 1861.
10—John Howard, corporal; mustered in, May 13, 1861; discharged, August 8, 1861.
11—Samuel M. Howard, corporal; mustered in, May 13, 1861; discharged, August 8, 1861.
12—Nicholas Hager, musician; mustered in, May 13, 1861; discharged, August 8, 1861.
13—Joseph Chaddock, musician; mustered in, May 13, 1861; discharged, August 8, 1861.
14—Allum, Harrison, private; mustered in, May 13, 1861; discharged, August 8, 1861.
15—Burch, John, private; mustered in, May 13, 1861; discharged, August 8, 1861.
16—Burley, Thomas H., private; mustered in, May 13, 1861; discharged, August 8, 1861.
17—Bieletor, Amager, private; mustered in, May 13, 1861; discharged, August 8, 1861.
18—Criswell, Charles, private; mustered in, May 13, 1861; discharged, August 8, 1861.

19—Criswell, Daniel, private; mustered in, May 13, 1861; discharged, August 8, 1861.
20—Chambers, James, private; mustered in, May 13, 1861; discharged, August 8, 1861.
21—Chambers, G. W., private; mustered in, May 13, 1861; discharged, August 8, 1861.
22—Damon, Norman, private; mustered in, May 13, 1861; discharged, August 8, 1861.
23—Fordyce, Solomon H., private; mustered in, May 13, 1861; discharged, August 8, 1861.
24—Fox, John E., private; mustered in, May 13, 1861; discharged, August 8, 1861.
25—Fox, William, private; mustered in, May 13, 1861; discharged, August 8, 1861.
26—Gray, William, private; mustered in, May 13, 1861; discharged, August 8, 1861.
27—Gray, Samuel, private; mustered in, May 13, 1861; discharged, August 8, 1861.
28—Gallaher, James, private; mustered in, May 13, 1861; discharged, August 8, 1861.
29—Harris, Elias R., private; mustered in, May 13, 1861; discharged, August 8, 1861.
30—Harris, Wm. P., private; mustered in, May 13, 1861; discharged, August 8, 1861.
31—Howard, James, private; mustered in, May 13, 1861; discharged, August 8, 1861.
32—Howard, Wiley, private; mustered in, May 13, 1861; discharged, August 8, 1861.
33—Hubbs, Isaac, private; mustered in, May 13, 1861; discharged, August 8, 1861.
34—Helms, Martin B., private; mustered in, May 13, 1861; discharged, August 8, 1861.
35—Knapp, Robert, private; mustered in, May 13, 1861; discharged, August 8, 1861.
36—Leonard, Allison G., private; mustered in, May 13, 1861; discharged, August 8, 1861.
37—Lydick, Samuel, private; mustered in, May 13, 1861; discharged, August 8, 1861.
38—Murphy, Salathiel, private; mustered in, May 13, 1861; discharged, August 8, 1861.
39—Murphy, David T., private; mustered in, May 13, 1861; discharged, August 8, 1861.
40—Myers, Henry, private; mustered in, May 13, 1861; discharged, August 8, 1861.

HISTORY OF MARSHALL COUNTY, W. VA. 191

41—Mellon, William, private; mustered in, May 13, 1861; discharged, August 8, 1861.
42—Mellon, Samuel N., private; mustered in, May 13, 1861; discharged, August 8, 1861.
43—Miller, Andrew, private; mustered in, May 13, 1861; discharged, August 8, 1861.
44—Miller, Gabriel, private; mustered in, May 13, 1861; discharged, August 8, 1861.
45—Moore, Ezekiel, private; mustered in, May 13, 1861; discharged, August 8, 1861.
46—McClelland, William, private; mustered in, May 13, 1861; discharged, August 8, 1861.
47—McFarland, Thomas, private; mustered in, May 13, 1861; discharged, August 8, 1861.
48—McGee, John, private; mustered in, May 13, 1861; discharged, August 8, 1861.
49—Marshall, Thomas, private; mustered in, May 13, 1861; discharged, August 8, 1861.
50—Marshall, Jesse, private; mustered in, May 13, 1861; discharged, August 8, 1861.
51—Martin, Joseph, private; mustered in, May 13, 1861; discharged, August 8, 1861.
52—Merchant, Benjamin F., private; mustered in, May 13, 1861; discharged, August 8, 1861.
53—Ogle, Jacob, private; musteredein, May 13, 1861; discharged, August 8, 1861.
54—Ogle, Daniel S., private; mustered in, May 13, 1861; discharged, August 8, 1861.
55—Parkinson, James M., private; mustered in, May 13, 1861; discharged, August 8, 1861.
56—Parkinson, Benoni, private; mustered in, May 13, 1861; discharged, August 8, 1861.
57—Riggs, Andrew, private; mustered in, May 13, 1861; discharged, August 8, 1861.
58—Ross, Samuel, private; mustered in, May 13, 1861; dsicharged, August 8, 1861.
59—Reed, Levi, private; mustered in, May 13, 1861; discharged, August 8, 1861.
60—Reed, Ezra M., private; mustered in, May 13, 1861; discharged, August 8, 1861.
61—Reed, Alpheus, private; mustered in, May 13, 1861; discharged, August 8, 1861.
62—Rollston, Chas. A., private; mustered in, May 13, 1861; discharged, August 8, 1861.
63—Sanders, James C., private; mustered in, May 13, 1861; discharged, August 8, 1861.

HISTORY OF MARSHALL COUNTY, W. VA.

64—Stricklin, John, private; mustered in, May 13, 1861; discharged, August 8, 1861.
65—Sands, Freeman P., private; mustered in, May 13, 1861; discharged, August 8, 1861.
66—Sands, George, private; mustered in, May 13, 1861; discharged, August 8, 1861.
67—Stewart, Jesse, private; mustered in, May 13, 1861; discharged, August 8, 1861.
68—Tarr, Brice, private; mustered ni, May 13, 1861; discharged, August 8, 1861.
69—Talbert, Anthony W., private; mustered in, May 13, 1861; discharged, August 8, 1861.
70—Thomas, Elias, private; mustered in, May 13, 1861; discharged, August 8, 1861.
71—Woods, Preston H., private; mustered in, May 13, 1861; discharged, August 8, 1861.
72—Whipkey, Alexander, private; mustered in, May 13, 1861; discharged, August 8, 1861.
73—White, John W., private; mustered in, May 13, 1861; discharged, August 8, 1861.
74—White, David C., private; mustered in, May 13, 1861; discharged, August 8, 1861.
75—Williams, Andrew J., private; mustered in, May 13, 1861; discharged, August 8, 1861.
76—Willard, Henry, private; mustered in, May 13, 1861; discharged, August 8, 1861.
77—Little, David, private; mustered in, May 11, 1861; discharged, Benwood.
78—Work, Alfred, private; mustered in, May 11, 1861; discharged, Dallas.

ROLL of Company D, First Regiment of West Virginia Volunteer Infantry, recruited at Cameron:
McElroy, James, captain; age, 39; mustered in, November 1, 1862; discharged, November 26, 1864.
Helms, Martin B., first lieutenant; age, 22; mustered in, October 3, 1862.
Hall, Chester B., second lieutenant; age, 22; mustered in, October 31, 1861.
Donley, James F., captain; mustered in, October 17, 1861.
McDonald, John S., captain; mustered in, February 7, 1862.
Logsdon, Wm. D., second lieutenant; mustered in, October 17, 1861; resigned, January, 1862.
Connelly, Jas. C., second lieutenant; mustered in, February 7, 1861; resigned, January, 1862.
Wilson, James, first lieutenant; mustered in, February 8, 1862; resigned.

HISTORY OF MARSHALL COUNTY, W. VA. 193

Bonar, Thomas S., sergeant; age, 20; mustered in, October 17, 1861; discharged, November 26, 1864.
Merchant, Benj. F., sergeant; age, 20; mustered in, October 17, 1861; discharged, November 26, 1864.
Allen, John P., corporal; age, 20; mustered in, October 17, 1861; discharged, November 26, 1864.
Fish, Wm., corporal; age, 25; mustered in, October 17, 1861; discharged, November 26, 1864.
Harris, Amos, corporal; age, 21; mustered in, October 17, 1861; discharged, November 26, 1864.
Cohen, James, private: age, 24; mustered in, October 17, 1861; discharged, November 26, 1864.
Earliwine, Wm., private; age, 18; mustered in, October 17, 1861; discharged, November 26, 1864.
Fish, Benj. F., private; age, 27; mustered in, October 17, 1861; discharged, November 26, 1864.
Fullerton, John B., private; age, 38; mustered in, October 17, 1861; discharged, November 26, 1864.
Holmes, Wm. H., private; age, 26; mustered in, October 17, 1861; discharged, November 26, 1864.
Hammond, Geo. W., private; age, 24; mustered in, October 17, 1861; discharged, November 26, 1864.
Harris, Henry J., private; age, 18; mustered in, October 17, 1861; discharged, November 26, 1864.
Hughes, Barney, private; age, 33; mustered in, October 17, 1861; discharged, November 26, 1864.
Myers, George M., private; age, 23; mustered in, October 17, 1861; discharged, November 26, 1864.
Martin, Joseph H., private; age, 18; mustered in, October 17, 1861; discharged, November 26, 1864.
Ogle, Daniel S., private; age, 21; mustered in, October 17, 1861; discharged, November 26, 1864.
Reed, Levi, private; age, 21; mustered in, October 17, 1861; discharged, November 26, 1864.
Sands, Freman P., sergeant; age, 20; mustered in, October 17, 1861; discharged, November 26, 1864.
Dunn, Samuel N., private; age, 20; mustered in, October 17, 1861; discharged, November 26, 1864.
Fox, Henry C., private; age, 18; mustered in, October 17, 1861; discharged, November 26, 1864.
Lowery, Jeremiah, private; age, 18; mustered in, October 17, 1861; discharged, November 26, 1864.
Miller, Andrew, private; age, 22; mustered in, October 17, 1861; discharged, November 26, 1864.
Merchant, Sam'l L., private; age, 18; mustered in, October 17, 1861; discharged, November 26, 1864.

HISTORY OF MARSHALL COUNTY, W. VA.

VETERANS

Mellon, Sam'l N., sergeant; age, 20; mustered in, October 17, 1861; re-enlisted, January 26, 1864; discharged, March 31, 1865.
Howard, James, sergeant; age, 20; mustered in, October 17, 1861; re-enlisted, February 8, 1864; discharged, July 16, 1865.
Fordyce, Solomon, corporal; age, 23; mustered in, October 17, 1861; re-enlisted, February 8, 1864; discharged, July 16, 1865.
Ogden, Geo. W., corporal; age, 20; mustered in, October 17, 1861; re-enlisted, January 26, 1864; discharged, June 7, 1865.
Riley, Chas. W., corporal; age, 18; mustered in, October 17, 1861; re-enlisted, February 8, 1864; discharged, July 16, 1865.
Dilley, Leonard, corporal; age, 19; mustered in, October 17, 1861; re-enlisted, February 8, 1864; discharged, July 16, 1865.
Harris, Wm. P., corporal; age, 25; mustered in, October 17, 1861; re-enlisted, February 8, 1864; discharged, July 16, 1865.
Blake, John, private; age, 20; mustered in, October 17, 1861; re-enlisted, February 8, 1864; discharged, July 16, 1865.
Blake, Nathan, private; age, 19; mustered in, October 17, 1861; re-enlisted, January 28, 1864; discharged, July 16, 1865.
Burley, Declifford M.,. private; age, 18; mustered in, October 17, 1861; re-enlisted, February 8, 1864; discharged, July 16, 1865.
Dean, Geo. H., private; age, 22; mustered in, October 17, 1861; re-enlisted, February 8, 1864; discharged, July 16, 1865.
Easton, Henry C., private; age, 19; mustered in, October 17, 1861; re-enlisted, January 26, 1864; discharged, July 16, 1865.
Holmes, Geo. W., private; age, 20; mustered in, October 17, 1861; re-enlisted, January 26, 1864; discharged, July 16, 1865.
Sims, Silas, private; age, 22; mustered in, October 17, 1861; re-enlisted, February 8, 1864; discharged, July 16, 1865.
Whipkey, Alexander, private; age, 19; mustered in, October 17, 1861; re-enlisted, February 8, 1864; discharged, July 16, 1865.

RECRUITS

Barcus, Benjamin, private; age, 26; mustered in, February 19, 1864; discharged, July 16, 1865.
Blake, William, private; age, 43; mustered in, February 18, 1864; discharged, July 16, 1865.

HISTORY OF MARSHALL COUNTY, W. VA. 195

Blake, Jeremiah, private; age, 18; mustered in, March 1, 1864; discharged, July 16, 1865.
Burley, John A., private; age, 18; mustered in, February 25, 1864; discharged, July 16, 1865.
Busey, Erastus, private; age, 18; mustered in, February 25, 1864; discharged, July 16, 1865.
Buzzard, John, private; age, 19; mustered in, March 24, 1864; discharged, July 16, 1865.
Burkham, Stephen, private; age, 34; mustered in, March 24, 1864; deserted, 1865.
Criswell, Lloyd, private; age, 18; mustered in, December 2, 1862; discharged, July 16, 1865.
Cunningham, James, private; age, 18; mustered in, March 24, 1864; discharged, March 24, 1865.
Courtwright, John, private; age, 31; mustered in, February 18, 1862; discharged, July 16, 1865.
Dunlap, Wm. B., private; age, 18; mustered in, December 2, 1862; discharged, July 16, 1865.
Davis, Thomas, private; age, 43; mustered in, March 25, 1864; discharged, July 16, 1865.
Dowler, John W., private; age, 24; mustered in, March 24, 1864; discharged, July 16, 1865.
Dunkan, William, private; age, 20; mustered in, March 25, 1864; discharged, July 16, 1865.
Fish, James K. P., private; age, 18; mustered in, December 2, 1862; discharged, July 16, 1865.
Fitzgerald, Jerry A., private; age, 18; mustered in, March 24, 1864; discharged, July 16, 1865.
Gallentine, Wm., private; age, 24; mustered in, February 19, 1864; discharged, July 16, 1865.
Hicks, James W., private; age, 18; mustered in, February 26, 1864; discharged, July 16, 1865.
Hart, William, private; age, 23; mustered in, March 24, 1864; discharged, July 16, 1865.
Howard, George M., private; age, 20; mustered in, March 24, 1864; discharged, ...
Howard, Albert, private; age, 18; mustered in, March 31, 1864; discharged, ...
Huffner, Renhart, private; age, 35; mustered in, March 24, 1864; discharged, July 16, 1865.
Kimmons, Sam'l W., private; age, 18; mustered in, December 2, 1862; discharged, July 16, 1865.
Logsdon, James, private; age, 18; mustered in, December 2, 1862; discharged, July 16, 1865.
Logsdon, John P., private; age, 18; mustered in, March 3, 1864; discharged, July 16, 1865.

Lydick, Samuel, private; age, 23; mustered in, March 24, 1864; discharged, July 16, 1865.
Quigley, John, private; age, 25; mustered in, March 25, 1864; discharged, July 16, 1865.
Riggs, Edward, private; age, 20; mustered in, March 1, 1864; discharged, July 16, 1865.
Smith, David G., private; age, 18; mustered in, February 25, 1864; discharged, July 16, 1865.
Stetson, Edward, private; age, 19; mustered in, March 24, 1864; discharged, July 16, 1865.
Sivert, John, private; age, 32; mustered in, April 2, 1864; discharged, July 16, 1865.
Shepherd, A. A. H., private; age, 19; mustered in, March 24, 1864; discharged, July 16, 1865.
Schlonaker, David, private; age, 28; mustered in, February 25, 1864; discharged, July 16, 1865.
White, Vachel M., private; age, 19; mustered in, February 25, 1865; discharged, July 16, 1865.
Welling, Edward, private; age, 19; mustered in, March 24, 1864; discharged, July 16, 1865.
Chambers, Hamilton, private; age, 19; mustered in, March 24, 1864; died March 30, 1865.
Hartzell, Simon, private; age, 42; mustered in, February 2, 1864; discharged, November 15, 1864.
Riggs, James L., private; age, 20; mustered in, March 24, 1864.
Sands, Geo. W., private; age, 20; mustered in, December 2, 1862; discharged, September 28, 1864.
Whipkey, Eli, private; age, 23; mustered in, March 25, 1862; died in prison.
Westfall, John, private; age, 18; mustered in, November 20, 1863; discharged, May 31, 1865.
Stimmel, Henry, private; age, 27; mustered in, March 24, 1864.

DISCHARGED FOR DISABILITY

Barcus, Benjamin, private; age, 26, mustered in, October 17, 1861; discharged, date unknown.
Blake, Isaac, private; age, 23; mustered in, October 17, 1861; discharged, date unknown.
Burch, Jesse, private; age, 43; mustered in, October 17, 1861; discharged, date unknown.
Cox, Stephen, private; age, 22; mustered in, October 17, 1861; discharged, date unknown.
Davis, Squire, private; age, 24; mustered in, October 17, 1861; discharged, March 12, 1863.
Evans, John, private; age, 24; mustered in, October 17, 1861; discharged, date unknown.

HISTORY OF MARSHALL COUNTY, W. VA.

Evans, Gaius W., private, age, 19; mustered in, October 17, 1861; discharged, date unknown.
Fordyce, John M., private; age, 19; mustered in, October 17, 1861; discharged, date unknown.
Gray, William, private; age, 24; mustered in, October 17, 1861; wounded.
Gibson, John L., private; age, 19; mustered in, October 17, 1861; discharged, date unknown, D.
Howard, Wiley, private; age, 25; mustered in, October 17, 1861; discharged; date unknown, D.
Howard, Wm. M., private; age, 24; mustered in, October 17, 1861; discharged; date unknown, D.
Hartzell, Elias, private; age, 23; mustered in, October 17, 1861; discharged; date unknown, D.
Hendrixon, Wm., private; age, 18; mustered in, October 17, 1861; discharged; date unknown, D.
Helms, George M., private; age, 21; mustered in, October 17, 1861; discharged; date unknown, D.
Howard, Jacob; private; mustered in, October 17, 1861; discharged, date unknown, D.
Hicks, Wilson, private; age, 21; mustered in, October 17, 1861; promoted.
Moore, Ezekiel, private; mustered in, October 17, 1861; discharged, date unknown, D.
Masena, Samuel, private; age, 42; mustered in, October 17, 1861; discharged; date unknown, D.
Murphy, William, private; age, 32; mustered in, October 17, 1861; discharged; date unknown, D.
Martin, Andrew J., private; age, 21; mustered in, October 17, 1861; enlisted in cavalry.
Knight, George T., private; mustered in, October 17, 1861; charged, date unknown, D.
Parkinson, James, private; age, 20; mustered in, October 17, 1861 ;discharged, February 24, 1863, D.
Parkinson, Wm. L., private; age, 18; mustered in, October 17, 1861, discharged, date unknown, D.
Riggs, Edward, private; age, 21; mustered in, October 17, 1861; discharged; date unknown, D.
Whipkey, Alexander, Jr., private, age, 21; mustered in, October 17, 1861; discharged, March 22, 1863, D.
Woods, James, private; age, 25; mustered in, October 17, 1861, discharged, date unknown, D.
Hubbs, W. H., private; age, 30; mustered in, October 17, 1861; transferred to V. C.

DESERTED

Burch, Martin, private; age, 21.
Whipkey,. Jacob, private; age, 20; mustered in, October 17,

1861; discharged, July 16, 1865. Whipkey returned to the company and served out his full time.

Armstrong, W. H. E., private; age, 18; mustered in, February 25, 1864; died.
Basford, Randolph, private; age, 22; mustered in, October 17, 1861; killed.
Basford, William, private; age, 25; mustered in, October 17, 1861; died.
Burley, Thomas H., corporal; mustered in, October 17, 1861; killed.
Crow, Thomas J., private; age, 22; mustered in, October 17, 1861; killed.
Dunn, William H., private; age, 18; mustered in, October 17, 1861; died.
Dilley, Adison, private; age, 24; mustered in, October 17, 1861; died.
Davis, W. H. H., private; age, 20; October 17, 1861; died.
Evans, Jonathan E., sergeant; age, 22; mustered in, October 17, 1861; killed.
Fox, William, private; age, 22; mustered in, October 17, 1861; died.
Hollingshead, Samuel, private; age, 18; mustered in, October 17, 1861; died.
Harris, Henry C., private; age, 18; mustered in, October 17, 1861; died.
Holmes, Josiah, private; age, 21; mustered in, December 20, 1861; died.
Pyles, Jeremiah, private; age, 24; mustered in, October 17, 1861; died.
Spears, Sergeant, private; age, 20; mustered in, October 17, 1861; died.
Simms, Josiah, private; age, 35; mustered in, March 24, 1864; killed.
White, Edward, private; age, 35; mustered in, October 17, 1861; killed.
Woodburn, Alexander G., croporal; age, 32; mustered in, August 12, 1862; died.

Thomas S. Bonar was wounded at Fort Republic, June 5, 1862, and at Bull Run, August 30, 1862.

Henry J. Harris was shot through the front part of the head but was not killed by the gunshot.

Freman P. Sands was captured at Moorefield, September 11, 1863.

Samuel N. Dunn died in prison at Richmond at an unknown date.

HISTORY OF MARSHALL COUNTY, W. VA.

Henry C. Fox died in the Andersonville prison, Georgia, on the eighth day of May, 1864.

Jeremiah Lowery died in prison at Richmond, Va., date unknown.

Andrew Miller was killed by an explosion on a transport near Fortress Monroe, Va., at an unknown date.

John Buzzard was wounded in the shoulder at Newmarket, Va.

Stephen Burkham deserted June 2, 1865, at Cumberland, Maryland.

Lloyd Criswell was wounded in the breast at Snickers Ferry, Va.

Albert Howard was killed June 23, 1865, by B. & O. R. R.

A. A. H. Shepherd was wounded in the hand.

Hamilton Chambers died at Baltimore, Md., March 30, 1865. He was wounded at Piedmont, Va., and captured on the 5th of June, 1864.

James L. Riggs was captured at Winchester, Va., July 28, 1864.

Geo. W. Sands died in Andersonville prison.

Eli Whipkey died at Richmond, Va., in prison, at a date unknown.

John Westfall was wounded in action.

Henry Stimmel was wounded and captured July 24, 1864, and is supposed to have died in prison.

Isaac Blake was wounded in a foot at Romney, Va.

William Gray was wounded in action at Winchester, March 23, 1864, and lost a leg.

Elias Hartzell was wounded in a leg in Banks' retreat from Winchester, Va.

Wm. T. Hicks was promoted to assistant surgeon of 7th Regiment, W. Va. Infantry.

William Murphy was wounded at Winchester, March 23, 1862.

W. H. E. Armstrong died at Baltimore, Md., September 23, 1864.

Randolph Basford was killed in action at Columbia Furnace, May 9, 1862.

William Basford died at Annapolis, Md., date unknown.

Thomas H. Burley was killed in action at Winchester, Va., March 23, 1862.

Thomas J. Crow was killed in the same action.

Wm. H. Dunn died at Annapolis, Md., from effects of starvation in prison. He was, at the time of his death, a paroled prisoner.

Addison Dilley died at his home in Green County, Pa., at a date unknown.

W. H. H. Davis died in prison at Richmond, Va., December 30, 1863.

Jonathan Elmer Evans was killed in action at Winchester, Va., March 21, 1864.

William Fox died at Frederick, Md., at a date unknown.

Samuel Hollingshead died in the Andersonville prison on the 21st day of March, 1864.

Josiah Holmes died of wounds received at Piedmont, Va., June 5, 1864.

Henry C. Harris died at his home in Marshall County.

Jeremiah Pyles died at Washington, D. C., date unknon.

Sergeant Spears died at his home March 19, 1863, while at home on a furlough.

Josiah Simms was killed in action at Piedmont, June 5, 1864.

Edward White was killed in action at Winchester, Va., March 23, 1862.

Alexander G. Woodburn died in prison at Danville, Va., January 4, 1864. He was captured at Moorefield, Va., September 11, 1863.

Chester B. Hall was captured at Moorefield, September 11, 1863, and held a prisoner twenty-two months.

"D" appearing after the date of discharge indicates that the person discharged from service was discharged on account of disability.

ROLL of part of Company E of the First Regiment of West Virginia Volunteer Infantry recruited from Marhasll County:

Murrins, George A, sergeant; age, 20; mustered in, October 17, 1861; discharged, November 26, 1864.

Ebington, Benjamin, private; age, 20; mustered in, October 17, 1861; discharged, November 26, 1864.

Harrington, John, private; age, 22; mustered in, October 17, 1861; discharged, November 26, 1864.

Murrins, James, private; age, 26; mustered in, October 17, 1861; discharged, November 26, 1864.

Murriner, John, private; age, 18; mustered in, October 17, 1861; discharged, November 26, 1864.

Wilson, George D., private; age, 19; mustered in, October 17, 1861; discharged, November 26, 1864.

Wilson, Wm. D., private; age, 21; mustered in, October 17, 1861; discharged, November 26, 1864.

Kemple, John, private; age, 21; mustered in, October 17, 1861; discharged, November 26, 1864.

Garrison, Wm. A., private; age, 26; mustered in, September 14, 1862; discharged, June 25, 1865.

HISTORY OF MARSHALL COUNTY, W. VA.

Finsley, Frederick, private; age, 18; mustered in, October 17, 1861; discharged, July 16, 1865.
Huggens, Richard, sergeant; age, 35; mustered in, October 17, 1861; discharged, May 24, 1865; D.
Murriner, William; age, 31; mustered in, October 17, 1861; discharged, July 16, 1865.
McGilton, Nelson; age, 18; mustered in, October 17, 1861; discharged, July 16, 1865.
Smith, Thomas; age, 18; mustered in, October 17, 1861; discharged, July 16, 1865.
Wayt, Reuben; age, 18; mustered in, October 17, 1861; discharged, July 16, 1865.
Fox, John L.; age, 18; mustered in, October 17, 1861; discharged, date unknown.
Sivert, William, sergeant; age, 24; mustered in, October 17, 1861; discharged, date unknown.
Clark, Thadeus, Co. B, private; age, 27; mustered in, September 11, 1861; captured.
Davis, Albert, Co. G, private.
Goudy, Albert, Co. G, private; age, 21; mustered in, October 30, 1861; discharged, November 26, 1864.
Cruson, John, Co. G, private; age, 21; mustered in, October 30, 1861; discharged, July 16, 1865.

John Kemple was captured at Newmarket, October 7, 1864.

William Sivert was captured at Moorefield, September 11, 1863, and died at Richmond, November 4, 1864.

Thadeus Clark was transferred to Veteran Reserve Corps, April 10, 1864.

ROLL of Company K, of First Regiment of West Virginia Volunteer Infantry, enlisting from Marshall County:
Keller, Geo. W., sergeant; age, 28; mustered in, November 14, 1861; discharged, veteran.
Hosenfelt, Joseph, corporal; age, 21; mustered in, November 14, 1861; discharged, November 26, 1864.
Bennett, Samuel, private; age, 27; mustered in November 14, 1861; discharged, November 26, 1864.
Bird, John, private; age, 42; mustered in, February 15, 1864; discharged, July 16, 1865.
Crow, John, private; age, 20; mustered in, March 24, 1864; discharged, July 16, 1865.
Bird, Roseberry, private; age, 19; mustered in, February 15, 1864; discharged, July 16, 1865.
Criswell, Peter O., private; age, 32; mustered in, February 19, 1864; discharged, July 16, 1865.

HISTORY OF MARSHALL COUNTY, W. VA.

Eskey, John, private; age, 33; mustered in, February 25, 1864; discharged, July 16, 1865.
Gray, James, private; age, 23; mustered in, November 14, 1861; discharged, July 18, 1864.
Heston, Benjamin, private; age, 19; mustered in, March 25, 1864; discharged, July 16, 1865.
Johnson, Alexander, private; age, 41; mustered in, March 24, 1864; discharged, July 16, 1865.
Kemple, Henry C., private; age, 19; mustered in, August 11, 1862; discharged, July 16, 1865.
Leach, Clement V., private; age, 31; mustered in, March 24, 1864; discharged, July 16, 1865.
Leach, Ambros, private; age, 38; mustered in, February 25, 1864; discharged, July 16, 1865.
Magers, John W., private; age, 18; mustered in, March 24, 1864; discharged, July 16, 1865.
Marple, Joel D., private; age, 18; mustered in, March 24, 1864; discharged, July 16, 1865.
Orum, Peter, private; age, 37; mustered in, November 14, 1861; discharged, November 26, 1864.
Riggs, Lemuel, private; age, 31; mustered in, March 24, 1864; discharged, July 16, 1865.
Shepherd, Henry C., private; age, 20; mustered in, March 24, 1865; discharged, July 16, 1865.
Shilling, James, private; age, 38; mustered in, March 24, 1864; discharged, July 16, 1865.

VETERANS RE-ENLISTED

Criswell, Lewis B., private; age, 26; mustered in, November 14, 1861; discharged, July 16, 1865.
Gray, Robert, private; age, 30; mustered in, November 14, 1861; discharged, July 16, 1865.
Keller, Henry, private; age, 20; mustered in, November 14, 1861; discharged, July 16, 1865.
Keller, John W., private; age, 18; mustered in, November 14, 1861; discharged, July 16, 1865.
Kemple, Otis, private; age, 19; mustered in, November 14, 1861; discharged, July 16, 1865.
Leach, Samuel, corporal; age, 24; mustered in, November 14, 1861; discharged, July 16, 1865.
Leach, Benjamin, private; age, 28; mustered in, November 14, 1861; discharged, July 16, 1865.
Morgan, Wm. H., private; age, 18; mustered in, November 14, 1861; discharged, July 16, 1865.
McHenry, James, private; age, 22; mustered in, November 14, 1861; discharged, July 16, 1865.

HISTORY OF MARSHALL COUNTY, W. VA. 203

McCombs, John, corporal; age, 23; mustered in, November 14, 1861; discharged, July 16, 1865.
Pelley, James, sergeant; age, 23; mustered in, November 14, 1861; discharged, July 16, 1865.
Riggle, Charles, private; age, 20; mustered in, November 14, 1861; discharged, July 16, 1865.

DISCHARGED

Orum, George, private; age, 39; mustered in, November 14, 1861; discharged, January 27, 1863, D.
McCauslin, Robert, private; age, 36; mustered in, November 14, 1861; discharged, July 7, 1862, D.
Davis, Cephas, private; age, 21; mustered in, November 14, 1861; discharged, date unknown, D.
Gosney, Richard, private; age, 20; mustered in, November 14, 1861; dsicharged, November 18, 1862, D.
Talbert, John, private; age, 18; mustered in, November 14, 1861; died.
McGinnis, John J., sergeant; age, 33; mustered in, November 14, 1861; discharged, September 24, 1863.
Shaw, Joseph, private; age, 24; mustered in, November 14, 1861; killed.

Joseph Shaw was killed in action at Snickers Ferry, July 18, 1864.

John Eskey was wounded at the same engagement and lost a leg.

ROLL of Company L, Sixth Regiment of West Virginia Infantry, recruited at Cameron.

1—Treadway, Wm. M., captain; age, 44; mustered in, October 14, 1861; discharged, November 12, 1864.
2—Dickey, John H., captain; age, 55; mustered in, November 12, 1861; discharged, March 5, 1863.
3—McDonald, Wm. R., first lieutenant; age, 20; mustered in, November 12, 1861; discharged, ...
4—Yahrling, Chas. F. A., second lieutenant; age, 21; mustered in, February 18, 1862; discharged, November 12, 1864.
5—Criswell, Joseph, sergeant; age, 26; mustered in, October 14, 1861; re-enlisted.
6—Marshall, Jesse, sergeant; age, 26; mustered in, October 14, 1861; re-enlisted.
7—Cale, Isaac, corporal; age, 35; mustered in, November 24, 1862; re-enlisted.
8—Gaugh, Elijah D., musician; age, 30; mustered in, August 24, 1863.
9—Anderson, John C., wag'nr; age, 23; mustered in, October 14, 1861; veteran.

10—Alley, Wm. L., private; age, 26; mustered in, December 31, 1861; veteran.
11—Alley, Uriah T., private; age, 18; mustered in, September 9, 1864.
12—Arthur, John O., private; age, 19; mustered in, November 24, 1862.
13—Burton, John A., private; age, 22; mustered in, October 14, 1861.
14—Betesall, Frederick, private; age, 19; mustered in, November 24, 1862.
15—Boham, Matthias, private; age, 26; mustered in, March 1, 1864.
16—Criswell, John W., private; age, 21; mustered in, October 14, 1861; veteran.
17—Chambers, Henry, private; age, 18; mustered in, October 14, 1861; veteran.
18—Cale, Andrew J., private; age, 37; mustered in, November 24, 1862.
19—Cale, John, private; age, 33; mustered in, November 24, 1862.
20—Dumire, Andrew T., private; age, 18; mustered in, March 1, 1864.
21—Evans, Thomas G., private; age, 20; mustered in, November 12, 1861; veteran.
22—Evans, William, private; age, 18; mustered in, December 10, 1861; veteran.
23—Evans, Samuel, private; age, 20; mustered in, December 31, 1861; veteran.
24—Grimes, Hiram, private; age, 18; mustered in, December 14, 1861; veteran.
25—Gallantine, John, private; age, 19; mustered in, December 14, 1861; veteran.
26—Gorby, Richard P., private; age, 18; mustered in, December 14, 1861; veteran.
27—Hughes, Henry V., private; age, 18; mustered in, December 10, 1861; veteran.
28—Hartong, William, private; age, 21; mustered in December 10, 1861.
29—Ice, Isaac, private; age, 45; mustered in, January 2, 1862.
30—Ice, Andrew J., private; age, 18; mustered in, December 31, 1861.
31—Johnson, Wm. P., private; age, 19; mustered in, October 14, 1861; veteran.
32—Keyser, John L., private; age, 20; mustered in, November 24, 1862.
33—Lowe, David, private; age, 22; mustered in, October 14, 1861; veteran.

HISTORY OF MARSHALL COUNTY, W. VA. 205

34—Lindsey, Alex N., private; age, 22; mustered in, March 1, 1864.
35—Marshall, Thomas T., private; age, 21; mustered in, October 14, 1861; veteran.
36—Musgrove, David S., private; age, 18; mustered in, October 14, 1861; veteran.
37—Miller, John D., private; age, 30; mustered in, October 14, 1861; veteran.
38—Myers, Andrew, private; age, 18; mustered in, October 14, 1861; veteran.
39—Mellon, William, private; age, 26; mustered in, November 12, 1861; veteran.
40—Manion, Thomas W., private; age, 19; mustered in, December 31, 1861.
41—Myers, William, private; age, 18; mustered in, September 3, 1864.
42—Pletcher, Uriah, private; age, 19; mustered in, November 12, 1861; veteran.
43—Pletcher, Samuel, private; age, 20; mustered in, December 10, 1861; veteran.
44—Piper, Andrew J., private; age, 18; mustered in, March 1, 1864.
45—Ross, Thomas, private; age, 18; mustered in, November 12, 1861; veteran.
46—Ravenscroft, Wm., private; age, 19; mustered in, November 14, 1861; veteran.
47—Richter, Frederick, private; age, 18; mustered in, December 10, 1861; veteran.
48—Stewart, Joseph, private; age, 34; mustered in, October 14, 1861; veteran.
49—Sands, George W., private; age, 18; mustered in, October 14, 1861.
50—Sloan, Mordica, private; age, 43; mustered in, October 14, 1861; veteran.
51—Sloan, Sam'l H., private; age, 30; mustered in, December 10, 1861; veteran.
52—Sivert, Jacob, private; age, 37; mustered in, October 14, 1861; veteran.
53—Stout, Samuel, private; age, 18; mustered in, October 14, 1861; veteran.
54—Sprouse, William, private; age, 28; mustered in, November 24, 1862.
55—Smith, Levi, private; age, 18; mustered in, August 2, 1864.
56—Whipkey, Josiah, private; age, 28; mustered in, October 14, 1861; veteran.

57—Wayt, Thomas, private; age, 18; mustered in, November 12, 1861; veteran.
58—Whipkey, John, private; age, 28; mustered in, August 24, 1863.
59—Wilson, George W., private; age, 20; mustered in, March 1, 1864.

DISCHARGED

60—Criswell, Charles, second lieutenant; age, 22; mustered in, November 12, 1861; discharged, January 15, 1863.
61—Dick, David, first lieutenant; age, 21; mustered in, October 14, 1861; discharged, November 15, 1863.
62—Stewart, Robert, first sergeant; age, 23; mustered in, October 14, 1861; discharged, November 12, 1864.
63—Anderson, Benjamin, first lieutenant; age, 22; mustered in, October 14, 1861; discharged, November 12, 1864.
64—Gillispie, Cornelius, first lieutenant; age, 31; mustered in, October 14, 1861; discharged, November 12, 1864.
65—Stewart, Sam'l M., corporal; age, 22; mustered in, October 14, 1861; discharged, November 12, 1864.
66—Starkey, John W., corporal; age, 21; mustered in, October 14, 1861; discharged, November 12, 1864.
67—Earl, Elias, corporal; age, 40; mustered in, October 14, 1861; discharged, November 12, 1864.
68—Ryan, Jasper, corporal; age, 20; mustered in, October 14, 1861; discharged, November 12, 1864.
69—Richter, Sam'l F., corporal; age, 19; mustered in, December 10, 1861; discharged, November 12, 1864.
70—Williams, Peter, musician; age, 21; mustered in, October 14, 1861; discharged, November 12, 1864.
71—Murch, Enoch, private; age, 25; mustered in, October 14, 1861; discharged, November 12, 1864.
72—Burt, Robert, private; age, 33; mustered in, October 14, 1861; discharged, November 12, 1864.
73—Baker, Lewis, private; age, 20; mustered in, October 14, 1861; discharged, November 12, 1864.
74—Criswell, William, private; age, 19; mustered in, October 14, 1861; discharged, November 12, 1864.
75—Criswell, John, Jr., private; age, 18; mustered in, October 14, 1861; discharged, November 12, 1864.
76—Criswell, John, Sr., private; age, 44; mustered in, October 14, 1861; discharged, February 10, 1864, D.
77—Doty, Micajah, private; age, 28; mustered in, October 14, 1861; discharged, November 12, 1864.
78—Darrow, Wm., private; age, 24; mustered in, October 14, 1861; discharged, November 12, 1864.
79—Darrow, Jacob, private; age, 19; mustered in, November 12, 1861; discharged, November 12, 1864.

HISTORY OF MARSHALL COUNTY, W. VA.

80—Dickey, Robert, private; age, 25; mustered in, October 14, 1861; discharged, November 12, 1864.
81—Dixon, William, private; age, 26; mustered in, November 12, 1861; discharged, November 12, 1864.
82—Garry, James, private; age, 28; mustered in, October 14, 1861; discharged, November 12, 1864.
83—Hewes, Shipley, private; age, 44; mustered in, October 14, 1861; discharged, November 12, 1864.
84—Henderson, John, private; age, 26; mustered in, November 12, 1861; discharged, November 12, 1864.
85—Lancaster, Henry, private; age, 35; mustered in, October 14, 1861; discharged, November 12, 1864.
86—Kolp, Christian, private; age, 28; mustered in, October 14, 1861; discharged, November 12, 1864.
87—Miller, David K., private; age, 21; mustered in, October 14, 1861; discharged, November 12, 1864.
88—Muldrew, Abram, private; age, 18; mustered in, October 14, 1861; discharged, November 12, 1864.
89—Marshall, William, private; age, 20; mustered in, October 14, 1861; discharged, November 12, 1864.
90—Marshall, Asbury, private; age, 40; mustered in, November 20, 1861; discharged, November 12, 1864.
91—Musgrove, James G., private; age, 21; mustered in, November 20, 1861; discharged, November 12, 1864.
92—McElvain, James, private; age, 21; mustered in, October 14, 1861; discharged, November 12, 1864.
93—McGrath, John J., private; age, 19; mustered in, October 14, 1861; discharged, November 12, 1864.
94—McBroom, Robert, private; age, 19; mustered in, October 14, 1861; discharged, November 12, 1864.
95—Ross, Joseph, private; age, 25; mustered in October 14, 1861; discharged, November 12, 1864.
96—Richmond, Charles, private; age, 28; mustered in, October 14, 1861; discharged, November 12, 1864.
97—Richmond, Isaac J., private; age, 31; mustered in, October 14, 1861; discharged, November 12, 1864.
98—Richmond, Silas, private; age, 22; mustered in, October 14, 1861; discharged, November 12, 1864.
99—Reynolds, Franklin, private; age, 23; mustered in, October 14, 1861; discharged, October 26, 1863.
100—Spears, Thomas, private; age, 33; mustered in, October 14, 1861; discharged, November 12, 1864.
101—Stewart, Wm. A., private; age, 18; mustered in, October 14, 1861; discharged, November 12, 1864.
102—Standiford, Skelton, private; age, 24; mustered in, October 14, discharged, November 12, 1864.

103—Sands, William, private; age, 44; mustered in, October 14, 1861; discharged, November 12, 1864.
104—Tracy, David, private; age, 35; mustered in, October 14, 1861; discharged, November 12, 1864.
105—Venus, William, private; age, 38; mustered in, November 12, 1861; discharged, November 12, 1864.
106—Wilson, David, private; age, 19; mustered in, October 14, 1861; dischaged, June 27, 1864.
107—Wilson, John, private; age, 21; mustered in, December 10, 1861; discharged, December 10, 1864.
108—Magruder, Thomas, sergeant; age, 26; mustered in, October 14, 1861; promoted.
109—Magruder, Daniel, corporal; age, 35; mustered in, October 14, 1861; promoted.

DIED

110—Burge, Andrew J., corporal; age, 23; mustered in, Oc- 14, 1861; re-enlisted.
111—Ball, Richard, private; age, 42; mustered in, October 1861; died.
112—Burge, Harvey, private; age, 26; mustered in, December 31, 1861; died.
113—Cain, Madden, private; age, 18; mustered in, January 1, 1862; killed.
114—McCracken, Alex, private; age, 21; mustered in, October 14, 1861; killed.
115—McCloskey, James, private; age, 40; mustered in, October 14, 1861; re-enlisted.
116—Roach, Jesse, private; age, 21; mustered in, December 10, 1861; died.
117—Shilling, David, private; age, 18; mustered in, December 10, 1861; re-enlisted.
118—Lancaster, John, private; age, 22; mustered in, December 10, 1861; died.
119—Thompson, Joseph, private; age, 19; mustered in, December 28, 1863; re-enlisted.

Joseph Stewart died at Annapolis, Maryland, February 19, 1865, a paroled prisoner.
Andrew J. Burge died September 28, 1864.
Richard Ball died March 16, 1863, at Grafton Hospital.
Harvey Burge died at the same place on the 16th of March, 1863.
Madden Cain was killed in action in Tucker County, West Virginia, October 28, 1863.
Alex McCracken was killed at Rowlsburg, W. Va., July 9, 1863.

HISTORY OF MARSHALL COUNTY, W. VA.

James McCloskey re-enlisted and was killed in action at New Creek, W. Va., August 4, 1864.

Jesse Roach died at a General Hospital at Parkersburg, W. Va., November 20, 1863.

David Shilling re-enlisted and was killed in action at New Creek, W. Va., August 4, 1864.

John Lancaster died at his home in Marshall County, November 19, 1863.

Joseph Thompson re-enlisted and died March 31, 1865, in the General Hospital at Parkersburg, W. Va.

ROLL of Company B, Seventh Regiment of West Virginia Infantry, recruited at Cameron:

Thomas, Morris, captain; age, 39; mustered in, August 7, 1861; discharged, October 12, 1862.

Head, Wm. T., first lieutenant; age, 35; mustered in, August 7, 1861; discharged, June 17, 1862.

Kraus, Samuel, second lieutenant; age, 28; mustered in, August 7, 1861; discharged, July 1, 1865.

Hendershot, Jas. M., private; age, 35; mustered in, August 7, 1861.

Chambers, Geo. W., private; age, 22; August 7, 1861.

Ridman, Isaac., private; age, 35; mustered in, August 7, 1861; discharged, July 1, 1865.

Fullerton, W. R. C., private; age, 18; mustered in, August 7, 1861; discharged, July 1, 1865.

Galloway, Nicholas, private; age, 18; mustered in, September 1, 1861; discharged, July 1, 1865.

Tarr, Brice Howard, private; age, 19; mustered in, September 23, 1861; discharged, May 8, 1865.

Fry, James, private; age, 20; mustered in, September 23, 1861; discharged, July 1, 1865.

Smith, Benj. F., private; age, 23; mustered in, October 4, 1861; discharged, February 27, 1865, D.

Good, George, private; age, 21; mustered in, January 21, 1862; dishchaged, December 24, 1862.

Good, David, private; age, 29; mustered in, January 21, 1862; discharged, July 1, 1865.

Good, Samuel, private; age, 26; mustered in, January 21, 1862; discharged, December 8, 1862.

Mathews, David, private; age, 22; mustered in, January 23, 1862; discharged, July 1, 1865.

Stewart, Irvin, private; age, 28; mustered in, August 7, 1861; dischaged, July 1, 1865.

Stewart, Thomas, private; age, 32; mustered in, August 7, 1861; discharged, July 1, 1865.

Sanders, John, private; age, 19; mustered in, August 7, 1861; discharged, July 1, 1865.

HISTORY OF MARSHALL COUNTY, W. VA.

Stewart, William J., corporal; age, 18; mustered in, August 7, 1861; discharged, July 2, 1863.
Scott, Martin L., private; age, 23; mustered in, August 7, 1861; discharged, September 17, 1862.
Sherman, Robert, pivate; age, 25; mustered in, August 7, 1861; discharged, September 17, 1862.
Freeman, William, private; age, 18; mustered in, August 7, 1861; discharged, June 24, 1863, D.
Vanderhoof, Cornelius, private; age, 30; mustered in August 7, 1861; transferred.
Woods, John, private; age, 19; mustered in, August 7, 1861; dischaged, October 3, 1863, D.
Whitely, Albert H., private; age, 32; mustered in, August 7, 1861; discharged, February 3, 1863.
Wetzel, John T., private; mustered in, August 7, 1861; discharged, July 1, 1865.
Walton, Hiram, corporal; age, 27; mustered in, August 7, 1861; discharged, July 1, 1865.
West, John C., corporal; age, 24; mustered in, August 7, 1861; dischaged, February 12, 1863.
Whipkey, Freeman, corporal; age, 18; mustered in, August 7, 1861; discharged, July 1, 1865.
Gadus, Zacharias, private; age, 21; mustered in, August 7, 1861; discharged, December 16, 1862, D.
Masters, Jesse, private; age, 24; mustered in, August 7, 1861; discharged, July 1, 1863.
Masters, Mathew, private; age, 27; mustered in, August 7,
Moose, George W., private; age, 21; mustered in, August 7, 1861.
Morris, Hiram K., private; age, 35; mustered in, August 7, 1861; discharged, June 29, 1862.
Morris, William G., private; age, 40; mustered in, August 7, 1861; discharged, June 8, 1862.
Miller, Jacob, private; age, 18; mustered in, August 7, 1861; discharged, October 17, 1862.
Mathews, William H., private; age, 20; mustered in, August 7, 1861; discharged, February 15, 1862, D.
Ormsby, John H., private; age, 18; mustered in, August 7, 1861; discharged, January 12, 1863.
Parker, Oliver, private; age, 31; mustered in, August 7, 1861; discharged, October 30, 1862.
Pratt, Alexander, private; age, 44; mustered in, August 7, 1861; discharged, February 7, 1863, D.
Rush, James, private; age, 20; mustered in, August 7, 1861.
Ross, Mathias M., private; age, 23; mustered in, August 7, 1861; discharged, February 14, 1863, D.

HISTORY OF MARSHALL COUNTY, W. VA. 211

Roberts, James M., private; age, 18; mustered in, August 7, 1861; discharged, July 1, 1865.
Sayers, Wm. M., private; age, 34; mustered in, August 7, 1861; discharged, July 1, 1865.
Stewart, Perry P., private; age, 18; mustered in, August 7, 1861; discharged, February 13, 1863, D.
Graham, William, private; age, 25; mustered in, August 7, 1861; discharged, April 17, 1863, D.
Good, Jacob, private; age, 25; mustered in, August 7, 1861; discharged, February 19, 1863, D.
Gregg, Jacob, private; age, 43; mustered in, August 7, 1861; dischaged, October 18, 1863.
Hunt, David, private; age, 39; mustered in, August 7, 1861; discharged, June 15, 1865, D.
Good, Thomas, private; age, 23; mustered in, August 7, 1861; discharged, July 1, 1865.
Jackson, William, private; age, 43; mustered in, August 7, 1861; discharged, February 9, 1864.
Kuhn, Abraham, private; age, 24; mustered in, August 7, 1861; discharged, April 4, 1863.
Kuhn, William, private; age, 22; mustered in, August 7, 1861; discharged, August 24, 1861.
Lewis, Jackson, private; age, 18; mustered in, August 7, 1861; discharged, July 1, 1865.
Lightner, Wm. H., private; age, 25; mustered in, August 7, 1861; discharged, July 1, 1865.
Miller, Samuel, private; age, 39; mustered in, August 7, 1861; discharged, July 1, 1865.
Myers, Martin S., private; age, 18; mustered in, August 7, 1861; discharged, May 29, 1865.
Myers, John M., private; age, 44; mustered in, August 7, 1861; discharged, February 15, 1862.
McGary, John, private; age, 27; mustered in, August 7, 1861; discharged, July 1, 1865.
Matheng, Elias, private; age, 18; mustered in, August 7, 1861; discharged, July 1, 1865.
Prickett, James, first sergeant; age, 42; mustered in, August 7, 1861; discharged, February 3, 1862.
Denny, John, private; age, 27; mustered in, August 7, 1861; discharged, May 10, 1863.
Tarr, Nathan B., private; age, 44; mustered in, August 7, 1861; discharged, July 1, 1865.
Leichter, Emery, sergeant; age, 20; mustered in, August 7, 1861; discharged, December 12, 1862, D.
Sander, Joseph, private; age, 28; mustered in, August 7, 1861; discharged, July 1, 1865.

HISTORY OF MARSHALL COUNTY, W. VA.

Hendershot, A. W., private; age, 23; mustered in, August 7, 1861.
Mathews, John, sergeant; age, 22; mustered in, August 7, 1861; discharged, September 12, 1862.
Fry, Christian S., sergeant; age, 24; mustered in, August 7, 1861.
Strickland, Reuben, corporal; age, 18; mustered in, August 7, 1861; discharged, July 1, 1865.
Bruhn, Frederick, private; age, 19; mustered in, August 7, 1861.
Canan, Chales, sergeant; age, 30; mustered in, August 7, 1861; discharged, September 12, 1863.
Moore, Thomas, private; age, 26; mustered in, August 7, 1861; discharged, March 28, 1863, D.
Sisson, David S., private; age, 22; mustered in, August 7, 1861.
Boyd, Levi, musician; age, 44; mustered in, August 7, 1861; discharged, October 18, 1862, D.
Lowery, Abraham, private; age, 26; mustered in, August 7, 1861.
Ramsey, Milton R., wagn'r; age, 32; mustered in, August 7, 1861; dischaged, February 2, 1862, D.
Ashby, James, private; age, 18; mustered in, August 7, 1861.
Alltop, George W., private; age, 31; mustered in, August 7, 1861.
Baldwin, Francis W. H., corporal; age, 20; mustered in, August 7, 1861; discharged, July 16, 1864.
Barnett, Jesse L., corporal; age, 22; mustered in, August 7, 1861; discharged, October 27, 1864.
Chambers, James A., private; age, 20; mustered in, August 7, 1861; discharged, July 1, 1865.
Chippie, Samuel W., private; age, 40; mustered in, August 7, 1861; discharged, February 28, 1863, D.
Chambers, Calbert D., private; age, 34; mustered in, August 7, 1861; discharged, January 5, 1863.
Cowel, Julius, private; age, 18; mustered in, August 7, 1861; discharged, February 13, 1863.
Chambers, Hamilton, private; age, 18; mustered in, August 7, 1861; discharged, November 14, 1862, D.
Crow, George, private; age, 18; mustered in, August 7, 1861; discharged, July 1, 1865.
Cooper, Samuel H., private; age, 18; mustered in, August 7, 1861; discharged, July 1, 1865.
Clark, Thomas, private; age, 22; mustered in, August 7, 1861; discharged, July 1, 1865.
Clouston, James, private; age, 20; mustered in, August 7, 1861; discharged, July 1, 1865.

HISTORY OF MARSHALL COUNTY, W. VA. 213

Clark, William H., private; age, 19; mustered in, August 7, 1861; discharged, July 1, 1865.
Clark, Asa, private; age, 18; mustered in, August 7, 1861; discharged, Jully 1, 1865.
Coe, John, private; age, 43; mustered in, August 7, 1861; discharged, July 1, 1865.
Dougherty, Chas., private; age, 38; mustered in, August 7, 1861; discharged, November 14, 1862, D.
Davis, George W., private; age, 22; mustered in, August 7, 1861; discharged, July 1, 1865.
Delaney, Jonathan, private; age, 19; August 7, 1861; discharged, July 1, 1865.
Davis, James, private; age, 18; mustered in, August 7, 1861; discharged, July 1, 1865.
Emory, Hiram, private; age, 21; mustered in, August 7, 1861; discharged, July 3, 1863, D.
Fry, Abraham, sergeant; age, 27; mustered in, August 7, 1861; discharged, August 25, 1864.
Fry, William H., sergeant; age, 19; mustered in, August 7, 1861; discharged, September 12, 1863.
Fletcher, Thomas, corporal; age, 19; mustered in, August 7, 1861; discharged, May 3, 1863.
Grunnell, Levi, private; age, 44; mustered in, August 7, 1861; discharged, October 18, 1862, D.
Grandstaff, Wm. H., private; age, 18; mustered in, August 7, 1861; discharged, July 1, 1865.
Gray, Elias, W., private; age, 26; mustered in, August 7, 1861; discharged, July 1, 1865.
Grim, Lebbeus, private; age, 25; mustered in, August 7, 1861; discharged, January 8, 1863, D.
Crow, Andrew J., private; age, 19; mustered in, August 7, 1861; discharged, July 1, 1865.

(D) following the date of discharge indicates that the soldier discharged was physically unable for military duty.

Captain Thomas Morris resigned on the 12th of October, 1862, to accept promotion to the rank of Lieutenant Colonel, Fifteenth W. Va. Infantry, and was killed in action at Snickers Gap.

Samuel Kraus was promoted to captain and mustered out at the expiration of term of service.

James M. Hendershot deserted in May, 1862.

George W. Chambers enlisted in Battery C., U. S. Artillery.

Brice Howard Tarr was promoted to Second Lieutenant in Company F., May 8, 1865.

Samuel Good died December 6, 1862.

George Good died December 24, 1862.

William Stewart was killed in action at Gettysburg, July 2, 1863.

Martin L. Scott was killed in action at Antietam, September 17, 1862.

Robert Sherman was killed in action at Antietam, September 17, 1862.

Cornelius Vanderhoof was transferred to V. R. C.

Oliver Parker died October 30, 1862.

Thomas Good was wounded but date not given.

David Hunt lost an arm but no particulars are given.

Martin S. Myers was promoted to Second Lieutenant, May 29, 1865.

James Prickett was promoted to Second Lieutenant, June 19, 1862, and mustered out from wounds received at Fredericksburg, Va., February 3, 1863.

John Masters was mustered out by reason of consolidation of regiment.

Christian S. Fry deserted May 17, 1862.

Frederick Bruhn was transferred to Battery C., 4th U. S. Artillery, October 22, 1862, and killed by cars at Glen Easton, W. Va., 1865.

A. W. Hendershot was killed in action at Cold Harbor, June 3, 1864.

David S. Sisson died of wounds received at Fredericksburg, February 13, 1862.

Abraham Lowery was killed in action at Fredericksburg, December 13, 1862.

James Ashby died of disease October 19, 1864.

George W. Altop died of wounds received at Locust Grove, June 23, 1864.

Francis W. H. Baldwin was promoted to First Lieutenant October 27, 1864; promoted to Captain, February 6, 1865, and promoted to Lieutenant Colonel.

Jesse L. Barnett was promoted to Second Lieutenant, February 18, 1865, and promoted to Captain.

James Davis was killed in action at Gettysburg, July 3, 1863.

Abraham Fry was killed in action August 25, 1864.

William H. Fry was mustered out by reason of consolidation.

Hiram Walton was wounded.

Mathew Masters was killed in action May 12, 1864.

George W. Moose died of disease March 2, 1864.

James Rush was killed in action May 12, 1864.

Jacob Miller was transferred to Battery C., 4th U. S. Artillery.

HISTORY OF MARSHALL COUNTY, W. VA. 215

Thomas Fletcher was killed in action at Chancellorsville, Virginia, May 3, 1863.

ROLL of Company A of the Eleventh Regiment of West Virginia Volunteer Infantry enlisted in Marshall County, June, 1861.

1—Cummins, William, captain; age, 27; mustered in, June 1, 1863; discharged, June 17, 1865.
2—Mountz, Andrew, first lieutenant; age, 23; mustered in, September 12, 1863; discharged, June 17, 1865.
3—Ayers, Michael A., second lieutenant; age, 21; mustered in, November 5, 1864; discharged, June 17, 1865.
4—Purdy, Geo. H., sergeant; age, 22; mustered in, March 21, 1864; discharged, June 17, 1865; veteran.
5—Lemasters, A. W., sergeant; age, 29; mustered in, January 2, 1864; discharged, June 17, 1865.
6—Reed, Oscar, sergeant; age, 20; mustered in, February 12, 1864; discharged, June 17, 1865.
7—Cole, John S., sergeant; age, 19; mustered in, August 11, 1863; discharged, June 17, 1865.
8—Gossett, John T., sergeant; age, 26; mustered in, January 3, 1864; discharged, June 17, 1865; veteran.
9—Villars, James, corporal; age, 25; mustered in, February 1, 1864; discharged, June 17, 1865.
10—Henry, Robert S., corporal; age, 23; mustered in, January 27, 1863; discharged, June 17, 1865.
11—Kelley, Amos, corporal; age, 35; mustered in, August 20, 1862; discharged, June 17, 1865.
12—Leach, Abraham, corporal; age, 19; mustered in, May 7, 1863; discharged, June 17, 1865.
13—Greer, John, corporal; age, 25; mustered in, December 26, 1863; discharged, June 17, 1865.
14—Smith, Joseph D., corporal; age, 21; mustered in, August 11, 1863; discharged, June 17, 1865.
15—Long, Lewis, corporal; age, 21; mustered in, February 1, 1864; discharged, June 17, 1865; veteran.
16—Smith, Arnold, musician; age, 15; mustered in, August 11, 1863; discharged, June 17, 1865.
17—Gwynn, Thomas, wgn'r; age, 30; mustered in, March 1, 1864; discharged, June 17, 1865; veteran.
18—Baker, James, private; age, 27; mustered in, March 1, 1864; discharged, June 17, 1865.
19—Ballard, John D., private; age, 29; mustered in, September 21, 1862; discharged, June 17, 1865.
20—Barger, Jackson L., private; age, 32; mustered in, December 26, 1863; discharged, June 17, 1865.
21—Bell, Israel J., private; age, 25; mustered in, February 8, 1864; discharged, June 17, 1865.

HISTORY OF MARSHALL COUNTY, W. VA.

22—Biddle, John F., private; age, 22; mustered in, March 1, 1864; discharged, June 17, 1865.
23—Cunningham, W. R., private; age, 20; mustered in, February 23, 1864; discharged, June 17, 1865; veteran.
24—Chapman, Geo. W., private; age, 25; mustered in, December 28, 1863; discharged, June 17, 1865.
25—Cooper, William, private; age, 21; mustered in, August 11, 1863; discharged, June 17, 1865.
26—Cunningham, E. J., private; age, 18; mustered in, December 26, 1863; discharged, June 17, 1865.
27—Coplinger, William, private; age, 18; mustered in, February 23, 1864; discharged, June 17, 1865.
28—Collett, Chester, private; age, 18; mustered in, September 5, 1864; discharged, June 17, 1865.
29—Drake, Samuel, private; age, 22; mustered in, December 28, 1864; discharged, June 17, 1865.
30—Deems, George, private; age, 18; mustered in, September 21, 1862; discharged, June 17, 1865.
31—Davis, Charles W., private; age, 53; mustered in, September 21, 1862; discharged, June 17, 1865.
32—Brown, Edward A., private; age, 18; mustered in, August 11, 1863; discharged, June 17, 1865.
33—Exline, John, private; age, 28; mustered in, September 21, 1862; discharged, June 17, 1865.
34—Elliott, Charles W., private; age, 18; mustered in, December 26, 1863; discharged, June 17, 1865.
35—Gump, James, private; age, 26; mustered in, December 28, 1863; discharged, June 17, 1865; veteran.
36—Gump, Daniel S., private; age, 27; mustered in, December 26, 1863; discharged, June 17, 1865.
37—Griffin, Wm. H., private; age, 20; mustered in, August 11, 1863; discharged, June 17, 1865.
38—Henderson, Isaac M., private; age, 18; mustered in, December 28, 1863; discharged, June 17, 1865.
39—Hind, David R., private; age, 18; mustered in, December 28, 1863; discharged, June 17, 1865.
40—Haggerty, Jas. G., private; age, 35; mustered in, December 28, 1863; discharged, June 17, 1865.
41—Howard, Arthur F., private; age, 18; mustered in December 28, 1863; discharged, June 17, 1865.
42—Harden, Burr, private; age, 30; mustered in, August 11, 1863; discharged, June 17, 1865.
43—James, Geo. C., private; age, 46; mustered in, September 21, 1862; discharged, June 17, 1865.
44—James, Geo. L., private; age, 18; mustered in, March 1, 1864; discharged, June 17, 1865.

HISTORY OF MARSHALL COUNTY, W. VA.   217

45—Kimble, Daniel, private; age, 23; mustered in, December 26, 1863; discharged, June 17, 1865.
46—Keener, David, private; age, 44; mustered in, August 11, 1863; discharged, June 17, 1865.
47—Kerwood, Jas. P., private; age, 20; mustered in, August 11, 1863; discharged, June 17, 1865.
48—Kerwood, Thomas, private; age, 18; mustered in, December 26, 1863; discharged, June 17, 1865.
49—Kelley, Alex, private; age, 28; mustered in, September 21, 1862; discharged, June 17, 1865.
50—Loufman, John, private; age, 18; mustered in, March 23, 1864; discharged, June 17, 1865.
51—Lyons, Geo. W., private; age, 24; mustered in, December 26, 1863; discharged, June 17, 1865.
52—McWilliams, F. M., private; age, 22; mustered in, December 27, 1863; discharged, June 17, 1865.
53—Mountz, Richard C., private; age, 19; mustered in, May 9, 1864; discharged, June 17, 1865.
54—Miller, Wm. G., private; age, 23; mustered in, March 1, 1864; discharged, June 17, 1865.
55—Morgan, Jas. B., private; age, 21; mustered in, March 1, 1864; discharged, June 17, 1865.
56—Nash, William, private; age, 20; mustered in, August 11, 1863; discharged, June 17, 1865.
57—Nixon, Benj. F., private; age, 18; mustered in, December 26, 1863; discharged, June 17, 1865.
58—Plum, Joseph, private; age, 18; mustered in, August 11, 1863; discharged, June 17, 1865.
59—Plum, John W., private; age, 18; mustered in, December 26, 1863; discharged, June 17, 1865.
60—Pepler, John H., private; age, 23; mustered in, September 26, 1862; discharged, June 17, 1865.
61—Posthlewait, John N., private; age, 19; mustered in, August 11, 1863; discharged, June 17, 1865.
62—Prettyman, J. J., private; age, 24; mustered in, August 11, 1863; discharged, June 17, 1865.
63—Prettyman, Perry, private; age, 20; mustered in August 11, 1863; discharged, June 17, 1865.
64—Prettyman, Leven T., private; age, 18; mustered in, December 26, 1863; discharged, June 17, 1865.
65—Price, Moses, private; age, 18; mustered in, December 26, 1863; discharged, June 17, 1865.
66—Ruble, Peter A., private; age, 18; mustered in, December 26, 1863; discharged, June 17, 1865.
67—Roby, Godfrey A., private; age, 31; mustered in, March 1, 1864; discharged, June 17, 1865.

68—Sexton, Armstrong, private; age, 24; mustered in, February 24, 1864; discharged, June 17, 1865; veteran.
69—Smith, Martin V., private; age, 23; mustered in, August 11, 1863; discharged, June 17, 1865.
70—Smith, Joseph S., private; age, 22; mustered in, December 26, 1863; discharged, June 17, 1865.
71—Smith, Solomon F. M., private; age, 18; mustered in, August 11, 1863; discharged, June 17, 1865.
72—Sayers, Isaac T., private; age, 18; mustered in, August 11, 1863; discharged, June 17, 1865.
73—Sayers, Richard C., private; age, 21; mustered in, December 26, 1863; discharged, June 17, 1865.
74—Sayers, George, private; age, 18; mustered in, December 26, 1863; discharged, June 17, 1865.
75—Strickling, John W., private; age, 20; mustered in, August 11, 1863; discharged, June 17, 1865.
76—Seely, Allen, private; age, 18; mustered in, December 26, 1863; discharged, June 17, 1865.
77—Smith, Warren, private; age, 23; mustered in, August 11, 1863; discharged, June 17, 1865.
78—Showalter, E. H., private; age, 27; mustered in, August 11, 1863; discharged, June 17, 1865.
79—Stewart, Jefferson, private; age, 27; mustered in, August 11, 1863; discharged, June 17, 1865.
80—Taylor, Thomas, private; age, 18; mustered in, August 11, 1863; discharged, June 17, 1865.
81—Trout, Joseph H., private; age, 30; mustered in, September 21, 1862; discharged, June 17, 1865.
82—Villers, Albert, private; age, 20; mustered in, December 28, 1863; discharged, June 17, 1865.
83—Vincent, Wm. H., private; age, 18; mustered in, March 1, 1864; discharged, June 17, 1865.
84—Wolfe, John, private; age, 18; mustered in, August 11, 1863; discharged, June 17, 1865.
85—Wood, Newton, private; age, 21; mustered in, December 26, 1863; discharged, June 17, 1965.
86—Wood, William, private; age, 18; mustered in, December 26, 1863; discharged, June 17, 1865.
87—Hight, Bryson D., private; age, 23; mustered in, June 29, 1861; discharged, June 17, 1865.
88—Ullum, Stephen, private; age, 23; mustered in, June 29, 1861; discharged, June 17, 1865.

DISCHARGED

90—Baggs, John P., captain; age, 38; mustered in, June 29, 1861; discharged, April 4, 1863.
91—Baggs, Geo. W., second lieutenant; age, 26; mustered in, October 1, 1861; discharged, October 9, 1862; res.

HISTORY OF MARSHALL COUNTY, W. VA.   219

92—McGill, Jas. H., second lieutenant; age, 19; mustered in, September 15, 1863.
93—Carman, Benj. F., private; age, 23; mustered in, June 29, 1861; expiration term.
94—Dardinger, John S., private; age, 18; mustered in, June 29, 1861; discharged, November 26, 1864.
95—Fowler, Richard, corporal; age, 44; mustered in, June 29, 1861; discharged, January 22, 1864, D.
96—Greer, Geo. W., private; age, 23; mustered in, October 1, 1861; discharged, November 23, 1864.
97—Gump, Daniel, private; age, 38; mustered in, June 29, 1861; discharged, November 23, 1864.
98—Grandstaff, Jacob, private; age, 23; mustered in, June 29, 1861; discharged, September 29, 1862, D.
99—Loy, William, private; age, 18; mustered in, June 29, 1861; discharged, July 1, 1862, D.
100—Loy, Edward, private; age, 25; mustered in, June 29, 1861; discharged, July 1, 1864.
101—McReynolds, Wm., private; age, 25; mustered in, June 29, 1861; discharged, November 23, 1864.
102—Mooney, Andrew L., private; age, 23; mustered in, June 29, 1861; discharged, November 23, 1864.
103—McGill, Samuel, private; age, 18; mustered in, June 29, 1861; discharged, December 13, 1863, D.
104—Owens, Milton, private; age, 24; mustered in, June 29, 1861; discharged, September 20, 1862, D.
105—Price, John, private; age, 23; mustered in, June 29, 1861; discharged, August 31, 1862, D.
106—Riggs, James J., private; age, 18; mustered in, June 29, 1861; discharged, November 23, 1864.
107—Roome, John, private; age, 28; mustered in, June 29, 1861; discharged, June 20, 1862, D.
108—Sayer, William, private; age, 23; mustered in, June 29, 1861; discharged, October 28, 1861, D.
109—Schoonover, Jesse, private; age, 20; mustered in, June 29, 1861; discharged, March 20, 1862, D.
110—Turney, John, private; age, 24; mustered in, June 29, 1861; discharged, February 20, 1863, D.
111—Allen, John P., private; age, 18; mustered in, June 29, 1861; transferred.
112—Hollingshead, Samuel, private; age, 18; mustered in, June 29, 1861; transferred.

DIED

113—Bell, George, private; age, 18; mustered in, February 8, 1864; died April 23, 1864.
114—Davis, Samuel, private; age, 42; mustered in, June 29, 1861; died September 10, 1861.

HISTORY OF MARSHALL COUNTY, W. VA.

115—Lash, John B., private; age, 32; mustered in, December 26, 1863; died May 17, 1864.
116—Miller, Richard, private; age, 50; mustered in, May 28, 1863; died August 4, 1863.
117—Malsed, Wm. H., sergeant; age, 23; mustered in May 28, 1863; died, July 1, 1864; vet.
118—Paxton, William, private; age, 18; mustered in, March 1, 1862; died April 8, 1862.
119—Smith, Thomas F., private; age, 22; mustered in, Oc- 1, 1861; died October 1, 1862.
120—Watkins, Daniel, private; age, 25; mustered in, October 1, 1861; died November 9, 1861.
121—Amos, John D., sergeant; age, 22; mustered in, June 29, 1861; died July 17, 1861.
122—Baird, Stephen, private; age, 23; mustered in, June 29, 1861; died October 29, 1861.
123—Branner, Jacob, private; age, 45; mustered in, July 14, 1862; died September 24, 1862.
124—Baker, John A., private; age, 19; mustered in, June 29, 1861; died September 24, 1864.
125—Bayles, Maxwell, private; age, 19; mustered in, June 29, 1861; died September 24, 1862.
126—Duncan, George, private; age, 25; mustered in, August 11, 1863; died August 10, 1864.
127—Gray, James, private; age, 18; mustered in, June 29, 1861; died September 24, 1862.
128—Gray, Franklin, private; age, 18; mustered in, October 1, 1862; died May 12, 1863.
129—Mayfield, Anson, private; age, 24; mustered in, June 1, 1862; died September 24, 1862.
130—Mede, Benjamin, private; age, 23; mustered in, June 29, 1861; died November 9, 1861.
131—Richardson, Joshua, private; age, 27; mustered in, June 29, 1861; died October 20, 1861.
132—Rush, Isaac, private; age, 20; mustered in, June 29, 1861; died December 10, 1861.
133—Shields, William, private; age, 26; mustered in, June 12, 1863; died July 10, 1863.
134—Snider, Noah, private; age, 21; mustered in, August 11, 1863; died January 1, 1864.
135—Smith, Samuel B., private; age, 24; mustered in, June 29, 1861; died August 20, 1864.
136—White, Alpha O., corporal; age, 26; mustered in, August 11, 1863; died October 8, 1863.
136—Myers, James, private; age, 18; mustered in, August 11, 1863; died May 7, 1864.

HISTORY OF MARSHALL COUNTY, W. VA. 221

Samuel Drake was captured at Cedar Creek, October 19, 1864.

Edward A. Brown was captured at the same place and at the same date.

Isaac M. Henderson was wounded August 1, 1864.

(D) after dates indicates disability.

J. F. H. McWilliams was wounded at Cedar Creek, October 19, 1864.

William Nash was wounded at the same place, October 12, 1864.

J. J. Prettyman was wounded at the same place, October 19, 1864.

Moses Price was wounded at the same time and place.

John S. Dardinger was mustered out on account of wounds received while in the service. He was discharged on the 26th of November, 1864.

ROLL of Company H, Eleventh West Virginia Infantry, who were recruited from Marshall County:

Parriott, Geo. W., captain; age, 27; mustered in, October 21, 1863; discharged, November 14, 1864.

Pyles, B. .A C., lieutenant; mustered in, September 21, 1862; discharged, March 1, 1863.

Blake, Thomas, private; age, 18; mustered in, September 21, 1862; discharged, June 17, 1865.

Blake, Solomon, private; age, 18; mustered in, March 19, 1864; discharged, June 17, 1865.

Bloyd, Jas. W., private; age, 18; mustered in, November 10, 1862; discharged, June 17, 1865.

Crawford, Oliver, private; age, 19; mustered in, December 26, 1863; discharged, June 17, 1865.

Carothers, H. H., private; age, 27; mustered in, September 21, 1862; discharged, June 17, 1865.

Evans, Perry, private; age, 18; mustered in, February 10, 1863; discharged, June 17, 1865.

Evans, Frank M., private; age, 24; mustered in, March 5, 1864; discharged, June 17, 1865.

Fowler, Noah C., private; age, 25; mustered in, September 17, 1864; discharged, June 17, 1865.

Gorby, David, private; age, 23; mustered in, January 5, 1864; discharged, June 17, 1865; veteran.

Gillispy, Alexander, private; age, 19; mustered in, September 21, 1862; discharged, June 17, 1865.

Hutchison, Thos. S., private; age, 37; mustered in, January 5, 1863; discharged, June 17, 1865; veteran.

Headly, James, private; age, 20; mustered in, February 26, 1864; discharged, June 17, 1865.

Heatherly, David H., private; age, 20; mustered in, March 30, 1864; discharged, June 17, 1865.
Heatherby, Adrain, private; age, 19; mustered in, September 21, 1862; discharged, June 17, 1865; veteran.
Johnson, John H., private; age, 21; mustered in, January 5, 1862; discharged, June 17, 1865.
.ohnson, Abraham, private; age, 23; mustered in, January 20, 1862; discharged, June 17, 1865.
Johnson, Adam, private; age, 18; mustered in, October 30, 1863; discharged, June 17, 1865.
Jillett, Jackson, private; age, 20; mustered in, January 5, 1864; discharged, June 17, 1865.
King, Alexander, private; age, 35; mustered in, January 5, 1864; discharged, June 17, 1865.
Leach, James, A., private; age, 18; mustered in, August 10, 1863; discharged, June 17, 1865.
Whitlatch, Jesse B., private; age, 21; mustered in, January 27, 1864; discharged, June 17, 1865; veteran.
Crow, William, private; age, 33; mustered in, February 20, 1864; discharged, June 17, 1865.
Anderson, Samuel, sergeant; age, 46; mustered in, November 14, 1861; discharged, November 14, 1864.
Banning, Ephraim, sergeant; age, 27; mustered in, September 26, 1861; discharged, November 14, 1864.
Crawford, I. N., sergeant; age, 28; mustered in, October 4, 1861; discharged, November 14, 1864.
Blake, John, corporal; age, 44; mustered in, November 26, 1861; discharged, November 26, 1864.
Crawford, Jos. S., private; age, 21; mustered in, September 30, 1861; discharged, November 14, 1864.
Stern, Wm. H., private; age, 21; mustered in, September 30, 1861; discharged, November 14, 1864.
Daugherty, John W., private; age, 27; mustered in, November 14, 1861; discharged, December 2, 1862, D.
Crawford, John T., private; age, 24; mustered in, November 14, 1861; discharged, December 2, 1862, D.
Tarr, John B., private; mustered in, September 20, 1861; discharged, December 2, 1862, D.
Bloyd, Joseph C., corporal; age, 20; mustered in, February 20, 1864; discharged, May 19, 1864; veteran.*
Blake, Geo. W., private; age, 45; mustered in, September 30, 1861; discharged, February 1, 1863; died.
Daugherty, John P., private; age, 45; mustered in, September 30, 1861; discharged, September 30, 1862; died.*
Geho, Samuel W., private; age, 18; mustered in, October 4, 1861; discharged, February 11, 1862; killed.

HISTORY OF MARSHALL COUNTY, W. VA.

Pyles, Wm. H., private; age, 28; mustered in, November 14, 1861; discharged, August 11, 1864; died.

Whitlatch, Noah, private; age, 20; mustered in, February 25, 1864; discharged, August 4, 1864; veteran.*

James, Ephraim, private; age, 18; mustered in, September 21, 1862; discharged, October 25, 1862; deserted.

(*) Died at dates given.

ROLL of Company A of the Twelfth West Virginia Volunteer Infantry recruited at Moundsville, August, 1862:

1—Burley, Will J., captain; age, 22; mustered in, November 20, 1864; discharged, ...

2—Rigg, W. H., first lieutenant; age, 19; mustered in, August 16, 1862; discharged, ...

3—Caldwell, Joseph, sergeant; age, 24; mustered in, August 16, 1862; discharged, ...

4—Tomlinson, Joseph, sergeant; age, 24; mustered in, August 16, 1862; discharged, June 16, 1865.

5—Jones, John G., sergeant; age, 26; mustered in, August 16, 1862; discharged, June 16, 1865.

6—Mathews, C. C., sergeant; age, 18; mustered in, August 16, 1862; discharged, June 16, 1865.

7—Leach, Joseph, corporal; age, 26; mustered in, August 16, 1862; discharged, June 16, 1865.

8—Jones, Abraham, corporal; age, 21; mustered in, August 16, 1862; discharged, June 16, 1865.

9—Carr, Edward, corporal; age, 22; mustered in, August 16, 1862; discharged, June 16, 1865.

10—Jones, Geo. A., corporal; age, 24; mustered in, August 16, 1862; discharged, June 16, 1865.

11—Orum, George, corporal; age, 19; mustered in, August 16, 1862; killed.

12—Geurin, Alexander, corporal; age, 22; mustered in, August 16, 1862; discharged, June 16, 1865.

13—Crow, Absalom, corporal; age, 24; mustered in, August 16, 1862; discharged, June 16, 1865.

14—Allison, Oscar L., corporal; age, 19; mustered in, August 16, 1862; discharged, June 16, 1865.

15—Coe, Jas. W., drummer; age, 18; mustered in, August 16, 1862; discharged, June 16, 1865.

16—Auten, William, private; age, 18; mustered in, February 16, 1864; discharged, June 16, 1865.

17—Byrnes, W. F., private; age, 17; mustered in, August 16, 1862; discharged, March 11, 1865.

18—Burch, John, private; age, 20; mustered in, August 16, 1862; discharged, June 16, 1865.

19—Barnhart, B. F., private; age, 28; mustered in, August 16, 1862; discharged, June 16, 1865.
20—Baker, John C., private; age, 45; mustered in, August 16, 1862; discharged, December 31, 1864.
21—Baker, T. B., private; age, 25; mustered in, August 16, 1862; discharged, June 16, 1864.
22—Brown, Samuel, private; age, 23; mustered in, August 16, 1862; discharged, June 16, 1865.
23—Bryson, John A., private; age, 19; mustered in, August 16, 1862; discharged, June 16, 1865.
24—Crow, John, private; age, 22; mustered in, August 16, 1862; discharged, June 16, 1865.
25—Criswell, Oliver, private; age, 17; mustered in, August 16, 1862; discharged, June 16, 1865.
26—Conner, Alexander, private; age, 17; mustered in, August 16, 1862; discharged, June 16, 1865.
27—Conaway, George, private; age, 26; mustered in, August 16, 1862; discharged, June 16, 1865.
28—Cecil, Andrew, private; age, 23; mustered in, August 16, 1862; discharged, June 16, 1865.
29—Dorsey, W. H., private; age, 18; mustered in, August 16, 1862; discharged, June 16, 1865.
30—Dorsey, Bassil, private; age, 20; mustered in, August 16, 1862; discharged, June 16, 1865.
31—Dorman, Norman E., private; age, 20; mustered in, August 16, 1862; discharged, June 16, 1865.
32—Devoir, John N., private; age, 18; mustered in, August 16, 1862; discharged, June 16, 1862.
33—Derrah, James, private; age, 18; mustered in, August 16, 1862; discharged, June 16, 1865.
34—Echols, W. H., private; age, 23; mustered in, August 16, 1862; discharged, June 16, 1865.
35—Edwards, John W., private; age, 20; mustered in, August 16, 1862; discharged, June 16, 1865.
36—Flanagan, John M., private; age, 20; mustered in, August 16, 1862; discharged, June 16, 1862.
37—Gossett, George, private; age, 19; mustered in, August 16, 1862; discharged, June 16, 1865.
38—Gregg, Isaac, private; age, 23; mustered in, August 16, 1862; discharged, June 16, 1865.
39—Gamble, Wm. C., private; age, 22; mustered in, August 16, 1862; discharged, June 16, 1865.
40—Gillett, Wm., private; age, 22; mustered in, August 16, 1862; died.
41—Geurrin, Mahlon, private; age, 24; mustered in, August 16, 1862; deserted.

42—Holmes, Henry, private; age, 18; mustered in, August 16, 1862; discharged, May 28, 1865.
43—Kane, Jeremiah, private; age, 18; mustered in, August 16, 1862; discharged, June 16, 1865.
44—King, Francis, private; age, 18; mustered in, February 25, 1864; discharged, June 16, 1865.
45—Logsdon, James, private; age, 21; mustered in, August 16, 1862; discharged, June 16, 1865.
46—Logsdon, John E., private; age, 18; mustered in, August 16, 1862; discharged, June 16, 1865.
47—Magers, James A., private; age, 19; mustered in, August 16, 1862; discharged, June 16, 1865.
48—Magers, David, private; age, 22; mustered in, August 16, 1862; discharged, June 16, 1865.
49—Mathews, A. J., private; age, 18; mustered in, August 16, 1862; discharged, June 16, 1865.
50—Miller, James N., private; age, 18; mustered in, August 16, 1862; discharged, June 16, 1865.
51—Morris, Daniel, private; age, 24; mustered in, August 16, 1862; discharged, June 16, 1865.
52—Massena, Samuel, private; age, 41; mustered in, August 16, 1862; discharged, June 16, 1865.
53—McGarvy, Thomas, private; age, 19; mustered in, August 16, 1862; discharged, December 19, 1864.
54—Magers, William F., private; age, 18; mustered in, August 16, 1862; discharged, June 16, 1865.
55—McKnight, John, private; age, 34; mustered in, August 16, 1862; discharged, June 16, 1865.
56—Noice, William, private; age, 21; mustered in, August 16, 1862; discharged, June 16, 1865.
57—Porter, John S., private; age, 20; mustered in, August 16, 1862; discharged, May 3, 1865.
58—Pratt, John D., private; age, 36; mustered in, February 4, 1864; discharged, June 16, 1865.
59—McPelley, Philip, private; age, 19; mustered in, August 16, 1862; discharged, June 16, 1865.
60—Riggs, A. B., private; age, 26; mustered in, August 16, 1862; discharged, June 16, 1865.
61—Riggle, George, private; age, 18; mustered in, August 16, 1862; discharged, June 16, 1865.
62—Riggs, Alfred, private; age, 18; mustered in, February 18, 1864; discharged, June 16, 1865.
63—Sims, John, private; age, 16; mustered in, August 16, 1862; discharged, June 16, 1865.
64—Stine, William, private; age, 16; mustered in, August 16, 1862; discharged, June 16, 1865.

65—Schofield, Edward, private; age, 27; mustered in, August 16, 1862; discharged, June 16, 1865.
66—Shook, Israel, private; age, 31; mustered in, August 16, 1862; discharged, June 16, 1865.
67—Shilling, Alexander, private; age, 24; mustered in, August 16, 1862; discharged, June 16, 1865.
68—Trenter, John, private; age, 17; mustered in, August 16, 1862; discharged, June 16, 1865.
69—Talbert, John R., private; age, 24; mustered in, August 16, 1862; discharged, June 16, 1865.
70—Wyrick, J. W., private; age, 22; mustered in, August 16, 1862; discharged, June 16, 1865.
71—Winsel, James L., private; age, 25; mustered in, January 13, 1864; discharged, June 16, 1865.
72—Younken, Samuel F., private; age, 19; mustered in, August 16, 1862; discharged, June 16, 1865.
73—Morgan, Thomas R., private; age, 30; mustered in, August 16, 1862; discharged, June 16, 1865.

DISCHARGED

74—Tomlinson, Hager, captain; age, 24; mustered in, August 16, 1862; discharged, November 6, 1864, res.
75—Magruder, Thomas, first lieutenant; age, 26; mustered in, August 16, 1862; discharged, June 17, 1863, res.
76—Bier, Philip G., second lieutenant; age, 20; mustered in, January 17, 1863; promoted, killed.
77—Manning, Thomas W., second lieutenant; age, 22; mustered in, April 12, 1864; discharged, November 16, 1864, res.
78—Gregg, Gans, private; age, 19; mustered in, August 16, 1862; discharged February —, 1863, D.
79—Sims, Martin, private; age, 44; mustered in, August 16, 1862; discharged, February —, 1863, D.
80—Chambers, Morrison, private; age, 36; mustered in, August 16, 1862; discharged, February —, 1863, D.
81—Baird, J. H., private; age, 24; mustered in, August 16, 1862; discharged, June —, 1863, D.
82—Dunlap, James, private; age, 19; mustered in, August 16, 1862; discharged, February —, 1863, D.
83—Williams, C. W., private; age, 34; mustered in, August 16, 1862; discharged, June —, 1863, D.
84—Argo, Wm., private; age, 28; mustered in, August 16, 1862; discharged, June 13, 1864, D.
85—Scantling, John, private; age, 48; mustered in, August 16, 1862; transferred, V. R. C.

DIED

86—Hammond, George, private; age, 20; mustered in, August 16, 1862; died, February 2, 1863.
87—Moslander, Wm., private; age, 24; mustered in, August 16, 1862; died, February 7, 1863.
88—Criswell, John A., private; age, 29; mustered in, December 4, 1863; killed, May 15, 1864.
89—Leach, Wm. H., first lieutenant; age, 21; mustered in, August 16, 1862; killed, June 5, 1864.
90—Boyd, R. G., private; age, 18; mustered in, August 16, 1862; killed, June 5, 1864.
91—Jones, George L., private; age, 22; mustered in, August 16, 1862; killed, June 5, 1864.
92—Manning, Louis, private; age, 30; mustered in, August 16, 1862; killed, June 5, 1864.
93—Turner, Thomas M., private; age, 17; mustered in, August 16, 1862; died, July 11, 1864.
94—Stine, Jacob, private; age, 23; mustered in, August 16, 1862; died, August 10, 1864.
95—Kempfher, August, private; age, 23; mustered in, August 16, 1862; killed, September 3, 1864.
96—Holms, Peter, private; age, 18; mustered in, August 16, 1862; died, July 4, 1863.
97—Coe, Isaac, private; age, 39; mustered in, August 16, 1862; died, November .., 1863.
98—Brockway, Thomas, private; age, 22; mustered in, August 16, 1862; died, November 22, 1863.
99—James, Isaac, private; age, 39; mustered in, August 16, 1862; died, December .., 1863.

Will J. Burley was mustered in as second lieutenant, August 16, 1862, and was promoted to first lieutenant, February 3, 1863, and promoted to major, January 25, 1865.

W. H. Riggs was commissioned first lieutenant, December 16, 1864.

Joseph Caldwell was wounded at Winchester, Virginia, July 24, 1864, and promoted to second lieutenant, December 16, 1864, and killed in action at Fort Gregg, Va.

John G. Jones was wounded at Piedmont, Va., June 5, 1864.

W. F. Byrnes was wounded in a hand at Winchester, Va., June 15, 1863, and discharged on account of the wound.

Henry Holmes was wounded at New Market, Va., May 15, 1864.

Thomas McGarvey had a hand shot off in an engagement at Strasburg, Va., May, 1864.

John S. Porter died at Fortress Monroe at a general hospital from the effect of a gunshot wound received in action April 2, 1865.

Philip McPelley was wounded at Snicker's Ferry, Va., July 18, 1864.

John R. Talbert was wounded at New Market, Va., May 15, 1864.

Thomas R. Morgan was wounded at Snicker's Ferry, Va., July 15, 1864.

Philip G. Bier was promoted to captain and to A. A. G., April, 1864, and killed at Cedar Creek, October 19, 1864.

Wm. H. Leach, R. G. Boyd, George L. Jones, Louis Manning and John A. Criswell were killed on June 5, 1864, at Piedmont.

August Kempfher was killed at Berryville, Va., September 3, 1864.

Thomas M. Turner died of wounds, July 11, 1864, at Staunton, Va.

Corporal George Orum was killed at Fort Gregg near Petersburg, Va., on April 2, 1865.

ROLL of Company B, Twelfth Regiment of West Virginia, Volunteer Infantry, recruited in Marshall County, August, 1862:

1—Roberts, John C., captain; age, 27; mustered in, January 25, 1863; mustered out, June 16, 1865.
2—Wallace, Henry C., first lieutenant; age, 19; mustered in, August 20, 1862; mustered out, June 16, 1865.
3—Anshutz, Henry T., second lieutenant; age, 23; mustered in, February 17, 1863; mustered out, June 16, 1865.
4—Kimmins, Wm. R., sergeant; age, 36; mustered in, August 20, 1862; mustered out, June 16, 1865.
5—Games, Alfred, sergeant; age, 35; mustered in, August 20, 1862; mustered out, June 16, 1865.
6—Bryson, Abraham, sergeant; age, 31; mustered in, August 20, 1862; mustered out, June 16, 1865.
7—Blake, Thomas, sergeant; age, 24; mustered in, August 20, 1862; mustered out, June 16, 1865.
8—Fletcher, David A., sergeant; age, 40; mustered in, August 20, 1862; died, February 6, 1865.
9—Reed, Ezra M., corporal; age, 25; mustered in, September 20, 1862; died, October 17, 1864.
10—Reed, Josephus, corporal; age, 25; mustered in, February 8, 1863; died, July 17, 1864.
11—Manning, Wm. M., corporal; age, 18; mustered in, September, 1862; mustered out, June 16, 1865.

HISTORY OF MARSHALL COUNTY, W. VA.

12—Coffield, Wm. M., corporal; age, 22; mustered in, August 20, 1862; mustered out, June 16, 1865.
13—Marple, George, corporal; age, 18; mustered in, September, 1862; mustered out, June 16, 1865.
14—Allen, Leander, corporal; age, 21; mustered in, August 20, 1862; mustered out, June 16, 1865.
15—Whetzal, Martin, corporal; age, 25; mustered in, August 20, 1862; mustered out, June 16, 1865.
16—Harbinson, John W., corporal; age, 19; mustered in, August 20, 1862; mustered out, June 16, 1865.
17—Allman, Joshua, private; age, 44; mustered in, September .., 1862; mustered out, June 16, 1865.
18—Anderson, Joseph H., private; age, 18; mustered in, August 20, 1862; mustered out, June 16, 1865.
19—Blake, Joseph, private; age, 26; mustered in, September, 1862; mustered out, June 16, 1865.
20—Blair, James M., private; age, 21; mustered in, August 20, 1862; mustered out, June 16, 1865.
21—Burris, John W., private; age, 20; mustered in, August 20, 1862; mustered out, June 16, 1865.
22—Booth, John J., private; age, 21; mustered in, August 20, 1862; wounded.
23—Bonar, Wm. N., private; age, 18; mustered in, August 20, 1862; mustered out, June 16, 1865.
24—Burch, James, private; age, 34; mustered in, August 20, 1862; mustered out, June 16, 1865.
25—Crow, Henry, private; age, 32; mustered in, August 20, 1862; mustered out, June 16, 1865.
26—Coulter, Andrew, private; age, 28; mustered in, August 20, 1862; mustered out, June 16, 1865.
27—Coffman, Adam, private; age, 27; mustered in, August 20, 1862; mustered out, June 16, 1865.
28—Cecil, Geo. W., private; age, 18; mustered in, August 20, 1862; mustered out, June 16, 1865.
29—Collins, Wm. H., private; age, 24; mustered in, August 20, 1862; mustered out, June 16, 1865.
30—Clayton, John W., private; age, 20; mustered in, January 14, 1864; mustered out, June 16, 1865.
31—Criswell, Charles, private; age, 23; mustered in, January 14, 1864; mustered out, June 16, 1865.
32—Criswell, Wm. H., private; age, 18; mustered in, January 8, 1864; mustered out, June 16, 1865.
33—Criswell, John C., private; age, 20; mustered in, January 8, 1864; mustered out, June 16, 1865.
34—Craig, Samuel, private; age, 20; mustered in, August 20, 1862; mustered out, June 16, 1865.

35—Evans, William, private; age, 18; mustered in, August 20, 1862; mustered out, June 16, 1865.
36—Francis, Emanuel, private; age, 43; mustered in, August 20, 1862; mustered out, June 16, 1865.
37—Francis, Joseph T., private; age, 20; mustered in, August 20, 1862; mustered out, April 28, 1865, D.
38—Fuller, Geo. W., private; age, 29; mustered in, August 20, 1862; mustered out, June 16, 1865.
39—Goodrich, Nelson, private; age, 44; mustered in, August 20, 1862; mustered out, June 16, 1865.
40—Goodrich, Nathan D., private; age, 42; mustered in, September, 1862; mustered out, June 16, 1865.
41—Goodrich, T. M., private; age, 18! mustered in, August 20, 1862; mustered out, June 16, 1865.
42—Goodrich, Franklin, private; age, 19; mustered in, August 20, 1862; mustered out, June 16, 1865.
43—Griffith, Benjamin, private; age, 40; mustered in, August 20, 1862; mustered out, June 16, 1865.
44—Griffith, Amos, private; age, 18; mustered in, August 20, 1862; mustered out, June 16, 1865.
45—Griffith, John, private; age, 18; mustered in, August 20, 1862; mustered out, June 16, 1865.
46—Greathouse, Amos, private; age, 30; mustered in, August 20, 1862; mustered out, June 16, 1865.
47—Greathouse, John, private; age, 19; mustered in, August 20, 1862; mustered out, June 16, 1865.
48—Greathouse, Hiram, private; age, 18; mustered in, August 20, 1862; mustered out, June 16, 1865.
49—Greathouse, Thomas, private; age, 21; mustered in, March 11, 1864; mustered out, June 16, 1865.
50—Hollingshead, Venus, private; age, 33; mustered in, August 20, 1862; mustered out, June 16, 1865.
51—Henry, Robert A., private; age, 23; mustered in, August 20, 1862; mustered out, June 16, 1865.
52—Hartzell, John, private; age, 18; mustered in, August 20, 1862; mustered out, June 16, 1865.
53—Johnston, John W., private; age, 19; mustered in, August 20, 1862; mustered out, June 16, 1865.
54—Knapp, Andrew, private; age, 34; mustered in, August 20, 1862; mustered out, June 16, 1865.
55—Moore, John L., private; age, 40; mustered in, August 20, 1862; mustered out, June 16, 1865.
56—Kidder, Ira, private; age, 25; mustered in, February 19, 1864; mustered out, June 16, 1865.
57—Miner, Alexander, private; age, 34; mustered in, August 20, 1862; mustered out, June 16, 1865.

HISTORY OF MARSHALL COUNTY, W. VA. 231

58—Morgan, Jas., private; mustered in, August 20, 1862; mustered out, June 16, 1865.
59—Morgan, David L., private; age, 18; mustered in, August 20, 1862; mustered out, June 16, 1865.
60—Morgan, Oliver H. P., private; age, 18; mustered in, September, 1862; mustered out, June 16, 1865.
61—McHenry, James N., private; age, 25; mustered in, August 20, 1862; mustered out, June 16, 1865.
62—Manning, Jas. B., private; age, 20; mustered in, August 20, 1862; mustered out, June 16, 1865.
63—Muldrew, Andrew, private; age, 18; mustered in, August 20, 1862; mustered out, June 16, 1865.
64—Parsons, Thomas, private; age, 44; mustered in, September, 1862; mustered out, June 16, 1865.
65—Pyles, Joshua, private ;age, 26; mustered in, August 20, 1862; mustered out, June 16, 1865.
66—Peters, Samuel W. M., private; age, 22; mustered in, February 19, 1864; mustered out, June 16, 1865.
67—Ritchey, Crozier, private; age, 35; mustered in, August 20, 1863; mustered out, June 16, 1865.
68—Reece, George W., private; age, 30; mustered in, January 14, 1864; mustered out, June 16, 1865.
69—Rulong, Wm. H., private; age, 23; muteresd in, August 20, 1862; mustered out, March 12, 1865.
70—Rulong, Morris, private; age, 28; mustered in, February 16, 1864; mustered out, June 16, 1865.
71—Robinson, James, private; age, 32; mustered in, August 20, 1862; mustered out, June 16, 1865.
72—Roberts, Jacob J., private; age, 25; mustered in, August 20, 1862; mustered out, June 16, 1865.
73—Riggs, Thomas G., private; age, 21; mustered in, August 20, 1862; mustered out, June 16, 1865.
74—Reed, Dolphus, private; age. 22; mustered in, August 20, 1862; mustered out, June 16, 1865.
75—Rine, David, private; age, 18; mustered in, August 20, 1862; mustered out, June 16, 1865.
76—Sibert, Barney, private; age, 44; mustered in, August 20, 1862; mustered out, April 10, 1865.
77—Sears, John, private; age, 34; mustered in, August 20, 1862; mustered out, June 16, 1865.
78—Snider, Wilson, private; age, 22; mustered in, August 20, 1862; mustered out, June 16, 1865.
79—Sutter, Jacob, private; age, 18; mustered in, August 20, 1862; mustered out, June 16, 1865.
80—Stilwell, Joseph, private; age, 19; mustered in, February 19, 1864; mustered out, June 16, 1865.

81—Stilwell, Timothy C., private; age, 18; mustered in, February 19, 1864; mustered out, June 16, 1865.
82—Truman, Elias, private; age, 19; mustered in, August 20, 1862; mustered out, June 16, 1865.
83—Taylor, Francis, private; age, 21; mustered in, August 20, 1862; mustered out, June 16, 1865.
84—Van Scyoc, Joshua, private; age, 18; mustered in, February 8, 1863; mustered out, June 16, 1865.
85—Wilson, James, private; age, 42; mustered in, August 20, 1862; mustered out, June 16, 1865.
86—Wilson, Samuel, private; age, 20; mustered in, August 20, 1862; mustered out, June 16, 1865.
87—Wilson, Samuel H., private; age, 18; mustered in, August 20, 1862; mustered out, June 16, 1865.
88—Wallace, Wm. F., private; age, 18; mustered in, August 20, 1862; mustered out, June 16, 1865.
89—Wallace, Joseph, private; age, 44; mustered in, February 16, 1864; mustered out, June 16, 1865.
90—Robinson, Phillip, private; age, 18; mustered in, August 20, 1862; mustered out, June 16, 1865.

DISCHARGED

91—Bonar, Martin P., captain; mustered in, August 20, 1862; mustered out, January 16, 1863, res.
92—Fish, Nathan S., first lieutenant; mustered in, July 23, 1862; mustered out, February 3, 1863, res.
93—Allen, Wm. M., private; age, 25; mustered in, August 20, 1862; mustered out, February 24, 1863, D.
94—Burch, Talbert, private; age, 32; mustered in, August 20, 1862; mustered out, April 7, 1863.
95—Hall, Daniel C., private; age, 43; mustered in, January 8, 1864; mustered out, October 6, 1864, D.
96—McDonald, Jas. A., private; age, 36; mustered in, August 20, 1864, D.
97—Bush, William, private; age, 32; mustered in, August 20, 1862; mustered out, April 1, 1863, D.

DIED IN SERVICE

98—Blinque, Thomas, corporal; age, 24; mustered in, August 20, 1862; died, September 29, 1862.
99—Conley, Wm. H., corporal; age, 20; mustered in, August 20, 1862; died, December 14, 1862.
100—Standiford, Wm. S., corporal; age, 23; mustered in, August 20, 1862; died, July 24, 1864.
101—Allen, Samuel, private; age, 19; mustered in, August 20, 1862; died, February 24, 1863.

HISTORY OF MARSHALL COUNTY, W. VA. 233

102—Biles, John, private; age, 22; mustered in, February 22, 1864; died, November 29, 1864.
103—Crow, James M., private; age, 18; mustered in, August 20, 1862; died, June 13, 1863.
104—Davis, Wilson, private; age, 19; mustered in, August 20, 1862; died, December 7, 1862.
105—Griffith, Zachariah, private; age, 20; mustered in, August 20, 1862; died, June 20, 1863.
106—Giles, Hamilton, private; age, 24; mustered in, August 20, 1862; died, October 12, 1864.
107—Myers, Joseph, private; age, 24; mustered in, August 20, 1862; died, February 20, 1863.
108—Mullen, Joseph, private; age, 20; mustered in, August 20, 1862; died, July 24, 1864.
109—Robinson, George, private; age, 22; mustered in, August 20, 1862; died, February 23, 1863.
110—Richey, Andrew K., private; age, 18; mustered in, August 20, 1862; died, November 30, 1862.
111—Taylor, John, private; age, 23; mustered in, August 20, 1862; died, January 24, 1863.
112—Truman, James M., private; age, 25; mustered in, August 20, 1862; died, August 12, 1863.
113—White, Alexander, private; age, 41; mustered in, August 20, 1862; died, June 18, 1863.
114—Wilson, Joseph G., private; age, 20; mustered in, August 20, 1862; died, December 26, 1862.
115—Truman, Robert T., private; age, 23; mustered in, August 20, 1862; died, December 14, 1862.
116—Enix, Brice, private; age, 40; mustered in, August 20, 1862; deserted, 1862.

John C. Roberts was promoted to captain from second lieutenant and resigned on account of a wound received January 20, 1865.

Henry Wallace was promoted from sergeant to second lieutenant, August 20, 1864.

Ezra M. Reed was captured at New Market, Va., May 15, 1864, and died at Andersonville, Ga., December 7, 1864.

Joseph Anderson was missing in the action at Cedar Creek, Va., August 14, 1864.

John M. Booth was wounded in action at Winchester, Va., June 13, 1863, and lost a leg by amputation from effect of the wound.

Wm. N. Bonar was wounded in action at Hatcher's Run, Va., the bullet cutting the windpipe and through a shoulder.

James B. Manning was wounded at Piedmont, Va., June 5, 1864.

Wm. Standiford was missing at Winchester, Va., July 24, 1864.

James M. Crow was killed at Winchester, Va., June 13, 1863.

Zachariah Griffith died on June 22, 1863, from wounds received in action at Winchester, Va., June 13, 1863.

Joseph Mullen was killed in action at Winchester, Va., July 24, 1864.

ROLL of Company C of the Twelfth Regiment of West Virginia Volunteer Infantry, recruited from Marshall County:

1—Bartlett, Erastus G., captain; age, 33; mustered in, August 23, 1862; mustered out, June 16, 1865.
2—Roberts, Wm. L., first lieutenant; age, 29; mustered in, August 23, 1862; mustered out, June 16, 1865.
3—McCord, H. R., second lieutenant; age, 31; mustered in, November 2, 1864; mustered out, June 16, 1865.
4—Hadsall, John E., first sergeant; age, 18; mustered in, August 23, 1862; mustered out, June 16, 1865.
5—Hubbs, Isaac N., sergeant; age, 26; mustered in, August 23, 1862; mustered out, June 16, 1865.
6—Gardner, Michael, sergeant; age, 24; mustered in, August 23, 1862; mustered out, June 16, 1865.
7—Bane, Henry, sergeant; age, 27; mustered in, August 23, 1862; mustered out, June 16, 1865.
8—Ormsby, Thomas J., sergeant; age, 22; mustered in, August 23, 1862; mustered out, June 16, 1865.
9—Harris, Geo. W., corporal; age, 22; mustered in, August 23, 1862; mustered out, June 16, 1865.
10—Marple, Thomas W., corporal; age, 22; mustered in, August 23, 1862; mustered out, June 16, 1865.
11—Chambers, Benjamin, corporal; age, 21; mustered in, August 23, 1862; mustered out, June 16, 1865.
12—Knapp, Robert, corporal; age, 29; mustered in, August 23, 1862; mustered out, June 16, 1865.
13—Richmond, Wm. Mc., corporal; age, 24; mustered in, August 23, 1862; mustered out, June 16, 1865.
14—Chambers, Wilson, corporal; age, 20; mustered in, August 23, 1862; mustered out, June 16, 1865.
15—Hicks, Wm. H., corporal; age, 23; mustered in, August 23, 1862; mustered out, June 16, 1865.
16—Crouch, James C., corporal; age, 18; mustered in, August 23, 1862; mustered out, June 16, 1865.
17—Aston, Thomas, private; age, 18; mustered in, August 23, 1862; mustered out, June 16, 1865.
18—Abercrombie, W. H., private; age, 21; mustered in, August 23, 1862; mustered out, September 15, 1864.

HISTORY OF MARSHALL COUNTY, W. VA. 235

19—Briggs, James M., private; age, 30; mustered in, August 23, 1862; mustered out, June 16, 1865.
20—Bane, Jesse, private; age, 18; mustered in, August 23, 1862; mustered out, June 16, 1865.
21—Bane, George, private; age, 23; mustered in, August 23, 1862; mustered out, May 16, 1865.
22—Bassett, Jacob W., private; age, 20; mustered in, February 27, 1864; mustered out, June 16, 1865.
23—Clegg, Thomas, private; age, 18; mustered in, August 23, 1862; mustered out, May 16, 1864.
24—Clegg, John E., private; age, 22; mustered in, August 23, 1862; mustered out, June 16, 1865.
25—Crow, John W., private; age, 19; mustered in, August 23, 1862; mustered out, June 16, 1865.
26—Coffield, J. H., private; age, 22; mustered in, August 23, 1862; mustered out, June 16, 1865.
27—Conner, J. H., private; age, 22; mustered in, August 23, 1862; mustered out, June 16, 1865.
28—Crow, Harmon, private; age, 21; mustered in, August 23, 1862; mustered out, June 16, 1865.
29—Cross, William, private; age, 36; mustered in, August 23, 1862; mustered out, June 16, 1865.
30—Chambers, John, private; age, 22; mustered in, August 23, 1862; mustered out, June 16, 1865.
31—Carothers, J. P., private; age, 34; mustered in, August 23, 1862; mustered out, June 16, 1865.
32—Chaddock, J. J., private; age, 23; mustered in, August 23, 1862; mustered out, June 16, 1865.
33—Clegg, John, private; age, 43; mustered in, February 15, 1864; mustered out, June 16, 1865.
34—Clegg, Thomas B., private; age, 18; mustered in, March 15, 1864; mustered out, June 16, 1865.
35—Degarmo, James, private; age, 24; mustered in, August 23, 1862; mustered out, June 16, 1865.
36—Dakan, John, private; age, 35; mustered in, August 23, 1862; mustered out, June 16, 1865.
37—Deitz, Andrew, private; age, 19; mustered in, August 23, 1862; mustered out, June 16, 1865.
38—Dardinger, Stephen, private; age, 44; mustered in, August 23, 1862; mustered out, June 16, 1865.
39—Earliwine, Reuben, private; age, 19; mustered in, August 23, 1862; mustered out, June 16, 1865.
40—Founds, John W., private; age, 19; mustered in, August 23, 1862; mustered out, June 16, 1865.
41—Fish, Isaac N., private; age, 18; mustered in, August 23, 1862; mustered out, June 16, 1865.

HISTORY OF MARSHALL COUNTY, W. VA.

42—French, Samuel, private; age, 37; mustered in, August 23, 1862; mustered out, June 16, 1865.
43—Gorby, Josephus, private; age, 18; mustered in, August 23, 1862; mustered out, June 16, 1865.
44—Gosney, James, private; age, 18; mustered in, August 23, 1862; mustered out, June 16, 1865.
45—Grimes, James, private; age, 23; mustered in, August 23, 1862; mustered out, June 16, 1865.
46—Gray, Francis M., private; age, 21; mustered in, August 23, 1862; mustered out, June 16, 1865.
47—Gunn, Wm. R., private; age, 18; mustered in, August 23, 1862; mustered out, June 16, 1865.
48—Hagerman, Joseph, private; age, 17; mustered in, August 23, 1862; mustered out, June 16, 1865.
49—Hicks, John A., private; age, 18; mustered in, August 23, 1862; mustered out, June 16, 1865.
50—Harris, Samuel, private; age, 18; mustered in, August 23, 1862; mustered out, June 16, 1865.
51—Knapp, Alvah, private; age, 23; mustered in, August 23, 1862; mustered out, June 16, 1865.
52—Koch, Joseph, private; age, 18; mustered in, February 15, 1864; mustered out, October 26, 1864.
53—Logsdon, J. R., private; age, 18; mustered in, August 23, 1862; mustered out, June 16, 1865.
54—Logsdon, Anthony, private; age, 28; mustered in, August 23, 1862; mustered out, June 16, 1865.
55—Logsdon, J. F., private; age, 27; mustered in, August 23, 1862; mustered out, June 16, 1865.
56—Moore, William, private; age, 37; mustered in, August 23, 1862; mustered out, June 16, 1865.
57—Miller, M. W., private; age, 20; mustered in, August 23, 1862; mustered out, June 16, 1865.
58—Miller, M. D. L., private; age, 24; mustered in, August 23, 1862; mustered out, June 16, 1865.
59—McKnight, G. S., private; age, 18; mustered in, August 24, 1862; mustered out, June 16, 1865.
60—McCon, J. W., private; age, 18; mustered in, August 23, 1862; mustered out, June 16, 1865.
61—Nice, Thomas, private; age, 38; mustered in, August 23, 1862; mustered out, June 16, 1865.
62—Powell, Melvin, private; age, 18; mustered out, August 23, 1862; mustered out, June 16, 1865.
63—Ruckman, Isaac D., private; age, 29; mustered in, August 23, 1862; mustered out, June 16, 1865.
64—Roberts, John A., private; age, 34; mustered in, August 23, 1862; mustered out, June 16, 1865.

HISTORY OF MARSHALL COUNTY, W. VA.

65—Roberts, Jacob D., private; age, 18; mustered in, August 23, 1862; mustered out, June 16, 1865.
66—Redd, John S., private; age, 25; mustered in, August 23, 1862; mustered out, June 16, 1865.
67—Redd, Parker S., private; age, 30; mustered in, August 23, 1862; mustered out, April 1, 1864.
68—Richmond, J. F., private; age, 18; mustered in, March 26, 1864; mustered out, June 16, 1865.
69—Standiford, Benj., private; age, 18; mustered in, August 23, 1862; mustered out, June 16, 1865.
70—Stump, Albert, private; age, 29; mustered in, August 23, 1862; mustered out, June 16, 1865.
71—Sparh, John, private; age, 26; mustered in, August 23, 1862; mustered out, June 16, 1865.
72—Shipley, Robert, private; age, 17; mustered in, August 23, 1862; mustered out, June 16, 1865.
73—Stewart, L. C., private; age, 32; mustered in, August 23, 1862; mustered out, June 16, 1865.
74—Sisson, A. M., private; age, 30; mustered in, August 23, 1862; mustered out, June 16, 1865.
75—Shepherd, J. W., private; age, 18; mustered in, February 20, 1864; mustered out, June 16, 1865.
76—Standiford, Jacob, private; age, 18; mustered in, March 12, 1864; mustered out, June 16, 1865.
77—Sockman, F. M., private; age, 19; mustered in, February 27, 1864; mustered out, June 16, 1865.
78—Williams, Wesley, private; age, 27; mustered in, August 23, 1862; mustered out, June 16, 1865.
79—Williams, Marion, private; age, 19; mustered in, August 23, 1862; mustered out, June 16, 1865.
80—Whetzal, James, private; age, 19; mustered in, August 23, 1862; mustered out, June 16, 1865.
81—Williams, S. H., private; age, 37; mustered in, August 23, 1862; mustered out, June 16, 1865.
82—Williams, W. H., private; age, 25; mustered in, August 23, 1862; mustered out, June 16, 1865.
83—Wright, W. S., private; age, 18; mustered in, August 23, 1862; mustered out, June 16, 1865.
84—Lydick, John B., second lieutenant; mustered in, August 23, 1862; mustered out, December 25, 1862.
85—Whittingham, James, second lieutenant; mustered in, August 2, 1862; D.
86—Kirkendall, John A., private; age, 36; mustered in, August 23, 1862; D.
81—Pritchet, Wesley W., private; age, 18; mustered in August 23, 1862; D.

DIED

88—White, Milton B., sergeant; age, 19; mustered in, August 23, 1862; died, March 7, 1863.
89—Nixon, James, corporal; age, 21; mustered in, August 23, 1862; died, December 15, 1862.
90—Wayt, Allen N., private; age, 19; mustered in, August 23, 1862; died, January 11, 1863.
91—Lowe, Alexander, private; age, 18; mustered in, August 23, 1862; died, December 13, 1862.
92—Knapp, Stewart, private; age, 20; mustered in, August 25, 1862; died, June 3, 1863.
93—Hummel, Jonas, private; age, 38; mustered in, August 23, 1862; died, June 13, 1863.
94—Lowery, Benjamin C., private; age, 23; mustered in, August 23, 1862; mustered out, November 12, 1863.*
95—Workman, Benj. M., private; age, 23; mustered in, August 23, 1862; mustered out, November 12, 1863.*
96—Billeter, Aunger, private; age, 23; mustered in, August 23, 1862; mustered out, January 27, 1864.*

The three names followed by (*) deserted at the dates given above.

H. R. McCord was promoted from sergeant major November 2, 1864.

W. H. Abercrombie died a prisoner at Andersonville, Ga., September 15, 1864.

John Dakan was wounded and captured at Piedmont.

Isaac N. Fish was wounded at Piedmont.

Francis M. Gray was wounded. His leg was broken above the knee.

Joseph H. Koch died October 26, 1864, at Andersonville, Georgia.

J. R. Logsdon was killed while planting a flag on Fort Gregg near Petersburg in a desperate charge.

Parker S. Redd was killed in action at Hatcher's Run, Va., April 1, 1865.

Milton B. White died at Winchester of typhoid fever on March 7, 1863.

Jonas Hummel was killed at Winchester, Va., June 13, 1863.

(D) following dates indicates disability.

ROLL of the members of Company I of the Fifteenth West Virginia Infantry, raised in Marshall County:
1—McGruder, Daniel, first lieutenant; age, 35; mustered in, December 14, 1863.

HISTORY OF MARSHALL COUNTY, W. VA. 239

2—Flack, David E., first lieutenant; age, 27; mustered in, October 11, 1862; discharged, April 1, 1863.
3—Winters, Isaac, second lieutenant; age, 25; mustered in, November 14, 1864; discharged, June 14, 1865.
4—Dague, Frederick, sergeant; age, 22; mustered in, October 11, 1862; discharged, June 14, 1865.
5—McGruder, Thos. S., sergeant; age, 28; mustered in, December 12, 1863; discharged, June 14, 1865.
6—Reed, Henry, sergeant; age, 28; mustered in, October 11, 1862; discharged, June 14, 1865.
7—Winters, Alonzo, sergeant; age, 23; mustered in, October 11, 1862; discharged, June 14, 1865.
8—Taylor, John, corporal; age, 21; mustered in, October 11, 1862; discharged, June 14, 1865.
9—Armstrong, John C., corporal; age, 32; mustered in, October 11, 1862; discharged, June 14, 1865.
10—Ewing, Geo. M., corporal; age, 23; mustered in, October 11, 1862; discharged, June 14, 1865.
11—Winters, Harvey, corporal; age, 21; mustered in, October 11, 1862; discharged, June 14, 1865.
12—Marsh, Abram, musician; age, 30; mustered in, March 10, 1864; discharged, June 14, 1865.
13—Blake, Robert, private; age, 23; mustered in, October 11, 1862; discharged, June 14, 1865.
15—Beymer, Frederick, private; age, 22; mustered in, October 11, 1862; discharged, June 14, 1865.
16—Bruce, Nathan T., private; age, 20; mustered in, October 11, 1862; discharged, June 14, 1865.
17—Burris, William, private; age, 20; mustered in, October 11, 1862; discharged, June 14, 1865.
18—Couty, John V., private; age, 24; mustered in October 11, 1862; discharged, June 14, 1865.
19—Cunningham, Geo. W., private; age, 23; mustered in, October 11, 1862; discharged, June 14, 1865.
20—Carr, William, private; age, 42; mustered in, October 11, 1862; discharged, June 14, 1865.
21—Crickborn, Edward, private; age, 44; mustered in, October 11, 1862; discharged, June 14, 1865.
22—Chidester, John, private; age, 31; mustered in, October 11, 1862; discharged, September 13, 1864.
23—Crim, William, corporal; age, 30; mustered in, February 17, 1863; discharged, October 19, 1864.
24—Daugherty, Jas. W., private; age, 22; mustered in, October 11, 1862; discharged, June 14, 1865.
25—Daugherty, Robert M., private; age, 24; mustered in, October 11, 1862; discharged, June 14, 1865.

HISTORY OF MARSHALL COUNTY, W. VA.

26—Daugherty, John H., private; age, 23; mustered in, October 11, 1862; discharged, June 14, 1865.
27—Dague, Robert L., private; age, 22; mustered in, October 11, 1862; discharged, June 14, 1865.
28—Davidson, James H., private; age, 27; mustered in, February 6, 1864; discharged, June 14, 1865.
29—Davis, John H., private; age, 20; mustered in, October 11, 1862; discharged, date unknown, D.
30—Elliott, Joseph, private; age, 24; mustered in, October 11, 1862; discharged, September 29, 1864.
31—Gardener, Wm., private; age, 40; mustered in, October 11, 1862; discharge date unknown, D.
32—Gunn, George H., private; age, 23; mustered in, October 11, 1862; discharged, July 17, 1863.
33—Gray, Henry A., private; age, 18; mustered in, October 11, 1862; discharged, December 3, 1862.
34—Hill, Thomas, private; age, 19; mustered in, October 11, 1862; discharged, June 14, 1865.
35—Hartley, Daniel, private; age, 31; mustered in, October 11, 1862; discharged, April 8, 1863, D.
36—Jackson, Simeon, private; age, 44; mustered in, October 11, 1862; discharged, September 12, 1863, D.
37—Kantriner, Jacob, private; age, 40; mustered in, October 11, 1862; discharged, July 18, 1864.
38—Kiger, James, private; age, 37; mustered in, October 11, 1862; discharged, ...
39—Littleton, James, private; age, 24; mustered in, August 30, 1862; discharged, ...
40—Marsh, George W., private; age, 28; mustered in, October 11, 1862; discharged, January 4, 1862.
41—Marsh, John W., private; age, 23; mustered in, October 11, 1862; discharged, ...
42—Menix, Jonathan, private; age, 30; mustered in, October 11, 1862; discharged, ...
43—Moore, Franklin, private; age, 19; mustered in, October 11, 1862.
44—Nickerson, Francis, private; age, 28; mustered in, October 11, 1862; discharged, June 14, 1865.
45—Nichols, Geo. W., sergeant; age, 30; mustered in, October 11, 1862; discharged, September 19, 1864.
46—Roseberry, John T., private; age, 20; mustered in, October 11, 1862; discharged, June 14, 1865.
47—Rogers, James, private; age, 28; mustered in, October 11, 1862; discharged, April 7, 1863.
48—Sherman, Thomas, private; age, 23; mustered in, October 11, 1862; discharged, June 14, 1865.

HISTORY OF MARSHALL COUNTY, W. VA. 241

49—Turner, Samuel, private; age, 32; mustered in, October 11, 1862; discharged, June 14, 1865.
50—Thompson, Wm., private; age, 27; mustered in, October 11, 1862; discharged, June 14, 1865.
51—Workman, Daniel, private; age, 24; mustered in, October 11, 1862; discharged, June 14, 1865.
52—Whorton, John, private; age, 44; mustered in, October 11, 1862; discharged, June 14, 1865.
53—Howe, John W., Co. D., private; age, 18; mustered in, January, 1864; discharged, June 14, 1865.

Isaac Winters was promoted to second lieutenant, November 19, 1864.

John Chidester was wounded at Berryville, September 3, 1864, died.

William Crim was killed in action at Cedar Creek, October 19, 1864.

Joseph Elliott died at Annapolis, Md., September 19, 1864.

Geo. H. Gunn died at Sr. John's Run, July 17, 1863.

Henry A. Gray died at Cumberland, Md., December 3, 1862.

Jacob Kantriner was killed in action July 18, 1864, at Snicker's Ferry.

George W. Marsh died at Sr. John's Run, West Virginia.

Jonathan Menix was wounded.

George W. Nichols was killed in action at Winchester, Va., September 19, 1864.

(D) following dates indicates disability.

ROLL of Company A of the Seventeenth West Virginia Infantry, recruited in Marshall County, August, 1864:

1—Baker, Arthur O., captain; age, 36; mustered in, September 2, 1864; mustered out, June 30, 1865.
2—Parriott, Samuel A., first lieutenant; age, 24; mustered in, September 2, 1864; mustered out, June 30, 1865.
3—Griffith, Geo. W., second lieutenant; age, 20; mustered in, September 2, 1864; mustered out, June 30, 1865.
4—Robinson, John R., first sergeant; age, 29; mustered in, September 2, 1864; mustered out, June 30, 1865.
5—Fordyce, John, sergeant; age, 22; mustered in, September 2, 1864; mustered out, June 30, 1865.
6—Harris, John A., sergeant; age, 26; mustered in, September 2, 1864; mustered out, June 40, 1865.
7—Gatts, Silas W., sergeant; age, 23; mustered in, September 2, 1864; mustered out, June 30, 1865.
8—Hubbs, Geo. W., first corporal; age, 22; mustered in, September 2, 1864; mustered out, June 30, 1865.

HISTORY OF MARSHALL COUNTY, W. VA.

9—Marple, John, second corporal; age, 24; mustered in, September 2, 1864; mustered out, June 30, 1865.
10—Clouston, Wm. J., third corporal; age, 19; mustered in, September 2, 1864; mustered out, June 30, 1865.
11—Carney, Wm., fourth corporal; age, 23; mustered in, September 2, 1864; mustered out, June 30, 1865.
12—Lemasters, Isaac D., fifth corporal; age, 22; mustered in, September 2, 1864; mustered out, June 30, 1865.
13—Henry, James, sixth corporal; age, 21; mustered in, August 24, 1864; mustered out, June 30, 1865.
14—Gatts, Samuel E., seventh corporal; age, 19; mustered in, September 2, 1864; mustered out, June 30, 1865.
15—Williamson, F. L., musician; age, 18; mustered in, September 2, 1864; mustered out, June 30, 1865.
16—Conley, Jacob A., musician; age, 18; mustered in, September 19, 1864; mustered out, June 30, 1865.
17—Ayers, John G., private; age, 33; mustered in, September 2, 1864; mustered out, June 30, 1865.
18—Burley, Lindsey, private; age, 34; mustered in, September 2, 1864; mustered out, June 30, 1865.
19—Burleigh, Presley M., private; age, 35; mustered in, September 2, 1864; mustered out, June 30, 1865.
20—Baker, James M., private; age, 18; mustered in, September 2, 1864; mustered out, June 30, 1865.
21—Bush, John W., private; age, 18; mustered in, September 2, 1864; mustered out, June 30, 1865.
22—Buttler, Thomas, private; age, 37; mustered in, September 2, 1864; mustered out, June 30, 1865.
23—Bonar, James C., private; age, 17; mustered in, September 2, 1864; mustered out, June 30, 1865.
24—Bonar, Jasper W., private; age, 16; mustered in, September 2, 1864; mustered out, June 30, 1865.
25—Buzzard, Theodore, private; age, 18; mustered in, September 2, 1864; mustered out; June 30, 1865.
26—Basford, Melvin, private; age, 18; mustered in, September 2, 1864; mustered out, June 30, 1865.
27—Chambers, Eli, private; age, 18; mustered in, September 2, 1864; died, February 8, 1865.
28—Criswell, John W., private; age, 17; mustered in, September 2, 1864; mustered out, June 30, 1865.
29—Coe, Wm. R., private; age, 18; mustered in, September 2, 1864; mustered out, June 30, 1865.
30—Chambers, James E., private; age, 21; mustered in, September 2, 1864; mustered out, June 30, 1865.
31—Chambers, Amos, private; age, 36; mustered in, September 2, 1864; mustered out, June 30, 1865.

HISTORY OF MARSHALL COUNTY, W. VA. 243

32—Chambers, Alexander, private; age, 18; mustered in, September 2, 1864; mustered out, June 30, 1865.
33—Doyle, Hiram, private; age, 18; mustered in, September 2, 1864; mustered out, June 30, 1865.
34—Daugherty, Robert H., private; age, 19; mustered in, September 2, 1864; mustered out, June 30, 1865; Vet.
35—Daugherty, John W., private; age, 29; mustered in, September 2, 1864; mustered out, June 30, 1865.
36—Duncan, John, private; age, 37; mustered in, September 2, 1864; mustered out, June 30, 1865.
37—Earnest, Isaac, private; age, 41; mustered in, September 2, 1864; mustered out, June 30, 1865.
38—Earnest, Peter, private; age, 22; mustered in, September 2, 1864; mustered out, June 30, 1865.
39—Earliwine, Joseph, private; age, 19; mustered in, September 2, 1864; mustered out, June 20, 1865.
40—Earliwine, Ebenezer, private; age, 20; mustered in, September 2, 1864; mustered out, June 30, 1865.
41—Earliwine, Stewart, private; age, 19; mustered in, September 2, 1864; mustered out, June 30, 1865.
42—Founds, David, private; age, 18; mustered in, September 2, 1864; mustered out, June 30, 1865.
43—Geho, Jacob, private; age, 19; mustered in, September 2, 1864; mustered out, June 30, 1865.
44—Gray, Samuel, Jr., private; age, 18; mustered in, September 2, 1864; mustered out, June 30, 1865.
45—Gray, Samuel, Sr., private; age, 27; mustered in, September 2, 1864; mustered out, June 30, 1865.
46—Gilbert, Aquilla, private; age, 41; mustered in, August 24, 1864; mustered out, June 30, 1865.
47—Gallaher, Levi, private; age, 42; mustered in, September 1, 1864; mustered out, June 30, 1865.
48—Gamble, Wm. W., private; age, 21; mustered in, September 26, 1864; mustered out, June 30, 1865.
49—Hartzell, John G., private; age, 43; mustered in, September 6, 1864; mustered out, June 30, 1865.
50—Harbison, Thos. B., private; age, 18; mustered in, August 24, 1864; mustered out, June 30, 1865.
51—Harris, John W., private; age, 18; mustered in, September 6, 1864; mustered out, June 30, 1865.
52—Harris, Jas. K. P., private; age, 18; mustered in, September 2, 1864; mustered out, June 30, 1865.
53—Johnson, Franklin, private; age, 19; mustered in, September 2, 1864; mustered out, June 30, 1865.
54—Johnson, David B., private; age, 29; mustered in, September 2, 1864; mustered out, June 30, 1865.

55—Johnson, Henry, private; age, 23; mustered in, October 1, 1864; mustered out, June 30, 1865.
56—Maris, Wm. T., private; age, 44; mustered in, September 2, 1864; mustered out, June 30, 1865.
57—McCracken, David, private; age, 30; mustered in, September 2, 1864; mustered out, June 30, 1865.
58—Myers, David, private; age, 18; mustered in, August 24, 1864; mustered out, June 30, 1865.
59—Mason, William, private; age, 21; mustered in, August 24, 1864; mustered out, June 30, 1865.
60—Mitchel, Moses M., private; age, 18; mustered in, September 7, 1864; mustered out, June 30, 1865.
61—Moore, Thomas, private; age, 33; mustered in, September 2, 1864; mustered out, June 30, 1865.
62—Neely, Edwin, S., private; age, 31; mustered in, September 1, 1864; mustered out, June 30, 1865.
63—Kimball, Abraham, private; age, 20; mustered in, September 27, 1864; mustered out, June 30, 1865.
64—Lydick, Noah, private; age, 19; mustered in, September 15, 1864; mustered out, June 30, 1865.
65—Logsdon, Joseph W., private; age, 25; mustered in, October 4, 1864; mustered out, June 30, 1865.
66—Ott, John T., private; age, 26; mustered in, September 2, 1864; mustered out, June 30, 1865.
67—Potts, George W., private; age, 35; mustered in, September 2, 1864; mustered out, June 30, 1865.
68—Purdy, Rufus S., private; age, 17; mustered in, September 2, 1864; mustered out, June 30, 1865.
69—Piles, Salem L., private; age, 18; mustered in, September 2, 1864; mustered out, June 30, 1865.
70—Pierce, Wm. L., private; age, 18; mustered in, September 2, 1864; mustered out. June 30, 1865.
71—Ross, Joseph R., private; age, 21; mustered in, September 2, 1864; mustered out, June 30, 1865.
72—Ross, Matthias B., private; age, 24; mustered in, September 2, 1864; mustered out, June 30, 1865.
73—Reynolds, Lewis, private; age, 19; mustered in, September 2, 1864; mustered out, June 30, 1865.
74—Reynolds, William, Jr., private; age, 16; mustered in, September 2, 1864; mustered out, June 30, 1865.
75—Richmond, Taylor, private; age, 19; mustered in, September 2, 1864; mustered out, June 30, 1865.
76—Roseberry, John E., private; age, 21; mustered in, September 7, 1864; mustered out, June 30, 1865.
77—Reed, Alex H., private; age, 18; mustered in, August 19, 1864; mustered out, June 30, 1865.

HISTORY OF MARSHALL COUNTY, W. VA.

78—Reilly, Hyder, private; age, 18; mustered in, September 2, 1864; mustered out, June 30, 1865.
79—Sibert, Barney, private; age, 25; mustered in, September 2, 1864; mustered out, June 30, 1865.
80—Stewart, James P., private; age, 19; mustered in, September 2, 1864; mustered out; June 30, 1865.
81—Standiford, John J., private; age, 18; mustered in, August 24, 1864; mustered out, June 30, 1865.
82—Thornberry, Leander, private; age, 18; mustered in, September 7, 1864; mustered out, June 30, 1865.
83—Talbert, Anthony W., private; age, 22; mustered in, September 2, 1864; mustered out, June 30, 1865.
84—Venus, Joseph Allen, private; age, 19; mustered in, September 2, 1864; mustered out, June 30, 1865.
85—Wilson, Joseph H., private; age, 19; mustered in, August 21, 1864; mustered out, June 30, 1865.
86—Williamson, Thos. H., private; age, 21; mustered in, September 2, 1864; mustered out, June 30, 1865.
87—Wright, Josephus, private; age, 16; mustered in, September 2, 1864; mustered out, June 30, 1865.
88—Welch, Thos. D., private; age, 42; mustered in, September 2, 1864; mustered out, June 30, 1865.
89—Harris, Hamilton C., sergeant; age, 21; mustered in, September 2, 1864; mustered out, June 30, 1865.

DESERTED

90—Curtis, John, private; age, 20; mustered in, September 2, 1864.
91—Rains, Noah, corporal; age, 21; mustered in, September 7, 1864.
92—Rains, Henry C., private; age, 23; mustered in, September 7, 1864.
93—White, Edward, private; age, 26; mustered in, September 7, 1864.
94—McGown, John O., private; age, 13; mustered in, September 7, 1864.

RECRUITS

95—Bland, Richard A., private; age, 18; mustered in, March 22, 1865; mustered out, June 30, 1865.
96—Bland, Simeon, private; age, 20; mustered in, March 2, 1865; mustered out, June 30, 1865.
97—Brown, Jesse, private; age, 19; mustered in, February 25, 1865; mustered out, June 30, 1865.

98—Cole, Stephen, private; age, 44; mustered in, February 28, 1865; mustered out, June 30, 1865.
99—Davis, Abner, private; age, 27; mustered in, March 2, 1865; mustered out, June 30, 1865.
100—Earnest, Henry, private; age, 34; mustered in, February 20, 1865; mustered out, June 30, 1865.
101—Miller, Cephus, private; age, 22; mustered in, February 28, 1865; mustered out, June 30, 1865.
102—Miller, Levi, private; age, 28; mustered in, February 28, 1865; mustered out, June 30, 1865.
103—Mackey, Robert F., private; age, 18; mustered in, March 2, 1865; mustered out, June 30, 1865.
104—Midcap, Walter, private; age, 29; mustered in, February 23, 1865; mustered out, June 30, 1865.
105—Postlethwait, Joseph, private; age, 36; mustered in, February 28, 1865; mustered out, June 30, 1865.
106—Postlethwait, M. V., private; age, 20; mustered in, February 28, 1865; mustered out, June 30, 1865.
107—Postlethwait, J., private; age, 26; mustered in, February 28, 1865; mustered out, June 30, 1865.
108—Sheets, Elias, private; age, 18; mustered in, March 28, 1865; mustered out, June 30, 1865.

ROLL of Company G of the Seventeenth Regiment of West Virginia Volunteer Infantry recruited in Marshall County in February, 1865:

1—Criswell, Hanson, captain; age, 30; mustered in, February 22, 1865; mustered out, June 30, 1865.
2—Jones, Geo. McM., first lieutenant; age, 37; mustered in, February 6, 1865; mustered out, June 30, 1865.
3—Vickers, Andrew, second lieutenant; age, 27; mustered in, February 22, 1865; mustered out, June 30, 1865.
4—Dorsey, Samuel, Jr., sergeant; age, 34; mustered in, February 20, 1865; mustered out, June 30, 1865.
5—Brantner, David A., sergeant, age, 37; mustered in, February 18, 1865; mustered out, June 30, 1865.
6—Conner, Philip M., sergeant; age, 22; mustered in, February 20, 1865; mustered out, June 30, 1865.
7—Conner, Geo. W., sergeant; age, 19; mustered in, February 20, 1865; mustered out, June 30, 1865.
8—Lowe, Alexander, sergeant; age, 44; mustered in, February 18, 1865; mustered out, June 30, 1865.
9—Pearson, Benj. F., corporal; age, 44; mustered in, February 18, 1865; mustered out, June 30, 1865.
10—Wells, David, corporal; age, 29; mustered in, February 18, 1865; mustered out, June 30, 1865.

HISTORY OF MARSHALL COUNTY, W. VA. 247

11—Moore, John H., corporal; age, 21; mustered in, February 18, 1865; mustered out, June 30, 1865.
12—Hubbs, Elijah, corporal; age, 38; mustered in, February 18, 1865; mustered out, June 30, 1865.
13—Staley, James, corporal; age, 24; mustered in, February 18, 1865; mustered out, June 30, 1865.
14—Stilwell, Elias, corporal; age, 44; mustered in, February 18, 1865; mustered out, June 30, 1865.
15—Chaddock, Richard, corporal; age, 42; mustered in, February 18, 1865; mustered out, June 30, 1865.
16—Hostettler, Daniel M., corporal; age, 20; mustered ni, February 21, 1865; mustered out, June 30, 1865.
17—McMullen, John, musician; age, 43; mustered in, February 20, 1865; mustered out, June 30, 1865.
18—Bradshaw, Almon O., wagoner; age, 37; mustered in, February 18, 1865; mustered out, June 30, 1865.
19—Bowen, Job, private; age, 27; mustered in, February 18, 1865; mustered out, June 30, 1865.
20—Butler, Robert, private; age, 31; mustered in, February 18, 1865; mustered out, June 30, 1865.
21—Butler, William J., private; age, 25; mustered in, February 18, 1865; mustered out, June 30, 1865.
22—Butcher, Geo. W., private; age, 36; mustered ni, February 15, 1865; mustered out, June 30, 1865.
23—Cannon, John L., private; age, 29; mustered in, February 17, 1865; mustered out, June 30, 1865.
24—Butcher, Robert W., private; age, 33; mustered in, February 11, 1865; mustered out, June 30, 1865.
25—Conner, Wm. L., private; age, 21; mustered in, February 20, 1865; mustered out, June 30, 1865.
26—Clayton, David G., private; age, 40; mustered in, February 21, 1865; mustered out, June 30, 1865.
27—Cunningham, John W., private; age, 20; mustered in, February 23, 1865; mustered out, June 30, 1865.
28—Cunningham, Philip, private; age, 23; mustered in, February 20, 1865; mustered out; June 30, 1865.
29—Dague, William, private; age, 21; mustered in, February 25, 1865; mustered out, June 30, 1865.
30—Dobbs, William, private; age, 44; mustered in, February 20, 1865; mustered out, June 30, 1865.
31—Edgar, David, private; age, 42; mustered in, February 17, 1865; mustered out, June 30, 1865.
32—Ewing, William, private; age, 21; mustered in, February 20, 1865; mustered out, June 30, 1865.
33—Ford, Benjamin F., private; age, 24; mustered in, February 18, 1865; mustered out, June 30, 1865.

34—Gallaher, Joseph, private; age, 26; mustered in, February 17, 1865; mustered out, June 30, 1865.
35—Gatts, Wm. S., private; age, 23; mustered in, February 20, 1865; mustered out, June 30, 1865.
36—Harris, Leander B., private; age, 21; mustered in, February 20, 1865; mustered out, June 30, 1865.
37—Hall, George W., private; age, 19; mustered in, February 20, 1865; mustered out, June 30, 1865.
38—Himelrick, Alexander, private; age, 21; mustered in, February 15, 1865; mustered out, June 30, 1865.
39—Hixenbaugh, Wm. H., private; age, 19; mustered in, February 18, 1865; mustered out, June 30, 1865.
40—Hostuttler, David, private; age, 30; mustered in, February 14, 1865; mustered out, June 30, 1865.
41—Hostuttler, Lewis, private; age, 21; mustered in, February 17, 1865; mustered out, June 30, 1865.
42—Hostuttler, Jackson, private; age, 27; mustered in, February 15, 1865; mustered out, June 30, 1865.
43—Himelrick, Francis, private; age, 40; mustered in, February 11, 1865; mustered out, June 30, 1865.
44—Homer, Josiah, private; age, 33; mustered in, February 17, 1865; mustered out, June 30, 1865.
45—Hammond, James, private; age, 42; mustered in, February 20, 1865; mustered out, June 30, 1865.
46—Hammond, Francis M., private; age, 35; mustered in, February 21, 1865; mustered out, June 30, 1865.
47—Hinerman, Jesse, private; age, 25; mustered in, February 25, 1865; mustered out, June 30, 1865.
48—Jefferson, Wm., private; age, 30; mustered in, February 20, 1865; mustered out, June 30, 1865.
49—Johnson, Anthnoy, private; age, 27; mustered in, February 20, 1865; mustered out, June 30, 1865.
50—Jones, Daniel, private; age, 25; mustered in, February 20, 1865; mustered out, June 30, 1865.
51—Jenkins, Henry, private; age, 18; mustered in, February 25, 1865; mustered out, June 30, 1865.
52—King, Enoch, private; age, 18; mustered in, February 17, 1865; mustered out, June 30, 1865.
53—Lemon, Jasper N., private; age, 28; mustered in, February 18, 1865; mustered out, June 30, 1865.
54—Lewis, James, private; age, 37; mustered in, February 18, 1865; mustered out, June 30, 1865.
55—Luke, James F., private; age, 17; mustered in, February 25, 1865; mustered out, June 30, 1865.
56—Lydick, Wm. H., private; age, 18; mustered in, February 15, 1865; mustered out, June 30, 1865.

HISTORY OF MARSHALL COUNTY, W. VA. 249

57—Logsdon, Thomas, private; age, 32; mustered in, February 18, 1865; mustered out, June 30, 1865.
58—Mathews, Andrew D., private; age, 21; mustered in, February 20, 1865; mustered out, June 30, 1865.
59—Morrow, Alexander, private; age, 18; mustered in, February 20, 1865; mustered out, June 30, 1865.
60—Mane, Stephenson, private; age, 27; mustered in, February 15, 1865; mustertd out, June 30, 1865.
61—McMahon, Perry, private; age, 25; mustered in, February 18, 1865; mustered out, June 30, 1865.
62—Miles, James, private; age, 35; mustered in, February 20, 1865; mustered out; June 30, 1865.
63—McMillen, Benj. V., private; age, 27; mustered in, February 25, 1865; mustered uot, June 30, 1865.
64—Olney, Joel L., private; age, 37; mustered in, February 18, 1865; mustered out, June 30, 1865.
65—Price, Thomas J., private; age, 24; mustered in, February 18, 1865; mustered out, June 30, 1865.
66—Porter, George A., private; age, 18; mustered in, February 20, 1865; mustered out, June 30, 1865.
67—Powell, Thompson, private; age, 17; mustered in, February 21, 1865; mustered out, June 30, 1865.
68—Parriott, Robert A., private; age, 18; mustered in, February 20, 1865; mustered out, June 30, 1865.
69—Phillips, Wm. O., private; age, 37; mustered in, February 17, 1865; mustered out, June 30, 1865.
70—Rutan, John, private; age, 31; mustered in, February 20, 1865; mustered out, June 30, 1865.
71—Rine, John S., private; age, 21; mustered in, February 20, 1865; mustered out, June 30, 1865.
72—Robertson, Chas. C., private; age, 35; mustered in, February 18, 1865; mustered out, June 30, 1865.
73—Shriver, Leslie, private; age, 35; mustered in, February 14, 1865; mustered out, June 30, 1865.
74—Stump, Adam, private; age, 27; mustered in, February 17, 1865; mustered out, June 30, 1865.
75—Stilwell, Timothy, private; age, 16; mustered in, February 18, 1865; mustered out, June 30, 1865.
76—Sloan, Henry, private; age, 20; mustered in, February 25, 1865; mustered out, June 30, 1865.
77—Tuttle, Joel, private; age, 26; mustered in, February 21, 1865; mustered out, June 30, 1865.
78—Taylor, Caleb, private; age, 42; mustered in, February 25, 1865; mustered out, June 30, 1865.
79—Ullum, Alfred, private; age, 39; mustered in, February 20, 1865; mustered out, June 30, 1865.

80—Vaughn, Eli, private; age, 27; mustered in, February 18, 1865; mustered out, June 30, 1865.
81—Wallace, Isaiah, private; age, 39; mustered in, February 17, 1865; mustered out, June 30, 1865.
82—Woodburn, Charles D., private; age, 18; mustered in, February 20, 1865; mustered out, June 30, 1865.
83—Whitlatch, George L., private; age, 18; mustered in, February 21, 1865; mustered out, June 30, 1865.
84—Willison, Amos, private; age, 41; mustered in, February 20, 1865; mustered out, June 30, 1865.
85—Wolfe, John, private; age, 30; mustered in, February 20, 1865; mustered out, June 30, 1865.
86—Wychoff, William, private; age, 40; mustered in, February 25, 1865; mustered out, June 30, 1865.
87—Youst, Jacob, private; age, 30; mustered in, February 20, 1865; mustered out, June 30, 1865.
88—Yoho, James D., private; age, 18; mustered in, February 20, 1865; mustered out, June 30, 1865.
89—Yoders, George, private; age, 22; mustered in, February 25, 1865; mustered out, June 30, 1865.
90—Zink, Joseph, private; age, 28; mustered in, February 18, 1865; mustered out, June 30, 1865.

DISCHARGED FOR DISABILITY

91—Dague, Fred A., corporal; age, 20; mustered in, February 20, 1865; mustered out, June 3, 1865.
92—Cage, Samuel, private; age, 23; mustered in, February 20, 1865; mustered out, June 13, 1865.
93—Harris, Peter, private; age, 36; mustered in, February 11, 1865; mustered out, June 3, 1865.
94—Jones, Geo. McM., private; age, 37; mustered in, February 18, 1865; mustered out, June 26, 1865.
95—Rodocker, William, private; age, 42; mustered in, February 18, 1865; mustered out, June 3, 1865.
96—White, Charles, private; age, 19; mustered in, February 18, 1865; mustered out, June 3, 1865.
97—Wilson, Samuel W., private; age, 38; mustered in, February 18, 1865; mustered out, June 6, 1865.
98—Wilson, Samuel W., Jr., private; age, 23; mustered in, February 18, 1865; mustered out, June 3, 1865.
99—Lowery, Calvin F., private; age, 32; mustered ni, February 21, 1865; died.
100—Reed, James W., private; age, 24; mustered in, February 21, 1865; deserted, May 17, 1865.
101—Wood, Asa, private; age, 26; mustered in, February 18, 1865; deserted, June 6, 1865.

HISTORY OF MARSHALL COUNTY, W. VA.   251

102—Wood, Sanford, private; age, 30; mustered in, February 18, 1865; deserted, June 20, 1865.

George McM. Jones was discharged by order of the Secretary of War to accept promotion to first lieutenant.

ROLL of Company H of the Seventeenth Regiment of West Virginia Volunteer Infantry, recruited in Marshall County, February, 1865:

1—Logsdon, Wm. D., captain; age, 37; mustered in, March 1, 1865; mustered out, June 30, 1865.
2—Harris, Francis, first lieutenant; age, 28; mustered in, March 1, 1865; mustered out, June 30, 1865.
3—Grimes, Oliver, first sergeant; age, 21; mustered in, February 18, 1865; mustered out, June 30, 1865.
4—Foster, James C., first sergeant; age, 36; mustered in, February 17, 1865; mustered out, June 30, 1865.
5—Bonar, John W., first sergeant; age, 34; mustered in, February 20, 1865; mustered out, June 30, 1865.
6—Allen, John P., first sergeant; age, 24; mustered in, February 20, 1865; mustered out, June 30, 1865.
7—Knox, Wm. A., first sergeant; age, 42; mustered in, February 17, 1865; mustered out, June 30, 1865.
8—Barnett, Wm. H., corporal; age, 23; mustered in, February 20, 1865; mustered out, June 30, 1865.
9—Ritchea, George, corporal; age, 40; mustered in, February 18, 1865; mustered out, June 30, 1865.
10—Jones, Wm. P., corporal; age, 20; mustered in, February 17, 1865; mustered out, June 30, 1865.
11—Cummins, Noble T., corporal; age, 33; mustered in, February 17, 1865; mustered out, June 30, 1865.
12—Davis, Robert H., corporal; age, 37; mustered in, February 17, 1865; mustered out, June 30, 1865.
13—Quigley, Jacob, corporal ;age, 21; mustered in, February 17, 1865; mustered out, June 30, 1865.
14—Calvert, William, musician; age, 45; mustered in, March 4, 1865 ;mustered out, June 30, 1865.
15—Kershner, David; musician; age, 35; mustered in, February 15, 1865; mustered out, June 30, 1865.
16—Bowers, John, private; age, 19; mustered in, February 18, 1865; mustered out, June 30, 1865.
17—Bondy, Jonathan, private; age, 18; mustered in, February 17, 1865; mustered out, June 30, 1865.
18—Burge, Elijah, private; age, 22; mustered in, February 20, 1865; mustered out, June 30, 1865.
19—Buchanan, William, private; age, 42; mustered in, February 17, 1865; mustered out, June 30, 1865.
20—Cummins, John S., private; age, 36; mustered in, February 17, 1865; mustered out, June 30, 1865.

HISTORY OF MARSHALL COUNTY, W. VA.

21—Carney, Martin, private; age, 21; mustered in, February 21, 1865; mustered out, June 30, 1865.
22—Carney, Hiram, private; age, 21; mustered in, February 16, 1865; mustered out, June 30, 1865.
23—Capito, Christian, private; age, 39; mustered in, February 17, 1865; mustered out, June 30, 1865.
24—Connelly, Clark, private; age, 25; mustered in, February 18, 1865; mustered out, June 30, 1865.
25—Cummins, James R., private; age, 20; mustered in, February 17, 1865; mustered out, June 30, 1865.
26—Cummins, F. A., private; age, 38; mustered in, February 17, 1865; mustered out, June 30, 1865.
27—Dowler, Edward, private; age, 30; mustered in, February 17, 1865; mustered out, June 30, 1865.
28—Dermose, Robert, private; age, 30; mustered in, February 17, 1865; mustered out, June 30, 1865.
29—Enix, Wm. H., private; age, 18; mustered in, February 17, 1865; mustered out, June 30, 1865.
30—Fletcher, Abraham, private; age, 24; mustered in, February 18, 1865; mustered out, June 30, 1865.
31—Fish, Wm. V., private; age, 24; mustered in, February 20, 1865; mustered out, June 30, 1865.
32—Gosney, Richard, private; age, 24; mustered in, February 17, 1865; mustered out, June 30, 1865.
33—Gamble, James L., private; age, 19; mustered in, February 17, 1865; mustered out, June 30, 1865.
34—Hughes, Samuel D., private; age, 18; mustered in, February 18, 1865; mustered out, June 30, 1865.
35—Huggins, Eli, private; age, 18; mustered in, February 17, 1865; mustered out, June 30, 1865.
36—Harris. George C., private; age, 27; mustered in, February 18, 1865; mustered out, June 30, 1865.
37—Holmes, John, private; age, 27; mustered in, February 17, 1865; mustered out, June 30, 1865.
38—Hughes, Silas N., private; age, 20; mustered in, February 20, 1865; mustered out, June 30, 1865.
39—Harris, John C., private; age, 31; mustered in, February 17, 1865; mustered out, June 30, 1865.
40—Harris, Elias R., private; age, 26; mustered in, February 20, 1865; mustered out, June 30, 1865.
41—Howard, Thomas, private; age, 37; mustered in, February 20, 1865; mustered out, June 30, 1865.
42—Hendrickson, D. J., private; age, 19; mustered in, February 20, 1865; mustered out, June 30, 1865.
43—Harris, Elijah, private; age, 24; mustered in, February 18, 1865; mustered out, June 30, 1865.

HISTORY OF MARSHALL COUNTY, W. VA. 253

44—Higgins, Stephen, private; age, 27; mustered in, February 25, 1865; mustered out, June 30, 1865.
45—Knapp, Wm. E., private; age, 29; mustered in, February 17, 1865; mustered out, June 30, 1865.
46—King, Joshua J., private; age, 29; mustered in, February 17, 1865; mustered out, June 30, 1865.
47—Kirkpatrick, I. T., private; age, 19; mustered in, February 16, 1865; mustered out, June 30, 1865.
48—Lemasters, Jas. A., private; age, 22; mustered in, February 21, 1865; mustered out, June 30, 1865.
49—Lancaster, Thos. M., private; age, 19; mustered in, February 21, 1865; mustered out, June 30, 1865.
50—Marshall, Jas. W., private; age, 18; mustered in, February 18, 1865; mustered out, June 30, 1865.
51—Miller, William, private; age. 35; mustered in, February 16, 1865; mustered out, June 30, 1865.
52—Miller, Eli, private; age, 38; mustered in, February 16, 1865; mustered out, June 30, 1865.
53—Marple. Joseph, private; age, 18; mustered in, February 15, 1865; mustered out, June 30, 1865.
54—Marple, Wm. H., private; age, 21; mustered in, February 15, 1865; mustered out, June 30, 1865.
55—Nelson, David, private; age, 27; mustered in, February 17, 1865; mustered out, June 30, 1865.
56—Orum, Peter, private; age, 18; mustered in, February 17, 1865; mustered out, June 30, 1865.
57—Ogle, Jacob W., private; age, 22; mustered in, February 18, 1865; mustered out, June 30, 1865.
58—Parks, William H., private; age, 39; mustered in, February 17, 1865; mustered out, June 30, 1865.
59—Rayl, James, private; age, 18; mustered in, February 17, 1865; mustered out, June 30, 1865.
60—Reed, John, private; age, 26; mustered in, February 18, 1865; mustered out, June 30, 1865.
61—Stricklin, Humphry, private; age, 45; mustered in, February 17, 1865; mustered out, June 30, 1865.
62—Summerville, J. J., private; age, 41; mustered in, February 15, 1865; mustered out, June 30, 1865.
63—Williams, Edward, private; age, 44; mustered in, February 17, 1865; mustered out, June 30, 1865.
64—Winesburg, Barney, private; age, 44; mustered in, February 18, 1865; mustered out, June 30, 1865.
65—West, Isaac, private; age, 36; mustered in, February 20, 1865; mustered out, June 30, 1865.
66—Whitlatch, George, private; age, 18; mustered in, February 20, 1865; mustered in, June 30, 1865.

67—Wright, Nathan, private; age, 23; mustered in, February 17, 1865; mustered out, June 30, 1865.
68—Welling, Henry, private; age, 23; mustered in, February 17, 1865; mustered out, June 30, 1865.
69—Willard, Porter, private; age, 27; mustered in, February 18, 1865; mustered out, June 30, 1865.
70—Riddle, James, private; age, 50; mustered in, February 16, 1865; mustered out, May 19, 1865, D.
71—Logsdon, Jas. W., private; age, 26; mustered in, February 17, 1865; died, April 5, 1865.
72—Yoho, Samuel, private; age, 36; mustered in, February 16, 1865; mustered out, June 30, 1865.

ROLL of Company L of the Fourth Regiment of West Virginia Cavalry recruited in Marshall County, August, 1863, to serve six months:

1—McDonald, John S., captain; age, 26; mustered in, August 30, 1863; mustered out, March 10, 1864.
2—Harris, Thomas, first lieutenant; age, 27; mustered in, August 30, 1863; mustered out, March 10, 1864.
3—Varley, William, second lieutenant; age, 40; mustered in, August 30, 1863; mustered out, March 10, 1864.
4—Myers, James W., first sergeant; age, 19; mustered in, August 30, 1863; mustered out, March 10, 1864.
5—McFarland, Thos. B., second sergeant;; age, 33; mustered in, August 30, 1863; mustered out, March 10, 1864.
6—Collins, Thos. J., com. sergeant.; age, 28; mustered in, August 30, 1863; mustered out, March 10, 1864.
7—Crow, William, sergeant; age, 23; mustered in, August 30, 1863; mustered out, March 10, 1864.
8—Parriott. Samuel A., sergeant; age, 23; mustered in, August 30, 1863; mustered out, March 10, 1865.
9—Parkinson, Henry, sergeant; age, 22; mustered in, August 30, 1863; mustered out, March 10, 1864.
10—Cummins, Francis A., sergeant; age. 27; mustered in, August 30, 1863; mustered out; March 10, 1864.
11—Roberts, Irvin F., sergeant; age, 21; mustered in, August 30, 1863; mustered out, March 10, 1864.
12—Foster, James, corporal; age. 34; mustered in, August 30, 1863; mustered out, March 10, 1864.
13—Gibson, John L., corporal; age, 21; mustered in, August 30, 1863; mustered out, March 10, 1864.
14—Griffith, Geo. A., corporal; age, 18; mustered in, August 30, 1863; mustered out, March 10, 1864.
15—Robinson, John R., corporal; age. 28; mustered in, August 30, 1863; mustered out, March 10, 1864.

HISTORY OF MARSHALL COUNTY, W. VA. 255

16—Bowen, James H., corporal; age, 22; mustered in, August 30, 1863; mustered out, March 10, 1864.
17—Evans, George W., corporal; age, 36; mustered in, August 30, 1863; mustered out, March 10, 1864.
18—Spoon, Jacob, corporal; age, 44; mustered in, August 30, 1863; mustered out, March 10, 1864.
19—Dorsey, Cornelius, corporal; age, 22; mustered in, August 30, 1863; mustered out, March 10, 1864.
20—Smalley, Jacob, bugler; age, 32; mustered in, August 30, 1863; mustered out, March 10, 1864.
21—Harris, Jas. K. P., bugler; age, 18; mustered in, August 10, 1863; mustered out, March 10, 1864.
22—Shepherd, David, farrier; age, 25; mustered in, August 30, 1863; mustered out, March 10, 1864.
23—Ackels, George W., private; age, 19; mustered in August 30, 1863; mustered out, March 10, 1864.
24—Arnold, Willie, private; age, 19; mustered in, August 30, 1863; mustered out, March 10, 1864.
25—Arnold, John, private; age, 18; mustered in, August 30, 1863; mustered out, March 10, 1864.
26—Bowen, Brice, private; age, 19; mustered in, August 30, 1863; mustered out, March 10, 1864.
27—Biles, Fleming, private; age, 33; mustered in, August 30, 1863; mustered out, March 10, 1864.
28—Baker, James M., private; age, 18; mustered in, August 30, 1863; mustered out, March 10, 1864.
29—Bonar, James, private; age, 35; mustered in, August 30, 1863; mustered out, April 9, 1864.
30—Brock, Jacob, private; age, 18; mustered in, August 30, 1863; mustered out, March 10, 1864.
31—Crow, John W., private; age, 25; mustered in, August 30, 1863; mustered out, March 10, 1864.
32—Crow, Isaac, private; age, 18; mustered in, October 16, 1863; mustered out, March 10, 1864.
33—Cummins, John H., private; age, 34; mustered in, August 30, 1863; mustered out, March 10, 1864.
34—Charlton, Edward J., private; age, 19; mustered in(August 30, 1863; mustered out, March 10, 1864.
35—Conner, Philip, private; age, 21; mustered in, August 30, 1863; mustered out, March 10, 1864.
36—Conner, Wm. L., private; age, 20; mustered in, August 30, 1863; mustered out, March 10, 1864.
37—Carmichael, Silas, private; age, 20; mustered in, August 30, 1863; mustered out, March 10, 1864.
38—Cross, Andrew, private; age, 29; mustered in, August 30, 1863; mustered out, March 10, 1864.

256　HISTORY OF MARSHALL COUNTY, W. VA.

39—Carr, Thomas O., private; age, 23; mustered in, August 30, 1863; mustered out, March 10, 1864.
0 —Carr Joseph L., private; age. 18; mustered in, August 30, 1863; mustered out, March 10, 1864.
41—Cain, Joseph, private; age, 28; mustered in, August 30, 1863; died, April 2, 1864.
42—Clark, James, private; age, 40; mustered in, August 30, 1863; mustered out, March 10, 1864.
43—Chambers, James, private; age, 20; mustered in, August 30, 1863; mustered out, March 10, 1864.
44—Carney, William, private; age, 22; mustered in, August 30, 1863; mustered out, March 10, 1864.
45—Carney, Mathew, private; age, 21; mustered in, August 30, 1863; mustered out, March 10, 1864.
46—Carney, Hiram, private; age, 24; mustered in. August 30. 1863; mustered out, March 10, 1864.
47—Clegg, Elijah, private; age, 18; mustered in, October 16, 1863; mustered out, March 10, 1864.
48—Enix, W. H., private; age, 18; mustered in, August 30, 1863; mustered out, March 10, 1864.
49—Fitzgerald, B., private; age, 23; mustered in, October 16, 1863; mustered out, March 10, 1864.
50—Gregg, Edward S., private; age, 25; mustered in, August 30, 1863; mustered out, March 10, 1864.
51—Grimes, John W., private; age, 20; mustered in, August 30, 1863; mustered out, March 10, 1864.
52—Harris, Hamilton, private; age, 20; mustered in, August 30, 1863; mustered out, March 10, 1864.
53—Harris, John F., private; age. 21; mustered in, August 30, 1863; mustered out, March 10, 1864.
54—Harris, George, private; age, 27; mustered in, August 30, 1863; mustered out, March 10, 1864.
55—Harris, Eli, private; age, 22; mustered in, August 30, 1863; mustered out, March 10, 1864.
56—Hendrickson, David, private; age, 28; mustered in, August 30, 1863; mustered out, March 10, 1864.
57—Howard, Albert, private; age, 18; mustered in, August 30, 1863; mustered out, March 10, 1864.
58—Johnson, David B., private; age, 19; mustered in, August 30, 1863; mustered out, March 10, 1864.
59—Kelley, Hamilton, private; age, 28; mustered in, August 30, 1863; mustered out, March 10, 1864.
60—Kent, John M., private; age, 30; mustered in, August 30, 1864; mustered out, March 10, 1864.
61—Lydick, William, private; age, 32; mustered in, August 30, 1863; mustered out, March 10, 1864.

HISTORY OF MARSHALL COUNTY, W. VA. 257

62—Lydick, Noah, private; age, 18; musttred in, August 30, 1863; mustered out, March 10, 1864.
63—Logsdon, John P., private; age, 18; mustered in, August 30, 1863 ;mustered out, March 10, 1864.
64—Logsdon, Joseph, private; age, 24; mustered in, August 30, 1863; mustered out, March 10, 1864.
65—Meyers, George M., private; age, 18; mustered in, August 30, 1863; mustered out, March 10, 1864.
66—Messacher, Thomas, private; age, 18; mustered in, August 30, 1863; mustered out; March 10, 1864.
67—Manning, Samuel B., private; age, 18; mustered in, August 30, 1863; mustered out, March 10, 1864.
68—Manning, Franklin, private; age, 25; mustered in, August 30, 1863; mustered out, March 10, 1864.
69—May, Levi, private; age, 22; mustered in, August 30, 1863; mustered out, March 10, 1864.
70—Morgan, John L. V., private; age, 18; mustered in, August 30, 1863; mustered out, March 10, 1864.
71—Purdy, Rufus, private; age, 18; mustered in, August 30, 1863; mustered out, March 10, 1864.
72—Porter, Arthur, private; age, 18; mustered in, August 30, 1863; mustered out; March 10, 1864.
73—Porter, William, private; age, 23; mustered in, August 30, 1863; mustered out, March 10, 1864.
74—Pyles, Thomas W., private; age, 19; mustered in, August 30, 1863; mustered out, March 10, 1864.
75—Pyles, Jacob B., private; age, 18; mustered in, August 30, 1863; mustered out, March 10, 1864.
76—Richmond, Wm. M., private; age, 21; mustered in, August 30, 1863; mustered out, March 10, 1864.
77—Riser, Charles, private; age, 18; mustered in, August 30, 1863; mustered out, March 10, 1864.
78—Richmond, Taylor, private; age, 18; mustered in, August 30, 1863; mustered out, March 10, 1864.
79—Ray, Alexander, private; age, 18; mustered in, August 30, 1863; mustered out, March 10, 1864.
80—Stilwell, Silas, private; age, 39; mustered in, August 30, 1863; mustered out, March 10, 1864.
81—Stansberry, John W., private; age, 34; mustered in, August 30, 1863; mustered out, March 10, 1864.
82—Stewart, James, private; age, 19; mustered in, August 30, 1863; mustered out, March 10, 1864.
83—Stewart, Irwin, private; age, 23; mustered in, August 30, 1863; mustered out, March 10, 1864.
84—Sivert, John, private; age, 39; mustered in, August 30, 1863; mustered out, March 10, 1864.

HISTORY OF MARSHALL COUNTY, W. VA.

85—Terrill, Thomas S., private; age, 28; mustertd in, August 30, 1863; mustered out, March 10, 1864.
86—Varley, Robert M., private; age, 18; mustered in, August 30, 1863; mustered out, March 10, 1864.
87—Williamson, Frank, private; age, 18; mustered in, August 30, 1863; mustered out, March 10, 1864.
88—Shaw, Leroy, private; age, 19; mustered in, August 30, 1863; mustered out; March 10, 1864.
89—Lightner, James A., private; age, 18; mustered in, August 30, 1863; mustered out, October 15, 1863.
90—Terrell, Daniel, private; age, 24; mustered in, August 30, 1863; mustered out, September 15, 1864.
91—Brock, Abraham, private; age, 25; mustered in, August 30, 1863; deserted, September 14, 1864.

Willie Arnold was wounded severely at Medley Farm, Va., January 30, 1864.

James Bonar was captured at Medley Farm, Va., January 30, 1864, and died at Andersonville, April 9, 1864.

Joseph Cain was captured at Medley Farm, Va., and died at Andersonville, Ga., April 2, 1864.

Robert M. Varley was wounded at Medley Farm, Va., January 30, 1864, leg broken above the knee.

ROLL of Company I of the Sixth West Virginia Cavalry, formerly the Third West Virginia Infantry, and was recruited at Moundsville:

Purdy, Lewis B., captain; age, 20; mustered in, April 1, 1864.
Lindsey, Robert F., second lieutenant; age, 20; mustered in, January 18, 1863.
Price, Moses B., sergeant; age, 23; mustered in, July 10, 1861; mustered out, August 17, 1864.
Clark, Jacob C., sergeant; age, 42; mustered in, July 17, 1861; mustered out, August 17, 1864.
Alexander, John R., sergeant; age, 19; mustered in, July 10, 1861; mustered out, August 17, 1864.
Dunlap, Charles, sergeant; age, 18; mustered in, July 10, 1861; mustered out, August 17, 1864.
Pierce, Arthur D., sergeant; age, 18; mustered in, July 10, 1861; mustered out, August 17, 1864.
Trian, Charles, corporal; age, 31; mustered in, July 10, 1861; mustered out, August 17, 1864.
Brany, Samuel, corporal; age, 29; mustered in, July 10, 1861; mustered out, August 17, 1864.
Aston, Joseph, corporal; age, 21; mustered in, July 10, 1861; mustered out, August 17, 1864.
Shepherd, Nathan B., corporal; age, 19; mustered in, July 10, 1861; mustered out, August 17, 1864.

HISTORY OF MARSHALL COUNTY, W. VA.

Burley, Joseph A.; age, 28; mustered in, July 10, 1861; mustered out, August 17, 1864.
McPeek, Joseph B., sad'lr; age, 25; mustered in, July 10, 1861; mustered out, August 17, 1864.
Porter, James A., wagoner; age, 20; mustered in, July 10, 1861; mustered out, August 17, 1864.
Blake, Harrison, private; age, 21; mustered in, July 10, 1861; mustered out, August 17, 1864.
Blake, George W., private; age, 18; mustered in, July 10, 1861; mustered out, August 17, 1864.
Bowers, John P., private; age, 24; mustered in, July 10, 1861; mustered out, August 17, 1864.
Clayton, William, private; age, 37; mustered in, July 10, 1861; mustered out, August 17, 1864.
Criswell, Enoch, private; age, 25; mustered in, July 10, 1861; mustered out, August 17, 1864.
Davis, Adam R., private; age, 44; mustered in, July 19, 1861; mustered out, August 17, 1864.
Evans, George W., private; age, 22; mustered in, July 10, 1861; mustered out, August 17, 1864.
Gans, Henry C., private; age, 18; mustered in, July 10, 1861; mustered out, August 17, 1864.
Games, Isaac, private; age, 19; mustered in, July 10, 1861; mustered out, August 17, 1864.
Grimes, Oliver, private; age, 18; mustered in, July 10, 1861; mustered out, August 17, 1864.
Geho, Robert, private; age, 20; mustered in, July 10, 1861; mustered out, August 17, 1864.
Games, David A., private; age, 24; mustered in, July 10, 1861; mustered out, August 17, 1864.
Hurley, James, private; age, 25; mustered in, July 10, 1861; mustered out, August 17, 1864.
Hartley, Joshua, private; age, 20; mustered in, July 10, 1861; mustered out, August 17, 1864.
Hartley, Isaac S., private; age, 23; mustered in, July 10, 1861; mustered out, August 12, 1864, D.
Hammond, William, private; age, 35; mustered in, July 10, 1861; mustered out, August 17, 1864.
Hammond, Joseph, private; age, 18; mustered in, July 10, 1861; mustered out, August 17, 1864.
Leach, Sumner E., private ;age, 18; mustered in, July 10, 1861; mustered out, August 17, 1864.
Lindsey, William H., private; age, 19; mustered in, July 10, 1861; mustered out, August 17, 1864.
Luster, William H., private; age, 18; mustered in, August 9, 1861; mustered out, August 17, 1864.

McGee, Edward, private; age, 28; mustered in, July 19, 1861; mustered out, August 17, 1864.
Mosslander, Joseph E., private; age, 23; mustered in, July 10, 1861; mustered out, August 17, 1864.
Mills, James D., private; age, 21; mustered in, July 10, 1861; mustered out, August 17, 1864.
Magers, James W., private; age, 21; mustered in, July 10, 1861; mustered out, August 17, 1864.
Moore, John H., private; age, 18; mustered in, July 29, 1861; mustered out, August 17, 1864.
Porter, Abner S., private; age, 19; mustered in, July 10, 1861; mustered out, August 17, 1864.
Price, G. B. M., private; age, 18; mustered in, July 29, 1861; mustered out, August 17, 1864.

William Carr was discharged May 22, 1862, on account of disability.
Jonathan Barcus was discharged April 17, 1863, on account of disability.
Peter B. Catlett was discharged August 5, 1862, on account of disability.
Stephen Gallaher was discharged April 1, 1863, on account of disability.
Louis L. Hyman was discharged November 3, 1862, on account of disability.
Adam Helms was discharged April 10, 1863, on account of disability.
John Lightner was discharged November 22, 1862, on account of disability.
James W. Myers was discharged March 20, 1863, on account of disability.
Robert C. Purdy was discharged July 11, 1862, on account of disability.
George W. Patterson was discharged April 10, 1862, on account of disability.
William Tomlinson was discharged January 16, 1862, on account of disability.
Hager Tomlinson was promoted to captain, Co. A, 12th W. Va. Infantry, August 16, 1862.
George Thomas was promoted March 20, 1862.
Captain William J. Purdy resigned February 6, 1862.
Louis H. Smith died July 15, 1864, at Cumberland, Md., of wounds.
I. D. Bartlett died July 18, 1862, at Middletown, Va.
L. G. Geho died April, 1862, on Allegheny Mountains.
William B. Johnson was killed in action at Rocky Gap, Va., August 26, 1863.

HISTORY OF MARSHALL COUNTY, W. VA. 261

Jackson Pride died October 31, 1861, at Moundsville.
Henry J. Reynolds was drowned near Grafton, August 23, 1861.
Thomas Williams died May 22, 1862, at Rosebys Rock.

VETERANS

Daugherty, Wm. H., sergeant; age, 18; July 10, 1861; January 28, 1864; June 10, 1865.
Hanen, Samuel R., lieutenant; age, 22; July 10, 1861; January 28, 1864; June 10, 1865.
Deitz, Louis A., sergeant; age, 19; July 10, 1861; February 1, 1864; June 10, 1865.
Purdy, William S., corporal; age, 21; July 10, 1861; February 20, 1864; June 10, 1865.
Ray, William H., corporal; age, 21; September 21, 1861; March 27, 1864; June 10, 1865.
Wayt, Joseph, corporal; age, 18; July 10, 1861; February 1, 1864; June 10, 1865.
Thurber, D. A., corporal; age, 18; July 10, 1861; March 27, 1864; June 10, 1865.
Fountain, Jas., blacksmith; age, 19; July 10, 1861; March 27, 1864; June 10, 1865.
Berry, Charles D., private; age, 19; July 19, 1861; January 28, 1864; June 10, 1865.
Boran, Wade H., private; age, 18; July 10, 1861; March 27, 1864, June 10, 1865.
Dunlap, Wm. H., private; age, 18; July 10, 1861; February 1, 1864; June 10, 1865.
Dolan, James, private; age, 19; July 10, 1861; February 1, 1864; June 10, 1865.
Dilly, James A., private; age, 19; July 10, 1861; February 1, 1864; June 10, 1865.
Davis, Benj. C., private; age, 30; August 25, 1861; March 27, 1864; June 10, 1865.
Dobbs, Nathan C., private; age, 21; July 9. 1861; March 27, 1864; June 10, 1865.
Gorby, Jasper B., private; age, 18; July 10, 1861; August 28, 1864; June 10, 1865.
Johnson, John T., private; age, 24; July 10. 1861; February 1, 1864; June 10, 1865.
Lydick, O. H. P., private; age, 18; July 10, 1861; January 28, 1864; June 10, 1865.
McGill, William, private; age, 18; July 10, 1861; February 1, 1864; June 10, 1865.
McGown, Patrick, private; age, 28; July 19, 1861; March 27, 1864; June 10, 1865.

HISTORY OF MARSHALL COUNTY, W. VA.

Manning, Beeler, private; age, 23; July 31, 1861; February 1, 1864; June 10, 1865.
Nuss, John C., private; age, 25; July 10, 1861; February 1, 1864; June 10, 1865.
Purdy, Simeon T., private; age, 19; July 29, 1861; January 28, 1864; June 10, 1865.
Powell, John E., private; age, 21; July 29, 1861; February 20, 1864; June 10, 1865.

Pugh, Lewis, private; age. 29; mustered in, July 29, 1861; died, August 8, 1864.
Riggs, Jerry D., private; age, 20; mustered in, July 10, 1861; mustered out, August 17, 1864.
Sealah, William H., private; age, 20; mustered in, August 9, 1861; mustered out, August 17, 1864.
Sayers, Alex S., private; age, 28; mustered in, July 10, 1861; mustered out, August 17, 1864.
Tomlinson, Simeon, private; age, 29; mustered in, July 10, 1861; mustered out, August 17, 1864.
Wells, Stewart, private; age, 21; mustered in, July 10, 1861; mustered out, August 17, 1864.
Games, John D. Recruit, private; age, 33; mustered in December 4, 1861; mustered out, June 10, 1865.
Lindsey, Johnson C., recruit, private; age, 17; mustered in, June 1, 1863; mustered out, June 10, 1865.
Sayler, John W., recruit, private; age, 37; mustered in, July 6, 1863; mustered out, June 10, 1865.
Venus, Samuel V., recruit, private; age, 23; mustered in, July 1, 1863; mustered out, June 10, 1865.
Wilson, Ephraim, recruit, private; age, 30; mustered in, April 1, 1864; mustered out, June 10, 1865.
Tomlinson, Alfred, recruit, private; age, 27; mustered in, December 12, 1861; mustered out, June 10, 1865.

DISCHARGED

Purdy, William J., captain; age, 27; mustered in July 10, 1861; discharged, February 6, 1862.
Hunter, Hanson W., captain; age, 24; mustered in, July 10, 1864; promoted.
Lydick, Benjamin T., second lieutenant; age, 39; mustered in, July 10, 1861; discharged, January 18, 1863, D.
Carr, William, private; age, 42; mustered in, July 10, 1861; discharged, May 22, 1862, D.
Barcus, Jonathan, private; age, 19; mustered in, July 10, 1861; discharged, April 17, 1863, D.
Catlett, Peter B., private; age, 43; mustered in, July 10, 1861; discharged, August 5, 1862, D.

HISTORY OF MARSHALL COUNTY, W. VA. 263

Gallaher, Stephen, private; age, 28; mustered in, July 10, 1861; discharged, April 1, 1863, D.

Hyman, Louis, private; age, 18; mustered in, July 19, 1861; mustered out, November 3, 1862, D.

Helms, Adam, private; age, 40; mustered in, July 10, 1861; mustered out, April 10, 1863, D.

Lightner, John, private; age, 19; mustered in, July 29, 1861; discharged, November 22, 1862, D.

Myers, James W., private; age, 18; mustered in, July 10, 1861; mustered out, March 20, 1863, D.

Purdy, Robert C., private; age, 41; mustered in, December 11, 1861; mustered out, July 11, 1863, D.

Patterson, George W., private; age, 19; mustered in, July 10, 1861; mustered out, April 10, 1863, D.

Tomlinson, William, private; age, 21; mustered in, December 4, 1861; mustered out, January 16, 1863, D.

Tomlinson, Hager, private; age, 22; mustered in, July 10, 1861; promoted.

Thomas, George, private; age, 18; mustered in, July 10, 1861.

Smith, Louis H. (died), corporal; age, 23; mustered in, July 10, 1861; discharged, July 15, 1864.

Bartlett, I. D. (died), drummer; age, 21; mustered in, July 10, 1861; discharged, July 18, 1862.

Geho, L. G. (died), private; age, 20; mustered in, October 1, 1861; discharged April 19, 1862.

Johnson, William B. (died), private; age, 20; mustered in, July 10, 1861; discharged, August 26, 1862.

Pride, Jackson (died), private; age, 18; mustered in, July 10, 1861; discharged, October 31, 1861.

Reynolds, Henry J. (died), private; age, 22; mustered in, December 8, 1861; discharged, March 10, 1864.

Trueman, Thomas J. (died), private; age, 19; mustered in, July 10, 1861; discharged, August 23, 1861.

Williams, Thomas (died), private; age, 22; mustered in, July 10, 1861; discharged, May 22, 1862.

Robert F. Lindsey was promoted to second lieutenant and from that to captain, December 24, 1864.

George W. Blake was wounded at Rocky Gap, August 26, 1863, in a thigh, and died at a date unknown.

Isaac S. Hartley died August 12 in Andersonville prison.

Lewis Pugh died in prison at Andersonville, Ga., August 8, 1864, of diarrhea.

Simeon Tomlinson died July 24, 1864, in prison at Andersonville, Ga.

Hanson W. Hunter promoted to major, March 20, 1864.

Benjamin T. Lydick resigned January 18, 1863, wounded at Bull Run, August 29, 1862.

Ritchie, George, private; age, 19; July 10, 1861; March 13, 1864; June 10, 1865.
Tagg, Stewart, private; age, 30; July 10, 1861; March 27, 1864; June 10, 1865.
Tomlinson, John G., private; age, 19; July 10, 1861; March 27, 1864; June 10, 1865.
Wilkinson, James M., private; age, 25; July 10, 1861; February 1, 1864; June 10, 1865.

Stewart Tagg died at Moundsville on May 11, 1865, from the effects of treatment while a prisoner.

MISCELLANEOUS

Burgess, William, private; age, 44; mustered in, February 16, 1865; member of Co. I, 6th Infantry, W. Va.
Gorby, Jesse J., private; age, 44; mustered in, February 16, 1865; member of Co. I, 6th Infantry, W. Va.
Griffith, Joseph, private; age, 34; mustered in, February 8, 1865; member of Co. P, 6th Infantry, W. Va.
Cooper, Samuel W., private; member of Co. B, 1st Cavalry, W. Va.
Cooper was killed in action at Wythville, Va.

Members of Company D of the First W. Va. Artillery from Marshall County:
Brown, Frederick M., private; age, 20; mustered in, February 19, 1864.
Dowler, Gustavus A., private; age, 18; mustered in, February 19, 1864.
Helms, Adam, private; age, 44; mustered in, February 25, 1864.
Hammond, Thos. G., private; age, 18; mustered in, March 24, 1864.
McCombs, Jos. T., private; age, 17; mustered in, February 25, 1864.
Bird, Francis, private; age, 35; mustered in, February 19, 1864.

Company H of the First W. Va. Artillery:
Bowen, Corbly H., private; age, 21; mustered in, September 1, 1864.
Riggs, Elias E., private; age, 18; mustered in, September 1, 1864.

Members of Company C of the First West Virginia Cavalry:
Davis, John, private; age, 17; mustered in, February 8, 1864.
Mathews, S. W., private; age, 20; mustered in, February 22, 1864.

HISTORY OF MARSHALL COUNTY, W. VA.

Riggs, I. D., private; age, 18; mustered in, February 22, 1864.
Ray, John, private; age, 21; mustered in, February 21, 1864.
Shimp, W. H., private; age, 19; mustered in, February 12, 1864.

Company B, First W. Va. Cavalry:
Younken, Daniel, private; age, 21; mustered in, September 19, 1861.

Jonathan H. Lockwood was mustered into the United States service on the 1st of September, 1861, and was commissioned major and was promoted to lieutenant-colonel of the Seventh Regiment of West Virginia Volunteer Infantry.

Thomas Finn enlisted at Wheeling Island on the first day of September, 1861, in Company G, Seventh West Virginia Infantry. He entered the service as corporal and was promoted to first lieutenant in 1863; was wounded at the battle of Cold Harbor, near Richmond, Va., on June 3, 1864, from which he lost a leg.

Company M, First West Virginia Cavalry:
Israel, Jacob E., second lieutenant; age, 44; mustered in, March 15, 1865; mustered out, July 8, 1865.
Wiedebusch, August, private; age, 21; mustered in, February 21, 1865; mustered out, July 8, 1865.

Company I, First West Virginia Cavalry:
Kinney, Cephus, a private, entered the war in 1861 and served until it closed in 1865. He was in a number of battles and was wounded three times.

Samuel McMillan served in the United States Navy and was on the Battleship Cumberland when it was sunk by the Merrimac on the 8th of March, 1862, when that ironclad attacked the United States fleet in Hampton Roads.

CONFEDERATE STATE SOLDIERS

Frank Morris, William Blakemore, *Quincy Cresap, William Martin, Ephraim Owen Wells, Wm. H. H. Powell, *B. F. Standiford.

Ephraim Owen Wells served in 36th Virginia Infantry under Stonewall Jackson and later was promoted to first lieutenant in the cavalry under General Jenkins.

He was wounded in one of the many engagements in which he participated.

Wm. H. H. Powell served in the same command and was wounded in three places in the second battle at Bull Run,

* Still living 1924.

August 30, 1862; he was also wounded at an engagement at Wytheville later when serving in the cavalry.

B. F. Standiford went to Marshall, Texas, in November, 1860, and enlisted in the southwest and served until the close of the war and returned to Marshall County and later located at St. Mary's, West Virginia.

SPANISH-AMERICAN WAR

1898

ROSTER of members of Company M of the 1st West Virginia Regiment of Volunteer Infantry from Marshall County, enlisted May, 1898, for service in the Spanish-American War:

Captain, R. N. Humphreys
First Lieutenant, A. L. Hooton
Second Lieutenant, C W. Conner
First Sergeant, James Neilson
First Sergeant, Wm. F. Taylor
First Sergeant, Samuel Parkinson
First Sergeant, P. E. Conner
First Sergeant, R. C. Yoho
Corporal, Charles Evans
Corporal, E. E. Donley
Corporal, Wm. E. Conner
Corporal, Thadeus Wright
Corporal, W. E. Keyser
Corporal, W. G. Lutes
Corporal, Harry McGill
Buglers, W. E. Stultz and Clarence Echols
Wagoner, James Purtiman

Privates

Shirley Pattee
John Donley
Howard Edwards
Charles Kull
Wm. W. Wade
Mort Flanagan
Harry L. Purdy
Harry Rogers
John Mangold
Elmer Booth
Wm. S. Powell
Harry Goudy
Wm. O. Ewing
Samuel Lancaster

Charles Gamble
Wm. H. Conner
Edward Litton
John Fry
Arthur Litton
Alton Jones
Enos Bertrand
Harry Thomas
William Price
Foster Rine
Elias Charlton
Houston Henretta
B. F. Duncan
Charles Brantner

HISTORY OF MARSHALL COUNTY, W. VA.

Arch T. Martin
Charles Moser
Jesse Mathews
R. B. Koch
Mart Goodwin

George Barker
James Hagerman
John Slipner
H. M. Salters
William Marple

James Neilson was promoted to sergeant-major of the battalion and R. C. Yoho was promoted to first sergeant to fill the vacancy.

Lieutenant A. L. Hooton was detailed as ordnance officer, then as commissary officer and from that was promoted to captain of Company K.

Houston Henretta died at Knoxville, Tennessee, September 20, 1898, and was interred at Mount Rome Cemetery at Moundsville.

Roster of members of Company G of the 1st Regiment of West Virginia Volunteers, May, 1898, in the Spanish-American War:

Frank Hubbs
C. H. Wilson
Richard Bartley
Albert Ingram

George Lowe
Wm. L. Stilwell
Daniel L. Wilson
C. S. Hubbs

Members of Company D of the Second West Virginia Volunteers:

S. E. Doty   S. E. Phillips   George C. Conner

Philip Schafer, major, first battalion, First Regiment of West Virginia Volunteer Infantry.

Samuel R. Hanen, Jr., was in the United States Navy and did service on the Battleship Brooklyn.

WORLD WAR

1914-1918

COMMISSIONED OFFICERS

Major in Line Service

Freed, Horace

Captains in Line Service

Wilson, Stanley B.
McCamic, Chas.

Snedeker, Wm.
Blankford, W. B.

Lieutenants in Line Service

Ransom, Ira
Arnold, Lloyd

Stilwell, Herbert
Cope, Walter A.

Bondy, Ralph
Buzzard, Howard
Spurr, Clinton
Beer, Edwin
Proelss, O.
Stewart, Melville
Mountain, W. A.

Conaway, Edmund
Henderson, Byron
Rogerson, Bemis
Booher, Wilford
Bottome, Sterling
Peoples, Guy

Captains in Medical Service

Compton, Filmore
McGlumphy, C. B.
Crow, W. F.
Howard, M. F.

Barlow, C. A.
Lake, S T.
Covert, O. F.

Lieutenants in Medical Service

Yoho, Sidney
Streibich, J. A.
Stidger, Reed
Woodruff, Ralph
Sheets, Luther G.
Rinehart, A. B.
Ealy, D. B.
Williamson, C. D.

Steele, Byron W.
Riggs, Lawrence B.
Luikart, J. H.
Morgan, C. G.
Sammons, W. P.
Ferguson, J. H.
Roberts, Erett
McGuffy, Dr.

Gaunt, H. G., Chaplain
Lewis, J. M., Cadet

WORLD WAR
1914-1918
ROSTER OF VOLUNTEERS
Infantry

Alexander, Ralph
Burge, Patrick J.
Coffman, William
Chalk, Harry
Crim, Harry
Daily, Cecil E.
Engle, James T.
Halley, Verne
Jones, Ray
Kensle, John
Lough, Charles C.
Melott, Wm. Henry
Nemek, Louis
Ryan, Gilbert
Savell, Carl

Koski, Alex
Karcher, Fred K.
Manning, Jacob A.
Mountain, Albert A.
O'Hara, Frank
Ricci, Frank
Shimp, John
Wucelich, John
Boston, Okey M.
Brannen, Wm. Fremont
Baldassana, Albert
Cecil, Wylie Rinehart
Downing, Wm. H.
Darman, Chester
Hackenburg, Wm. J.

HISTORY OF MARSHALL COUNTY, W. VA.

Snedeker, Will Leroy
Bond, James Francis
Burge, Herbert L.
Carr, Fred Winford
Cohen, Clyde
Crape, Jack
Dayton, Lindsey F.
Gilbert, Earl
Hurd, Ben

Helms, John Morgan
Kimberly, Ralph
Kimple, Harry Alex
Mountain, Thomas Jas.
Montgomery, James C.
Richmond, Alliance Q.
Rodgers, Patrick J.
Saner, Michael Victor

Artillery

Arn, Frank
Bonar, David
Brandon, Charles
Clutter, Ray
Doyle, Ellwood
Gladys, Peter
Kittlewell, Albert
Melott, John A.
Morrison, Walter
Potts, Louis
Riggs, J. Hanen
Sigafoose, Ralph
Sullivan, Roy
Van Dine, Chester
Bennett, John B.
Blanford, Ray
Curry, Wm.
Curtis, W. F.
Evans, Walter
Kerby, James A.
Melott, Thomas

Martin, Ross
Nice, Wm. H.
Pyles, Michael
Roberts, E. L.
Shimp, Ralph
Shepherd, James B.
Wood, Asa T.
Berry, Marion
Bonar, William
Chambers, Earl C.
Downing, Chester
Fogle, Arch
Kull, Lawrence
Mix, Edward
Martin, Clay N.
Offterdinger, Wm.
Rex, Rek H.
Rumble, Prentis
Straight, Henry
Virgin, J. M.

Navy

Jones, Dorsey
Oliver, Alva
Price, Justin B.
Simpson, Frank C.
Sullivan, John C.
Toner, Charles J.
Woodward, Roy
Walton, Sam'l W. G.
Yeager, George
Roth, Robert Leroy
Chaddock, Robert N.
Chaddock, Wm. E.
Clyde, Arthur Harrison

Blake, Edward Leo
Bogard, George
Cousins, Frank
Crow, Victor
Crow, Artie
Dowler, Clarence W.
Fullerton, Geo. H.
Hicks, John A.
Harris, Hubert H.
McMullen, Clyde J.
Parsons, Wm. Lester
Robinson, John F.
Seese, Arthur J.

Daugherty, Ernest C.
Headley, Edmund P.
Hicks, Joseph I.
Howard, Rowland Reed
McDaniel, Marion R.
Paterick, Louis H.
Rafferty, Russel R.
Smith, Milton Lloyd
Thompson, Hugh W.
Williams, Robert T.
Yokum, Clarence E.

Seltner, Edwin
Wilson, Harry W.
Yokum, Thomas L.
Brown,. Gerald H.
Burcey, Harry
Crow, Archie Noble
Chapman, Arley
Dorsey, Valentine
Eller, Wm. Herbert
Haythorn, Wm. A.
Hill, Ambros H.

Marines

Hill, Isaac
McElroy, Joe M.
Orum, John R.
Travis, James Wesley
Whitlatch, J. V.
Wilhelm, Archie R.
Lowe, Wm. R.
Brown, Paul J.
Duffy, Martin Terrell
Durbin, Lester Delmo
Geho, David W.
Gregory, Floyd Riley
Gaughan, John Joseph
Huffman, Rob
Mallott, William Lewis
Rinehart, John C.
Watkins, Albert H.
Walton, George
Yokum, Thurman
Logsdon, Alwin W.

Burton, James Okey
Bromelow, Edward
Datzko, Mike
Ernst, Frank A.
Gillispie, W. E.
Gray, Walker L.
Geogeline, Samuel
Hill, Isaac, Jr.
Harris, Carlton W.
McDowell, Bruce R.
Siburt, Willard C.
Walton, George Earl
Walton, Wm. F.
King, Emmons T.
Booher, Samuel
Crepe, Joe
Elrod, Joseph
Fry, Leo Joseph
Gray, Austin E.
Hill, Felix Warren

Cavalry

Antil, Gruber
Vajvzek, John

Buzzard, Howard

National Guards

Burch, Clarence
Founds, David
Lark, George
Baker, William

Graham, Sam
Null, Earl
Brock, Ray
Graham, Harold

Field Artillery

Bryant, Alvie E.
Moran, Paul M.

Vano, Benedict
Kerby, James A.

HISTORY OF MARSHALL COUNTY, W. VA.

Siburt, James B.
Poluttis, Gus

Dukes, John W.

Coast Artillery

Duffy, Thomas J.

Coast Artillery Corps

Chaddock, William
Howard, Joseph L.
O'Tool, Patrick
Fair, Roscoe
Meek, E. Grover A.

Pond, Frank
Sickles, George
Gruber, John
Melott, James J.
Roscoe, George

Medical Reserve Corps

Wells, Vane Constant

Officers' Training Camp

Arnold, Lloyd J.
Freed, Horace
Henderson, Byron
Rogerson, Bemis
Williams, Price
Booher, Wilford J.
Ganby, Ralph

Goodman, Lawrence
Stewart, Melville
Wilson, Stanley Bruce
Bottome, Sterling B.
Conoway, Edmund M.
Peoples, Guy
Sammons, Wm. P.

Reserve Officers' Training Camp

Bondy, Austin

Proelss, O. A., Jr.

Medical Department

Ayers, Benj. R.
Conner, Joseph A.
Ealy, D. B.
Luikart, J. H.
Pleshkob, Paul
Strebich, Joseph A.
Wilson, Wm. A.
Young, Guy
Barlow, C. A.
Cover, O. F.
Fry, Leo Joseph
Morgan, C. G.

Rinehart, A. B.
Tyson, David Willis
Woodruff, Ralph
Crow, W. F.
Crow, J. Randall
Compton, Fillmore
Ferguson, J. H.
Myers, Roy Daton
Shepherd, Walter G.
Woodrug, R. L.
Williamson, C. D.
Yoho, Sidney F.

Medical Enlisted Reserve Corps

Covert, Leo D.
Kaufman, E. L.
McCuskey, C. F.

Yeater, Harvey U.
Fisher, Earl T.
Mackey, W. K.

HISTORY OF MARSHALL COUNTY, W. VA.

Evans, Harold
Klug, Thomas M.

Niedemyer, J. W.

Aero Sector Signal Corps

Bloyd, Joe
Downs, Eugene S.
Perl, James Leo
Snook, Martin A.
Schuse, Joseph
Sigler, Harold
Wright, Charles
Conner, Troy B.
Hood, Wm. C.
Ransom, Ira A.

Sadler, Edward J.
Tagg, Earl
Wick, John James
Yost, Joseph
Carson, Wm. T.
Hemphill, Clyde L.
Richmond, A. C.
Sockman, James W.
Watson, Wm. J.
Young, Clarence R.

Engineers

Ellis, George Lewis
Miller, Ben
Hammond, David M.

Wilson, Thos. G.
Murry, James Walker

Naval Reserve Force

Crow, Orie W.

Transportation Department

Tomlinson, W. H.

UNCLASSIFIED

Burkey, James Wm.
Eller, William T.
James, Albert I.
Korgans, Dominick
Martin, Harry
Poochacky, Oldrich
Parriott, Harold
Supler, John M.
Tribett, Earl
Crim, Jesse P.
Gray, Walter Leroy
Jones, Arthur L.
Lejek, Paul.
Miller, Earl

Price, Judd
Patterson, Ray
Taylor, Curtis E.
Whiteside, Lester T.
White, Richmond Lee
Crawford, John Glasby
Hart, Jeff J.
Krepelka, Karl
Lancaster, Lawrence
McCosh, Rex H.
Price, Wm.
Pleus, Robt. Read, Jr.
Tucker, Samuel
Wilkinson, Jas. R.

MISCELLANEOUS CLASSIFICATION

Baker, John F., Draftsman.
Stewart, Neil, French-American Army Corps.
Madell, Joseph C., Ordnance Department.

HISTORY OF MARSHALL COUNTY, W. VA.

McCamic, Charles, Quartermaster Department.
Bierce, John F., Signal Corps.
Cornish, Robert C.
Gaokell, Mrs. Daisy, Nurse Reserve.
McNemar, Alma, Yeowoman.

RED CROSS NURSES

Winters, Miss Myrtle, Camp Wheeler, Georgia.
Miller, Miss Effie, Walter Reed, Washington.
Chaddock, Miss Laura, Debarkation, Hampton, Virginia.
Clouse, Miss Orpha, Camp Hancock, Georgia.
Knight Miss Dora, Savenay, France.
Marsh, Miss Mary, Camp Lee, Virginia.
Samples, Miss Carrie, Savenay, France.
Dunlap, Miss Alberta, Camp Lee, Virginia.
Joliffe, Miss Olive, Walter Reed Hospital, Washington.
Gillispie, Miss Florence, Camp Meade, Base Hospital No. 4.
Lindsey, Miss Ella B., El Paso, Texas.
Mourot, Miss Nan, a Secretary, served n iFrance and Italy.
Taylor, Miss Alice, served in England and France.
Lewis, Miss Naomi, Dietitian, Camp Gordon, Georgia.
Newman, Miss Dora, Y. M. C. A. work in France.
Bowman, Florence G., served in France.

ROSTER OF SELECTED MEN

Entrained for Camp Lee, Va., September 5, 1917

Jesse Wilhelm   Whitelaw Reed South
Thomas Brannen

Entrained for Camp Lee, Va., September 6, 1917

Creston Clark Burley   Thomas Perkins
James Raymond Murphy

Entrained for Camp Lee, Va., September 7, 1917

Louis J. Chaddock   John Servia
Stephen J. Martinkovic

Entrained for Camp Lee, Va., September 8, 1917

Oliver Earl Francis   Lou E. McHenry
Wm. French Church

Entrained for Camp Lee, Va., September 10, 1917

Harry R. Brannen   Wm. Paul Scully
Wm. Thomas Blake

Entrained for Camp Lee, Va., September 20, 1917

Harley Lloyd Gatts
Mike Di Felice
William Wodiske
Arch L. Parks
Konstanz Vengdinski
Frank Oduila
John Wesley Crow
Orion Yoho
Nick Ferrera
Edward Hyatt
Joseph Kostka
Mike Morhovich
Mike Brazdovich
John Isaac Filben
Chas. Edward Ray
Wm. H. McClellan
Ward Jewel Calvert
Forest Lee Delany
Raymond Smallwood
Mike Campagnia
Alex Habak
Vinton W. Lindsey
Harry L. Crow
Frederick A. Hertzog
Luiggi Campagnia
Amanoilis Zamantaski
Nick Vigndicik
Andy Papula
John White
Asa Shepherd
Benjamin Doyle
Milton Hill
John Begovich
John Robert Crow
Joe Roytek
John Venljarich
Albert Golia Ray
Edward Morningstar
Winford Woodburn
John Lalor Ernst
Steve Bankovich
Roscoe Simpson
John Stolarchich
Stephen Neuseth
Joseph Kluchan
W. Lester Burton
Rocco Mirabella
Frank Studen
Chas. Conn Wilson
Chas. Alfred Fish
Paul Szymnski
Harry Clyde Richmond
Louis Niebergall
Burch C. Kiger
Patrick J. Scully
Harry Taylor Gray
Thos. James Butler
Wm. Rogers Holmes
Stanley Charles Crow
Jacob Lloyd McCracken
Joshua Earl Yoho
Edward Francis Kelley
Chas. Robert McCombs
Andrew Hlasko
Mike Stomek
Dwight Dorian Kelley
George Sonewald
Bertram B. Conley
John Cannell
Jacob Underdonk
Walter Chapman
William Filben
Veto Campo Bianco
Joseph Henry Koltz
Emil George Walk
Raymond Storm
Clyde L. Daily
Marko Tusin
Jesse Lloyd Rush
Otis Stern
James Edgar Sole
Vacil Locak
Harry Hyde
William Nightler
Elmer Gump
Joseph Henry
Phillip Brannen
Paul Matovich
Pasquale Fallova
Harry Martin Neer
Clarence E. Rush
Clinton Whitlatch

HISTORY OF MARSHALL COUNTY, W. VA. 275

John Vorderbrueggen
Earl Staley
Stanko Ceronis
George Rukavina
George Sodat
Norman Reed Jackson
Thomas Edgar Clark
Lester McSwain
Floyd Elsworth Sine
Martin Fred Riggle
Charles C. Riggs
Carl Robert Cousins
Joseph Kluch
Wm. Thomas O'Connell
Charles Leek
Lawrence Terrell
Louis Warner
George H. Kauakakis
Charles Schrader Winter
Claude C. Bonar
Jesse Bond Hewett
Harry William Bartels
Herbert Montgomery Hull
Raymond Harvey Dunlap
Jesse Edgar Yonkins
Charles Brockman Daily
Chas. William Meyers
H. Goffe Chambers
Peter Paul Templin
Robert Sylvus Mariner
James Patrick Matthews

Entrained for Camp Lee, Va., October 4, 1917

Steve Gongola
Steve Horvatt
William L. Cosser
Adam Markeoik
Carmono Martino
Chasles A. Gebert
Matthew Green
John M. Conners
Herbert Stilwell
Orvil D. Kidd
Nicola Di Mario
Ray Nease
Jesse Willis
Frank Gasparevic
Henry Erit Strober
Petro Di Carlo
Ervin Edwin Bell
Joe S. Wiblin
Chas. H. Anderson
Jack Dibykowski
Roy Wells Arreck
Lennie Gardner
Samuel B. Wilson
John Edgar Anderson
George A. Long
Rosco Floyd Yoho
Florian Gracik
Wylie Wilson
Roy Edward Powell
Clyde Bacon
Mat Spisich
Harry J. Kettler
Presley W. Hill
Gaspar Pavlic
Guisseppe Cocco
Carl Magers
Marco Iarquinio
Thomas Clark Raber
Tony Bumbuti
Otis Ray Galentine
Oren Everett Arthur
John William Slokan
Jacob Presley Loy
Vinton T. Bogard
Charles W. Pond
Charles Alfred Henry
William Houston Higgins
Martin S. Furbee
Joseph Guarmere
Roy Guy Smith
John William Elliott
Joseph Van Syoc
Thomas Frank Hughes
Edward G. Hossman
William Scott Bell
Stephen Brnjas
Tony Serechis
Lyle Cobard Anderson
William Leurie King
Diomjasius A. Horan

Entrained for Camp Sherman, Ohio, October 11, 1917

McKinley Donkan

Entrained for Camp Devens, Ayers, Mass., October 17, 1917

Michael Romano

Entrained for Camp Lee, Va., October 27, 1917

Earnest Echart Armstrong (Col.)

Shirley Eggleston Wade (Col.)

Entrained for Camp Sherman, Ohio, December 5, 1917

Marciey Dobosy

Entrained for Fort Screven, Ga., December 20, 1917

Amil Carl Bartels
Louis Langmyer
Elias Abraham
Thomas Conner
William W. White
Jesse Clinton Icard
George Strait
Manford Kerns
Harry Peter Klug
Harry Crow
Clem James Yoho
Leslie Taylor
Earl Parks
Raymond Guy Everett
Thomas Reed Games
Steve Cilli
James P. Wasmuth
Lester Brown
Orie E. Crow
Elmer Brown
Leslie Van Syoc
Ralph E. Lowe
Ben Frank Myers
Edwin Beer
Edward Renik
Stidger Polen
Henry Bartrug
Francis Marion Maine
Artimous Oldfield
Glen Cunningham
Herbert Dray
Harrison Custick

Paul Hagerman
Gaetam Porcari
Jesse D. H. Sullivan
Harry Lloyd Lowe
Harry Wilbur Vick
Roy Samuel Hubbs
Lewis Bell
William Alfred Rigfgle
Robert Wm. Robinson
John A. McKee
Alva Miller
John Parker Harris
Chas. Cunningham
Mikaible Shkuratow
Quiller Braden Huffner
Jesse Clyde Parsons
Michael Iemma
John M. Hazlett
John Gorby
Allen Aaron Gump
Pasquale Ricci
Everett Zane Rupp
John Dado
Frank Whitlatch
Charles Edgar West
Okey F. Harris
George W. Becker
Edgar Losen Roberts
Vincenzo Di Gaspero
Frank Francis Yoho
Angelo Marchine
Charles Howard Shipley

HISTORY OF MARSHALL COUNTY, W. VA. 277

Harry Clark Rogerson
William Richard Schmitz
Charles Wesley Shimp
Curtis Ray McCullough
Lawrence F. Shaffer
Bayard McClean Roberts
Charles Marion Lehew
Frank Joseph Rushman
Ersie Van R. Teagarden
Edward Emmit Tasker
Harrison Kline East
William Patrick Folley
Charles Julius Hammel
William Joseph Riggle
Stanley Thomas Patton
Clarence Eastman Goodrich
William H. Fletcher
Edward B. Cecil
William Edgar Foster
Roy Scott Daugherty
Warren Montgomery
Thomas McLand Yates
Harold Byron Fitzsimmons
Walter Clifford Courtwright
James Francis Gallaher
John Leonard Church
William Edward Archey
Joseph Aston

Entrained or Camp Dodge, Iowa, January 22, 1918

Henry Brooks (Colored)

Entrained for Fort Screven, Ga., January 25, 1918

Oscar Yost
Ballard H. Shipley
Nick Valirakis

Entrained for Fort Oglethorp, Ga., February 2, 1918

Guy Edwin Young
Lester Ray Hayes
James Leo Peel

Entrained for Camp American University, Washington, D. C., February 10, 1918

Thomas Samuel Wilson

Entrained for Camp Greenleaf, Ga., February 25, 1918

Olen Rutan
Roy Ewell Hood
Matthew P. Wick
James W. Mellon

Entrained for Camp Kelley Field, San Antonio, Texas, February 25, 1918

Walter Duncan

Entrained or Camp Kelley Field, San Antonio, Texas, March 9, 1918

William P. Brennan
Marion Steele Berry
Edward Joseph Doyle
James Franklin Gately

Entrained for Camp Greenleaf, Lytle, Ga., March 10, 1918

Edward Lee Dunlap
Jesse Earl Stewart

Entrained for Camp Greenleaf, Lytle, Ga., March 13, 1918

Howard Isaac Booher

HISTORY OF MARSHALL COUNTY, W. VA.

Entrained for Camp Kelley Field, San Antonio, Texas, March 25, 1918

John Edward Morris   Thomas Joseph Cooper

Entrained for Camp Kelley Field, San Antonio, Texas, April 1, 1918

Joseph Wm. Bosley

Entrained for Camp Lee, Va., April 2, 1918

James Wm. Voltz   Jacob S. Baumberger
Louis Kershkey   Gilbert W. Wiatt
Ralph Niedemyer   Frank Conley
Lawrence Smitt   Ben F. Peabody
Elmer E. McKitrick   Ross Edgar Flanagan
Axel Herman Grenberg   Joseph Tkach
Ralph Edwin Gunn   Charles A. Rider, Jr.
Ottis Wm. Rush   Thomas Oliver Pyles
Anderson Clark   Charles Bier
Ray Strawn   Jacob F. Hall
John Wm. Rigby   Michael Stefanski
Joseph Earl Duffy   Domineco Nscozlios
Samuel James Crahan   Daniel Wilson
John Burke   Michael J. Pendergast
David Carl Simms   Richard Baxter Raney
Chester Clyde Walen   Edward Russell Parker
Mura Guiseppe   Stanley Kello
William C. Wallace   Guy N. Shafferman
Stafano Di Domenio   Donald Skelton Scroggins

Entrained for Camp Dix, Watertown, N. J., March 28, 1918

Louis C. Reidel

Entrained for Camp Wadsworth, Spartinsburg, N. C., May 22, 1918

Albert Conrad Carle

Entrained for Camp Meade, Md., April 26, 1918

William Nelson Weekly   Everett Whipkey
Homer Frank Davis   John Mason Gibson
Zina Constantino   Samuel E. Stone
James W. Acres   John T. Oliver
Clyde Anderson   Wm. Delbert Snyder
Alexander Bier   Daxutres Whypamabi
Thomas F. Hazlett   George Grayson Calvert
Harold Burgiss   Carl Leroy Rodocker
Charles Marion Cook   Leonard M. Morningstar
Silvus Appolomio   John Maywood Williams
Carle Prince   John Francis Rushman

HISTORY OF MARSHALL COUNTY, W. VA.

Tgnacy Gonsicbowski
Lee A. Long
James Wm. Lemasters
Floyd Bonar

Harry Wm. Long
Jesse Eldridge Gittings
Edward Melvin Dennis
Ralph Arthur Galentine

Entrained for Camp Lee, Va., April 4, 1918

Charles Wosick

Entrained for Camp Lee, Va., April 7, 1918

Harry Warner Jones

Entrained for Camp Dix, Watertown, N. J., April 16, 1918

Edgar Rogers Hughes

Entrained for Camp Dodge, Iowa, April 29, 1918

James Ernest

Entrained for Camp Dix, Watertown, N. J., May 6, 1918

George L. Muldrue

Entrained for Ft. Leavenworth, Kans., May 8, 1918

Edward Voight

Entrained for Ft. Thomas, Ky., May 13, 1918

James W. Byrnes
Wylie Erwin Parsons
Peter Zerras
Pasquale Gibilisco
Harry Alloway
Robert Shepherd
August Kerscha
Lawrence Wilson

Louis De Carlo
Antonio Fiarino
Scaffidi Castantino
Carl Covert Wayman
William Ernest
Oakley Lemuel Wood
Andrae Di Domineco

Entrained for University of Akron, Ohio, May 15, 1918

Frank G. Berry
Elmer Rickey
Edward E. Weaver
Chas. T. Gallaher
Eugene A. Ward
Earl Wm. Smith
Lester C. Pyles
Chester Arthur Olson

Wm. R. Deegan
Donald E. Grimes
Frank Cecil Robinson
Benedict Edward Murphy
Chas. Michael Callahan
Robert H. McGlumphy
Ralph Holderman

Entrained for Camp Sevier, Greenville, S. C., May 17, 1918

George Williams

HISTORY OF MARSHALL COUNTY, W. VA.

Entrained for Ft. Benjamin Harrison, Ind., May 17, 1918

George Sheets
Frank Jeffers
William Webb
Daniel J. Hanley
Charles A. Curran
Archie R. Bayles
Leo J. O'Conner
Richard B. Nolan

Everett L. Mahood
Samuel R. Mahood
Frank A. Young
Richard F. Conners
John Elwood Morris
Harry F. Davis
John J. Butterfield
James Little

Entrained for Camp Meade, Md., May 20, 1918

Arleigh O. Wilson

Entrained for Medical Supply Depot, Philadelphia, Pa., May 22, 1918

Charles McCune Bloyd
Robert E. Blankensop

Entrained for Columbus Barracks, Columbus, Ohio, May 23, 1918

John Storm
William A. Polley
Presley Durig
Ross Al Durig
Everett Lee Darrah
Chas. Wagner
John Kolinski
John Spears
Carl Fred Bom

Saul Moore
John Wm. Mowder
Raymond M. Barney
James Lester Anderson
Lawrence E. Nangle
John Harris Fleming
George Raymond White
Thomas L. Daugherty
Emmett Q. Rogerson

Entrained for Camp Sherman, Ohio, May 24, 1918

Joseph Christopher Duffy

Entrained for Camp Lee, Va., May 26, 1918

Pete Barovic
Carl A. O'Connel
Arthur Perrin
Earl E. Bowers
Slater Chambers
Felice Cerrone
W. L. Nolan
Charles Gould
John Wesley Noble
John C. Hopkins
Harry Chambers
Grover C. Crawford
Louis V. Carpenter
William T. Yates

Vere R. Todd
John J. Heagin
Leroy Huff
Herman Specht, Jr.
Silas Lee Gittings
Salvator Carboni
Robert Cash Safreed
Herbert Edward Barker
Cornelius F. Hall
John Francis Truax
Sam Sushocloesky
John Elwood Rabre
Talmage Jas. Ingersall
Oliver Franklin Paith

HISTORY OF MARSHALL COUNTY, W. VA. 281

Paul Howard Parsons
Albert Littman
Okey Espey Yoho
Frank W. Slokan
Louis J. Romel
Lester Crow
Ross Berry
William Hatina
Lloyd Rankin
Louis Joseph Oberg
William Kelley
James Alfred Welling
Denver Pear Martin
Walter Ray Hartley
Wesley Cosser
Guisseppi Rea
William Jacob Yoho
John Hoyt
William R. Chambers
Harry Tedrow
Hugh Knight
Donato Chista
Orange Leek
Halford High
Tony Samel
Thomas Fox
Emmett Robinson
Sabatino Laneria
Carl Fisk Bonar
Elbert Whorton
John Bell Yuzapos
John Elmer Fish
Albert Croll
George Brown
Dovener Lafferty
Jesse Amos
Boyd Sine
George C. Stewart
John Groff
Walter Sheakatrike
Edward West
William K. Richmond
George Myers
John Garfield Mix
Russell Howard Blair
Charles E. Sheets
J. F. Hunt

Robert McClain Linch
Bonnie Herbert Boso
Robert Vinton Weaver
Albert Warsinski
William Parker
Ransel Yoho
Tomaso Pocci
Thomas Earl Gilbert
Francisco Lancio
Robert E. McCombs
Paul Melko
Herbert R. Fuller
Louis C. Whetzel
Herman R. Bowers
Orla H. Snedeker
Charles E. Anderson
Floyd A. Siers
Hugh McShane
John Evashko
Frank Marion Tagg
Emmett Hinerman
William Decker
John Gray
James Earl Magers
Jacob Herman Eifler
John W. Whitlatch
Leo Dombrowskie
Jesse Clinton Cunningham
John Frederick Young
Charles Lambracht
William McKinley Garrison
Luther Francis Clark
Joseph Henry Schmid
Robert Lee Robinson
Floyd Jasper Richardson
John Heghie Erlewine
Guiseppe Zuaranta
George William Wisenbaler
Raymond Albert Scanlon
William Winford Baker
John Francis Callihan
John Herbert Jackson
Chancy L. Yeater
Vincent John Wayman
James Lindsay Robinson
Harry Rayland Caldwell
Clarence Terrell Lutes

Thomas Moore Parker
John B. Galentine
Raymond Milton McCann
Everett Elwood Goodwin
Albert Carrol Jablinske
Fred Forest Castilow
Siloesio Catalano
Elbert B. Dittmires

Leslie C. Howard
Encil Milton Degarmo
Benjamin Franklin Stephens
Roylance Richard Terrell
Clarence Benton McCann
Charles Everett Barker
Lee George Brannon

Entrained for Camp Humphreys, Va., May 28, 1918

George Kessler

Entrained for Camp Jackson, S. C., May 28, 1918

J. B. Dorsey

Entrained for Camp Gordon, Ga., May 29, 1918

Tony Mazurick

Entrained for Columbus Barracks, Columbus, Ohio, May 29, 1918

Joe Euclid Garbesi, Jr.

Entrained for Camp Zachary Taylor, Ky., May 29, 1918

Vance Halley

Entrained for Camp Grant, Ill., June 3, 1918

Frank Bloom

Entrained for Camp Greenleaf, Ga., June 6, 1918

Leo A. Kaschke

Entrained for Columbus Barracks, Columbus, Ohio, June 13, 1918

William Encil Lucas

Entrained for Camp Lewis, American Lake, Washington, June 17, 1918

Absolom Cecil

Entrained for Vancouver Barracks, Washington, June 17, 1918

Ray R. O'Niel

Entrained for Walter Reed Gen. Hosp., Tacoma, D. C., June 19, 1918

Edwin Fitzsimmons   Thomas J. Wilson

Entrained for Vancouver Barracks, Washington, June 21, 1918

Charles Thompson

Entrained for Camp Greenleaf, Ga., June 25, 1918

Joe Burdulis

HISTORY OF MARSHALL COUNTY, W. VA.

Entrained for Camp Lee, Va., June 26, 1918

Allick Goletts
Alec Bodekosky
James Shay
Lloyd Bane
Edward Ray
Oliver H. Day
George Varlas
Harry Spears
William Warner

Foster Noble
Edward Leo Conners
Harry McCune
Anthony Frank Ticich
Harry Raymond Anderson
Luther Walker Porter
Earl Willard Ransom
Charles Foster Vandyne

Entrained for Base Hospital No. 58, Camp Grant, Ill., July 5, 1918

Felix Cecil Staeck

Entrained for Normal School, Murfreesboro, Tenn., July 14, 1918

Lee K. Rose
Louis J. Carskaden
George Sparry Weaver
Lynn Elliott Jones
Glen M. Ganier

Russell Rowland Blake
Llewellyn Niebergall
Joseph Walter Chaddock
Harley Friend Richmond
Harry Bartlett Haddox

Entrained for Camp Sherman, Ohio, July 26, 1918

Peter Camilli

Entrained for Camp Meade, Md., July 26, 1918

Thomas Earl Conoway
Oren E. Rulong
Ray C. Joliff
Clarence Long
James T. Lilley
Encil Leslie Cecil
Abraham Ellis
James Demetrakis
Cecil Floyd Potts
Tony Polutis
Forrest Kent
Edwin Logan
Spray Burley
Philip E. Jones
Steve Kellar
Jacob S. Crow
George E. Rush
Walter G. Allen
Herman H. Mason
Raymond Robertson
Joseph Vokovich
Harry Logsdon

Herbert Leroy Fish
Allen Cunningham
Adam Ciesrecki
Paul Leon Dorsey
Guy Laster Knapp
Charles Minor
Frank Lewis
Charles J. Garey
Robert M. Charlton
Cecil E. Daily
Joseph D. Woods
Charles J. Roach
Russell Pierce
Tony Ruzinski
Sam Braden
Charles H. Sloan
Elmer R. Huss
Charles E. Mooney
William D. Mercer
Charles Raper
Joseph E. Parker
Luiggi Palisco

Joseph A. Nolan
James Mickey
Chancey Roy Clylor
Robert Little
Ralph S. Kaufield
Frand C. Redd
John Hall
James W. Schaffer
Thomas F. Logsdon
Oscar J. W. Ryan
Oscar E. Steen
Frank Lis
Herbert Johnson
Ralph Lancaster
Henry Leasure
William Watson
Carl Tochilenkow
Clyde Louis Lutes
Henry Robert Yates
Oscar Siburt
William Finch
Edgar J. Noland
Sedry Earl West
Wilbert Harry Fisher
Carmine Padula
Francisco Balito
Harry Shook
John Hubert Brown
Walter Glenn Day
Ivan Dempsey Kelley
Wilber H. Everett
Chester Lee Fisher
Mangior Salvatoria
Frank William Blake
Archie L. Snedeker
James O. Howard
Andrew Sarvel
Wtadystow Thwaitek
Angello Muscette
Louis Edwin Gatts
Clarence B. Allman
Roy E. Smith
Wylie Roe Fish
Okley Ray Vandine
Michael Buksa
Louis R. Voitel
Sergey Skuratoo

Brooks Polen
Russell Crim
Elijah Blake
Edward Samuel Dowler
Ercel Hullian Loy
Leslie Nathan Bartlett
Roy William Chambers
Edmond A. Kloetzly
Herbert Clemens Fisher
John Robert Christie
Jasse Parsons McHenry
Alvin James Kettlewell
Arthur Hampton Sibert
Eli Mercer
Onward E. Burge
Clifford H. Rogerson
Harley Cramer Emery
Steve Borland
John L. Woodruff
Charles Eugene Barr
Harry August Wendt
William Wester Nicolan
Charles Raymond Milliken
Edward Beecher
Ernest Ward Berisford
Clyde Lincoln Kaercher
Charles Laird Gittings
Lisle Edgar Hawkins
Ernest M. Craighton
Roy Leonard Anderson
William Edgar Ruckman
Carl Wayne Snedeker
Milton Arthur Gable
John Kennedy McCully
Archibald J. Lafferty
Jesse C. Cunningham
Vincenzo Pulsinelli
August H. Sunderman
Clarence B. Whitlatch
George L. McCracken
Charles J. Conners
Bence C. Rogerson
Grafton E. Williams
Wilford Richmond
David M. Hammond
Lawrence W. O'Connell
Grover Franklin Auten

HISTORY OF MARSHALL COUNTY, W. VA. 285

Clyde Clarence Anderson
Hugh Alexander Mercer
James Lawrence Crogan
John Capper
John R. Howard
Joseph Skazuiski
John W. Gossett
James W. Ray
Salvator Scalora
Ernest Riggs
Edmond E. Craig
Herman B. Riggs
Bruce E. Riggs
Luggi Meura

Elmer Blake
Francisco Yanni
Charles M. Grandon
Albert F. Coffield
Joseph P. Kissel
William Henry Behrens
Forrest William Flouhouse
Charles Buzzard
Jonathan I. Rush
Patrick J. Hughes
Howard Payne Cox
William Charles Beucke
Fred J. Lambrecht

Entrained for Camp Forrest, Lytle, Ga., July 29, 1918

Charles Vernon Du Bois
Jesse J. Hart

Entrained for Surgeon General O..ce, Washington, D. C., Aug. 17, 1918

Karl Dix Louden

Entrained for Columbus Barracks, Columbus, Ohio, August 17, 2918

Manie Shore
Dorsey Woodruff
William H. Kolz
John Wesley Martin
Leroy Patterson
Charles F. Logsdon
Charles Blake

Orvil Mason
George Newby
George Selby Powell
Robert Graham Lindsey
Raymond W. Parriott
William Russell Crawford
George Everett Barker

Entrained for the University of West Virginia, Morgantown, W. Va., August 15, 1918

Hubert Dewey Lutes
John B. Yeater
Frank H. Turvey
Clarence L. Bonar
Thomas Welch
Olga G. Ramsey
George M. McGary
William Leo Hughes
Willard B. Decker
Luke Heil

Harry L. Duncan
Roy Berisford
Clarence M. Spear
Charles C. McCracken
Francis Perry Searls
John W. Horan
Benjamin S. Lindsey
William F. Bartlett
Marcus A. Bowman

Entrained for Camp Lee, Va., August 29, 1918
Frank Gorh

Entrained for Camp Lee, Va., August 29, 1918
Jan Minchenko

HISTORY OF MARSHALL COUNTY, W. VA.

Entrained for Camp Greenleaf, Lytle, Ga., August 29, 1918

William H. Hill
Charles A. Bloyd
Emery Cross
Carl Austin Wellman
George Braske
Fred C. Phillips

Brady F. Rine
Louis B. Castilow
Charles A. Young
Frank Elmer Greathouse
Kenneth Walter Evans
Clarence Robert Craft

Entrained for Camp Green, Charlotte, S. C., August 30, 1918

John K. Billetter
Roy W. Joliffe
Everett F. Seyler
Earl Wisenbaler
Harry Roseberry
Robert L. Robinson
Clyde Loper

Denton Albaugh
Chester A. Cohen
Barzillia Wirt Riley
Byron Harrison Gardner
Hue E. Lucas
Sherman Welsch

Entrained for Richmond Commercial Club, Richmond, Ind., August 31, 1918

Hugh J. O'Malley

Alfred M. McConnell

Entrained for Camp Custer, Battle Creek, Mich., Sept. 1, 1918

Malen Laurel Walters

Entrained for Camp Taylor, Louisville, Ky., Sept. 2, 1918

Grover Cleveland Musgrove

Entrained for Camp Sherman, Ohio, Sept. 4, 1918

George E. Bruce

Entrained for Camp Lee, Va., Sept. 4, 1918

William Donovan
Paul E. Lowe
James Hubert Foust
Timothy John Lucey
John David Hanna
Grant Hilberry
William P. Green
Thomas C. Fisher
Foster A. Jefferson
Argyle Ogle Mason
Jason Brice Johnson
Donald L. Wayne
Sabiteno Epifnao
Leland Coffield
David T. Murphy

Albert Gelner
Earl James Brennen
Michael Dado
Denny R. Crow
Edwin Lemont Shriver
William James Burley
Albert William Lass
William Anderson
Lioniel Andreas
Charles Wade
Peter John Muhart
Charles Snyder
Ralph B. Fuller
Raymond Frank Fish
James Otis Lutes

Oscar Crow
Silvia Voorhies
Guy Delbert Horner
John H. Kettlewell
Michael Wm. Cusack
Joseph Fred Clayton
Orvill L. Riggle
Webster McKimmie
Andrew Lester
William Carl Koch
Walter Francis Ryan
James Wm. Downing
Pearl Robert Yates
Denny Albert Murry
Frank Michael Meyers
Bruce Robert Evans
Sidney Shirley Mason
Cyrus McHenry
Roy D. Taylor
Nicholas Lecko
Ralph Caldwell Williams
Charles Otto Villers
Samuel Randall Simmons
Homer Charles Parriott
Peter Francis Bierce
William Wesley Phillips
Friend Leonidas Blake
William Lee Armstrong
Lawrence J. Pelley
William Francis Chambers
Charles Orion Campbell
George Frank Russell
Harry R. O. Richmond
Anthony Henry Becker
Forrest William Alley
Bryan Thomas Clark
Harry McKinley Miles
Harley Otto Whittingham
Earl McClelland Trump
Reymond Furbee
Sidney Shirley Mason

Willie Franklin Remke
Raymond Prentice Stone
Charles H. V. Workman
James Robert Maxwell
Frank Lewis Supan
Howard J. Barth
James K. Davis
John Lehew, Jr.
Albert C. Von Philip
Joseph Fragasso
Archie A. Baine
Okey Atewart
Stanley Gray
Thomas C. Truman
Lawrence B. Riggs
George Whitlatch
William H. Anderson
Frank Whitlatch
Perry Auter
Everett William West
Antonio Tiritilla
James Walter Arn
Walter E. Wilson
Ottie Kirby
Frank Ferris
Louis Elbert Clark
Joseph Johns, Jr.
Verner Curtis Oliver
Elmer Elsworth Yoho
John Leonard Morris
Friend N. Porterfield
Erett Edwin Buzzard
Thomas James Virgin
James Randall Lancaster
James Archie Gillingham
Curtis Clay Watkins
Thomas C. Truman
Henry Ernest Oberg
Millard D. Logsdon
Wesley Elwood Mariner

Entrained for Camp Humphreys, Va., Sept. 6, 1918

Fred R. Louden
Harry Meyers
John Wesley Boble
Ralph C. Kettler

Otis Rush
John Roiso
Clifford Earl O'Niel
Charles M. Anderson

HISTORY OF MARSHALL COUNTY, W. VA.

Charles Whipkey
Wylie F. Bondy
Augustus A. Horne
Sheldon R. Van Brugh

Raymond U. Marple
Clarence B. Yeater
John L. Byard

Entrained for Camp Humphreys, Va., Sept. 10, 1918

Harry C. Morris

Entrained for Camp Lee, Va., September 13, 1918

Nelson Richard
Curtis Darrah
Stephen C. Namaek
Walter Mays
Harry A. Bryson
Luther Gay Sheets
Charles O. Glover
Elmer R. Richmond
Alfred R. Icenhour
James E. Hipkins
John S. Turner

Oscar Burton
Peter Makarow
Charles L. Mercer
Frank N. Longstreth
Elsworth R. Richmond
Clarence W. Van Dyne
Huse Voss Campbell
Clyde H. McCombs
William Patrick Dixon
Thomas J. Morris

Entrained for Camp Sherman, Ohio, Sept. 15, 1918

George James Stultz

Entrained for Columbus Barracks, Columbus, Ohio, October 1, 1918

Jesse Burnard Orum

Entrained for Pitt. University, Pittsburgh, Pa., October 1, 1918

Donald McMahon Reynolds   Percy Coxen

Entrained for West Virginia University, Morgantown, West Virginia, October 2, 1918

Paul Revere Wellman
Ralph H. Hemphill
William Ward McMasters
Wayne Eldron Mason
Herbert Dean Garvin
Victor Raymond Jones
Stanley George Fisher
Hugh Barger Wellman

Russell James Hamilton
Herman Leroy Baker
Louis Danford Conner
Fred Lother Miller
Victor Anvil Riggs
Ralph Fitzsimmons
John Peter McDermott
Martin Francis Hopkins

Entrained for Wesleyan, Buchannon, W. Va., October 3, 1918

Ross Bonar
Charles A. Watkins

W. W. Kinsey

Entrained for Ohio Wesleyan, Delaware, Ohio, October 5, 1918

James Alvin Baker

Entrained for Pennsylvania State College

Harry Webster Moore

Entrained for Ohio Wesleyan, Delaware, Ohio, October 9, 1918

Raymond L. Lowe

Entrained for Bethany College, Bethany, W. Va., October 10, 1918

Jesse T. Barnum   Harold Kenneth Snyder

Entrained for Marietta College, Marietta, Ohio, October 11, 1918

Louis McFarland Timblin

Entrained for University of Pennsylvania, Philadelphia, Pa.,
October 11, 1918

Edward H. Burke

Entrained for Bethany College, Bethany, W. Va., October 15, 1918

George Elwood Strobel

Entrained for Camp Humphreys, Va., October 15, 1918

Clarence H. Slaughter

Entrained for Baltimore Dental College, Baltimore, Md., Oct. 21, 1918

Bernard James McGinnis

Entrained for Camp Taylor, Louisville, Ky., October 23, 1918

Harlan Ross Courtwright

Entrained for Camp Sherman, Ohio, October 23, 1918

Erwin H. Cochran

Entrained for West Virginia University, Morgantown, W. Va.,
October 29, 1918

Luke Burdett Ross   John Martin Chenoweth
Joseph Lawrence Burley

Entrained for West Virginia University, Morgantown, W. Va.,
November 5, 1918

William Peter Hall	Gordon Criswell
Morris Edward Brant	Sumner N. Linch
Charles Carlton Fish	Conrad Ellsworth Chaddock
Wesley Harrison Ward	Harold Floyd Montgomery
Louis Edwin Weekly	James Raymond Burley
Wilbur James Burge	George Lawrence Davis

Entrained for Ohio College of Surgery, Cincinnati, Ohio,
November 11, 1918

George W. Bone

Entrained for U.S. Marine Corps Station, Pittsburgh, Pa.,
November 11, 1918

Roy Glen Davis

CASUALTY LIST
KILLED IN ACTION
Moundsville

Forest Lee Delaney
Elbert Whorton
George Varlis
John T. Oliver
Ralph Alexander
Albert I. Jones
Austin E. Gray

Chester Vandine
Lawrence Lancaster
John W. Gray
George Grayson Calvert
Oliver Earl Francis
John Gray
Earl Staley

Benwood

Patrick J. Rogers
William Thomas Blake

John Dobias
Michael Romano

Cameron

Howard M. Fisher
Lester Delmo Durbin
John M. Williams

Jesse Grim
James R. Wilkinson

Loudensville

Walter H. Hartley

Miscellaneous

Mike V. Saner, Rosby's Rock
Albert A. Mountain, McMechen
James R. Fitzgerald, Elm Grove

John Orum, Sherrard
Mike Datzo, Glendale
David Geho, Bellton

KILLED BY ACCIDENT

William H. Nice, Moundsville

DIED OF WOUNDS
Moundsville

Samuel Tucker
John Shimp

William Offterdinger
Joe S. Wiblin

Miscellaneous

Alvin W. Logsdon, McMechen
Lester Crow, Glen Easton
Lester Scott, Dallas

Mathew Green, Wheeling, R. F. D. 2
Paul Lejek, Benwood

WOUNDED

Moundsville

William Baker
Felix Warren Hill
Arthur W. Jones
Alexander Bier
Edward West
Charles Leek
Peter Gladys
William Bonar
Ralph Kimberly
Lennie Gardner
Joseph Thack
Louis Romel
James E. Magers
Orange Leek

Lester McSwain
William N. Garrison
Thomas Fox
Atlee H. Miller
John Gray
Arthur L. Jones
David Bonar
Creston C. Burley
George Myers
Sam Suhodalsky
Oldrich Prochanzy
Jesse Lloyd Rush
Donald Skelton Scroggins
Albert G. Safreed

Benwood

William P. Scully
Thomas N. Parker
John Wucelich
Karl Krepelka

Michael Vucelich
Lewis V. Carpenter
Silveo Appoloni
Samuel Geogeline

Cameron

Earl Miller
Leslie C. Howard
Jesse Amos
Ralph E. Gunn

C. E. Anderson
John Maywood Williams
James L. Robinson
Talmage James Ingersoll

McMechen

Earl Tribett
William Wodiske
Henry Erit Strober

William T. Yates
William Q. Richmond
Leo Dombroskie

Rock Lick

John M. Supler

Earl S. Bowers

Bellton

Lee A. Long
Milton Hill

Lindsey F. Dayton

Miscellaneous

George Skiterelich, Bogg's Run
Otis Stern, Silver Hill
William J. Hackenburg, Wheeling,
R. F. D. 2
Chas. H. Weaver, Delaware, Ohio
William Decker, Bellaire, Ohio

DIED IN CAMP

Ralph E. Lowe, Glen Easton, Fort Screven
Pearl R. Yates, Benwood, Camp Lee
Francis Thomas Logsdon, Moundsville, Camp Meade
John Hanna, Moundsville, Camp Lee
Slater Chambers, Cameron, Camp Meade
William T. Eller, Moundsville, Great Lakes
Guy Peoples. Cameron, Camp Sherman
William Alfred Riggle, Dallas, Fort Screven
Robert William Robinson, Sherrard, Fort Screven
Elsworth Richmond, Dallas, Camp Lee
Frank Turvey, McMechen, Morgantown
Walter C. Courtwright, Cameron, Fort Screven

LOST AT SEA

Paul Norrington, Moundsville, lost on Otranto
Jesse Bond Hewitt, Moundsville, died at sea
Edward Leo Blake, Benwood, lost on Cyclops
Roy Samuel Hubbs, Glen Easton, lost on Otranto

MISSING IN ACTION

William T. Eller, Cameron, R. F. D. 2
Curtis E. Taylor, Silver Hill
Archie N. Cook, Cameron
Denver P. Martin, Mannington

CAPTURED BY GERMANS

Chester Darman, Moundsville

HISTORY OF MARSHALL COUNTY, W. VA.

MARSHALL COUNTY AID IN WAR FUND

MARSHALL COUNTY contributed liberally of both men and means in support of the World War. The amount of government war bonds purchased by the citizens of this county was certainly creditable to it. The following reports made by the banks of this county, of quotas estimated for the county and the amount subscribed to the several LIBERTY BOND LOANS cannot fail to be interesting to the patriotic people and one of which future generations will look upon with commendable pride.

THE FIRST LIBERTY LOAN, 1917, the quota estimated for this county was $208,500, and the amount subscribed was $99,100.

THE SECOND LIBERTY LOAN, 1917, the quota estimated for this county at $473,850, and the amount subscribed by the citizens was $672,750.*

THE THIRD LIBERTY LOAN, 1918, the quota was fixed for this county at $540,400, and the amount subscribed was $831,100.*

THE FOURTH LIBERTY LOAN, 1918, was conducted upon the plan of a regular campaign, and was of unusual interest and was, beyond a doubt, well managed and the people were instructed and interested in many thing connected with bond issues that were of much benefit to them. It was a campaign of patriotism and instruction in matters of business interest and it was made plain that investment in Liberty Bonds was a matter of business and an opportunity for investment people should seek. It was a new method of thrift and an opportunity to save. The result of three weeks' campaign will tell the story of success of the campaign in few words and few figures.

The quota estimated or the county was $1,042,100, and the amount subscribed was $1,331,250. Oversubscribed $289,150.*

THE FIFTH LIBERTY LOAN or the FIFTH LIBERTY VICTORY LOAN was in the spring of 1919. The quota as estimated for this county was $742,350. The amount subscribed by the citizens amounted to the sum of $773,000.*

* The above amounts are as reported by Federal Reserve Banks.

WAR HERO CLUB

In memory and honor of these illustrious brave Marshall County boys who have made the last sacrifice, even unto death, and the fifteen hundred Marshall County boys, many of whom are now in the front line trenches, and all of whom now stand ready to make that same supreme sacrifice for the cause of humanity, THE MARSHALL COUNTY HERO CLUB is hereby organized.

To entitle one to supporting membership in this club, individual subscription to the FOURTH LIBERTY LOAN must be at least $2,000.

Martin Brown	$2,000.00	Mrs. Mary Etta Weaver	$2,000.00
C. B. Roe	2,000.00	T. S. Riggs	2,000.00
W. D. Alexander	2,500.00	C. A. Showacre	2,000.00
M. F. Compton	2,500.00	W. A. B. Dalzell	5,000.00
J. A. Bloyd	5,000.00	B M. Spurr*	2,500.00
B. F. Hodgeman	2,000.00	H. J. Zink	2,000.00
W. Martin Riggs	2,000.00	E. C. Yoho	3,000.00
Friend Yoho	4,000.00	V. A. Weaver	2,000.00
Mrs. Mary E. Smith	5,000.00	W. D. Dunn	2,000.00
I. Gordon	5,000.00	John Chapman, Jr	2,000.00
Joseph Nolte	3,000.00	W. H. Hubbs	2,000.00
R. D. Miller	2,000.00	John Dague	2,000.00
S. A. Walton	2,000.00	B. M. Spurr*	2,000.00
Chas. McCamic	2,000.00	John Johnson	2,000.00
M. A. Sybert	2,000.00	T. E. Young	2,000.00
J. M. Sanders	5,000.00	Elmer W. Bonar	2,000.00

Equitable Life Assurance Society	$8,500.00
Manufacturers' Light & Heat Co.	7,000.00
Carnegie Natural Gas Company	2,000.00
Wheeling Electric Company	2,000.00
S. H. Woodruff and family	3,000.00
J. C. Bardall Company	5,000.00
Sullivan Bros.	2,200.00

WOMEN'S WAR SAVING STAMP CLUB

MEMBERS of the Women's War Saving Stamp Club were each required to purchase W. S. S. to the amount of one hundred dollars face value when matured January 1, 1923.

Cameron

Mrs. Ella Benedum	Mrs. Caddie Grimes
Mrs. J. T. Baxter	Mrs. Emma Crow
Mrs. J. I. Elbin	Mrs. O. Benedum
Mrs. F. Hays Fish	Mrs. Loper
Mrs. Etta D. Leach	Miss Clara Peoples
Mrs. Geo. Platt	Miss Blanche Durbin
Mrs. Harvey Hicks	Miss Emma M. Crow
Mrs. Elizabeth Crow	Miss Laura Church

Miss Helen S. Nowell
Mrs. C. D. Fish
Mrs. A. Richter

Miss Alta Bungard, R. D. No. 3
Mrs. C. M. Phillips, R. D. No. 3
A. F. Knight

Captina

Miss Tola Yoho
Mrs. G. W. H. Gatts

Mrs. Cecil Timmons
Mrs. Eugene V. Gatts

Cresap

Mrs. Elizabeth Cresap

Miss Elizabeth T. Cresap

Dallas

Miss Leota J. Steele
Mrs. Amanda Harsh
Mrs. Maggie M. Mooney
Mrs. A. D. Mooney

Mrs. Cora Campbell
Mrs. W. A. Harsh
Mrs. W. A. Campbell
Miss Mary Harsh

Glendale

Mrs. Charles Morningstar
Mrs. Wallace Smith
Mrs. Harry Schafer
Mrs. Frank Cotton
Miss Clara Morningstar
Miss Ida Still
Miss Ada Beal

Miss Helen Morningstar
Dr. Harriet B. Jones
Mrs. Mary C. Dowler
Mrs. J. A. Clark
Mrs. Nannie Beal
Mrs. Meta Gilmore

Glen Easton

Miss Edith Jefferson

Mrs. Allie Chapman

R. D. No. 1

Mrs. Mary B. Rine
Mrs. Samuel Chapman
Mrs. W. A. Chambers
Mrs. Eliza C. Wayt
Mrs. G. W. Kelley
Mrs. A. M. Anguish

Mrs. G. B. Games
Mrs. T. T. Bonar
Mrs. John Chapman
Mrs. J. G. Kelley
Miss Olive Bonar

R. D. No. 2
Mrs. Jacob Coffield

Kausooth

Mrs. Leonard Hartley

Mrs. Nancy Cain

Moundsville

Mrs. Evan Roberts
Mrs. H. L. McCuskey
Mrs. Vera Newman

Miss Sebasteen Rafferty
Miss Dess Turner
Mrs. Mary E. Smith

Miss Lou Turner
Miss Ethel Woodburn
Mrs. V. A. Weaver
Mrs. Anna B. McGlumphy
Mrs. A. L. Francis
Mrs. Tom Kelley
Mrs. Frank Peters
Mrs. Parry Miller
Miss Francis McCamic
Miss Bess E. Shaw
Miss Julia Campbell
Mrs. J. A. Morrison
Mrs. W. M. Riggs
Miss Rose Litman
Mrs. L. H. Denosky
Miss Emma L. Walton
Mrs. J. G. Walton
Mrs. S. J. Echols
Miss Pluma Jenkins
Miss Violet Smith
Miss A. Ewing
Mrs. Chas. E. Carrigan
Mrs. Harry A. Bowers
Mrs. J. W. Moorehead
Mrs Charles Kull
Miss Nellie Showacre
Miss Gertrude Shaw
Miss Jessie Martin
Mrs. J. E. Hughes
Miss Ella M. Brantner
Mrs. W. S. Powell
Mrs. Margaret Swift
Miss Maude Riggs
Mrs. A. F. Francis
Mrs. W. A. Luikart
Miss Rose Maurot
Miss Sarah Margaret Woodruff
Mrs. Louis Ramser
Miss Mabel Nanna
Mrs. Robert McCoy
Mrs. S. W. Mathews
Miss Eliza Dotta
Mrs. R. A. Ashworth
Miss Lena McDaniel
Mrs. Emma Clemens
Mrs. O. F. Covert
Mrs. R. G. Blankensop

Mrs. Will Hicks
Mrs. Myrtle Haynes
Mrs. Fred McMullen
Miss Emma Francis
Mrs. Louisa Schumacher
Mrs. W. C. Ferguson
Mrs. S. T. Courtwright
Miss Virginia Francis
Mrs. Lillie Marple
Mrs. M. A. Sanders
Mrs. Mary Reilly
Mrs. John Johnson
Mrs. Spencer White
Mrs. Erastus Miller
Mrs. S. C. Montgomery
Miss Lena Lauffer
Miss Grace Woodburn
Mrs. L. R. Potts
Miss Mary Nesbitt
Mrs. Mary Etta Weaver
Mrs. Laura Kelley
Miss Helen Henderson
Mrs. J. T. Jefferson
Mrs. James T. Miller
Mrs. W. P. Fish
Mrs T. L. Rogerson
Mrs. C. J. Barth
Miss Eula Barth
Miss Elsie Smith
Miss Agnes Lacy
Mrs. L. O. Jones
Mrs. A. R. Laing
Mrs. W. D. Alexander
Mrs. Chas. Stahl
Mrs. J. M. Cecil
Miss Retta Founds
Mrs. E. E. Henderson
Mrs. Anna Klug
Mrs. S. D. Ault
Mrs. A. C. Scroggins, Jr.
Mrs. W. P. Gorby*
Mrs. Arthur Francis
Miss Antoine Vorderbrueggen
Miss Jane Elizabeth Roe
Miss Toilla Houston
Miss Etta Courtwright
Miss Genevieve Barth

HISTORY OF MARSHALL COUNTY, W. VA.

Mrs. Harry Kerns
Mrs. H. G. Klink
Mrs. Amelia Karcher
Mrs. L. H. Coffield
Mrs. Rose Gordon
Mrs. Phebe Jane Cain
Mrs. C. B. Roe
Mrs. J. M. Weekly
Mrs. Frank Patton
Mrs. Mattie Nesbitt
Mrs. F. L. Yoho
Miss Myrtle Vandyne
Miss Mary Etta Hoskinson
Mrs. James A. Sigafoose
Miss Helen McCuskey

Mrs. M. L. Brantner
Miss Isabel McConnel
Mrs. B. L. Lowe
Miss Daisy Gorby
Mrs. Russell Ransom
Mrs. John McGary
Mrs. E. V. Burley
Miss Norma Scott
Miss Nettie Riggs
Miss Ella Harris
Miss Mary Ellen Dorsey
Mrs. H. L. Bauer
Mrs. T. J. Frohnapfel
Mrs. Mary Schafer
Mrs. Bess Yoho

R. D. No. 1

Mrs. Clara Dowler
Mrs. N. E. Daugherty
Miss Gertrude Jones

Miss Carrie Powell
Miss Henrietta Mason

R. D. No. 2

Mrs. Ida Rulong
Mrs. S. M. Wellman
Mrs. J. K. Lindsey
Mrs. F. L. Roberts
Mrs. Blane Bonar
Mrs. Geo. Darrow
Mrs. J. L. Woods

Mrs. Clara Doty
Mrs. Stella Lancaster
Mrs. Mary E. Cecil
Mrs. R. M. Gossett
Mrs. W. B. Wayt
Miss Mary Roberts

McMechen

Mrs. C. L. Snodgrass
*P. O. uncertain.

Miss Margaret Snodgrass

Proctor

Miss Regina Klug
Mrs. George Shutler
Mrs. Eliza Hyder
Mrs. Harry M. Graham
Mrs. Ellen Wilson
Miss Theresa Klug
Mrs. Sarah E. Wayne

Mrs. C. E. Bassett
Mrs. Joseph Vorderbrueggen
Mrs. E. C. Yoho
Mrs. Lucy Moore
Mrs. Emily Burton
Mrs. S. Earliwine

R. D. No. 3

Mrs. S. S. Clark

Mrs. Alice Flouhouse

Round Bottom

Mrs. J. W. Travis

Mrs. Morris Snedeker

Mrs. A. A. Horne
Miss Goldie Powers

Mrs. Millie Snedeker
Miss Marie Snedeker

Sherrard

Mrs. Josie McCleary
Miss Dora Behrens
Mrs. Emma V. McCombs
Mrs. Elizabeth Orum
Mrs. C. K. McCombs
Mrs. William Klages
Miss Minnie Behrens
Mrs. Rebecca Meriner
Miss Stella Marsh
Miss Mollie Marsh
Mrs. Elmira McConnell
Mrs. Ella Campbell
Mrs. Margaret Phillips
Mrs. Laura Pelley Smith
Miss Genevieve McCleary

Miss Reka Behrens
Mrs. J. F. Kiger
Mrs. Harry Marsh
Mrs. Charles Goetze
Miss Augusta Behrens
Miss Elizabeth Orum
Mrs. Samuel Hall
Mrs. E. J. Harris
Mrs. H. G. Marsh
Mrs. W. H. Johnson
Mrs. Elizabeth Phillips
Mrs. Edna Klages
Mrs. Wilhelmina Behrens
Miss Lena Behrens

Webster District

Mrs. W. H. Moore
Mrs. A. A. Hewett
Mrs. W. J. Martin
Mrs. Mabel Scott
Mrs. Adam Francis
Miss Ella Riggs
Mrs. Mary Norris
Miss Ella S. Brown
Miss Minnie Johnson

Mrs. W. T. Norris
Miss Jane Brown
Mrs. Shelvy B. Miner
Mrs. Caroline V. Francis
Mrs. James Fitzsimmons
Mrs. W. E. Moore
Miss Nannie Martin
Mrs. Jennie Fitzsimmons
Mrs. B. B. Elder

Woodlands

Miss Eva Sims
Miss Elsie Gatts

Mrs. D. W. Boston
Mrs. Ella Yoho

Miscellaneous

Mrs. Ira B. Pyles, Bellton
Mrs. B. Evans, Board Tree
Mrs. Eveline R. Pyles, Littleton
Mrs. J. H. Yoho, Howard
Mrs. Rose Booth, Welcome
Mrs. J. L. Hood, Roseby's Rock
Mrs. Sarah V. Lilley, Benwood, R. D. No. 2
Mrs. H. L. Clark, Grave Creek
Miss Emma Frohnapfel, St. Joseph

Miss Olive Campbell, Washington District
Miss Emma Allen, Union District
Miss Ella Caldwell, Union District
Mrs. W. C. Caldwell, Union District
Mrs. John Lemuel Garvin, Wheeling, R. D. No. 2
Mrs. Margaret Garvin, Wheeling, R. D. No. 2

HISTORY OF MARSHALL COUNTY, W. VA. 299

Miss May Caldwell, Wheeling, R. D. No. 2
Miss Alberta Caldwell, Wheeling, R. D. No. 2
Miss Ella Jones, Benwood
Miss Olive Crow, Washington District
Miss Lottie Riggle, Washington District
Mrs. Lulu Meyers, Wheeling, R. D. No. 2
Mrs. Marie Meier, Wheeling, R. D. No. 2
Miss Mary Meyers, Wheeling, R. D. No. 2
Miss Helen Garvin, Wheeling, R. D. No. 2

ONE THOUSAND DOLLAR BOND CLUB

This club was composed of those who purchased of the FOURTH LIBERTY LOAN BONDS to the amount of one thousand dollars or more but not to the amount of two thousand dollars.

C. M. Hood
Charles McCamic
R. G. Dakan
J. E. McCleary
O. P. Wilson
George P. Wasmuth
A. C. Scroggins, Jr.
E. C. Wayne
M. A. Sybert
B. F. Beer
John M. Cecil
J. W. Wellman
S. T. Courtwright
A. H. Ferris
W. F. Burgess
B. F. Beer
Jason Parsons
Van Ruckman
Oscar Wilson
George Ellis
Fred McNinch
I. B. Wilson
Dr. J. A. Miller
Mrs Clara Rife
Max Levy
A. R. Isiminger
Harry A. Bowers
A. G. Bonar
John W. Cunningham
L. H. McCuskey
M. Bachenheimer
A. F. Francis
Thomas Cochran
Louis Dressel
Sam Dorsey
Elizabeth Francis
Charles Kull
Anthony Frohnapfel
E. W. Lohr
Edward S. Dowler
J. W. Henderson
John L. Pelky
Mike Albert
J. T. Francis
W. W. Henderson
W. K. Mason
A. N. Holmes
Arabel Lilley
Frank H. Cecil
Thomas Scott
M. B. Pierce
William Offterdinger
J. B. Catlett
Friend Cox
John M. Johnson
Z. L. Simmons
James T. Miller
J. W. Moorehead
Samuel McGary
W. H. Hubbs
Dr. C. E. Hutchinson
H. L. Henderson

Fred Limlie
Earl L. Evans
C. H. Hunter
E. J. Harris
Frank Allen
Joe F. Voitle
John W. Crow, Jr.
J. M. Poyles
S. W. Booher*
Mrs. John W. Fish
Alex Purdy
Parry Miller
V. C. Yoho
E. G. Roberts
Miss Georgia Karcher
The J. A. Schwob Company
Mound City Council No. 6, Jr. O. U. A. M.

St. Francis Xavier Catholic Church
Suburban Brick Company
Wilson Miller, Woodruff
J. I. Hubbs, Nauvoo
B. B. Elder, Calis
S. W. Riggs, Webster District
Mound City Dry Goods Co., by Ferris Bros.
Little Prince Lodge 79, Knights of Pythias
P. B. O. Elks No. 282
Garvin & Ault
J. E. Sivert & Co.
I. C. Dowler, Calis
James I. Lutes, Glen Easton
W. E. Mason, Limestone
John Shepherd, Pleasant Valley

James Holmes $1,500.00
D. L. Logan............. 1,200.00
Andrew Lilley 1,500.00
S. Risinger 1,500.00

N. R. Yoho..............$1,500.00
Riley Workman 1,500.00
C. F. Kelley............. 1,500.00
W. S. Powell............ 1,600.00

A. B. Barnett
Lewis P. Riggle
John E. Wilson
E. D. Crow
Frank F. Boerner
Mary J. Cole
Lloyd Strope
Harry Burkley
Willard Chapman
T. C. Pipes
H. H. Pipes
Milton McCusky
Chris E. Yeater
Earnest Cully

B. E. McCuskey
W. M. Nowell
G. E. Fish
Margaret Hughes
S. E. Leech
Thomas Hopkins
J. McClean Phillips
Mrs. Olive Straub
Edward P. Cully
F. C. Yoho
Minor Grossman
James A. Whelan
J. W. Baily
Sinsel Hardware Company

GENERAL PERSHING CLUB

THIS CLUB was named in honor of General Pershing and required each member to purchase WAR SAVING STAMPS to the full limit allowed any one person to buy, one thousand dollars value, when matured January 1, 1923.

Cameron

Walter Loper
W. M. Nowell

H. W. Walton
Jane Leach

HISTORY OF MARSHALL COUNTY, W. VA.

Benjamin Patterson
J. M. Phillips
Minor Grossman
E. H. Lawrence
T. C. Pipes
John Thiel
George B. Patterson
John Nicholas
H. Burkey, Sr.
J. R. Jones
Lloyd Strope
J. N. Howard
T. E. Willard
Dave Bonar
William Miller
John Wendt
W. A. Ingram
S. E. Leach

L. L. Phillips
J. B. McNinch
W. S. Phillips
Martin Allen

C. A. Kessebring
James H. Wolfe

A. N. Holmes

Louis Gocke
James Launon
A. E. Nolte
Dr. W. J. Black
Paul Reidel
Louis M. Schad

John R. Roth

W. E. Hamilton
Everett C. Pyles

E. L. Kimmins

Frank Leach
William Jones
Harry Howard
Martha Miller
Sinsel Hardware Company
Geo. McCuskey
Thomas S. Gallantine
George Huffner
Mrs. Clara Fisher
Mrs. Leota Benedum
Paul Benedum
Guy Patterson
S. B. Hinerman
Wilber Watson
David Murphy
Harley Howard
Charles H. Carpenter
Patterson Glass Company

R. D.

W. H. Chambers
J. E. Crow
J. A. Cunningham

Captina

Horatio Gatts

R. D.

T. W. Crow

Benwood

William Hall
J. P. James
J. Frank Boenner
Mrs. William Hall
L. D. Dolbeare

R. D.

Mrs. Emma Johnson

Bellton

L. F. Burley
J. N. Pyles

Dallas

W. W. Campbell

Glen Easton

T. T. Bonar
Isaac Crow
T. E. Young
Willard Chapman
J. M. Rine
T. S. Carmichael

W. A. Chambers
J. B. Richter
John Chapman
Samuel Chapman
W. A. Standiford
R. A. Fitzgerald

R. D.

V. S. Kelley
S. R. Lydick
J. H. Crow

Jacob Coffield
A. R. Isinminger

Nancy Cain
E. L. Robinson

Kausooth

Leonard Whitley

Moundsville

J. M. Sanders
Mrs. Chas. McCamic
M. A. Syburt
Frank Williams
Mrs. Paul Maurot
V. A. Weaver
C. C. Nagle
Mrs. Emma Smith
Henry Karcher
S. W. Mathews
F. F. Yoho
W. M. Riggs
Mrs. Alice Logan
R. J. Cotts
D. C. Lutes
S. F. Francis
I. D. Keyser
Thomas Scott
Mrs. M. A. Syburt
B. B. McMechen
Auten & Gandee
M. J. Callahan
Lyle B. Byrnes
S. T. Courtwright
Charles Kull
T. A. Kelley
Hugh Thompson
E. Wilkinson
Fred E. Rife

J. A. Forster
J. A. Bloyd
W. A. B. Dalzell
Evan G. Roberts
A. J. Jones
B. M. Spurr
J. B. Catlett
Blair Yoho
Joe Shetler
Max Levy
T. S. Riggs
I. Gordon
Dr. C. D. Williamson
D. L. Logan
Mrs. Margaret Swift
W. M. Garner
Mrs. B. F. Beer
N. R. Yoho
Andrew Lilley
J. Howard Holt
W. X. Rupp
C. G. Musgrove
J. T. Miller
W. H. Johnson
Philip Ebeling
W. P. Yoho
C. M. Hood
B. F. Bone
J. E. McCleary

HISTORY OF MARSHALL COUNTY, W. VA.

A. Buckleh
W. D. Alexander
Mrs. W. A. B. Dalzell
Martin Brown
Thos. Cochran
Gertrude Spurr
Edwin Fitzsimmons
Sarah Ella Smith
Cyrus Yoho
Rev. M. F. Compton
S. Dorsey
Mrs. Vera Newman
J. W. Moorehead
Dr. J. C. Peck
Mrs. Anna B. McGlumphy

Mrs. C. E. Hutchinson
H. E. Roberts
S. M. Cunningham
Parry Miller
Mrs. Mary Etta Weaver
Mrs. Emily V. Burley
Arch E. Conner
H. J. Zink
J. E. Chase
Mrs. Ella Zena Garner
Mrs. Mary E. Smith
Fred McMullen
Miss Edith Campbell
J. W. Cunningham
Mrs. Pearl Wasmuth

R. D.

M. C. Koontz
Harold Conner
Albert Leach
Wilbert Jones
Mrs. Mary A. Koontz
Mrs. E. W. Dorsey

Mrs. M. C. Koontz
John McGary
Hubert Conner
George A Koontz
H. V. Campbell

McMechen

Mrs. Anna Koch
S. P. Ullum
F. H. Goodwin
H. G. Klink
Mrs. Will Jones
Ida Schultz
P. Seltner
James T. Powell
J. L. McMechen
J. E. Gatewood
Milton Robinson

Charles C. Schane
E. W. Samon
James Baird
C. M. Logsdon
Mrs. Nancy B. Houck
John W. Lineberger
J. T. Muldrew
Joseph Gatewood
Samuel J. Hunter
Mrs. Matilda Schafer
Charles Edward Jones

Proctor
R. D.

Mrs. Laura L. Yoho
J. P. Cooper
T. J. Frohnapfel
Harry Lauffer
Mrs. Matilda Cooper
L. A. Klug

Harry J. Frohnapfel
A. J. Frohnapfel
Mrs. Bordora E. Frohnapfel
J. P. Hyder
Effie M. Jolly
Joe Verderbruggen

Roseby's Rock

Mrs. Kate Hood
Mrs. Emma C. Ruckman
Freeman Beebout

Dr. Harry Howard
Frank Hopkins

Sherrard

Vinton McCleary
W. M. Gamble

C. H. Robinson

St. Joseph

T. J. Shutler
John Shutler

Rev. Fr. Buchheit

Woodlands

Mrs. Nola Yoho
R. D. Miller
Jehu Yoho

Mrs. Leota Baker
John Wilson
F. C. Rine, R. D. 1

Welcome

Mrs. E. C. Yoho
Cecil May Yoho

Bismark C. Yoho

Miscellaneous

Clinton Spurr, France
D. L. Dague, Viola
James Darrow, Lynn Camp
H. J. Richmond, Fairview Franklin District
D. H. Arrack, Franklin District
Clarence Remke, Wheeling, R. D. No. 2
Alex D. Hood, Wheeling, R. D. No. 2
Wilson Richmond, Woodruff
R. W. Luke, Elm Grove, R. D. No. 5
W. A. Caldwell, Elm Grove, R. D. No. 5
James Cunningham, Calis

Henry Geiseler, Elm Grove, R. D. No. 5
Mrs. Marie Meier, Wheeling, R. D. No. 2
A. Turner, Woodruff
W. F. Wagner, Wheeling, R. D. No. 2
Henry Meier, Wheeling, R. D. No. 2
Sam Fisher, Elm Grove, R. D. No. 5
Mrs. Blanche Luke, Elm Grove, R. D. No. 5
W. A. Cole, Elm Grove, R. D. No. 5
G. N. Dague, Elm Grove, R. D. No. 5

RECAPITULATION

Subscribed to Liberty Bonds as reported by Federal Reserve Banks for the several bond issues:

I—May 15 to June 15, 1917	$ 99,100
II—October 1 to October 27, 1917	672,750
III—April 6 to May 4, 1918	831,100
IV—September 28 to October 19, 1918	1,331,250
V—April 12 to May 4, 1919	773,000
	$3,707,200

The amount subscribed by citizens of the county and reported by local authorities:

I—May 15 to June 15, 1917	$ 176,100
II—October 1 to October 27, 1917	672,750
III—April 6 to May 4, 1918	831,100
IV—September 28 to October 19, 1918	1,331,250
V—April 12 to May 4, 1919	773,000
	$3,784,200

The difference is accounted for by the purchase of Liberty Bonds from banks out of the county by citizens and credited to the counties in which the purchases were made.

The amount invested in Liberty Bonds and in War Saving Stamps was very creditable to the citizens of the county. War Saving Stamps were purchased to the amount of $628,640. The total amount, as reported, invested in government securities, amounted to the sum of $4,412,840, or nearly ten percentum of the total assesed valuation of all property in the county.

More than ONE HUNDRED THOUSAND DOLLARS were donated by the citizens of this county to the organizations that aided the soldiers, both over sea and in camps in the United States. The above amount does not include RED CROSS work and cost of material used in making many articles of comfort for the soldiers.

MOUND

THE MOUND that stands in the midst of Moundsville is certainly one of the wonders of the world. No one knows by whom it was built nor does he know when it was built nor how it was built. It was evidently built by the hands of man, and that being the case, it is entitled to be classified as one of the wonders of the world.

Joseph Tomlinson seems to have lived near it for some time before he saw it. It has been stated that the first time he saw it was one evening as he returned home from hunting, with a load of game. He came up to what appeared to him to be a hill and in the way of his progress in getting home with a heavy load. He laid down his game and started along the foot of the hill to make an investigation of the nature of the hill and find a gap through which he might pass homeward without climbing so rugged a side as was presented to him. He soon made the circuit and found it was not a hill at all but a mound. He brought his wife the next morning to see it. They ascended it and made a thorough examination of the exterior as far as they could. Mr. Tomlinson regarded it as a burying place of an ancient race of people and as long as he lived cared for it and protected it as such.

It may appear strange that he lived some time near it without having seen it but it must be remembered that the Flats of Grave Creek was at that time covered with a dense growth of large trees, so dense that one could see but a short distance into the gloom of the forest, especially when leaves were on the trees, and when this fact is considered it will be understood.

Mr. and Mrs. Tomlinson found the mound covered with trees as large as those of the surrounding forest and of the same varieties. There was a depression in the top of the mound and a large beech tree stood in the center of it. The tree had a number of names carved upon it when discovered, indicating that others had seen it before Mr. and Mrs. Tomlinson. Some of the dates carved on it were as early as 1736. Many names were found carved upon the tree and many visited the mound after it was discovered, and many visitors carved their names upon it so that it had somewhat the appearance of an autograph album. A white oak stood on the west side of the disk that died in the beginning of the past century that had a valid claim to being the monarch of the surrounding forest. It died apparently of old age and was cut down carefully and the growths counted and from the number of them the age of the tree was estimated at five hundred years. It carried its thickness about fiftey feet from the ground and at that point branched out. The entire length of the tree was seventy feet when standing. It is said that it was fifteen feet in circumference. A red oak stood on the east side of the mound and a short distance down the side, that from its size, was entitled to succeed the white oak as monarch, if size and age was the direct line of decent of monarchship.

The height of the mound was given as seventy-nine feet and more than nine hundred feet in circumference at the base and fiftey feet acros the top.

While Joseph Tomlinson lived he would not allow the mound to be molested in any way as he regarded it as a burying place. He died in 1825, and the land was left to his son who yielded to the persuasion of those who were anxious to examine the interior.

On the nineteenth of March 1838 the work of making an excavation to examine the interior of the mound was commenced. A tunnel was started on the north side on a level with the base of the mound and with level ground about it. It was ten feet high and seven feet wide and was driven directly south toward the center of the mound. At a distance of one hundred and eleven feet, a vault was found. It was eight feet wide by twelve feet long. The sides of the vault were in line with the cardinal points. Its greater length was north and south.

There had been an excavation made in the earth seven feet deep before the vault was made. The vault had been made by placing timbers upright on two sides and the ends and they were covered with timbers laid crosswise, and these were covered with loose stones such as are found anywhere in the Flats of Grave Creek. The timbers had rotted and fallen in and the stones had fallen into the vault. The outlines could easily be traced by the rotten wood which would crumble between the thumb and fingers. The vault was as dry as any room.

In this vault two human skeletons were found. One of the skeletons had no ornaments about it of any kind while in the other six hundred and fifty ivory beads and an ivory ornament were found. The ornament was six inches long, one and five-eighths inches wide in the middle and one and one-half inches wide at the ends, with two holes through it about one-eighth of an inch in diameter. It was flat on one side and oval on the other side.

The beads were flat and from three-eighths of an inch to five-eighths of an inch in diameter. They looked as if they had been sawed from a shaft of ivory and holes drilled in the center of them. Some were in a good state of preservation while others crumbled when touched.

The first skeleton found was lying down on the back and along the west side of the vault and near it. The feet were about the middle of it and the body extended the full length with the head towards the south. The left arm was lying along left side and the right arm as if raised over the head, the bones lying about the ear and over across the head. No ornaments of any kind were found about this skeleton. The earth had evidently fallen into the vault before the ceiling had fallen as it was well preserved. When the bones were placed in their proper place and compared, they indicated a human being about five feet and nine inches in height. The shape of the head indicated a high degree of intellect. The second skeleton was lying on the left side with its head to the east, the feet likewise near the center of the side. The earth had not fallen in on this skeleton as on the first one found. It was not much broken, though more than the first one found. It was about this skeleton that the beads and ivory ornament were found.

After reaching the vault, work below was suspended and a shaft ten feet in diameter was started at the top in the depression and sunk to a level with the base of the mound and the land around it. At a depth of thirty-four or thirty-five feet, a vault was found that contained a human skeleton and a number of ornaments and a stone upon which were carved some hieroglyphics that astounded scientists.

About seventeen hundred beads, five hundred small shells, one hundred and fifty pieces of isinglass from one and one-half to two inches square, and five copper bracelets were found in the vault. The pieces of isinglass had two or three holes in them about the size of a small awl. The copper bracelets were found to be in a good state of preservation and the five together weighed seventeen ounces, and appeared to have been made of round bars bent until the ends met. They were from one-fourth to one-half an inch in diameter. The bracelets were about the wrists and the beads

and shells were about the neck and breast. The shells had been strung and worn as beads. The shells were thought to have been sea shells and very small. The pieces of isinglass had apparently been joined together and worn as a coat. The beads were from the thickness of pasteboard to one-fourth of an inch thick.

The stone that has been a mystery, was found in the upper vault near the skeleton. It was sand stone of very fine grain, and about one-half of an inch thick. It had no holes in it to indicate that it had been worn as an ornament. It was smooth on one side with hieroglyphics carved on the other side. There were quite a number of copper beads found in the vault with ivory ones.

There were many things found in the mound usually found in graves opened elsewhere, such as arrow heads, hatchets of stone, etc. The beads counted were those that were in fairly good condition. Many of them were too much decayed to bear handling and were not counted. The earth, in general, appeared to be of the same as the ground around the mound. In the interior were found blue spots which evidently had been caused by burning bones. There were particles of burned bones found in many of the blue spots, which was all the evidence required to decide the cause of them. From the number of spots there must have been many bodies cremated there in the far past.

After the tunnel and shaft were completed an investigation was made of the interior where they met, about twenty-five feet in diameter. The openings were walled and arched and the central one was plastered. It was the intention to make the room in the center a museum in which it was proposed to exhibit the relics found in the mound and that as near the spots where they were found as possible. It was abandoned in a few years and the openings have fallen in and the work all lost.

A circular house or observatory was built on the top of the mound soon after the openings were made. It was three stories high. The first story was thirty-two feet in diameter, the second twenty-six feet and the third ten feet in diameter. The roofs were nearly flat and very strong so that a number of persons could stand on them without danger of the roofs falling in and injuring them. From the roofs of the building there was a fine view of the surrounding country. It was neglected and soon fell to pieces and many years ago disappeared entirely and no trace of it is left. The last seen of the house was over half a century ago. The relics found in the mound have been so scattered that it would be a difficult task to gather them together.

The land, which for many years constituted the mound property, contains more than one acre of land and is bounded on the south by Tenth Street and on the north by Jane Street, on the east by Morton Avenue and on the west by Tomlinson Avenue.

The property changed hands several times since the death of Joseph Tomlinson. It was purchased a number of years ago by Hon. G. S. McFadden and owned by him and his heirs many years. It lay as any other unoccupied and nonproducing property, and from the effect of weather and children playing on it, was greatly damaged. Gullies were washed in the sides by rains and holes dug into the sides by children.

There was much talk of purchasing it and placing it in the hands of the State that it might be restored so far as possible to its original size and shape, and otherwise improved. Nothing was done until the Legislature convened in regular session in January, 1909. The Legislature passed an act authorizing the purchase of the mound for the sum of twenty five thousand dollars. A deed from R. J. McFadden and wife et al., dated April 15, 1909, conveyed the property to the State of West Virginia for the sum of twenty-five thousand dollars, of which the McFadden heirs donated five thousand dollars as a memorial to Hon. G. S. McFadden.

It received no attention from the State for more than five years. In the spring of 1915, M. Z. White, warden of the penitentiary, set a force of men to work on it to make the improvements so much talked of in years past.

After restoring it to its former shape by filling the gullies, holes and depression at the top caused by the caving in of the tunnel and the shaft, the work of beautifying it was started. Grass seed and fertilizer was liberally used, trees were planted on the sides of it to hold the earth in place and prevent rains from washing gullies, the level ground about the base of it was planted with ornamental trees, shrubs and roses. A hedge of California privet was planted around the lot, walks were made, beds were prepared and in summer many beautiful foliage plants are grown in them.

Through the energy of Mr. White the mound has been made a thing of real beauty and should, in part, stand as a memorial of the interest he had in caring for a burying place of a pre-historic race of people.

THE MOUND that stands in a conspicuous place in Moundsville is not the only mound found by early settlers in the Flats of Grave Creek nor is it the only evidence of a pre-historic people.

A number of small mounds were found scattered over the flats and all of them that were opened were found to contain articles that clearly indicated that they were graves of a people who lived here at an early age. The plow has leveled these mounds so that they can no longer be located and no records of them other than what is given above, and if these lines are lost, in a few years only tradition will be handed down to future generations. The tradition will cease to be remembered and that much of the history of this beautiful valley will be lost forever—forgotten.

From the numerous graves the name of Grave Creek was given to each of the three sreams of water that flow through the flats now known as the Flats of Grave Creek.

All the pre-historic work was not in these mounds only. Some stone works of a kind and purpose not clear to the mind of man were found in several places. On the Burley Hill is found a pile of stones, some of which are large but most of the stones are small, much like the ordinary flag stones or loose stones found on the surface of the ground and formerly used in constructing foundations for houses or other building purposes.

The structure was circular in shape and from the ruins

appears to have been a circular building or fortification and through the influence of time and the elements of nature the structure fell in, making the circular pile of stones above mentioned.

On a point on the south side of Big Grave Creek on a farm owned by B. F. Holmes and formerly owned by William Collins, on Robert's Ridge, is another pile of stones of the same kind only differing in size and amount of stones found there.

On the top of a hill on the Ohio side of the river opposite the mouth of Little Grave Creek, is another heap of stones of the same kind, and in both of the latter cases, the works appear to have been of the same nature and purpose of the one on the Burley Hill. These piles of stones are still in evidence of an extinct people.

No records of any investigations of these ruins further than moving of a few stones by inquisitive boys, has ever been reported, and to the average resident of this country these piles of stones, evidently ruins, mean nothing, but to the antiquarian they are monuments of historical value equal probably to some of the pyramids of Egypt or mounds or ruins found in the Tigris-Euphrates Valley and it is possible that they have the same relation to the early history of this country that the latter have to the early history of Egypt or Babylon. Something of the nature of a Rosetta Stone, if found, might give a key to the history locked up in these ruins of an ancient people.

It is no idle thought or foolish words to say that the history of the Ohio Valley, ancient and modern, if carefully written, would be as interesting and as enlightening as that of the two great valleys mentioned above and give valuable information upon the rise and progress of civilization.

The Ohio Valley is rich in hsitory but it appears that it will never be fully collected and given to the public unless there is greater interest taken than is taken at present.

PIONEER INDUSTRIES

The manufacture of breadstuff in this country at an early day was by primitive processes. The first meal was made by pounding corn in a hominy-block into coarse meal.

The machinery was simple. A large block was cut from a log of hard wood about three and one-half feet long, the ends squared, on the larger of which it rested. A hole was cut in the upper end with an ax as deep as it could be cut and then it was burned as deep as needed and the burned wood was scraped out clean, leaving a clean, smooth surface. A pestle was made from a piece of wood about the size of

HISTORY OF MARSHALL COUNTY, W. VA.

a mattock handle, large at one end, around which was put a band of iron to keep it from splitting and an iron wedge was driven into this end and this ocmpleted the apparatus for making hominy and coarse corn meal. This was the first method used, as it was easily made and was about the only available method in the days of early settlement in the Ohio Valley, and such as it was, it was generally ready for use by the time the first crop of corn raised was ripe and ready for making hominy or meal.

The hand-mill came later and was some improvement, but would not suit the work today. It was a small mill and was operated by hand power, but it was an improvement on the pounding process, but was a very slow process of grinding grain.

The horse-mill was only a mill of the same kind, larger and operated by horsepower.

Mills of the first two kinds were all the mills found except in thickly settled sections of the country for many years after the first settlements were made.

It was more than a quarter of a century after the first settlements were made before a water-mill was built in this county. For many years the nearest mill to the Flats of Grave Creek was at Shepherd's near where Elm Grove now stands. It was about fourteen miles and no road other than a path through the forest.

After the close of the long and bloody war with the Indians water-mills were built on Big Wheeling Creek and on Big Grave Creek, Little Grave Creek and on Middle Grave Creek and on several large runs. None were ever built on Fish Creek as it was considered a navigable stream and a dam could not be erected as it would interfere with the navigation of the creek.

One of the early water-mills erected in the county was erected on Big Wheeling Creek about a mile below the Harsh Sugar Camp, by Phillip Conkle, who owned and operated it one-half of a century and then sold it to William Ruth. The mill was built in 1801 and sold to Mr. Ruth in 1851 and he and his heirs owned and operated it one-half of a century. But floods damaged the dam that the owners decided that the product of the mill would not justify them in keeping the dam in repair, and soon after it had passed the century mark it ceased to be used and was dismantled and the building torn down.

It was one of the best of its kind and in its day and did its work faithfully until nature seemed to cease to work in harmony with it as floods became so frequent and so disastrous that it could not keep up its usual work for mankind and furnish its part of the staff of life and it ceased to be operated. It was one of the old land-marks in the early years of the present century and was the last mill of the kind in this section of the country.

BY carefully noticing the report of the County Assessor for the year 1860, it will be seen that people were not so much dependent upon factories for many of their supplies as they are at the present day.

Spinning wheels and hand looms were very common and in general use. Cards for carding wool into rolls were much in use. Carding mills were in operation in connection with grist mills as an annex to them. A very large plant of this kind was run in connection with the old River Shore mill that stood west of Water Street in Moundsville just above the foot of Fifteenth Street. Thousands of pounds of wool were carded into rolls for spinning or spun into yard to be woven into wear on hand looms that were operated in many of the homes at that day, or was prepared at the homes for stocking yarn and knit into socks.

Hundreds of pounds of flax were raised and worked up into various kinds of ware for household use and for clothing but the last half of the past century ended the manufacturing of home-made wares of any kind and they are only remembered by the older people of today. The mills for manufacturing material for home-made ware have been dismantled and in most cases torn down and are now a thing of the past to be revived no more, and the old-time spinning wheel and the equipments for making home-made ware are matters of curiosity.

WEATHER RECORD

1816—There was frost every month of this year. A heavy fall of snow in the early part of November was taken off with rain. causing a flood and much low ground was inundated, especially along the Monongahela River. Many cornfields were well filled with an unusual good crop of pumpkins which were carried off by the flood, which gave the flood the name of PUMPKIN FLOOD, by which it is remembered.

1831—Winter set in early this year and was very cold. By the last of the year the Ohio River was frozen so that it was crossed by teams and coal was hauled from Pipe Creek to Elizabethtown for fuel in sleds drawn by oxen. A heavy fall of snow went off in February, which caused the flood of 1832.

1834—There was a heavy frost this year on the morning of the first day of June.

HISTORY OF MARSHALL COUNTY, W. VA.

1855—The heaviest fall of snow recorded, commenced falling late in the night of December 24. It was a white Christmas.

On the first day of January, 1856, the temperature was zero. On the ninth of January the thermometers at the Flats of Grave Creek registered eighteen degrees below zero. Cold continued and the Ohio River was frozen so that it was used for a road and mail was carried from Wheeling to Parkersburg in a sled on the ice.

On March 1st, thermometers registered twelve degrees below zero.

1859—There was a heavy frost on Sunday morning, June 5th, which did much damage.

1864—The first day of January of this year is remembered as the Cold New Year. The last day of December, 1863, was an unusually warm day for the time of the year. A rain after midnight was followed by sudden cold, which became severe and was accompanied by a high wind.

1875—The 15th day of February of this year was unusually cold. Thermometers registered as low as eighteen degrees below zero.

1890—Trees and bushes were in bloom in February of this year. The winter had been an unusually open one, especially the months of January and February. A cold wave the latter part of February killed bloom, fruit buds and did the trees much damage.

1891—The heaviest fall of sleet known to the oldest inhabitants of this section occurred in January of this year. It did much harm to trees of all kinds as the weight of the ice broke many limbs from them, strewing the woods with brush.

1899—The ninth and tenth days of February of this year were very cold days. On the morning of the ninth, thermometers in a number of places registered sixteen below zero and on the following morning they registered from about twenty-nine degrees to forty degrees below zero. Locations and conditions and also differences in thermometers may be accounted for part of the difference in the temperature.

1903—This was not an unusually cold winter but was unusually long. It set in on the 18th of November and continued until late in March.

A heavy rain in January caused a flood in the river covering the low ground with ice as if nature was preparing it for Polar Bears. The flood reached the crest on the 25th of January. The break in the cold did not

affect the ground and it remained frozen until in March.
1912—There was some very cold weather this year. On the morning of the 13th of January the government thermometer at the penitentiary registered twenty-one degrees below zero. It was followed by cold weather.
1913—On the morning of November 9th of this year, a rain turned to snow and continued to fall all day and when it ceased falling the ground was covered to a depth of eighteen inches and travel on the hills was closed for several days and rural mail carriers were prevented from making the usual daily delivery of mail for a week.
1917—This was not an unusually cold winter but was an unusually unpleasant one as there were so many cold, stormy days. The minimum temperature registered was seventeen degrees below zero in December.
1918—This was a mild winter with an unusual number of clear bright days and little snow. Until the 29th of March the entire fall of snow had not aggregated one inch (.95 of an inch). On the 30th a snow fell to the depth of three inches and three-tenths of an inch. The spring was cold and late.

ANTIQUATED TERMS

SQUAW WINTER, INDIAN SUMMER and POW-WOWING WEATHER were terms familiar to the early settlers of the Ohio Valley, but today they are nearly obsolete and have little, if any, significance, but to the early settler they had real important meanings that to them amounted to matters of life or death.

Squaw Winter was a cold spell of weather or an autumnal storm that occurred about a month after the autumnal equinox. Often there was a fall of snow and sometimes a few days of real winter weather. Squaws, who did all the work of planting, cultivating and gathering the crops, would hasten to gather the pumpkins and squashes frm the cornfields when such storms commenced and store them away in protected places and cover them with dry leaves to keep them from freezing and preserve them for winter use.

Indian Summer was mild weather, setting in a few weeks later and lasting from one or two to four or five weeks. The weather was distinguished particularly by the haze or smoke that appeared to such an extent it obscured the sun or made it appear as a ball of fire in the sky.

When the weather began to get cold and stormy in autumn and snow began to fall or was likely to fall at any time, Indians usually withdrew the warriors from hostilities

HISTORY OF MARSHALL COUNTY, W. VA.

and ceased to send war parties against their enemies especially against the whites, for various reasons. They did not care to encounter the cold storms of winter while on expeditions against the enemy, the white settlers, and also they were unable to conceal themselves from the whites as the snow gave them an opportunity to follow their trail without any difficulty and small parties were sure to be pursued and punished unless it was a very weak settlement and far from aid; they also would withdraw from hostilities to engage in their usual winter hunts to provide meat for food and furs and skins to exchange for guns, ammunition, blankets and other articles they procured from traders for their use.

The pleasant weather of Indian Summer was favorable for hostilities and at the same time not good weather for hunting, and they would frequently send out small parties—scalping parties—to harrass the settlements and commit murders, as the whites were likely to have returned to their farms from forts after a fall of snow, feeling safe from Indians for reasons given above.

Indians generally confined their hostilities to summer and the mild weather permitting them to return and renew hostilities was called INDIAN SUMMER.

Pow-wowing Weather was a short season of mild, pleasant weather in the latter part of winter, generally in February and which was generally good sugar making season and improved by both whites and Indians and while squaws were making maple sugar the chiefs and warriors would frequently hold councils and discuss proposed expeditions against their enemies the following summer, hence pow-wowing weather.

TEMPERATURE

	1906		1907		1908		1909		1910	
	Max.	Min.	Max.	Min.	Max.	Min.	Max.	Min.	Max.	Min.
January	76	4	71	12	58	3	71	3	60	4
February	72	3	55	5	67	6	64	11	57	4
March	67	8	85	21	83	22	66	18	88	23
April	86	23	84	20	89	26	85	20	87	26
May	90	31	88	31	94	24	89	32	87	29
June	94	47	93	42	96	42	94	42	94	51
July	92	51	92	50	95	51	93	42	95	50
August	92	53	91	51	99	46	94	45	95	45
September	89	43	88	38	95	32	94	35	91	42
October	80	22	80	26	88	28	86	24	91	21
November	76	21	66	19	77	14	79	20	68	19
December	64	2	63	11	65	9	73	2	58	1

HISTORY OF MARSHALL COUNTY, W. VA.

	1911		1912		1913		1914		1915	
	Max.	Min.	Max.	Min.	Max.	Min.	Max.	Min.	Max.	Min.
January	62	7	55	21	65	21	75	3	60	2
February	68	16	64	4	72	5	57	10	63	11
March	70	6	72	14	75	11	76	8	45	16
April	80	17	84	26	89	24	91	29	77	21
May	97	31	90	38	93	28	97	31	86	37
June	99	51	91	36	98	36	99	44	91	40
July	103	51	96	54	99	50	102	42	93	52
August	100	47	91	47	98	46	98	59	98	59
September	90	39	95	39	98	31	98	34	98	59
October	82	29	89	29	89	24	78	24	78	29
November	71	14	73	21	73	11	76	33	76	18
December	72	12	66	10	62	14	60	1	65	1

	1916		1917		1918		1919		1920	
	Max.	Min.	Max.	Min.	Max.	Min.	Max.	Min.	Max.	Min.
January	60	2	71	2	..	..	66	2	58	1
February	68	11	70	7	..	..	54	12	40	17
March	75	16	85	25	83	25	47	20	61	12
April	77	21	..	..	77	24	55	25	86	23
May	93	40	..	..	88	30	97	36	92	31
June	89	42	..	..	88	40	98	50	93	52
July	97	52	..	..	97	43	100	51	93	47
August	97	49	..	..	107	52	95	47	82	49
September	91	34	..	..	83	32	93	39	90	46
October	91	27	..	..	74	22	90	36	81	28
November	72	14	..	..	56	20	69	5	68	18
December	66	2	..	17	60	20	65	2	65	11

(..) By oversight the record was not kept at the station.

RAINFALL

	1906	1907	1908	1909	1910	1911	1912	1913
January	2.54	5.77	1.19	3.20	5.60	5.38	1.37	6.16
February	1.30	1.24	2.24	3.87	3.74	1.40	1.38	1.60
March	5.63	8.18	5.44	2.55	.08	1.64	4.90	3.80
April	3.41	3.25	4.08	3.48	2.45	3.85	2.96	2.14
May	2.11	4.28	4.72	4.80	3.89	1.22	1.42	3.16
June	4.31	3.85	2.43	4.06	1.52	4.39	2.29	2.82
July	3.99	9.27	4.03	3.16	4.33	1.59	6.90	4.05
August	3.21	2.69	3.80	2.14	1.99	5.68	2.02	2.07
September	2.53	4.41	.59	.85	3.20	6.31	2.71	2.15
October	3.19	3.02	2.10	2.02	2.03	5.13	1.55	3.54
November	1.32	1.81	.51	.95	1.16	1.81	.76	1.96
December	4.35	2.62	1.31	1.85	2.31	3.61	2.60	2.99
	37.89	50.39	32.44	32.93	32.30	42.01	30.86	38.44

	1914	1915	1916	1917	1918	1919	1920	1921
January	.94	3.08	1.47	2.84	....	1.05	3.30	4.01
February	1.39	2.46	2.44	....	....	2.18	1.27	1.45
March	.75	1.28	2.09	2.09	1.47	2.20	2.25	4.05
April	2.06	1.30	4.47	....	2.20	2.97	4.04	2.62
May	2.40	3.54	3.77	....	5.47	4.18	1.91	3.86
June	4.27	5.73	3.37	....	1.90	1.67	3.38	3.89
July	1.75	3.00	1.29	....	2.75	4.82	6.36	1.25
August	.80	1.57	3.59	....	4.50	7.35	2.07	6.52
September	.82	2.80	.89	....	2.85	2.30	3.16	8.30
October	.06	2.49	2.55	....	2.87	5.29	1.73	1.52
November	2.40	2.40	1.55	....	1.77	4.77	1.85	6.68
December	4.60	4.06	1.47	....	4.44	2.90	2.38	4.38
	22.40	34.25	26.60	....	30.22	41.68	33.20	48.53

	1922	1923
January	1.41	....
February	2.25	.70
March	5.30	5.10
April	4.42	1.13
May	3.11	3.33
June	4.51	2.72
July	2.09	4.60
August	2.40	2.50
September	6.90	3.50
October	2.40	1.80
November	.65	3.50
December	1.70	6.40
	37.14	

CENTURY FLOOD RECORD
1810 to 1910

	Pittsburgh	Wheeling	Parkersburg
1810—Saturday, November 10	32	48	....
1832—Friday, February 10	35	48.11	49.5
1852—Tuesday, April 20	31.9	48	44
1860—Friday, April 13	26.7	43	44.7
1861—Monday, September 30	30	44.2	45.1
1862—Wednesday, April 23	27.9	37	37
1865—Sunday, March 19	31.4	41	....
1873—Monday, December 15	25.6	40.8	38.7
1874—Tuesday, January 9	22.9	38.9	38.8
1878—Thursday, December 12	34.9	34.9	40
1881—Tuesday, June 21	25.6	40.9	34
1883—Monday, February 19	25.8	39.7	45.2

Date			
1884—Friday, February 8	33.6	52.4	52.9
1891—Wednesday, February 18	31.3	44.11	44.6
1895—Monday, January 8	25.9	36.1	37
1897—Wednesday, February 24	24.5	37.10	....
1898—Wednesday, March 23	28	44.6	48.1
1900—Thursday, November 29	27.7	37.7	30.4
1901—Monday, April 22	28	41.9	43.9
1902—Sunday, March 2	32.4	43.3	40
1903—Monday, March 2	24.3	34.6	39.9
1904—Sunday, January 24	30.1	44.1	42.4
1904—Friday, March 4	29.1	39.3	....
1905—Monday, March 22	29	42.3	42.4
1907—Saturday, January 12	23	37	39.9
1907—Friday, March 15	35.2	50.5	51.6
1908—Monday, February 17	30.8	42	....
1908—Friday, March 20	27.3	39.6	....
1910—Thursday, January 20	22.3	31.9	....
1910—Friday, March 4	22	27.3	....
January 15, 1911	....	36.6	....
January 31, 1911	25.2	35.5	....
September 17, 1911	20.1	29.5	....
March 22, 1912	28.1	38.6	....
January 10, 1913	31.3	44.3	....
January 13, 1913	26.3	39.2	....

ASSESSOR'S REPORT
Of Marshall County for 1860
LIVE STOCK

Number of horses	2,413
Number of milch cows	1,501
Number of work oxen and other cattle	3,686
Number of sheep	10,002
Number of hogs	8,447
Value of live stock	$ 253,063
Value of slaughtered animals	44,944

FARM LAND

Number of acres of improved land	59,136
Number of acres of unimproved land	62,543
Cash value of the farms	$2,499,909
Value of farm machinery and implements	58,262

FARM PRODUCTS

Number of bushels of wheat	74,750
Number of bushels of corn	241,911
Number of bushels of oats	133,617
Number of bushels of potatoes	46,634

Number of pounds of tobacco	10,590
Number of pounds of hemp	146
Number of pounds of flax	7,722
Number of bushels of flax seed	675
Number of pounds of silk cocoons	20
Number of pounds of maple sugar	19,520
Number of gallons of maple molasses	1,958
Number of gallons of sorghum molasses	13,954
Number of pounds of honey	7,707
Number of pounds of beeswax	213
Value of manufactured goods and wares	$ 14,179

ASSESSOR'S REPORT

1910

LIVE STOCK

Number of horses	4,708	Value	$475,580
Number of cattle	7,786	Value	382,560
Number of sheep	29,681	Value	238,570
Number of hogs	2,735	Value	51,356

ASSESSED VALUATION OF PROPERTY

1923

	Real Estate	Personal Property	Board P. W.	Total of all
Cameron District	$ 3,236,460	$ 1,356,810	$ 1,143,644	$ 5,736,914
Clay District	1,433,970	239,000	1,487,154	3,160,124
Franklin District	2,497,390	430,230	1,248,016	4,175,635
Liberty District	2,103,960	492,390	2,560,709	5,158,259
Meade District	1,771,030	393,789	964,410	3,129,220
Sand Hill District	1,205,460	223,620	290,817	1,819,896
Union District	7,046,380	3,794,760	4,400,813	15,241,953
Washington District	1,895,230	721,170	857,952	3,474,252
Webster District	1,868,580	263,420	247,764	2,379,764
Moundsville Independent District	7,269,140	3,297,860	1,126,591	11,693,591
	$30,427,500	$11,214,040	$14,327,870	$55,969,410
Cameron City	$ 1,294,690	$ 1,021,230	$ 136,317	$ 2,452,237
Benwood City	3,716,980	3,188,250	3,542,607	10,447,837
McMechen City	1,508,680	323,950	602,587	2,435,117
Moundsville City	6,894,720	3,141,420	1,093,836	11,129,976
	$13,415,070	$7,674,750	$5,375,347	$26,465,167

SALARIES OF COUNTY OFFICERS

The Board of Supervisors, at a regular session held on the twentieth day of May, 1864, fixed salaries for county officers for the year as follows:

For prosecuting attorney................per annum, $200
For clerk of the board of supervisors........per annum, 350
For clerk of the circuit court............per annum, 75
For sheriff ....per annum, 50
For members of the board of supervisors for
    time spent in actual service............per diem, 2

On the twentieth of August, 1864, the board of supervisors completed the work of fixing salaries for county and township officers:

For township clerk ....per annum, $ 25
For county superintendent of free schools...per annum, 200
For recorder ....per annum, 50

The county treasurer was allowed three per centum for all county levy.

The sheriff was allowed five per centum of all taxes collected except war tax, which per agreement with the board of supervisors, was fixed at two and one-half per centum of all collected.

At a regular meeting of the board of supervisors, held on the twenty-third of June, 1865, the salary schedule was amended:

For county superintendent of free schools....per annum, $400
For recorder ....per annum, 100
For sheriff ....per annum, 150
For clerk of the board of supervisors........per annum, 300

SALARIES OF COUNTY OFFICERS
1923

For many years county officials were remunerated for services by fees for such services rendered with a small salary paid them in addition to the fees received.

The sheriff of the county served also as treasurer. He received five per cent. of taxes he collected subject to a discount of two and one-half per cent. for taxes paid in a discount period of one month.

After 1916 all county officers were paid an annual salary, paid in equal monthly payments. The salary schedule for county officers for the year 1923, as fixed by the county court or otherwise provided for, was as follows:

Sheriff (and treasurer) $3,500
Clerk of the Circuit Court..................... 2,250
Clerk of the County Court..................... 2,750
Prosecuting Attorney 1,800

HISTORY OF MARSHALL COUNTY, W. VA.

Assessor of the county........................ 2,400
County Road Engineer (new office)............ 2,400

Commissioners of the County Court, each $1,200, with an additional remuneration of two dollars per day for each day in session as a court.

County Superintendent of Schools, $2,150 and expenses.

At the present day there are many assistants such as deputy sheriffs, deputy assessor, field assistants, deputy clerks and other assistants at salaries in proportion to those of the several officers named above.

Fifty years ago, 1873, under the fee system, the salary schedule for the several officers as fixed by the county court or otherwise was as follows:

Sheriff $200
Clerk of the Circuit Court......................... 200
Clerk of the County Court......................... 200
Prosecuting Attorney 400
Assessors (two) each 400
County Superintendent of Schools................. 300

Assessors were allowed ten cents for each birth or death reported.

No allowance was made for expenses of County Superintendent.

MISCELLANEOUS

Voting places as ordered by the Board of Supervisors on March 29, 1864:

Cameron Township—Cameron and Terrell's Schoolhouse.
Clay Township—Moundsville and Roseby's Rock.
Franklin Township—Mouth of Fish Creek and Fairview.
Liberty Township—Big Run Schoolhouse and Forks of Fish Creek.
Meade Township—Mouth of Lynn Camp and Gorby & Guffy's Store.
Sand Hill Township—Sand Hill Schoolhouse.
Union Township—Benwood and Chestnut Grove Schoolhouse.
Webster Township—Smart's Store and Cross Roads.
Washington Township—Courthouse and Limestone Schoolhouse.

Meeting Places of the County Court

From June 19, 1835, to April 23, 1836, at a hotel kept by Mrs. Susan Parriott in Moundsville, then called the Lower Town.

From May 19, 1836, to September 19, 1836, at the county jail.

From September 19, 1836, until the present day, it has always met in a room at the courthouse.

The County Court, in the year 1858, levied taxes for county purposes to the amount of $4,473.25.

For the year 1918, the County Court laid a levy for county purposes of $94,438.52.

EARLY RECORDS

The first marriage recorded in this county is recorded in the following letters and figures:

    I, John Parriott, do hereby certify that I celebrated the rite of matrimony between Alexander Ogle and Mary Ann Baker, both of Marshall County, on the 18th of June, 1835.

June 19, 1835.   John Parriott.

The first deed of conveyance of land recorded in the records of Marshall County is in the proceedings of the County Court in the following words and figures, and certified to by two justices of the peace present at a regular session of County Court.

    A deed from Shipley Martin and his wife Nancy to John Gallaher for lot No. ——, situated in the addition to Moundsville, the same being duly certified and admitted to record the 19th day of June, 1835.

The deed conveyed a lot situated on the east side of Water Street fronting sixty-two and one-half feet on that street and extending back one hundred and forty-five feet to a sixteen foot alley. The price paid was ninety-five dollars.

The lot was the one on which a brick house now stands and in which was formerly the store of Joseph Gallaher, later removed into a frame building at the corner of Fourteenth and Water Streets.

BREAK IN RECORDS

In preparing this work breaks in the county records prevented complete connection. Records show that Arthur O. Baker was elected sheriff of this county at a regular annual election held on the fourth Thursday of May, 1862, to serve a regular term of two years from the first day of January, 1863. Records further show that he entered upon the discharge of his official duties at the commencement of the year and served until some time in the latter part of the summer of 1864. He enlisted in the United States service and was commissioned Captain of Company A, Seventeenth West Virginia Infantry, on the second day of September of that year. Later records indicate that Jackson Reed served as sheriff of this county the latter part of that year and also the two years following, that is, from the first of January, 1865, until the thirty-first of December, 1866.

By what authority Jackson Reed served as sheriff for that time, especially the term of two years, from January 1, 1865, to December 31, 1866, is impossible to ascertain, as no record is found concerning it and it has passed beyond the recollection of the oldest citizens now living.

No record is found of any meeting of the County Court or any similar body, from a regular session of the County Court composed of justices of the peace of the county, held on the 19th of June, 1863, until the first meeting of the Board of Supervisors on the 26th of January, 1864, nor is there any county record of the results of the regular annual election held on the fourth Thursday of October, 1863, and it will be clearly seen that the work was attended with no little difficulty.

POPULATION

By Magisterial Districts

	1920	1910	1900
CAMERON, including city, town and villages	3,685	3,442	2,350
CLAY, including city and village	1,994	1,862	1,807
FRANKLIN	1,467	1,655	1,957
LIBERTY	1,487	1,874	2,297
MEADE	1,224	1,527	1,580
SAND HILL	969	1,066	1,300
UNION, including cities, town and villages	10,398	10,001	7,688
WASHINGTON, including city, town and village	11,266	9,656	5,986
WEBSTER	1,191	1,305	1,479

Incorporated Cities or Towns

	1920	1910	1900
BENWOOD	4,773	4,926	4,511
CAMERON	2,404	1,660	964
McMECHEN	3,356	2,291	1,465
MOUNDSVILLE	10,669	8,918	5,352

	1920	1910	1900
MARSHALL COUNTY	33,681	32,383	26,444

FULLNAME AND SUBJECT INDEX

----, Jacob 65 77
ABERCROMBIE, W H 234 238
ABOTT, Wm E 130
About Col Beeler And The Mohawk
   Tribe, 45
ABRAHAM, Elias 276
Account of Capt Foreman's Expedition
   To Grave Creek & Attack, 26
ACKELS, George W 255
ACKERMANN, Nick 13
ACRES, James W 278
ADAIR, J M 172
ADAMS, Thomas 187
AIHINE, James 187
ALBAUGH, Denton 286
ALBERT, Mike 299
ALEXANDER, Jas 117 John R 258
   Joseph 114 115 Leila 172 Mrs R J
   128 138 Mrs W D 296 Ralph 268
   290 Robert 176 W D 294 303
   William 181 Wm 183 Wm J 127
   153 155 158
ALLEN, D Augustus 187 Elizabeth
   137 Emma 298 Frank 300
   Harrison 130 John 120 126 137
   John P 140 193 219 251 Leander
   229 Martin 301 Richard 132 137
   138 Samuel 232 Thomas 121 126
   147 Walter G 283 Wm M 232
ALLEY, Forrest William 287 J F 185
   John 119 Uriah T 204 Wm L 204
ALLISON, James 120 Oscar L 223
ALLMAN, C B 170 Clarence B 284
   Joshua 229
ALLOWAY, Harry 279
ALLTOP, George W 212
ALLUM, Harrison 189
ALTOP, George W 214
Amendment to The Constitution
   Changes County Court, 148
Amendments to The School Laws, 155
AMOS, Jesse 281 291 John D 220
An Amusing Incident Affects
   Settlement, 8

ANDERSON, Benjamin 206 C E 291
   Charles E 281 Charles M 287
   Chas H 275 Clyde 278 Clyde
   Clarence 285 Gail 171 Harry
   Raymond 283 James 37 James
   Lester 280 John 109 John C 203
   John Edgar 275 Joseph 233 Joseph
   H 229 Lyle Cobard 275 Mrs 37
   Roy Leonard 284 Sam J 169
   Samuel 222 Thomas 184 William
   286 William H 287
ANDREAS, Lioniel 286
ANDREW, Henry 129
ANGUISH, A M 295 David 117 121
   122 126 127 136 Messr 132 Opal
   172
ANKRUM, Aaron 187 William 187
Another Account of The Baker Family,
   72
ANSHUTZ, Henry T 228
ANTIL, Gruber 270
Antiquated Names of Weather, 316
APPOLOMIO, Silvus 278
APPOLONI, Silveo 291
ARCHEY, William Edward 277
ARGO, Wm 226
ARMSTRONG, Earnest Echart 276 J
   Y 108 John 182 183 John C 239
   Mr 183 S T 181 W H E 198 199
   William Lee 287
ARN, Frank 269 James Walter 287
ARNOLD, Frank 184 J Lloyd 186
   John 120 181 255 Lloyd 267
   Lloyd J 271 Mr 182 V 132
   Vanlear 178
   Willie 255 258
ARRACK, D H 304
ARRECK, Roy Wells 275
ARTHUR, John O 204
   Oren Everett 275
ASHBY, James 212 214
ASHWORTH, Mrs R A 296
ASSESSED VALUATIONS of All
   Kinds of Property, 1923 321

ASSESSOR'S REPORT for 1860 320
    Report of Live Stock for 1910 321
ASTON, John B 142 Joseph 258 277
    Thomas 234
ATEWART, Okey 287
AUGUISH, David 126
AULT, 300 Mrs S D 296
AUTEN, 302 Grover Franklin 284
    William 223 Wm 130
AUTER, Perry 287
AYERS, Benj R 271 John G 133 242
    Michael A 215
BACHENHEIMER, M 299
BACON, Clyde 275
BAGGS, Geo W 218 John P 218
BAILY, J W 300 Penny 135
BAINE, Archie A 287
BAIRD, J H 89 149 183 226 James
    303 Stephen 220
BAKER, 71 73 A O 134 177 183
    Adda 169 Arthur O 241 324
    Benjamin 187 Capt 72 Elizabeth
    72 Family 70 Helen 169 Henry 70
    72 74 Henry & Kate Captured By
    Indians & Escape 74 Henry &
    Three Other Young Men Escape &
    Arrive Home 71 Henry Attacked
    By Indians 70 Henry Captured By
    Indians 70 Henry Runs Gauntlets
    71 Herman Leroy 288 James 215
    James Alvin 288 James M 134
    242 255 John 70 72 73 74 75 82
    135 187 John A 220 John Builds
    A Block House 72 John C 224
    John F 272 John Sr Killed By
    Indians 72 Kate 74 75 Kate &
    Henry Captured By Indians &
    Escape 74 Leota 304 Lewis 206
    Margaret 75 Martin 73 Martin
    Gives An Account of Battle of
    Captina 73 Mary Ann 324 May
    Jane 73 Mr 75 82 Mrs 79 S P 97
    Samuel P 70 T B 224 William 270
    291 William Winford 281
Baker's Station, 82
BALDASSANA, Albert 268
BALDWIN, Francis W H 212 214

BALITO, Francisco 284
BALL, Richard 208
BALLARD, John D 215
BANE, George 235 Henry 234 Jesse
    235 Lloyd 283 Mordacai 116
BANKOVICH, Steve 274
BANNING, Ephraim 222
BARCLY, Robert 188
BARCUS, Benj 129 Benjamin 194
    196 Jonathan 260 262
BARDALL, J C 294
BARGER, Jackson L 215
BARKER, Charles Everett 282 George
    267 George Everett 285 Herbert
    Edward 280
BARLOW, C A 185 268 271
BARNARD, Eva G 171
BARNES, John 141
BARNETT, A B 172 300 Jesse L 212
    214 Wm H 251
BARNEY, Raymond M 280
BARNHART, B F 224 S 146
BARNS, John 135
BARNUM, Jesse T 289 Susan 169
BAROVIC, Pete 280
BARR, Charles Eugene 284
BARTELS, Amil Carl 276 Harry
    William 275
BARTH, Eula 296 Genevieve 296
    Howard J 287 Mrs C J 296
BARTLEBAUGH, C J 120 121
BARTLETT, Erastus G 234 I D 260
    263 Leslie Nathan 284 William F
    285
BARTLEY, Richard 267
BARTO, John 109 112 116
BARTRUG, Henry 276
BASFORD, Melvin 242 Randolph 198
    199 William 198 199
BASSETT, Jacob W 235 Mrs C E 297
    W H 126 153
BAUER, Mrs H L 297
BAUMBERGER, Jacob S 278 Orville
    169
BAXTER, J T 294
BAYLES, Archie R 280 Maxwell 220
BEAGLE, W A 129

BEAL, Ada 295 Nannie 295
BEAR WALLOW, 12
BECK, E L 170
BECKER, Anthony Henry 287 George W 276
BEEBOUT, Freeman 304
BEECHER, Edward 284
BEELER, Col 11 45 46 47 82 and The Mohawk Tribe 45
BEELER'S STATION, 81
BEER, B F 299 Edwin 268 276 Mrs B F 302
BEGOVICH, John 274
BEHRENS, Augusta 298 Dora 298 Lena 298 Minnie 298 Reka 298 Wilhelmina 298 William Henry 285
BELFORD, 187
BELL, Ervin Edwin 275 George 219 Israel J 215 Lewis 276 Margaret 170 William 187 William Scott 275
BELLVILLE, Wm 138
BENEDUM, Ella 294 Leota 301 O 294 Paul 301
BENNETT, John B 269 Samuel 201
BERISFORD, E W 169 Ernest Ward 284 Roy 285
BERRY, Charles D 261 Frank G 279 John W 139 Marion 269 Marion Steele 277 Ross 281
BERTRAND, Enos 266
BEST, Emma 172 Irene 168
BETESALL, Frederick 204
BETTS, John 187
BEUCKE, William Charles 285
BEVANS, 36 37 83 Children Murder of 36 Cornelius 37 John 37
BEYMER, Frederick 239
BIANCO, Veto Campo 274
BIDDLE, Charles W 143 John F 216 Spencer 187
BIELETOR, Amager 189
BIER, Alexander 278 291 Charles 278 George W 182 Philip G 226 228
BIERCE, John F 273 Peter Francis 287

BIGGS, 24 Joseph 25 67 Mary L 173 Thomas 66
BILDERBOCK, Capt 20
BILES, Fleming 255 John 233
BILLETER, Aunger 238
BILLETTER, John K 286
BILLS, William 187
BIRD, Francis 129 264 John 129 201 Roseberry 201 Roseby 129
BLACK, W J 301 Wm 130
BLACKBURN, John R 134
BLACKFORD, J A 172 Zephiniah 15
BLAIR, James M 229 Olive 172 Russell Howard 281
BLAKE, A E 170 Charles 285 Charles L 172 Earl C 169 Edward Leo 269 292 Elijah 284 Elmer 285 Frank William 284 Friend Leonidas 287 Geo W 222 George W 259 263 Harrison 259 Isaac 187 196 199 James A 132 Jeremiah 195 John 131 194 222 Joseph 229 Nathan 194 Robert 132 239 Russell Rowland 283 Solomon 221 Thomas 221 228 William 180 194 William Thomas 290 Wm 120 146 Wm Thomas 273
BLAKEMORE, William 265
BLAND, Richard A 245 Simeon 245
BLANFORD, Ray 269
BLANKENSOP, Mrs R G 296 Robert E 280
BLANKFORD, W B 267
BLINQUE, Thomas 232
BLODGET, Benjamin 116
BLODGETT, Daniel 187
BLOODY FIGHT IN THE FOG, 17
BLOOM, Frank 282
BLOOMFIELD, E J 130
BLOYD, Charles A 286 Charles Mccune 280 J A 294 302 Jas W 221 Joe 272 Joseph C 222 S L 128 Stephan L 132 138 Stephen S 120
BLUE, 82 Franklin B 134
BOARD OF SUPERVISORS, Declare Result of Township Election 120 Hold 1st Session & Organize 119

BOBLE, John Wesley 287
BODE, Martha 171
BODEKOSKY, Alec 283
BOENNER, J Frank 301
BOERNER, Frank F 300
BOGARD, George 269 Jesse J 142
　John 187 Vinton T 275
BOGGS, Capt 30 31 34 42 Mr 42
BOHAM, Matthias 204
BOHANAN, James 114
BOLE, John B 147 148
BOM, Carl Fred 280
BONAR, A G 299 Carl Fisk 281
　Clarence L 285 Claude C 275
　Dave 301 David 158 173 269 291
　Elmer W 294 Ezekial 172 Floyd
　279 Hallie 171 J W 89 138 141
　149 150 183 James 255 258 James
　C 114 117 134 242 Jasper W 242
　Jesse 126 153 John W 251 Joseph
　W 133 Martin P 232 Miles 120
　126 Mrs Blane 297 Olive 295
　Ross 288 S Howe 186 T T 295
　302 Thomas S 182 189 193 198
　Thos B 169 Virginia 169 W N 183
　William 269 291 Wm N 229 233
BONCE, John 187
BOND, James Francis 269 John 187
BONDY, Austin 271 Jonathan 251
　Ralph 268 Wylie F 288
BONE, B F 302 George W 290
BONNETT, 8 9 36 John 187 John
　1814 Company of 187 Levi 114
　Lewis 111 Wm 141
BOOHER, Howard Isaac 277 S W 300
　Samuel 270 Wilford 268 Wilford J
　271
BOOTH, Elmer 266 John 172 John J
　229 John M 233 Rose 298
BORAN, Wade H 261
BORLAND, Steve 284
BOSHER, William 20
BOSLEY, Joseph Wm 278
BOSO, Bonnie Herbert 281
BOSTON, Mrs D W 298 Okey M 268
BOTTOME, Sterling 268 Sterling B
　271 Virginia 172

BOUNTY, Offered To Volunteers In
　The Civil War 123
BOUQUET, Col 76
BOWEN, Brice 255 Corbly H 133 264
　James H 255 Job 247 Jobe 140
BOWERS, Earl E 280 Earl S 291
　Harry A 299 Harvey 117 Herman
　R 281 Jacob 126 John 251 John P
　259 Mrs Harry A 296
BOWLER, George 135
BOWMAN, Anna 170 E P 184 185
　Florence G 273 Marcus A 285
BOYD, 21 John 17 Levi 212 R G 227
　228
BOYLES, M P 169
BRADDOCK, Gen 75
BRADEN, Sam 283
BRADSHAW, A O 138 139 Almon O
　247
BRANCHES, Taught In Schools 156
BRANDON, Charles 269
BRANNEN, Harry R 273 Phillip 274
　Thomas 273 Wm Fremont 268
BRANNER, Jacob 220
BRANNON, Lee George 282
BRANT, Morris Edward 289
BRANTNER, Charles 266 David 143
　David A 138 140 246
　Ella M 296
　Mrs M L 297
BRANY, Samuel 258
BRASKE, George 286
BRAZDOVICH, Mike 274
BREAK, In Records 324
BRENNAN, William P 277
BRENNEN, Earl James 286
BRIDGES, 89
BRIEMSON, Hilda 170
BRIGGS, James M 235
BRNJAS, Stephen 275
BROCK, Abraham 258
　Jacob 255
　Ray 270
BROCKWAY, Thomas 227
BROGHER, Alfred 139
BROMELOW, Edward 270
BROOKS, Henry 277

BROWN, Edward A 216 221 Ella S
170 298 Elmer 276 F M 129 F W
129 Fred M 138 Frederick M 264
George 281 Gerald H 270 Isaac
187 Jane 298 Jesse 245 John 109
128 142 John Hubert 284 Lester
276 Martin 185 294 303 Paul J
270 Samuel 224 Samuel D 140
Thomas 117
BRUCE, George E 286 Nathan T 239
BRUHN, Frederick 212 214
BRYANT, Alvie E 270
BRYSON, Abraham 228 Harry A 288
John A 224
BUCHANAN, John 187 Thomas 112
114 177 Thos 112 113 William
251 Wm 142 Wm B 116
BUCHANNAN, Thos 111
BUCHEIT, Fr 304
BUCKLEH, A 303
BUCKLEY, Mrs 75
BUKSA, Michael 284
BULLMAN, John 187
BUMBUTI, Tony 275
BUNGARD, Alta 295 Marie 170
BURCEY, Harry 270
BURCH, Clarence 270 James 229
Jesse 109 112 114 196 John 189
223 Martin 197 Ray 169 Talbert
232
BURDULIS, Joe 282
BURGE, Andrew J 208 Elijah 140 251
Harvey 208 Herbert L 269 Miner
116 117 Onward E 284 Patrick J
268 Wilbur James 289
BURGESS, W F 299
William 264
Wm 137 141
BURGISS, Harold 278
BURKE, Edward H 289
John 278
Mary 169
BURKEY, H Sr 301 James Wm 272
BURKHAM, Stephen 195 199
BURKHART, Fred 139
BURKLEY, Harry 300
BURLEIGH, Presley M 242

BURLEY, Creston C 291 Creston
Clark 273 D Clifford 131
Declifford M 194 Emily V 303
Hyden 134 Jacob 107 108 110 111
112 113 114 116 177 James 108
115 116 177 181 James Raymond
289 John 119 John A 195 Joseph
A 188 259 Joseph Lawrence 289
Joshua 116 149 L 132 L F 301
Lindsey 134 149 242 Mrs E V 297
Presley M 135 Spray 283 Thomas
H 189 198 199 W J 89 149 150
183 184 Will J 223 227 William
172 William James 286
BURNES, Francis M 133
BURNS, James 188
BURR, Jacob 127 Mary 127
BURRIS, Francis 187 John W 229
Samuel 109 William 239
BURT, Robert 206
BURTON, Emily 297 James Okey 270
John A 204 Oscar 288 W Lester
274
BUSEY, Erastus 195
BUSH, John W 134 242 Lloyd 170
William 232
BUTCHER, Geo W 247 Robert W
247
BUTLER, Robert 139 247 Thomas
121 135 Thos James 274 William
J 247 Wm 141
BUTTERFIELD, John J 280
BUTTLER, Thomas 242
BUZZARD, Charles 285 Daniel 127
Erett Edwin 287 Howard 268 270
John 195 199
Theodore 135 242
BYARD, John L 288
BYINGTON, Dixie N 171
BYRNES, Geo W 186 George 172
James W 279 Lyle B 302
W F 223 227
CAGE, Samuel 140 250
CAIN, Joseph 256 258
Madden 208
Nancy 295 302
Phebe Jane 297

CALDWELL, Alberta 299 Alexander 117 E H 111 176 177 Elbert H 108 175 177 Ella 298 Harry Rayland 281 John 25 Joseph 223 227 Mary 170 May 299 Mrs W C 298 W A 304
CALE, Andrew J 204 Isaac 203 John 204
CALLAHAN, Chas Michael 279 M J 302
CALLIHAN, John Francis 281
CALVERT, George Grayson 278 290 Ward Jewel 274 William 251
CAMERON, 323 Hugh 42 Hugh Death of 42
CAMILLI, Peter 283
CAMPAGNIA, Luiggi 274 Mike 274
CAMPBELL, Carrie C 169 Charles Orion 287 Cora 295 Edith 303 Ella 171 298 Francis C 108 H V 303 Henry 116 Huse Voss 288 Julia 296 Mabel 172 Olive 298 W A 295 W D 126 154 W W 301 Wm D 120
CANAN, Chales 212
CANNELL, John 274
CANNON, John L 247
CAPITO, Christian 252
CAPPER, John 285
CAPTO, W W 142
CARBONI, Salvator 280
CARLAND, Daniel 187
CARLE, Albert Conrad 278
CARLO, Louis De 279 Petro Di 275
CARMAN, Benj F 219 Mollie 173
CARMICHAEL, H E 158 186 John 187 Silas 255 T S 302 Wm 168
CARNEY, Hiram 252 256 Martin 252 Mathew 256 Samuel F 131 William 256 Wm 135 242
CAROTHERS, H H 221 J P 235
CARPENTER, 45 Charles H 301 Lewis V 291 Louis V 280 Robert 44 87 Robert Adventure With Indians 44

CARR, Edward 223 Fred Winford 269 Joseph L 256 Thomas O 256 William 239 260 262
CARRIGAN, Chas E 185 Mrs Chas E 296
CARROLL, F S 172 John 187 Mildred 170
CARSKADEN, Louis J 283
CARSON, Wm T 272
CARTRIGHT, John 140
CASTANTINO, Scaffidi 279
CASTILOW, Fred Forest 282 Louis B 286
CATALANO, Siloesio 282
CATLETT, J B 299 302 P B 29 Peter B 96 260 262
CAUGLIN, Margaret 109
CECIL, Absolom 282 Andrew 224 Edward B 277 Encil Leslie 283 Frank H 299 Geo W 229 John M 299 Mary E 297 Mrs J M 296 Robert 117 Wm 146 Wylie Rinehart 268
CENTURY FLOOD RECORD, 319
CERONIS, Stanko 275
CERRONE, Felice 280
CHADDOCK, Alice 169 Conrad Ellsworth 289 J J 235 Joseph 189 Joseph Walter 283 Laura 273 Louis J 273 Richard 139 143 247 Robert N 269 William 271 Wm E 269
CHALK, Harry 268
CHAMBERS, Alexander 243 Amos 134 242 Benjamin 234 Calbert D 212 Earl C 269 Eli 135 242 G W 190 Geo W 209 George W 213 H Goffe 275 Hamilton 196 199 212 Harry 280 Henry 204 James 190 256 James A 212 James E 135 242 John 235 Morrison 226 Pearl 169 Roy William 284 Slater 280 292 W A 295 302 W H 301 William Francis 287 William R 281 Wilson 234
CHANOT, Justus 187

CHAPMAN, Allie 295 Arley 270 Geo
  W 216 John 184 185 295 302
  John Jr 294 Samuel 295 302
  Walter 274
  Willard 300 302
CHARLTON, Edward J 255
  Elias 266
  Robert M 283
CHASE, C O 130 Henry 129 J E 185
  186 303 J K 184 185 Wm 130
CHENOWETH, John Martin 289
CHERRY, Opal 171
CHIDESTER, John 239 241
CHIPPIE, Samuel W 212
CHISTA, Donato 281
CHRISTIE, John Robert 284
CHURCH, John Leonard 277 Laura
  294 Wm French 273
CIESRECKI, Adam 283
CILLI, Steve 276
CITIZENS, Dissatisfied With Location
  of County Seat 100
CIVIL WAR RECORD, 189 Company
  A 11th Regiment of Wva 215
  Company A 12th Regiment of
  Wva 223 Company A 17th
  Regiment of Wva 241 Company B
  12th Regiment of Wva 228
  Company B 7th Regiment of Wva
  209 Company C 12th Regiment of
  Wva 234 Company D 1st
  Regiment of Wva 192 Company E
  1st Regiment of Wva 200
  Company F 1st Regiment of Wva
  189 Company G 17th Regiment of
  Wva 246 Company H 11th
  Regiment of Wva 221 Company H
  17th Regiment of Wva 251
  Company I 15th Regiment of Wva
  238 Company I 6th Regiment of
  Wva 258 Company K 1st
  Regiment of Wva 201
  Company L 4th Regiment of Wva
  254 Company L 6th Regiment of
  Wva 203
  Confederate States Soldiers 265
  Miscellaneous 264

CLARK, Anderson 278 Asa 213 B H
  173 Bryan Thomas 287 Harry 12
  36 83 J A 295 Jacob C 258 James
  256 James A 108 Louis Elbert 287
  Luther Francis 281 Mrs H L 298
  Mrs S S 297 Thadeus 201 Thomas
  212 Thomas B 144 Thomas Edgar
  275 William H 213
CLAYTON, David G 247 John W 229
  Joseph Fred 287 W E 185 William
  259
CLEGG, Elijah 256 John 129 235
  John E 235 Thomas 117 187 235
  Thomas B 235
CLEMENS, Emma 296 John 133
CLINE, John 187
CLOUSE, Orpha 273
CLOUSTON, James 212 Wm J 133
  242
CLUTTER, Ray 269
CLYDE, Arthur Harrison 269
CLYLOR, Chancey Roy 284
COCCO, Guisseppe 275
COCHRAN, Erwin H 289 Thomas
  299 Thos 303
COCKAYNE, Benjamin 97 108 109
  Samuel 109 Vincent 109
COE, Isaac 227 Jas W 223 John 213
  W R 134 Wm R 242
COFFIELD, Albert F 285 J H 235
  Jacob 295 302 Leland 286 Mrs L
  H 297 Thomas 117
  Wm M 229
COFFMAN, Adam 229 William 268
COHEN, Chester A 286
  Clyde 269
  James 193
COLE, John S 215 Mary J 300
  Stephen 246 W A 304
COLEMAN, Henry C 187
COLLETT, Chester 216
COLLINS, 28 John 27
  Thos J 254
  William 120 121 126 312
  Wm 128 132 139
  Wm H 229
COLTON, Joshua 130

COMMISSIONERS, of The County Court Meet And Organize 149
COMMITTEE, of Teachers Report A System of Grading 157 Reports On Navigation of Fish Creek 114
COMPANY M 1st Wva V I Spanish American War, 266
COMPANY of Capt John Bonnett 1814, 187
COMPTON, Fillmore 271 Filmore 268 M F 294 303
CONAWAY, Edmund 268 George 224
CONKLE, Phillip 313
CONLEY, Bertram B 274 Frank 278 J C 184 Jacob A 242 James C 189 Wm H 232
CONNELLY, Clark 142 252 Jas C 192
CONNER, Alexander 224 Arch E 303 C W 185 266 Geo W 246 George C 267 George W 140 Harold 303 Hubert 303 J H 235 James H 183 184 Joseph A 271 Louis Danford 288 Mary 171 P E 266 Philip 255 Philip M 140 246 Thomas 276 Troy B 272 William 120 Wm 127 Wm E 266 Wm H 266 Wm L 140 247 255
CONNERS, Charles J 284 Edward Leo 283 John M 275 Richard F 280
CONOWAY, Edmund M 271 Thomas Earl 283
CONSTANTINO, Zina 278
COOK, Archie N 292 Charles Marion 278 Wm 150
COOPER, George 137 George T 141 J P 303 Jackman 176 James 120 Matilda 303 Samuel H 212 Samuel W 264 Thomas Joseph 278 William 216
COPE, Walter A 267
COPLINGER, William 216
CORBUT, Joseph 121
CORDER, Ethel 171
CORNELL, Amos 135

CORNISH, Robert C 273
CORNWELL, Yates 15
CORRATHERS, George 111
COSSER, Wesley 281 William L 275
COTTON, Frank 295
COTTS, R J 302
COULTER, Andrew 229
COUNTY, Court Fixes Prices of Liquor At Retail Etc 112 Court Lays Annual Levy of Taxes 110 Court Resolves Against Granting Retail Liquor License 117 Divided Into Districts - Boundaries 117 Divided Into Townships And Named 118
COURTWRIGHT, Etta 296 Harlan Ross 289 John 195 Mrs S T 296 S T 299 302 Walter C 292 Walter Clifford 277
COUSINS, Carl Robert 275 Frank 269
COUTY, John V 239
COVER, O F 271
COVERT, Leo D 271 Mrs O F 296 O F 268
COVOLT, Abraham 117
COWEL, Julius 212
COX, Dessie 171 Friend 299 Howard Payne 285 Jacob F 120 Jacob T 126 James M 129 Joseph 187 M F 173 Stephen 196
COXEN, Percy 288
CRAFT, Clarence Robert 286
CRAGO, F H 172 Mrs F H 173
CRAHAN, Samuel James 278
CRAIG, David 187 Edmond E 285 Samuel 229
CRAIGHTON, Ernest M 284
CRAPE, Jack 269
CRAWFORD, Col 10 52 91 92 Grover C 280 I N 222 John Glasby 272 John T 222 Jos S 222 O W 172 Oliver 221 William Russell 285 Wm 135
CREPE, Joe 270

CRESAP, Elizabeth 93 295 Elizabeth T 295 Mary 93 Michael 90 91 92 93 Michael Jr 93 Mr 94 Mrs 92 Quincy 265 Sarah 93
CRICKBORN, Edward 239
CRIM, Harry 268 Jesse P 272 Russell 284 William 239 241
CRISWELL, Capt 143 Charles 189 206 229 Daniel 190 E H 183 Enoch 259 Gordon 289 Hanson 181 246 John 109 117 John A 227 228 John C 229 John Jr 206 John Sr 206 John W 133 204 242 Joseph 203 Lewis B 202 Lloyd 195 199 Mr 183 Oliver 224 Peter O 120 129 201 Richard 121 William 206 Wm H 229
CROGAN, James Lawrence 285
CROLL, Albert 281
CROSS, Andrew 255 Emery 286 William 235
CROUCH, James C 234
CROW, Absalom 223 Andrew J 213 Archie Noble 270 Arthur 170 Artie 269 B L 183 Carl 169 Catharine 40 Christina 41 Denny R 286 E D 300 Elizabeth 40 294 Emma 294 Emma M 294 Erma 171 Frederick 38 39 Gail 169 George 212 Harmon 235 Harry 276 Harry L 274 Henry 229 Isaac 255 302 J E 301 J H 302 J Randall 271 Jacob 117 187 Jacob S 283 James M 233 234 John 38 39 138 201 224 John Robert 274 John W 183 235 255 John W Jr 300 John Wesley 274 Lester 281 291 M 126 Martin 38 39 Mr 41 42 Mrs 41 Olive 299 Orie E 276 Orie W 272 Oscar 287 Philip 138 Sisters 39 Sisters Murder of By Indians And A White Man 39 Stanley Charles 274 Susan 40 T W 301 Thomas J 198 199 Victor 269 W F 268 271 William 222 254
CRUIKSHANK, Winifred 170
CRUSON, John 201

CULLY, Earnest 300 Edward P 300
CUMMINS, Ada Ruth 169 F A 138 141 252 Francis A 254 James R 252 John H 139 255 John S 251 Noble F 139 Noble T 251 William 215
CUMMONS, James R 139
CUNNINGHAM, Allen 283 Chas 276 E J 216 Geo W 239 Glen 276 J A 301 J J 138 J W 303 James 127 195 304 Jesse C 284 Jesse Clinton 281 John 131 137 John S 128 John W 247 299 Levi 128 132 Philip 138 141 247 S M 303 W R 216
CURRAN, Charles A 280
CURRY, Wm 269
CURTIS, John 133 245 Martha 13 W F 269
CUSACK, Michael Wm 287 Mildred 170
CUSTICK, Harrison 276
DADO, John 276 Michael 286
DAGUE, D L 304 Daniel 127 Fred A 250 Frederick 139 140 239 G N 304 John 294 Robert L 240 Samuel 154 William 247 Wm 140
DAILY, Cecil E 268 283 Charles Brockman 275 Clyde L 274
DAKAN, John 235 238 R G 299
DALZELL, Mrs W A B 303 W A B 294 302
DAMON, Norman 190
DANCER, Jesse 142
DANIEL, John 73
DANLEY, P R 172
DARDINGER, John S 219 221 Stephen 235
DARLING, Daniel 187
DARMAN, Chester 268 292
DARNEL, Levi 188
DARRAH, Curtis 288 Everett Lee 280
DARROW, Jacob 206 James 304 Mrs Geo 297 Wm 206
DATZKO, Mike 270
DATZO, Mike 290

DAUGHERTY, Ernest C 270 Jas W 239 John H 240 John P 222 John W 135 222 243 Mrs N E 297 Robert H 135 243 Robert M 239 Roy Scott 277 Thomas L 280 William 187 Wm H 130 261
DAVIDSON, James H 240 Margaret 132 137 Martin 132 133
DAVIS, 38 39 A R 188 Abner 246 Adam R 259 Albert 121 201 Benj C 261 Cephas 203 Charles W 216 Ella 172 Emma 172 George Lawrence 289 George W 213 Harry F 280 Homer Frank 278 James 213 214 James K 287 John 130 264 John H 240 Joshua 52 53 Luella 168 N 127 Robert 117 Robert H 142 251 Roy Glen 290 S R 184 Samuel 219 Samuel S 133 Squire 196 Thomas 195 W H H 198 200 Wilson 233
DAY, Daniel 187 Oliver H 283 Walter Glenn 284
DAYTON, Lindsey F 269 291
DEAN, Geo H 194
DEATH, of Adam Grandstaff 36 of Bazel Duke 22 of Hugh Cameron 42 of John Neiswanger 42 of John Wetzel And Son George 48
DECARLO, Louis 279
DECKER, Willard B 285 William 281 292
DEEGAN, Wm R 279
DEEMS, George 216
DEFELICE, Mike 274
DEFENDERS OF THE FORT, 24
DEGARMO, Encil Milton 282 James 235
DEHASS, Dr 8
DEITZ, Andrew 235 Lewis A 130 Louis A 261 Opal 169
DELANEY, Forest Lee 290 Jonathan 213
DELANY, Forest Lee 274
DEMETRAKIS, James 283
DENISON, James 187
DENNIS, Edward Melvin 279

DENNY, John 211
DENOON, Robert 142
DENOSKY, Mrs L H 296
DEPUTY SHERIFFS And Other Officers, 113
DERMOSE, Robert 252
DERRAH, James 224
DETERMINED RESISTANCE Saves The Fort, 19
DEVOIR, John N 224
DIBYKOWSKI, Jack 275
DICARLO, Petro 275
DICK, David 206
DICKERSON, 41 Kinzie 66 Veach 56 67 Veach & John Wetzel Go In Search of A Prisoner 67 Veach Captures Indian Prisoner 67 Veach Compelled To Kill Indian Prisoner 67 Veach Shoots At An Indian 56
DICKEY, J H 121 John 116 John H 146 148 178 182 203 Robert 207
DICKINSON, 42
DIDOMENIO, Stafano 278
DIDOMINECO, Andrae 279
DIGASPERO, Vincenzo 276
DILLEY, Addison 199 Adison 198 James 131 James A 129 Leonard 131 194
DILLY, James A 261
DIMARIO, Nicola 275
DISCONTENT DEVELOPS, 99
DITTMIRES, Elbert B 282
DIXON, William 207 William Patrick 288
DOBBS, Amos 146 Nathan C 261 William 120 247 Wm 126 138 140 153
DOBIAS, John 290
DOBOSY, Marciey 276
DOLAN, James 261
DOLBEARE, L D 301
DOLEN, James 129
DOMAN, W J 172
DOMBROSKIE, Leo 291
DOMBROWSKIE, Leo 281
DOMENIO, Stafano Di 278
DOMINECO, Andrae Di 279

DONKAN, Mckinley 276
DONLEY, E E 266 James F 192 John 266
DONNELLY, James F 189
DONOVAN, William 286
DORMAN, Norman E 224
DORSEY, Bassil 224 Catherine 138 Cornelius 255 D A 184 Dennis 128 137 J B 282 Mary Ellen 297 Mrs E W 303 Paul Leon 283 S 303 Sam 299 Samuel 110 117 132 138 149 Samuel Jr 138 140 246 Thomas 128 Valentine 270 W H 224
DOTTA, Eliza 296
DOTY, Chage 188 Clara 297 Micajah 117 206 S E 267
DOUGHERTY, Chas 213
DOWLER, Anna 172 Clara 297 Clarence W 269 Edward 114 117 138 141 252 Edward S 299 Edward Samuel 284 G A 129 George 116 Gustavus A 264 I C 300 Isaac 132 James 131 John W 195 M A 185 Mary C 295 Michael 117 119 138 177 181 Ocie 172 Ora 169 Thomas 120 126
DOWNEY, Flora 172
DOWNING, Chester 269 James Wm 287 Wm H 268
DOWNS, Eugene S 272
DOYLE, Benjamin 274 Edward Joseph 277 Ellwood 269 Hiram 133 243 J E 184
DRAKE, Samuel 216 221
DRAY, Herbert 276
DRESSEL, Louis 299
DRUMMOND, Earl 170
DUBOIS, Charles Vernon 285
DUFF, A J 172
DUFFY, Joseph Christopher 280 Joseph Earl 278 Martin Terrell 270 Thomas J 271
DUKE, Bazel 22 Death of 22
DUKES, John W 271
DUMIRE, Andrew T 204

DUNCAN, B F 266 George 220 Harry L 285 John 133 243 Walter 277
DUNKAN, William 195
DUNLAP, Alberta 273 Charles 258 Edward Lee 277 James 109 116 226 Raymond Harvey 275 W H 129 131 Wm B 135 195 Wm H 261
DUNLEVY, J M 184
DUNMORE, 11 Lord 76
DUNN, Michael 113 147 177 181 Samuel N 193 198 W D 294 William H 198 Wm H 199
DUNSON, John 137
DURBIN, Blanche 294 Lester Delmo 270 290
DURIG, Presley 280 Ross Al 280
DUTIES, of Teachers And School Officers 152
EACHUS, Ida 171
EALY, D B 268 271
EARL, Elias 206
EARLIWINE, 36 49 Abraham 117 Adam 121 Ebenezer 134 243 Frederick 64 Jacob 9 Joseph 135 243 Mrs S 297 Reuben 235 Stewart 243 Stewart F 133 Wm 193
EARLY RECORDS, 324
EARLY SETTLEMENT, 7
EARNEST, Henry 246 Isaac 243 Peter 243
EAST, Harrison Kline 277
EASTON, Henry C 131 194
EBELING, Philip 302
EBINGTON, Benjamin 200
ECHOLS, Clarence 266 George W 133 Mrs S J 296 W H 224
EDGAR, David 247
EDGING, Robert 188
EDUCATION, 151
EDWARDS, Anna 172 Geo 128 143 Geo Reports Loans for Bounties Negotiated 128 George 123 125 126 128 132 136 137 154 181 184 Howard 266 John W 224 Mr 129 T C 147 W L 139 150 Wenona 172

EIFLER, Jacob Herman 281
ELBIN, J I 294
ELDER, B B 300 Mrs B B 298
ELECTIONS, Under The First Constitution of West Virginia 178 Under The Second Constitution of West Virginia 182
ELIZABETHTOWN, 95
ELLER, F W 185 William T 272 292 Wm Herbert 270
ELLIOTT, Charles W 216 John William 275 Joseph 240 241
ELLIS, Abraham 283 George 299 George Lewis 272
ELMSLEY, J W 172
ELROD, Joseph 270
EMERY, Adam 130 Beulah 169 Harley Cramer 284 T D 169 Wilford 189
EMORY, Hiram 213
ENGLE, James T 268
ENIX, Brice 233 W H 142 256 Wm H 252
ENOCH, Adam 74 Bruce 188 Capt 74
EPIFNAO, Sabiteno 286
ERLEWINE, John Heghie 281
ERNEST, Isaac 135 James 279 Peter 135 William 279
ERNST, Frank A 270 John Lalor 274
ESKEY, John 202 203
EVANS, Bruce Robert 287 Charles 266 Earl L 300 Frank M 221 G W 119 120 150 Gaius W 197 George 188 George W 255 259 Harold 272 India 172 John 188 196 Jonathan E 198 Jonathan Elmer 189 200 Kenneth Walter 286 Mrs B 298 Perry 221 Samuel 204 Thomas G 204 Walter 132 181 182 269 William 204 230
EVASHKO, John 281
EVENTS OF 1777, 14
EVERETT, Raymond Guy 276 Wilber H 284

EWING, A Alex 183 Alice 172 Anna 171 Edith 172 Geo M 239 Henry 111 J Alex 146 James 114 187 James D 146 Miss A 296 William 247 Wm 138 140 Wm O 266
EXLINE, John 216
FAIR, Roscoe 271
FALLOVA, Pasquale 274
FARRAR, W W 172
FELICE, Mike Di 274
FERGUSON, Francis L 186 J H 268 271 John 181 Mrs W C 296
FERRERA, Nick 274
FERRIS, 300 A H 299 Frank 287
FIARINO, Antonio 279
FILBEN, John Isaac 274 William 274
FINCH, William 284
FINN, Thomas 149 181 182 183 265
FINSLEY, Frederick 201 Wm 137
FIRST PUBLIC EXAMINATION OF TEACHERS FOR THE COUNTY, 156
FIRST SETTLEMENT WEST OF THE MOUNTAINS, 7
FIRST TEACHERS' INSTITUTE HELD IN COUNTY, 157
FISH, Benj F 193 C D 295 Charles Carlton 289 Chas Alfred 274 F Hays 294 G E 300 Herbert Leroy 283 Isaac N 235 238 James K P 195 John Elmer 281 John W 300 Marjorie 168 Mrs W P 296 Nathan S 232 Raymond Frank 286 W P 172 Wm 193 Wm V 141 252 Wylie Roe 284
FISHER, Chester Lee 284 Clara 301 Earl T 271 Herbert Clemens 284 Howard M 290 Olive Lohr 172 R A 172 Sam 304 Stanley George 288 Thomas C 286 Wilbert Harry 284
FITZGERALD, B 256 James R 290 Jerry A 195 John 134 R A 302
FITZSIMMONS, Edwin 282 303 Harold Byron 277 Jennie 298 Mrs James 298 Ralph 288 W D 168
FLACK, David E 239

FLANAGAN, John M 224 Mort 266
    Ross Edgar 278
FLEMING, John Harris 280 S S 143
FLETCHER, Abraham 252 Alfred 141
    David A 228 Thomas 213 215
    William 188 William H 277
FLOTA, Ruth 170
FLOUHOUSE, Alice 297 Forest 169
    Forrest William 285
FOGLE, Arch 269
FOLLEY, William Patrick 277
FORBES, Gen 75
FORD, Benj F 140 Benjamin F 247
FORDICE, John M 133
FORDYCE, John 241 John M 197
    Solomon 194 Solomon H 190
FOREMAN, Capt 14 26 27 28 29
    Hambleton 29 Mr 27 Nathan 29 W
    H 171 William 12 26 29 96 Wm
    130
FORSTER, J A 302
FORT CLARK, 82
FORT TOMLINSON, 83
FORTS, 81
FOSTER, James 254 James C 138 139
    251 William Edgar 277
FOUNDS, David 134 243 270 John W
    235 Retta 171 296
FOUNTAIN, Jas 261
FOUST, James Hubert 286
FOWLER, Noah C 221 Richard 219
FOWNER, William 172
FOX, Henry C 193 199 John E 190
    John L 201 Thomas 127 281 291
    William 190 198 200
FRACTION, Henry 188
FRAGASSO, Joseph 287
FRANCIS, A F 299 Caroline V 298 E
    B 137 Earl 169 Elizabeth 299
    Emanuel 230 Emma 296 Gail 171
    J T 299 James 188 John K 120
    127 154 Joseph T 230 Mrs A F
    296 Mrs A L 296 Mrs Adam 298
    Mrs Arthur 296 Oliver Earl 273
    290 S F 302 Virginia 296 William
    120
FREED, Ella 172 Horace 267 271

FREELAND, 12
FREEMAN, William 210
FRENCH, Samuel 236
FRIEDLY, Helena 169 Twila 169
FROHNAPFEL, A J 303 Anthony 299
    Bordora E 303 Emma 298 Harry J
    303 Mrs T J 297 T J 303
FRY, Abraham 213 214 Christian S
    212 214 James 209 John 266 Leo
    Joseph 270 271 William H 213
    214 Wm 121
FULL PARTICULARS OF THE
    INDIAN ATTACK, 21
FULLER, Geo W 230 Herbert R 281
    Ralph B 286
FULLERTON, Geo H 269 John B 193
    W R C 209
FURBEE, Martin S 275 Reymond 287
GABLE, Milton Arthur 284
GADUS, Zacharias 210
GALENTINE, John B 282 Otis Ray
    275 Ralph Arthur 279
GALLAHER, Chas T 279 James 190
    James Francis 277 John 324
    Joseph 248 324 Levi 135 243
    Stephen 260 263
GALLANTINE, John 204 Thomas S
    301
GALLENTINE, Wm 195
GALLOWAY, Nicholas 209
GAMBLE, Charles 266 James L 139
    252 W M 304 Wm C 224 Wm W
    243
GAMES, Alfred 228 Carrie 169 David
    A 259 G B 184 295 George B 186
    Isaac 259 John D 262 Thomas
    Reed 276
GANBY, Ralph 271
GANDEE, 302
GANIER, Glen M 283
GANS, Henry C 259
GAOKELL, Daisy 273
GARBESI, Joe Euclid Jr 282
GARDENER, Wm 240
GARDNER, Byron Harrison 286
    Lennie 275 291 Michael 234
GAREY, Charles J 283

GARNER, Ella Zena 303 Joshua 114
    116 W M 302
GARRISON, William Mckinley 281
    William N 291 Wm A 200
GARRY, James 207
GARVIN, 300 Helen 299 Herbert
    Dean 288 Mrs John Lemuel 298
    Mrs Margaret 298 T J 143
GASPAREVIC, Frank 275
GASPERO, Vincenzo Di 276
GATELY, James Franklin 277
GATES, Belle 172
GATEWOOD, Beatrice 171 J E 303
    Joseph 303
GATHO, Minnie 170
GATTS, Elsie 298 Eugene V 295
    Floris Iva 169 G W H 295 Harley
    Lloyd 274 Horatio 301 Louis
    Edwin 284 Samuel 116 Samuel E
    134 242 Silas W 134 241 Wm S
    140 248
GAUGH, Elijah D 203
GAUGHAN, John Joseph 270
GAUNT, H G 268
GEBERT, Chasles A 275
GEHO, David 290 David W 270 Jacob
    135 243 Joseph 121 L G 260 263
    Robert 259 Samuel W 222
GEISELER, D F 184 Henry 304
GELNER, Albert 286
GENERAL ELECTIONS, 174
GENERAL PROVISIONS, for Free
    Schools 151 for Holding Elections
    179
GEOGELINE, Samuel 270 291
GEURIN, Alexander 223
GEURRIN, Mahlon 224
GIBILISCO, Pasquale 279
GIBSON, John L 197 254 John Mason
    278
GILBERT, Aquilla 133 243 Earl 269
    Thomas Earl 281
GILES, Dorothy 171
    Hamilton 233
    James 143
GILLETT, Wm 224
GILLINGHAM, James Archie 287

GILLISPIE, Cornelius 206 Florence
    273 Leona 169 W E 270
GILLISPY, Alexander 221
GILMORE, Meta 295
GIRTY, George 31 Simon 24 71
    Simon Pleads for His Life And
    Saves It 71
GIST, Christopher 7 Christopher
    Visits The West 7
GITTINGS, Charles Laird 284 Jesse
    Eldridge 279 Silas Lee 280
GIVEN, Neal 188
GLADYS, Peter 269 291
GLASGOW, Alma 172
GLASPY, John 188
GLASS, Alfred 129 130
GLENDENNING, J W 139
GLOVER, Charles O 288
GLUM, Mrs 19
GOCKE, Louis 301
GODDARD, Joshua 146
GOETZE, Mrs Charles 298
GOLETTS, Allick 283
GONGOLA, Steve 275
GONSICBOWSKI, Tgnacy 279
GOOD, David 209 George 209 213
    Jacob 211 Moses C 108 Samuel
    209 213 Thomas 211 214
GOODMAN, John A 141 Lawrence
    271
GOODRICH, 62 Clarence Eastman
    277 Franklin 230 George 188
    Nathan D 230 Nelson 230 T M
    230
GOODWIN, Everett Elwood 282 F H
    303 Mart 267
GORBY, 323 Daisy 297 Daniel 117
    David 221 Gladys 172 J B 131
    Jasper B 261 Jesse J 138 141 264
    John 276 Josephus 236 Leah 169
    Mrs W P 296 Phoebe J 173
    Richard P 204
GORDON, I 294 302
    Margaret 172
    Rose 297
GORH, Frank 285
GORRELL, John 126

GOSNEY, James 236 Richard 141 203 252
GOSSETT, George 224 John T 215 John W 285 Mrs R M 297
GOUDY, Albert 201 Harry 266
GOULD, Charles 280
GRACIK, Florian 275
GRADING, of County Schools Introduced - By Whom 157
GRAFFE, Helen 170
GRAHAM, Harold 270 Mrs Harry M 297 Sam 270 William 211 Wm 143
GRANDON, Charles M 285
GRANDSTAFF, Adam 9 36 Adam Death of 36 Jacob 117 219 John R 139 143 Moses 188 Wm H 213
GRAVE, And Monument To Massacre 28
GRAY, Arthur H 185 Austin E 270 290 Elias W 130 213 Francis M 236 238 Franklin 220 G F 184 Harry Taylor 274 Henry A 240 241 James 188 202 220 John 117 281 290 291 John W 290 Lindsey T 182 Robert 131 202 Samuel 132 134 135 190 Samuel Jr 243 Samuel Sr 243 Stanley 287 Walker L 270 Walter 97 99 110 114 116 117 Walter Leroy 272 William 190 197 199
GREATHOUSE, Amos 230 Frank Elmer 286 Hiram 230 John 230 Thomas 230
GREEN, James 99 Mathew 291 Matthew 275 William P 286
GREENE, James 29
GREER, Geo W 219 George 31 James B 178 John 215
GREGG, Benjamin S 117 Edward 109 116 Edward S 256 Gans 226 Isaac 224 Jacob 211 Levi 188
GREGORY, Floyd Riley 270 Martha 172
GRENBERG, Axel Herman 278
GREY, Walter 109
GRIFFIN, Wm H 216

GRIFFITH, Amos 230 Benjamin 230 Geo A 254 Geo W 241 George W 134 John 230 Joseph 137 264 Zachariah 233 234
GRIM, Jesse 290 Lebbeus 213
GRIMES, Caddie 294 Donald E 279 George O 129 Hiram 204 James 236 John W 134 256 Oliver 142 251 259
GRINDELL, Henry 121
GRISWELL, Hanson 146
GROFF, John 281
GROSSMAN, Minor 300 301
GROVES, Rachel 172
GRUBER, John 271
GRUNNELL, Levi 213
GUARMERE, Joseph 275
GUFFY, 323
GUISEPPE, Mura 278
GULLENTINE, Wm 130
GUMP, Allen Aaron 276 Blanch 169 Daniel 219 Daniel S 216 Elmer 274 James 216
GUNN, Geo H 241 George H 240 Ralph E 291 Ralph Edwin 278 Wm R 236
GUNPOWDER EXPLOIT of Betty Zane, 33
GUSTAFSON, C S 171
GWYNN, Thomas 215
HABAK, Alex 274
HACKENBERG, William J 292
HACKENBURG, Wm J 268
HADDOX, Harry Bartlett 283
HADSALL, John E 234 Messr 132 Mr 121 128 132 Noah 120 121 122 123 125 126 127 136
HAGER, J B 121 Jacob B 189 Nicholas 189
HAGERMAN, James 267 Joseph 236 Paul 276 Samuel 127
HAGGERTY, Jas G 216
HAHN, Esther 172

HALL, Chester B 192 200 Cornelius F
  280 Daniel C 232 G W 140
  George W 138 248 Jacob F 278
  John 284 Mrs Samuel 298 Mrs
  William 301 Thurman 131
  William 301 Williamm Peter 289
HALLEY, Vance 282 Verne 268
HAMILTON, 21 Gov 18 Russell
  James 288 W E 301
HAMMEL, Charles Julius 277
HAMMOND, Andrew 172 D S 172
  David M 272 284 Erastus 172
  Francis M 248 Geo W 193 George
  227 Jacob 128 138 Jacom 126
  James 248 Joseph 132 259
  Thomas G 143 Thos G 264
  William 259
HANAN, S R 184 Samuel R 184
HAND, Gen 16 25 26
HANDLAN, Richard 188
HANEN, S R 156 182 Samuel H 158
  Samuel R 155 261 Samuel R Jr
  267
HANKINS, Mildred 172
HANLEY, Daniel J 280
HANNA, John 292 John David 286
HARBINSON, John W 229
HARBISON, Thomas B 133 Thos B
  243
HARDEN, Burr 216
HARDING, Vachel 187
HARE, Jessie 170
HARKINS, J J 142
HARKNESS, 78 Elizabeth 10 John 27
  Robert 27
HARMER, Gen 55 56 57 58
  Compelled To Release Wetzel 58
HARPOLD, Edna 172
HARRINGTON, John 200
HARRIS, Amos 137 193 Carlton W
  270 Dorothy 168 E J 300 E R 140
  147 Eli 256 Elias R 138 190 252
  Elijah 140 252 Ella 172 297 F 143
  Francis 251 Frank 139 Geo W 234
  George 256 George C 140 252
  Hamilton 256 Hamilton C 133 245
  Henry C 198 200 Henry J 193 198

HARRIS (continued)
  Hubert H 269 Isaac 29 J P 134
  Jacob 134 Jas K P 243 255 John
  15 John A 134 241 John C 140
  252 John F 256 John Parker 276
  John W 135 243 Leander B 248
  Leonard B 140 Lucy 137 Mrs E J
  298 Okey F 276 Peter 250 Samuel
  15 236 Thomas 254 W H 185 Wm
  P 131 190 194
HARSH, Amanda 295 Mary 295 W A
  295
HARST, David P 142
HART, Jeff J 272 Jesse J 285 William
  195
HARTLEY, Daniel 240 Isaac S 259
  263 Joshua 259 Leonard 295
  Stewart E 133 Thomas A 133
  Walter H 290 Walter Ray 281
HARTONG, William 204
HARTZELL, Elias 197 199 John 230
  John G 135 243 Simon 196
HARVEY, Benjamin 109 117 James A
  171
HATINA, William 281
HAUGHT, D L 171 Edwin 171
HAWKINS, Lisle Edgar 284
HAYES, Lester Ray 277
HAYHURST, John 142
HAYNES, Myrtle 296
HAYTHORN, Wm A 270
HAZLETT, John 186 John M 276
  Thomas F 278 William 169
HEAD, C C 170 W T 121 Wm F 133
  Wm T 209
HEADLEY, Edmund P 270
HEADLY, James 221
HEAGIN, John J 280
HEALY, John 147
HEATHERBY, Adrain 222
HEATHERLY, David H 222
HEDGE, Sidney 172
HEDGES, Joseph 66
  Mary E 172
  Thomas 67
HEFFLER, Joseph 43
HEIL, Luke 285

HELMICK, David S 133
  Nathaniel D 133
HELMS, Adam 260 263 264 George
  M 197 John Morgan 269 Martin B
  190 192
HEMPHILL, Clyde L 272 Ralph H
  288
HENDERSHOT, A W 212 214 James
  M 213 Jas M 209 Nanon 172
HENDERSON, Byron 268 271 Earl
  169 H L 299 Helen 296 Isaac M
  216 221 J W 299 John 207 Mr 77
  Mrs E E 296 Samuel 112 W H 154
  W W 299
HENDRICKSON, D J 252 David 256
HENDRIXON, Wm 197
HENNEN, Ruth 172
HENRETTA, Houston 266 267
HENRY, Charles Alfred 275 James
  133 242 Joseph 274 Patrick 16
  Robert A 230 Robert S 215
HERTZOG, Frederick A 274 W Clyde
  171
HESS, Ford 141
HESTON, Benjamin 202 David 133
HEWES, Shipley 207
HEWETT, Jesse Bond 275 Mrs A A
  298
HEWITT, Jesse Bond 292
HICKS, Dora 171 G John 188 Geo W
  149 Harvey 294 J B 149 183
  James W 195 John A 149 236 269
  Joseph I 270 Mrs Will 296 W B
  134 Wilson 197 Wm H 234 Wm T
  199
HIGGINS, J M 172 J W 154 John 127
  Stephen 253 William Houston 275
HIGH, Halford 281
HIGHT, Bryson D 218
HILBERRY, Grant 286
HILEY, Hesikiah 142
HILL, Ambros H 270 Benjamin 128
  Felix Warren 270 291 Isaac 270
  Isaac Jr 270 Matilda 139
  Milton 274 291
  Presley W 275
  Thomas 240 William H 286

HIMELRICK, Alexander 248
  Francis 248
HIND, David R 216
HINERMAN, Doris 171 E M 185
  Emmett 281 Jesse 248 S B 301
HIPKINS, James E 288
HIPSLEY, Ruth 169
HIXENBAUGH, Wm H 248
HLASKO, Andrew 274
HODGEMAN, B F 294
HOFFMAN, 74 Marie 172
HOGE, Isaac Jr 108 James M 176
HOLBROOK, Leona 169
HOLDERMAN, Ralph 279
HOLLIDAY, M H 129 R C 137 146
  176 177 R H 146 173 Wm 117
  128 137 Wm Jr 128
HOLLINGSHEAD, Samuel 198 200
  219 Venus 230
HOLMES, A N 150 299 301 B F 312
  Geo W 194 Henry 225 227 James
  300 John 252 Josiah 198 200 Wm
  H 193 Wm Rogers 274
HOLMS, Peter 227
HOLT, J Howard 302 James 142
HOMER, Josiah 248
HOOD, Alex D 304 C M 299 302
  Kate 304 Mrs J L 298 Roy Ewell
  277 Wm C 272
HOOTON, A L 185 266 267
  J E 183
HOOVER, Samuel 188
HOPKINS, Frank 304 John C 280
  Martin Francis 288 Thomas 300
HORAN, Diomjasius A 275 John W
  285
HORNBROOK, John 121 126 153
  John P 139
HORNE, Augustus A 288
  Mrs A A 298
HORNER, Guy Delbert 287
HORVATT, Steve 275
HOSACK, W 126 William 121
HOSENFELT, 201
HOSKINSON, Mary Etta 297
HOSSMAN, Edward G 275
HOSTETTLER, Daniel M 247

HOSTUTTLER, David 248
  Jackson 248 Lewis 248
HOUCK, Florence 171 Nancy B 303
HOUSE, 32
HOUSEMAN, Mary 170
HOUSTON, Toilla 296
HOWARD, Albert 195 199 256
  Arthur F 216 Brice 121 Enos 176
  George M 195 Harley 301 Harry
  301 304 J N 301 Jacob 197 James
  131 190 194 James O 284 John
  189 John R 285 Joseph L 271
  Leslie C 282 291 M F 268 Messr
  132 Norma 170 Reason B 116
  Rowland Reed 270 S 114 115
  Samuel 99 107 108 110 111 112
  113 114 115 116 146 177 Samuel
  M 189 Samuel Sr 116 Thomas 116
  121 123 125 126 127 136 137 138
  139 252 Wiley 190 197 Wm J 178
  Wm M 197
HOWE, John W 241 W R 181
HOWELL, Jonathan 188
HOWSER, 34
HOYT, John 281
HUBBS, Blain 168 C S 267 Elijah 127
  138 141 247 Elsie 168 Ethel 170
  Frank 267 Geo 146 Geo W 241
  George 126 129 153 George W
  134 Georgia 170 Isaac 117 190
  Isaac N 234 J I 300 John 188 Leah
  172 Roy Samuel 276 292 W H
  184 197 294 299
HUFF, Leroy 280
HUFFMAN, Rob 270
HUFFNER, George 301 Quiller
  Braden 276 Renhart 195
HUGGANS, John 109
HUGGENS, Richard 201
HUGGINS, Eli 141 252 Richard 188
HUGHES, Barney 193 Carrie 170
  Edgar Rogers 279 Henry V 204
  Jesse V 116 Margaret 300 Mrs J E
  296 Patrick J 285 Samuel D 142
  252 Silas 138 141 Silas N 252
  Thomas Frank 275
  William Leo 285
HULL, Herbert Montgomery 275
  William 117
HUMMEL, Jonas 238
HUMPHREYS, R N 266
HUNT, David 211 214 J F 281
HUNTER, C H 186 300 Gladys 172 H
  W 98 182 183 Hanson W 262 263
  Samuel J 303 Virginia 170
HUNTERS, Attacked By Indians 38
HUPP, Ethel 169
HURBLY, Newton M 133
HURD, Ben 269
HURLEY, James 259
HUSS, Elmer R 283
HUTCHINSON, C E 185 186 299
  Mrs C E 303
HUTCHISON, Thos S 221
HYATT, Edward 274
HYDE, Harry 274
HYDER, Eliza 297 J P 303
HYMAN, Louis 263 Louis L 260
IARQUINIO, Marco 275
ICARD, Jesse Clinton 276
ICE, Andrew J 204 Isaac 204
ICENHOUR, Alfred R 288
IEMMA, Michael 276
INCIDENTS, In Early Settlement 13
INDIAN, George Girty 31 Half King
  12 Simon Girty 24 71 White Eyes
  16
INDIAN WARFARE, 34
INDIANS,
  Abandon Siege And Retire 34
  Attack Adam Rowe's Family At
  Grave Creek 14
  Attack Fort Henry 17 31
  Kill Stock 20
INGERSALL, Talmage Jas 280
INGERSOLL, Talmage James 291
INGLE, William 29
INGRAM, Albert 267
  W A 301
IRWIN, W D 172
ISIMINGER, A R 299
ISINMINGER, A R 302
ISRAEL, Jacob E 265
JABLINSKE, Albert Carrol 282

JACKSON, John C 141 John Herbert 281 Norman Reed 275 Simeon 240 Stonewall 265 William 211
JACOB, 65 77 Zachariah 108
JAMES, Albert I 272 Ephraim 223 Geo C 216 Geo L 216 Isaac 227 J P 301
JAMISON, James 120
JEFFERS, Frank 280
JEFFERSON, Edith 295 Foster A 286 Jacob 113 176 James 188 John 99 John Sr 97 Mrs J T 296 Tony 169 Wm 140 248
JEMMISON, James 127
JENKINS, Gen 265 Henry 248 Mary 171 Miss Pluma 296
JENNY, Andrew 116 Wellington 176
JILLETT, Jackson 222
JOHNS, Joseph Jr 287
JOHNSON, Abraham 222 Adam 222 Alexander 202 Anthnoy 248 Anthony 138 141 David B 133 243 256 Emma 301 Franklin 134 243 Henry 244 Herbert 284 Ira W 131 Jason Brice 286 John 294 John H 222 John M 299 John T 131 261 Minnie 298 Mrs John 296 Mrs W H 298 Richard M 139 Samuel 30 Sidney 12 W H 302 W M 142 William B 260 263 Wm P 204
JOHNSTON, John W 230
JOLIFF, Ray C 283
JOLIFFE, Olive 273 Roy W 286
JOLLY, Effie M 303
JONES, A J 302 Abraham 188 223 Albert I 290 Alton 266 Arthur L 272 291 Arthur W 291 Charles 120 Charles Edward 303 Daniel 140 248 David 120 127 Dorsey 269 Ella 299 Garrison 176 Geo A 223 Geo Mcm 246 250 George A 146 George L 227 228 George M 140 George Mcc 126 George Mcm 251 George W 142 Gertrude 170 297 Harriet B 295 Harry Warner 279 J R 301

JONES (continued) Jeremiah 119 120 121 122 123 125 126 127 136 138 John G 223 227 Lynn Elliott 283 Morgan 15 88 115 178 Morgan Writes of Conditions At Grave Creek 15 Mr 125 136 Mrs L O 296 Mrs Will 303 Philip 117 132 Philip E 283 Ray 268 Solomon 29 Victor Raymond 288 W P 138 139 Wilbert 184 303 William 301 Wm P 251
JUGSTON, William F 189
JUNKINS, Ethyl 169 Jos 117
JUSTICE OF THE PEACE Qualified, 112
JUSTICES COURT Meets Organizes And Classifies Justices, 146
KAERCHER, Clyde Lincoln 284
KANE, Jeremiah 225
KANNER, Beulah 169
KANTRINER, Jacob 240 241
KARCHER, Amelia 297 Fred K 268 Georgia 300 Henry 302
KASCHKE, Leo A 282
KAUAKAKIS, George H 275
KAUFIELD, Ralph S 284
KAUFMAN, E L 271
KEENER, David 217
KEITH, Mr 95
KELLAR, Steve 283
KELLER, Charles 134 F J 173 Geo W 201 Gertrude 171 Henry 202 Jacob 187 John W 202
KELLEY, Alex 217 Amos 215 Beulah 169 C F 300 Dwight Dorian 274 Edward Francis 274 Francis 113 114 177 G W 295 Hamilton 256 Ivan Dempsey 284 J F 126 J G 295 J W 172 James 144 Laura 296 Mrs Tom 296 T A 302 V S 302 William 281
KELLO, Stanley 278
KELTZ, H 143 Henry 120 121 122 123 125 126 127 132 136 137 181 Messr 128 Peter 126

KEMPFHER, August 227 228
KEMPLE, Alex 119 George 137 141 Henry C 202 John 200 201 Otis 202
KENNEDY, R W 169
KENSLE, John 268
KENT, Forrest 283 Gideon 130 John M 256
KENTON, Simon 68
KERBY, James A 269 270
KERNS, Manford 276 Mrs Harry 297
KERR, Hamilton 56 65 77
KERRAR, Margaret 171
KERSCHA, August 279
KERSHKEY, Louis 278
KERSHNER, David 140 251
KERWOOD, Jas P 217 Thomas 217
KESSEBRING, C A 301
KESSLER, George 282
KETCHAM, Dorothy 171
KETTLER, Harry J 275 Ralph C 287
KETTLEWELL, Alvin James 284 John H 287
KEYSER, Abraham 130 I D 302 John L 204 W E 266 Wm 127 154
KIDD, Orvil D 275
KIDDER, Ira 130 230
KIEDAISCH, Vera 171
KIGER, Burch C 274 James 240 Mrs J F 298
KIGGINS, Thomas 188
KIMBALL, Abraham 244
KIMBERLY, Ralph 269 291
KIMBLE, Daniel 217
KIMMINS, A R 127 154 E L 301 S W 184 Wm R 228
KIMMONS, Joseph 137 141 Sam'l W 195
KIMPLE, Alexander 120 Harry Alex 269
KING, Alexander 222 Emmons T 270 Enoch 248 Francis 225 J T 157 171 Joshua J 253 Thelma 171 William Leurie 275
KINGSBERRY, Capt 57 58
KINNEY, Cephus 265
KINSEY, W W 288

KIRBY, Ottie 287
KIRKENDALL, John A 237
KIRKPATRICK, I T 253
KISSEL, Joseph P 285
KITTLE, Wm 185
KITTLEWELL, Albert 269
KLAGES, Edna 298 Mrs William 298
KLINK, H G 303 Mrs H G 297
KLOETZLY, Edmond A 284
KLUCH, Joseph 275
KLUCHAN, Joseph 274
KLUG, Anna 296 Harry Peter 276 L A 303 Regina 297 Theresa 297 Thomas M 272
KNAPP, Alvah 236 Andrew 230 Guy Laster 283 Robert 190 234 Stewart 238 Wm E 141 253
KNIGHT, A F 295 Dora 273 George T 197 Hugh 281 Pierson 131
KNIGHT'S ACCOUNT of The Attack, 21
KNOTTS, Z R 168
KNOX, James 188 Wm A 141 146 251
KOCH, Anna 303 Joseph 236 Joseph H 238 R B 267 William Carl 287
KOLINSKI, John 280
KOLP, Christian 207
KOLTZ, Joseph Henry 274 Peter 121 154
KOLZ, William H 285
KOONTZ, George A 303 M C 303 Mary A 303 Mrs M C 303
KORGANS, Dominick 272
KOSKI, Alex 268
KOSTKA, Joseph 274
KRAUS, Samuel 209 213
KREPELKA, Karl 272 291
KUHN, Abraham 211 Margaret 172 William 211
KULL, Charles 266 299 302 Lawrence 269 Mrs Charles 296
KYGER, Andrew 188 John 188
KYLE, John 120 126 128 138
LACY, Agnes 296
LAFFERTY, Archibald J 284 Dovener 281

LAING, Mrs A R 296
LAKE, S T 268
LAMBRACHT, Charles 281
LAMBRECHT, Fred J 285
LANCASTER, C S 169 Henry 207
  James Randall 287 John 208 209
  Lawrence 272 290 Nellie 172
  Ralph 284 Samuel 266 Stella 297
  Thos M 253
LANCIO, Francisco 281
LAND, Moses 133
LANDFRIED, Olive 171
LANERIA, Sabatino 281
LANGMYER, Louis 276
LARK, George 270
LASH, John B 220
LASS, Albert William 286
LAUFFER, Harry 303 Lena 296
LAUNON, James 301
LAVELLE, Patrick 172
LAW, Alexander 141
LAWLER, Lt 58
LAWRENCE, E H 301
LAYFIELD, Gertrude 172
LAYMAN, Joshua 133 W E 135
LEACH, Abraham 215 Albert 303
  Ambros 202 Benjamin 202
  Clement V 202 Etta D 294 Frank
  301 James A 222 Jane 300 John W
  184 Joseph 223 S E 301 Samuel
  129 202 Sumner E 259 Virginia
  171 Wm H 227 228
LEASURE, Henry 284
LECKO, Nicholas 287
LEECH, S E 300
LEEDS, Helen 169
LEEK, Charles 275 291 Orange 281
  291
LEGG, Frank 184
LEHEW, Charles Marion 277 John Jr
  287
LEICHTER, Emery 211
LEJEK, Paul 272 291
LEMASTERS, A W 215 Elias 133
  Isaac D 135 242 James Wm 279
  Jas A 253
LEMON 24 Jasper N 248 Rob't 23 25

LENGTH OF SCHOOL TERM, 154
LEONARD, A G 129 Allison G 190
LESTER, Andrew 287
LEVY, Max 299 302
LEWIS, Aaron 188 E M 184 Edward J
  135 Frank 283 J M 268 Jackson
  211 Jacob 110 James 248 Naomi
  273
LIGHTNER, A J 130 James A 258
  John 260 263 Wm H 211
LILLEY, Andrew 300 302 Arabel 299
  James T 283 Sarah V 298
LIMLIE, Fred 300
LINCH, Robert Mcclain 281 Sumner
  N 289
LINDSEY, Alex N 205 Benjamin S
  285 Elisha 128 129 Ella B 273
  Johnson C 262 Mrs J K 297
  Robert F 258 263 Robert Graham
  285 Vinton W 274 William H 259
LINEBERGER, John W 303
LINTON, Mary Grace 171
LIQUOR LICENSE Granted, 127
LIS, Frank 284
LIST, Thomas 96 Thomas H 97 111
  112 113 114 Thos H 114
LITMAN, Rose 296
LITTLE, David 192 James 280 Robert
  284
LITTLETON, James 240
LITTMAN, Albert 281
LITTON, Arthur 266 Edward 266
LOCAK, Vacil 274
LOCAL, Rainfall 318 Temperature
  317
LOCKWOOD, Jonathan H 265
LOGAN, 79 Alice 302 D L 300 302
  Edwin 283
LOGSDON, Alvin W 291 Alwin W
  270 Anthony 236 Bennett 116 C
  M 303 Charles F 285 Francis
  Thomas 292 Harry 283 J F 236 J
  R 236 238 James 195 225 James
  W 142 Jas W 254 John 130 John E
  225 John P 195 257 Joseph 257
  Joseph W 244 M D 169 Millard D
  287 Thomas 141 249

LOGSDON (continued)
　Thomas F 284 Wm D 192 251
LOHR, E W 299
LONG, Clarence 283 George A 275
　Hardesty 146 Harry Wm 279
　Jerremiah 46 Lee A 279 291 Lewis
　215
LONGSTRETH, Frank N 288
LOPER, Clyde 286 Mrs 294 Walter
　300
LORAIN, John 155 158 181
LORD, Wm C 141
LOUDEN, Fred R 287 Karl Dix 285
LOUDENSLAGER, Joseph 117
LOUFMAN, John 217
LOUGH, Charles C 268 Vera 169
LOWE, Alexander 238 246 David 204
　George 267 Harry Lloyd 276 Mrs
　B L 297 Paul E 286 Ralph E 276
　292 Raymond L 289 Wm R 270
LOWERY, Abraham 212 214
　Benjamin C 238 Calvin F 250
　Jeremiah 193 199 Malcolm 172
　Samuel 30 Wm F 176
LOY, Edward 219 Ercel Hullian 284
　Jacob Presley 275 Virginia 169
　William 219
LOYD, John A 133
LUCAS, Hue E 286 William Encil 282
LUCEY, Timothy John 286
LUIKART, J H 268 271 Mrs W A 296
LUKE, Blanche 304 James F 248 R W
　304 W L 172 Wm 127
LUKENS, Margaret 170
LUSTER, William H 259
LUTES, Clarence Terrell 281 Clyde
　Louis 284 D C 302 David 116 121
　Elza 129 Hubert Dewey 285 Isaac
　173 James I 300 James Otis 286
　W G 266
LYDICK, Benjamim T 264 Benjamin
　T 262 264 J B 121 John B 237
　Noah 244 257 O H 261
　S R 169 302
　Samuel 190 196
　William 256
　Wm H 139 248

LYNN, 27 28 John 25 26 30 31 81
　John Discovers Indians And Gives
　Timely Alarm 30 William 66 67
LYON, Daniel 188 David 188
LYONS, Geo W 217
M'GREW, Robert 29
MACKEY, Lureta 169 Robert F 246
　W K 271
MADELL, Joseph C 272
MAGERS, Carl 275 David 133 225
　James A 225 James E 291 James
　Earl 281 James W 260 John W
　129 132 139 202 Joseph 116
　William F 225
MAGRUDER, Daniel 208 Thomas
　208 226
MAHOOD, Everett L 280 Samuel R
　280
MAINE, Francis Marion 276
MAKAROW, Peter 288
MALLOTT, William Lewis 270
MALONY, William 188
MALSED, Wm H 220
MALY, John 188
MAMMOTH MOUND, 306
MANE, Stephenson 249
MANGOLD, John 266
MANION, Thomas W 205
MANNING, Beeler 262 Franklin 257
　Jacob A 268 James B 233 Jas B
　231 Louis 227 228 Samuel B 134
　257 T W 149 Thomas W 183 226
　W L 184 Wm M 228
MANNNIG, Beeler 131
MARCHINE, Angelo 276
MARINER, Robert Sylvus 275 Wesley
　Elwood 287
MARIO, Nicola Di 275
MARIS, Wm T 244
MARKEOIK, Adam 275
MARLIN, Elijah 188
MARPLE, George 229 Joel D 202
　John 135 242 Joseph 140 253
　Lillie 296 Raymond U 288
　Thomas W 234 W H 137 143
　William 267 Wm 141
　Wm H 253

MARSH, Abram 239 George W 240
  241 John W 240 Joseph 121 138
  Mary 273 Mollie 298 Mrs H G
  298 Mrs Harry 298 Stella 298
MARSHALL, Asbury 207 Elvada 170
  Jas W 253 Jesse 191 203 John 106
  Thomas 191 Thomas T 205
  William 207
MARSHALL COUNTY CREATED
  BY GENERAL ASSEMBLY, 106
MARSHMAN, Thomas F 181
MARTIN, 34 35 Alexander 188 Alma
  172 Andrew J 197 Arch T 267 Asa
  188 Bonham 117 Clay N 269
  Denver P 292 Denver Pear 281
  Edda 172 Family Murder of 34
  Harry 272 Jefferson T 175 176
  John 77 78 John Wesley 285
  Joseph 191 Joseph H 193 L G 146
  Luther 93 Mary 93 Miss Jessie
  296 Mrs W J 298 Nancy 324
  Nannie 298 Rebecca 11 77 78
  Robert 111 Ross 269 Samuel 188
  Shipley 324 William 265
MARTINKOVIC, Stephen J 273
MARTINO, Carmono 275
MASENA, Samuel 197
MASON, Argyle Ogle 286 Capt 18 20
  Clarence E 169 G F 169 Henrietta
  297 Herman H 283 Hildred 169
  Jeremiah 147 Jerry 183 O G 121
  Orvil 285 Samuel 16 17 21 Sidney
  Shirley 287 W E 158 172 184 300
  W K 299 Wayne Eldron 288
  William 244 Wm 133
MASSACRE, of Captain Foreman
  And Men 26
MASSENA, Samuel 225
MASSEY, A E 172
MASTERS, Cynthia 137 Jesse 210
  John 214
  Mathew 210 214
  Nathan 12 45 87 117 Z 108 110
  112 113 114
  Zadock 107 108 110 111 114 116
  177
MATHENG, Elias 211

MATHEWS, A J 225 Andrew D 141
  249 C C 184 223 David 209 Jesse
  267 John 212 Mrs S W 296 S W
  184 264 302 W B 157 William H
  210
MATOVICH, Paul 274
MATTHEWS, James Patrick 275 Lola
  171
MATTSON, Ellen 171
MAUROT, Mrs Paul 302 Rose 296
MAVIS, Andrew 188
MAXWELL, James Robert 287
MAY, Levi 257
MAYFIELD, Anson 220
MAYHALL, Timothy 99 114 116
MAYS, Walter 288
MAZURICK, Tony 282
MCARTHUR, Duncan 74
MCBROOM, Robert 207
MCCAMIC, Charles 185 273 299
  Chas 267 294 Miss Francis 296
  Mrs Chas 302
MCCANN, Clarence Benton 282
  Raymond Milton 282
MCCARDLE, Horace 188
MCCARRIHER, J W 146
MCCARTHY, David 188 Veda 171
MCCARTNEY, Andrew 129
MCCAUSLIN, Robert 203
MCCLANAHAN, Florence 170
MCCLEAN, Abijah 87 Arch 95
  Archibald 92 93 Col 94 Horatio J
  115 John 15 Joseph 97 111 112
  115 116 174 178 Joseph Jr 110
  112 114 Mr 93 94 178
MCCLEARY, Genevieve 298 J E 299
  302 Josie 298 Vinton 304
MCCLELLAN, Wm H 274
MCCLELLAND, William 188 191
MCCLOSKEY, James 208 209
MCCOMBS, Alexander 137 141 Chas
  Robert 274 Clyde H 288 Emma V
  298 J T 184 James 126 143 John
  131 203 Jos T 264 Mary 172 Mrs
  C K 298 Robert E 281
MCCON, J W 236
MCCONAGHY, James 114

MCCONAHEY, Robert 111
MCCONAUGHEY, Robert 117
  William 121
MCCONNEL, Isabel 297
MCCONNELL, Alfred M 286 Cora
  172 Daniel 137 Elmira 298 Robert
  98 146 Ruth 169 William 108 Wm
  108
MCCORD, H R 234 238
MCCORMACK, Thomas 97
MCCOSH, Rex H 272
MCCOWN, Isaac 73
MCCOY, Dr 126 154 Jno 114 Mrs
  Robert 296
MCCRACKEN, Alex 208 Charles C
  285 David 133 244 George L 284
  Jacob Lloyd 274
MCCREARY, John T 111 Wm 127
  154
MCCULLOCK, John 99
MCCULLOUGH, Curtis Ray 277
  John 67 Maj 23 25 Samuel 20 22
  William 66
MCCULLOUGH'S LEAP, 22
MCCULLY, John Kennedy 284
MCCUNE, Harry 283
MCCUSKEY, B E 300 C F 271 Geo
  301 H L 295 Helen 297 L H 299
MCCUSKY, Milton 300
MCDANIEL, Lena 296 Marion R 270
  Nellie 172
MCDERMOTT, John Peter 288
MCDONALD, Alexander 109 Jas A
  232 John S 135 154 181 189 192
  254 William P 176 Wm R 203
MCDOWELL, Bruce R 270 David
  121 126 H W 158 185
MCELROY, James 192 Joe M 270
MCELVAIN, James 207
MCFADDEN, G C 126 G S 120 154
  183 310 311 Mrs 310 R J 186 310
MCFARLAND, Thomas 191 Thos B
  254 William 109 111 113 117 177
  Wm 116 Wm Sr 119
MCFARREN, John 108
MCGARVEY, Thomas 227
MCGARVY, Thomas 225

MCGARY, George M 285 John 211
  303 Mrs John 297 Samuel 299
  William 172
MCGAW, Maggie 172
MCGEE, Edward 260 John 191
MCGILL, Harry 266 James 129 Jas H
  219 Samuel 219 William 261 Wm
  130
MCGILTON, Nelson 201
MCGINNIS, Bernard James 289 John
  J 203
MCGINTY, William 172
MCGLENN, A H 172
MCGLUMPHY, Anna B 296 303 C B
  268 Francis 130 John 130 Robert
  H 279
MCGOWN, John O 245 Patrick 261
MCGRATH, John J 207
MCGRUDER, Daniel 238 Thos S 239
MCGUFFY, Dr 268
MCHENRY, Cyrus 287 James 188
  202 James N 231 Jasse Parsons
  284 Lou E 273 Thomas 169
MCINTIRE, George 143
MCINTOSH, Decoyed And Murdered
  By Indians 43 Mrs 44 William 43
  44
MCJILTON, Frank 146 147
MCKEAN, James 97
MCKEE, Henrietta M 172 John A 276
MCKIMMEY, G W 126
MCKIMMIE, Geo W 147 153
  Webster 287
MCKINY, Calvin 133
MCKITRICK, Elmer E 278
MCKNIGHT, 21 G S 236 John 225
MCLEAN, Col Letter From George
  Washington 94
MCMAHON, A 88 Maj 53 58 Perry
  140 249
MCMASTERS, William Ward 288
MCMECHEN, B 109 112 B B 184
  185 302 Benjamin 107 108 110
  111 112 113 117 Hiram 108 120 J
  L 303 James 17 25 Mr 13 Mrs 13
  Sidney 12
  William 12 25 100

351

MCMILLAN, Ruth 128 138 Samuel 265
MCMILLEN, Benedict 120 Benj V 249 Esther 170
MCMULLEN, Clyde J 269 Fred 303 John 139 247 Mrs Fred 296
MCNEMAR, Alma 273
MCNINCH, F A 185 Fred 299 Fred A 186 J B 301
MCPEEK, Joseph B 259
MCPELLEY, Philip 225 228
MCREYNOLDS, Wm 219
MCRICHMOND, Wm 234
MCSHANE, Hugh 281
MCSWAIN, Lester 275 291
MCVAY, Jacob 188
MCWILLIAMS, F M 217 J F H 221
MEDE, Benjamin 220
MEDLEY, David 188
MEEK, E Grover A 271 Nella 172
MEIER, Henry 304 Marie 299 304
MEIGHEN, B F 183 184
MELKO, Paul 281
MELLON, James W 277 Sam'l N 194 Samuel N 191 William 191 205
MELOTT, James J 271 John A 269 Thomas 269 Wm Henry 268
MELVIN, T 147
MEMORIAL, To General Assembly of Virginia 100
MENIX, Jonathan 240 241
MERCER, 8 9 Charles L 288 Eli 284 Hugh Alexander 285 William D 283
MERCHANT, Benj F 193 Benjamin F 191 Sam'l 193
MERINAR, E K 170
MERINER, Rebecca 298
MESSACHER, Thomas 257
MEURA, Luggi 285
MEYERS, Chas William 275 Frank Michael 287 George M 257 Harry 287 Lulu 299 Mary 299 Victor E 185
MICKEY, James 284
MIDCAP, Walter 246

MILES, Harry Mckinley 287 James 249
MILITARY RECORDS, 187 Report By Miller And Wilson 29
MILLER, 14 Adam 73 Alva 276 Andrew 191 193 199 Anthony 29 30 Atlee H 291 Ben 272 Cephus 246 David K 207 Earl 272 291 Effie 273 Eli 253 Elijah 135 Fred Lother 288 Gabriel 191 Henry 121 126 J A 299 J T 302 Jacob 210 214 James N 225 James T 299 John 127 John A 130 John D 205 Levi 246 Lt 29 M D L 236 M W 236 Margaret 171 Martha 301 Mrs Erastus 296 Mrs James T 296 Mrs Parry 296 Parry 300 303 R D 294 304 Report of 29 Richard 220 Samuel 211 W M 184 William 253 301 Wilson 300 Wm G 217
MILLIKEN, Charles Raymond 284
MILLS, 53 80 James D 260 Pauline M 170 Thomas 52 79
MINCHENKO, Jan 285
MINER, Alexander 230 Mrs Shelvy B 298
MINOR, Charles 283
MINSON, John 117
MIRABELLA, Rocco 274
MISCELLANEOUS, 323
MITCHEL, Moses M 244
MIX, Edward 269 John Garfield 281
MONIS, Morgan 188
MONTGOMERY, Francis 141 Harold Floyd 289 James C 269 John 131 Joseph 117 129 Michael 142 Mrs S C 296 Warren 277
MOODY, John S 143
MOON, John H 141
MOONEY, A D 295 Andrew L 219 Charles E 283 John 120 121 122 123 125 126 127 Maggie M 295 Messr 132
MOORE, Annalie 171 Charles D 134 Everett F 185 186 Ezekiel 191 197 Ferdinand 188 Franklin 240 Harry Webster 289 Jacob 135

MOORE (continued)
  John H 247 260 John L 230 John
  R 120 Lucy 297 Mrs W E 298 Mrs
  W H 298 O A 146 O H 146 S A
  169 Saul 280 Thomas 134 188
  212 244 William 236
MOOREHEAD, J W 299 303 Mrs J
  W 296
MOOREHOUSE, Margaret 169
MOOSE, George W 210 214 Vida 171
MORAN, B 111 Blair 100 107 111
  113 177 Paul M 270
MORELAND, Nicholas 188
MORGAN, C G 268 271 David L 231
  Jas 231 Jas B 217 John L V 257
  Oliver H P 231 Robert 120 126
  Thomas 126 154 Thomas R 226
  228 Uriah 188 Wm H 202
MORHOVICH, Mike 274
MORNINGSTAR, Charles 295 Clara
  295 Edward 274 Helen 169 295
  Leonard M 278
MORRIS, Daniel 225 Eli C 142 Frank
  265 Harry C 288 Hiram K 210
  James D 108 111 146 176 177 Jas
  D 108 John Edward 278 John
  Elwood 280 John Leonard 287
  John R 128 Mary 171 Stephen 144
  Thomas 209 213 Thomas J 288
  William G 210 Wm T 134
MORRISON, Mrs J A 296 Walter 269
MORROW, Alexander 140 249 John
  R 132
MORTON, Richard 110 178
MOSER, Charles 267
MOSLANDER, Wm 227
MOSSLANDER, Joseph E 260
MOUND, At Moundsville 306
MOUNTAIN, Albert A 268 290
  Thomas Jas 269 W A 268
MOUNTZ, Andrew 215 Richard C
  217
MOUROT, Nan 273
MOWDER, John Wm 280
MUHART, Peter John 286
MULDREW, Abram 207 Andrew 231
  J T 303

MULDRUE, George L 279
MULLEN, Joseph 233 234
MULLINOX, Robt F 142
MURCH, Enoch 206
MURDER, of Bevans Children 36 of
  Crow Sisters By Indians And A
  White Man 39 of Martin Family
  34 of Tush Family 35
MURDY, Lyda C 173
MURPHY, Benedict Edward 279
  David 301 David T 190 286 James
  Raymond 273 Salathiel 190
  William 188 197 199
MURRELL, Amos 130
MURRINER, John 200 William 201
MURRINS, George A 200 James 200
MURRY, Denny Albert 287 James
  Walker 272
MUSCETTE, Angello 284
MUSGROVE, C G 302 David S 205
  Grover Cleveland 286 James G
  207
MYERS, Andrew 205 Ben Frank 276
  Cora 172 David 244 George 281
  291 George M 193 Henry 190
  James 220 James W 254 260 263
  John M 211 Joseph 233 Martin S
  211 214 Roy Daton 271 Victor E
  185 William 205 Wm 135
NACE, David 97
NAGLE, C C 302
NAMAEK, Stephen C 288
NANGLE, Lawrence E 280
NANNA, Mabel 296
NASH, William 217 221
NEAL, Archibald 188
NEASE, Ray 275
NEELY, Edwin S 244
NEER, Harry Martin 274
NEGRO, Dady Sam 31 32 Kate 31
NEILSON, Anna 170
  James 266 267
NEISWANGER, 43 John 42
  John Death of 42
NELSON, David 142 253 Morgan 108
  Richard 288
NEMEK, Louis 268

NESBITT, Emmie 172 Mary 171 296 Mrs Mattie 297
NEUSETH, Stephen 274
NEW STATE, 118
NEWBY, George 285
NEWLAND, Andrew 140 J 143
NEWMAN, Alexander 175 176 B B 156 173 Chas C 185 Dora 273 L S 183 Lewis S 182 Vera 295 303
NEY, J W 120 123
NICE, Thomas 236 William H 290 Wm H 269
NICHOLAS, John 301
NICHOLS, Geo W 240 George 142 George W 241 Thomas 97
NICKERSON, Francis 240
NICOLAN, William Webster 284
NIEBERGALL, Llewellyn 283 Louis 274
NIEDEMYER, J W 272 Ralph 278
NIGHTLER, William 274
NIXON, Benj F 217 James 96 238 John 183 184
NOBLE, Foster 283 John Wesley 280
NOICE, William 225
NOLAN, Joseph A 284 Richard B 280 W L 280
NOLAND, Edgar J 284
NOLLER, Ruth 172
NOLTE, A E 301 Joseph 294
NOLTY, Wm 185
NORRINGTON, Paul 292
NORRIS, Mary 298 Mrs W T 298
NOWELL, Helen S 295 W M 300
NSCOZLIOS, Domenico 278
NULL, Earl 270 John 111
NUSS, J B 130 John C 131 262
O'CONNEL, Carl A 280
O'CONNELL, Lawrence W 284 Wm Thomas 275
O'CONNOR, Leo J 280
O'HARA, Frank 268
O'NIEL, Clifford Earl 287 Con 10 James 96 Ray R 282
O'TOOL, Patrick 271
OBERG, Henry Ernest 287 Louis Joseph 281

ODUILA, Frank 274
OFFICIALS, Elected And Reported By Board of Supervisors 180 Elected And Reported By Canvassing Board of The County 182
OFFTERDINGER, William 290 299 Wm 269
OGDEN, Cornelius 187 Geo W 194
OGLE, Alexander 324 Capt 16 18 20 21 23 24 26 27 Daniel S 191 193 Jacob 21 191 Jacob W 142 253 Joseph 16 17 21 Mary Ann 324
OLDFIELD, Artimous 276
OLDHAM, Wylie H 176
OLIVER, Alva 269 John T 278 290 Verner Curtis 287
OLNEY, Joel L 141 249
OLSON, Chester Arthur 279
ORMSBY, John H 210 Thomas J 234
ORR, Hiram 178 William 188
ORUM, Elizabeth 298 George 203 223 228 Jesse Burnard 288 John 290 John R 270 Joseph 184 185 Lloyd 133 Mabel 169 Peter 117 142 202 253
OTT, John T 135 244
OTTER, Wm 142
OWENS, John 188 Milton 219
PADULA, Carmine 284
PAITH, Oliver Franklin 280
PALISCO, Luiggi 283
PAPULA, Andy 274
PARKER, Edward Russell 278 Joseph E 283 Oliver 210 214 Thomas Moore 282 Thomas N 291 William 281
PARKINSON, Benoni 191 Clara 173 George 172 Henry 134 149 254 J L 146 182 James 134 197 James M 191 John L 182 Samuel 266 Wm L 197
PARKS, Arch L 274 Earl 276 William H 253 Wm 141
PARR, Nathaniel 13 14
  Nathaniel Encounters Indians And Kills Two 13
  Stephan 12

PARRIOTT, C C 115 Christopher 113 114 115 178 Geo W 221 Harold 272 Homer Charles 287 James D 158 185 Jas D 185 John 100 107 108 109 110 111 112 113 114 115 116 117 175 176 177 324 Raymond W 285 Robert A 249 Robt A 140 Samuel A 134 241 254 Susan 108 323 T E 185 W E 122 183
PARSONS, Henry 116 J F 150 173 183 Jason 299 Jesse Clyde 276 Paul Howard 281 Thomas 150 231 Thomas J 184 185 Wm Lester 269 Wylie Erwin 279
PATERICK, Louis H 270
PATTEE, Shirley 266
PATTERSON, 301 Benjamin 301 David 188 George B 301 George W 260 263 Guy 301 Leroy 285 Mattie 172 Ray 272 Robert 116 Virginia 171
PATTON, Mabelle 170 Mrs Frank 297 Stanley Thomas 277 Thomas 182
PAVLIC, Gaspar 275
PAXTON, William 220
PEABODY, Ben F 278
PEARSON, Alpheus 141 Benj F 246 Nicholas 141
PECK, J C 303 Mary 173
PEDLEY, John 126 Joseph 137 154 Thomas M 173
PEEL, James Leo 277
PELKY, John L 299
PELLEY, A L 146 George 177 181 James 203 Lawrence J 287
PENDERGAST, Michael J 278
PENN, William 78
PEOPLES, Clara 294 Guy 268 271 292
PEPLER, John H 217
PERKINS, Jacob 172 Thomas 273
PERL, James Leo 272
PERRIN, Arthur 280
PERSHING, Gen 300

PETERS, Mrs Frank 296 Samuel W 130 Samuel W M 231
PETERSON, Edward 29
PEW, Jacob 29
PHILIP, Albert C Von 287
PHILLIPS, C M 295 Fred C 286 J M 153 301 J Mcclean 300 J W 126 L L 301 Margaret 298 Mrs Elizabeth 298 S E 267 W S 301 William Wesley 287 Wm O 249
PICKETT, Leonard 142 Robt S 142
PIERCE, Arthur D 258 M B 299 Russell 283 W L 133 Wm L 244
PIERPOINT, Gov 179
PIERSON, Benj F 139
PILES, Salem L 244
PIONEER, County Superintendents of Marshall County 155 Industries 312 Life 84
PIPER, Andrew J 205
PIPES, H H 300 J H 126 J N 153 James W 181 T C 184 300 301
PITCHER, Henry C 135
PLATT, Geo 294
PLESHKOB, Paul 271
PLETCHER, Samuel 205 Uriah 205
PLEUS, Robt Read Jr 272
PLUM, John W 217 Joseph 217
POCCI, Thomaso 281
POLEN, Brooks 284 Stidger 276
POLLEY, William A 280
POLLOCK, Thomas 117
POLUTIS, Tony 283
POLUTTIS, Gus 271
POLY, Christian 143
POND, Charles W 275 Frank 271
POOCHACKY, Oldrich 272
POPULATION, of Marshall County 1920 325
PORCARI, Gaetam 276
PORTER, Abner S 260 Arthur 257 George A 139 249 James A 259 John S 225 228 Jonah 187 Luther Walker 283 Sarah 171 William 257
PORTERFIELD, Friend N 287
POSTHLEWAIT, John N 217

POSTLETHWAIT, J 246 Joseph 246
   M V 246
POTTS, Cecil Floyd 283 George 132
   George W 133 244 Louis 269 Mrs
   L R 296
POWELL, Abraham 29 Benjamin 29
   Carrie 297 George Selby 285
   James T 303 John E 131 262
   Melvin 236 Mrs W S 296 Roy
   Edward 275 Thompson 249 W S
   173 300 Wm H H 265 Wm O 116
   Wm S 266
POWERS, Goldie 298 J L 130
   Virginia 169
POYLES, J M 300
PRATT, Alexander 210 Capt 31 I D
   131 John D 225
PRETTYMAN, J J 217 221 Leven T
   217 Perry 217
PRICE, B W 97 120 184 Bushrod 176
   G B M 260 John 219 Judd 272
   Justin B 269 Moses 217 221
   Moses B 258 Silas 117 Thomas J
   141 249 William 266 Wm 272
PRICKETT, James 211 214
PRIDE, Jackson 261 263
PRINCE, Carle 278
PRITCHELL, James 120
PRITCHET, Wesley W 237
PROBASCO, J W 128
PROCEEDINGS, of First Session of
   County Court 107
PROCHANZY, Oldrich 291
PROELSS, O 268 O A Jr 271
PROVISIONS, for District High
   Schools 156
PUGH, Lewis 262 263 T J 172
PULSINELLI, Vincenzo 284
PURCELL, Francis 92
PURDY, Alex 300 Geo H 215 Harry L
   266 L B 184 Lewis B 258 Lewis C
   178 Robert C 260 263 Rufus 257
   Rufus S 133 244 Simeon 97 114
   177 Simeon B 110 112 113 116
   178 Simeon T 262 W J 180 W S
   130 Walter 185 William J 260 262
   William S 261

PURTIMAN, James 266
PYLES, B A C 221 Eveline R 298
   Everett C 301 J N 301 Jacob B
   257 Jeremiah 198 200 Joshua 231
   Lester C 279 Michael 269 Mrs Ira
   B 298 Salem L 135 Thomas Oliver
   278 Thomas W 257 Wm H 223
QUICK, J F 172
QUIGLEY, Jacob 139 251 John 196
QUIGLY, Andrew 147
RABER, Thomas Clark 275
RABRE, John Elwood 280
RADABAUGH, John W 142
RADCLIFF, Thomas M 133
RAFFERTY, Russel R 270 Sebasteen
   295 Virginia 172
RAILROADS, 90
RAINS, Henry C 245 Noah 245
RAMSER, Mrs Louis 296
RAMSEY, James 116 Milton R 212
   Olga G 285
RANEY, Richard Baxter 278
RANKAN, John 121
RANKIN, Lloyd 281
RANSOM, Earl Willard 283 Ira 267
   Ira A 272 Mrs Russell 297
RAPER, Charles 283
RAVENSCROFT, Wm 205
RAY, Albert Golia 274 Alexander 257
   Chas Edward 274 Edward 283
   James W 285 John 130 144 265
   Margaret 128 William H 261
RAYL, James 253
REA, Guisseppi 281
REDD, Frand C 284 John S 146 237
   Parker S 237 238
REDMAN, J W 130
REECE, George W 231
REED, Alex H 244 Alpheus 191
   Dolphus 231 Ezra M 191 228 233
   Henry 146 239 J C 128 Jackson
   123 132 176 177 325 James W
   250 John 117 132 253 Josephus
   228 Levi 191 193 Messr 128
   Oscar 215 Samuel 121 Wilma 170
REESE, John 128 Samuel A 133
REID, John W P 155 158 181

REIDEL, Louis 170 Louis C 278 Paul 301
REILLY, Hyder 245 Mary 296
REINFORCEMENTS ARRIVE, 20
RELIEF, for Wives of Soldiers In The War 124
REMKE, Clarence 304 Willie Franklin 287
REMMICK, C H 131
RENIK, Edward 276
REPORT, of Bounty Paid - To Whom 129 of First Grand Jury of Marshall County 109 of Third Loan On County Bonds And Disbursement 137
RESSEGER, Samuel 172
RETURNS, of Second Township Election 126
REVIEW, of Early Education And Pioneer Schools 158
REX, Lucy 171 Rek H 269
REYNOLDS, Donald Mcmahon 288 F W 126 Franklin 207 Henry J 261 263 John S 181 Lewis 134 244 William Jr 244 Wm Jr 135
RICCI, Frank 268 Pasquale 276
RICE, Blanche 171 Jacob 188 Luther 172
RICHARDS, George 141
RICHARDSON, Floyd Jasper 281 Joshua 220
RICHEA, George 137
RICHEY, Andrew K 233 James 121
RICHMOND, A C 272 Alliance Q 269 Charles 207 Elmer R 288 Elsworth 292 Elsworth R 288 Flora 169 H J 304 Harley Friend 283 Harry Clyde 274 Harry R O 287 Isaac J 207 J F 237 J W 121 126 154 James F 144 John 121 Silas 207 Taylor 134 244 257 Wilford 284 William K 281 William Q 291 Wilson 304 Wm M 257 Wm Mc 234
RICHTER, A 295 Frederick 205 G 154 J B 302 Sam'l 206
RICKEY, Elmer 279

RIDDLE, James 254
RIDER, Charles A Jr 278 Jessie Belle 170
RIDMAN, Isaac 209
RIFE, Clara 299 Fred E 302
RIFLE, Henry 130
RIGBY, John Wm 278 Thomas 142
RIGFGLE, William Alfred 276
RIGG, W H 223
RIGGLE, Charles 203 George 225 Henry 188 Lewis P 300 Lottie 299 Martin Fred 275 Orvill L 287 William Alfred 292 William Joseph 277 Wm 130
RIGGS, 12 A B 225 Alfred 128 129 225 Alfred R 129 138 Alma 169 Andrew 191 Bruce E 285 Charles C 275 Ed T 172 Edward 196 197 Elias E 134 264 Ella 298 Ernest 285 Herman B 285 I D 265 Isaac D 130 J Hanen 269 J S 180 James 109 James J 219 James L 196 199 Jerry D 262 John 109 114 120 147 Joseph 96 Labon 120 127 Lawrence B 268 287 Lemuel 132 202 Lizzie 172 Mahlen 150 Mahlon 120 127 Maude 296 Messr 132 Mr 122 124 125 128 Mrs W M 296 Nettie 297 S W 300 Samuel 120 121 122 123 125 126 127 132 136 137 138 143 T S 294 302 Thomas 129 138 Thomas G 231 Victor Anvil 288 W H 227 W M 302 W Martin 294 Wm 126 153
RILEY, Barzillia Wirt 286 Charles 131 Chas W 194 Phillip 172 Thomas 172
RINDERER, Lorena 170
RINE, Brady F 286 David 231 F C 304 Foster 169 266 George 121 126 153 172 Gilmore 169 J M 158 169 302 James 121 123 125 126 127 136 John 117 John S 140 249 Mary B 295 Micajah 172 Richard 130
RINEHART, A B 268 271 John C 270

357

RISER, Charles 257
RISERA, Henry 29
RISINGER, S 300
RITCHEA, George 251
RITCHEY, Crozier 231 John 127 154
RITCHIE, George 264
ROACH, Charles J 283 Jesse 208 209
ROAD SUPERVISORS APPOINTED, 116
ROADS, 87
ROBERTS, 12 Bayard Mcclean 277 E G 300 E L 269 Edgar Losen 276 Erett 268 Evan 295 Evan G 302 Evelyn 172 H E 303 Irvin F 254 J B 97 Jacob D 237 Jacob J 231 James M 211 John A 236 John C 228 233 Jonathan 93 117 Jonathan W 138 Levi 188 Mary 297 Mrs F L 297 Reuben 109 W W 130 Wm L 234
ROBERTSON, Chas C 249 Raymond 283
ROBINSON, C H 304 E L 302 Emmett 281 Frank Cecil 279 George 233 Jack 134 James 188 231 James L 291 James Lindsay 281 John 173 John F 269 John R 135 241 254 Milton 303 Phillip 232 R J 185 Robert L 286 Robert Lee 281 Robert William 292 Robert Wm 276
ROBISON, Charles C 140
ROBY, Godfrey A 217
RODGERS, Mary 170 Patrick J 269
RODOCKER, Carl Leroy 278 William 250 Wm 141
ROE, C B 294 Jane Elizabeth 296 Mrs C B 297
ROGER'S STORY OF THE INDIAN ATTACK, 23
ROGERS, 24 Abraham 23 25 Andrew 95 David 91 Harold 171 Harry 266 Helen 172 James 240 Mr 15 Patrick J 290
ROGERSON, Bemis 268 271 Bence C 284 Clifford H 284 Emmett Q 280 Harry Clark 277 Mrs T L 296

ROISO, John 287
ROLLSTON, Chas A 191
ROMANO, Michael 276 290
ROMEL, Louis 291 Louis J 281
RONEY, John 129
ROOME, John 219
ROSCOE, George 271
ROSE, Lee K 283
ROSEBERRY, Harry 286 J T 184 John E 244 John T 184 240
ROSS, Joseph 207 Joseph R 134 244 Luke B 171 Luke Burdett 289 Mathias B 133 Mathias M 210 Matthias B 244 Samuel 191 Thomas 205 Wm 134
ROSTER, of County Superintendents of Marshall County 158 of Officers Elected Under Commonwealth & Govt of Virginia 175 of Teachers for 1923 168
ROTH, John R 301 Robert Leroy 269
ROUND BOTTOM LITIGATION, 90
ROWAND, E C 157
ROWE, Adam 14 Adam's Family Attacked By Indians At Grave Creek 14 Jacob 14 Mrs 14 Robert 14
ROYTEK, Joe 274
RUBLE, Paul R 171 Peter A 217
RUCKMAN, Emma C 304 Isaac D 236 Thomas 126 Thos 153 Van 299 William Edgar 284
RUDE, Irene 171
RUDLE, Samuel 142
RUKAVINA, George 275
RULONG, Eliza 128 Ida 297 Morris 129 231 Oren E 283 Richard 116 Wm H 231
RUMBLE, Prentis 269
RUPP, Everett Zane 276 W X 302
RUSH, Bethuel 188 Clarence E 274 David 117 George E 283 Isaac 220 James 210 214 Jesse Lloyd 274 291 Jonathan I 285 Otis 287 Ottis Wm 278 Willis 111

RUSHMAN, Frank Joseph 277
　　John Francis 278
RUSSELL, George Frank 287
RUTAN, John 140 249 Olen 277
RUTH, Mary E 172 William 313
RUZINSKI, Tony 283
RYAN, Gilbert 268 Henry 188 Jasper
　　206 Lazarus 117 Oscar J W 284
　　Walter Francis 287
RYERSON, 46
RYNER, Olive 171
SADLER, Edward J 272
SAFREED, Albert G 291 Robert Cash
　　280
SAINTCLAIR, Laura 172 Robert G
　　120 123
SALARIES, of County Officials In
　　1864 322 of County Officials In
　　1923 322
SALTER, Eli 127 154
SALTERS, H M 267
SALTNAKER, Attacked By Indians
　　70
SALVATORIA, Mangior 284
SAMEL, Tony 281
SAMMONS, J J 185 W P 268 Wm P
　　271
SAMON, E W 303
SAMPLES, Carrie 273
SAMS, Dady Aids In Defense 32
SANDER, Joseph 211
SANDERS, Chris 170 J M 294 302
　　James C 191 John 209 Mrs M A
　　296 Samuel 142
SANDS, Freeman P 192 Freman P 193
　　198 Geo W 196 199 George 192
　　George W 205 William 208
SANER, Michael Victor 269 Mike V
　　290
SANFORD, Alice 171
SANTEE, J W 168
SARVEL, Andrew 284
SAVELL, Carl 268
SAYER, William 219
SAYERS, Alex S 262 George 218
　　Isaac T 218 Richard C 218
　　Wm M 211

SAYLER, John W 262
SCALORA, Salvator 285
SCANLON, Raymond Albert 281
SCANTLING, John 226
SCHAD, Elizabeth 170 Louis M 301
SCHAFER, Harry 295 Mary 297
　　Matilda 303 Philip 267
SCHAFFER, James W 284
SCHANE, Charles C 303
SCHLONAKER, David 196
SCHMID, Joseph Henry 281
SCHMITZ, William Richard 277
SCHOFIELD, Edward 226
SCHOOL OFFICERS Carrying Out
　　The Provisions of Free Schools,
　　153
SCHOONOVER, Jesse 219
SCHRODER, Clara 171
SCHULTZ, Donald 170 Ida 303
SCHUMACHER, Louisa 296
SCHUSE, Joseph 272
SCHWOB, J A 300
SCOTT, 49 Andrew 31 John 117
　　Lawrence 171 Lester 291 Mabel
　　298 Martin L 210 214 Mollie 31
　　Norma 297 Thomas 299 302
　　William 111
SCROGGINS, A C Jr 299 Donald
　　Skelton 278 291 Mrs A C Jr 296
SCULLY, Patrick J 274 William P 291
　　Wm Paul 273
SEALAH, William H 262
SEARLS, Francis Perry 285
SEARS, John 231
SECOND ATTACK Upon Fort Henry,
　　30
SECOND LOAN On County Bonds -
　　From Whom, 132
SECOND REPORT of Bounty Paid -
　　To Whom, 132
SECOND SESSION of County Court,
　　110
SEELY, Allen 218
SEESE, Arthur J 269
SELTNER, Edwin 270 P 303
SEMI-CENTENNIAL SURVEY of
　　Schools, 161

SERECHIS, Tony 275
SERVIA, John 273
SETTLEMENT, At Flats of Grave Creek 9 At Mcmechen 12 At Wheeling Creek 8 On The Ridge At The Head of Narrows 11
SETTLERS, Leave The Flats of Grave Creek for Safety 10 Return To Their Improvements 11
SEXTON, Armstrong 218
SEYLER, Everett F 286
SHAFFER, Lawrence F 277
SHAFFERMAN, Guy N 278
SHATTOCK, N K 121
SHATTUCK, N K 124 125 181
SHAW, Bess E 296 Gertrude 296 John G 142 Joseph 203 Leroy 258
SHAY, James 283
SHEAKATRIKE, Walter 281
SHEETS, Charles E 281 Elias 246 George 280 Luther G 268 Luther Gay 288 Mary 172
SHEPHERD, 49 A A H 196 199 Asa 274 Benjamin 117 Col 16 21 22 23 24 26 David 16 21 25 28 30 31 48 255 Henry C 202 J W 237 James B 269 John 300 Joseph 144 N 126 154 Nathan 121 Nathan B 258 Nathaniel 116 Robert 279 Walter G 271 William 21
SHERIFF, Gives Bond 146
SHERIFFS, Appointed By The Governor of Virginia 177
SHERMAN, Robert 210 214 Thomas 240
SHERRICK, J W 172
SHETLER, Joe 302
SHIELDS, William 220
SHILLING, Alexander 226 David 208 209 James 202
SHIMP, Charles Wesley 277 John 268 290 Ralph 269 W H 265 Wm H 130
SHIPLEY, Ballard H 277 Charles Howard 276 Robert 237
SHKURATOW, Mikaible 276
SHOEMAKER, Robert 113 116

SHOOK, Harry 284 Israel 226 Zebadee 133
SHOPTON, John 73
SHORE, Manie 285
SHOWACRE, C A 294 Nellie 296 W H 132 W H H 120 121 122 123 125 126 127 136 137 183
SHOWALTER, E H 218
SHREFFLER, Lydia 170
SHREVE, John C 171
SHRIVER, Edwin Lemont 286 Elisha 29 Leslie 249
SHUTLER, John 304 Mrs George 297 T J 304
SHUTTLEWORTH, Benj F 142
SIBERT, Arthur Hampton 284 Barney 134 231 245 David A 129
SIBURT, James B 271 Oscar 284 Willard C 270
SICKLES, George 271
SIERS, Floyd A 281
SIGAFOOSE, Margaret 171 Mrs James A 297 Ralph 269
SIGLER, Harold 272
SIMMONS, John 131 Joseph 141 Samuel Randall 287 Silas 131 Z L 299
SIMMS, David Carl 278 Josiah 198 200
SIMONTON, W S 183
SIMPSON, Frank C 269 R W 173 Roscoe 274
SIMS, Eva 298 John 188 225 Martin 226 Silas 194
SINCLAIR, Josiah 183 184 185 Phoebe 172
SINE, Boyd 281 Floyd Elsworth 275
SINSEL, 300 301
SISSON, A M 237 David S 212 214
SIVERT, Frederick 9 13 J E 158 300 Jacob 205 John 144 196 257 Martha 13 William 201
SKAZUISKI, Joseph 285
SKITERELICH, George 292
SKURATOO, Sergey 284
SLAUGHTER, Clarence H 289
SLIPNER, John 267

SLOAN, Charles H 283 Henry 249 Mordica 205 Sam'l H 205
SLOKAN, Frank W 281 John William 275
SMALLEY, Jacob 255
SMALLWOOD, Raymond 274
SMART, 323
SMITH, A P 127 Arnold 215 Benj F 209 Berlin O 169 D B 121 126 David G 196 Earl Wm 279 Elsie 296 Emma 302 Goldie 169 James 121 Job 116 Joe 143 John 188 Joseph D 215 Joseph M 142 Joseph S 218 Laura Pelley 298 Levi 205 Lewis H 130 Lillian 171 Louis H 260 263 Martin V 218 Mary E 294 295 303 Milton Lloyd 270 Nellie 168 Neva 169 Roy E 284 Roy Guy 275 Samuel 117 Samuel B 220 Sarah Ella 303 Solomon F M 218 Sylvia 171 Thelma 170 Thomas 201 Thomas F 220 Violet 296 Wallace 295 Warren 218 William 188
SMITT, Lawrence 278
SNEDEKER, Archie L 284 Carl Wayne 284 John 147 Marie 298 Millie 298 Mrs Morris 297 Orla H 281 Will Leroy 269 Wm 267
SNIDER, Noah 220 Wilson 231
SNODGRASS, Margaret 297 Mrs C L 297
SNOOK, Martin A 272
SNYDER, Charles 286 Harold Kenneth 289 Wm Delbert 278
SOCKMAN, F M 237 Henry 178 James W 272 Warren 134
SODAT, George 275
SOLDIERS, of The Mexican War 188
SOLE, James Edgar 274
SOMMERVILLE, J J 137 141
SONDERMAN, Harry 170 Nellie 169
SONEWALD, George 274
SPADDEN, John A 140
SPANISH AMERICAN WAR Company M 1st Wva V I, 266
SPARH, John 237

SPEAR, Clarence M 285
SPEARS, Harry 283 John 280 Sergeant 198 200 Thomas 207
SPECHT, Herman Jr 280
SPICER, 42
SPISICH, Mat 275
SPOON, Jacob 255
SPRAGUE, George 142
SPROUSE, William 205
SPURR, B M 294 302 Clinton 268 304 Gertrude 303
STAECK, Felix Cecil 283
STAHL, Mrs Chas 296
STALEY, Earl 275 290 James 247
STALNATER, 70
STANDIFORD, B F 265 266 Benj 237 Jacob 144 237 James 117 137 John J 133 245 Skelton 111 207 W A 302 Wm 234 Wm S 232
STANSBERRY, John W 257
STARKEY, John W 206
STARKS, Pardon 188
STEALEY, James 139
STEELE, Belle M 173 Byron W 268 Leota J 295 S M 184
STEEN, Oscar E 284
STEENROD, Lewis 108
STEFANSKI, Michael 278
STEPHENS, Benjamin Franklin 282
STERN, Otis 274 292 Wm H 222
STETSON, Edward 196
STEWART, George C 281 H M 185 Irvin 209 Irwin 257 James 137 257 James P 134 245 Jean 168 Jefferson 218 Jesse 192 Jesse Earl 277 Joseph 205 208 L C 237 Marietta 169 Melville 268 271 Neil 272 O H 186 Okey 168 Perry P 211 R G 171 Robert 206 Sam'l M 206 Thomas 209 William 214 William J 210 Wm 119 Wm A 207 Wm J 181
STIDGER, L L 184 Reed 268 S B 181 Samuel B 189
STILL, Ida 295

STILWELL, Elias 138 139 247
  Herbert 267 275 Joseph 130 231
  Silas 257 Timothy 130 141 249
  Timothy C 232 Wm L 267
STIMMEL, Henry 196 199
STINE, Jacob 227 William 225
STOLARCHICH, John 274
STOMEK, Mike 274
STONE, John 188 Joseph 188
  Raymond Prentice 287 Samuel E
  278
STORM, John 280 Raymond 274
STOUT, Samuel 205
STRAIGHT, Henry 269
STRAIT, George 276
STRAUB, Olive 300
STRAWN, M B 169 Ray 278
STREBICH, Joseph A 271
STREIBICH, J A 268
STRICKLAND, Reuben 212
STRICKLIN, C L 170 Humphrey 139
  Humphry 253 John 134 192
STRICKLING, John W 218
STROBEL, George Elwood 289
STROBER, Henry Erit 275 291 Jacob
  141
STROMBERG, Florence 170
STROPE, Lloyd 300 301
STUDEN, Frank 274
STULTZ, George James 288 W E 266
STUMP, Adam 249 Albert 237
STUTZMAN, E 170
SUHODALSKY, Sam 291
SULLIVAN, 294 Daniel 32 Daniel
  And Two Men Arrive At The Fort
  32 Elizabeth 72 Jesse D H 276
  John C 269 Roy 269
SUMMER, Gladys 171
SUMMERVILLE, J J 253
SUNDERMAN, August H 284
SUPAN, Frank Lewis 287
SUPERVISORS, Inquire When The
  Term of Office Expires 122
SUPLER, John M 272 291
SUSHOCLOESKY, Sam 280
SUTTER, Jacob 231
SWANN, Rembrance 177

SWEARINGEN, Andrew 22 Capt 34
  Col 20
SWEETEN, F B 98
SWERINGEN, Col 19
SWIFT, Margaret 296 302
SWIGGER, Wm 141
SWINEHART, W W 170
SYBERT, M A 294 299
SYBURT, M A 302
SYOC, Joseph Van 275 Leslie Van
  276
SZYMNSKI, Paul 274
TAGG, Earl 272 Frank Marion 281
  Stewart 264
TALBERT, Anthony W 134 192 245
  Eli 176 177 178 181 John 120 203
  John R 226 228
TALBOTT, Virginia 170
TARR, Brice 192 209 Brice Howard
  213 John B 222 Nathan B 211
TASKER, Edward Emmit 277
TATE, 31
TAYLOR, Alice 273 Caleb 249 Curtis
  E 272 292 Francis 232 I H 172
  James 188 John 109 233 239
  Leslie 276 Roy D 287 Thomas 218
  William 188 Wm F 266
TAZWELL, Littleton W 113 115
TEACHERS OF THE SCHOOLS In
  1873, 172
TEAGARDEN, Ersie Van R 277 Flo
  169
TEDROW, Harry 281
TEMPLE, John F 133
TEMPLIN, Peter Paul 275
TERRELL, 323
  Daniel 99 187 258
  Lawrence 275
  Roylance Richard 282
TERRILL, Hattie Bonar 169
  Thomas S 258
THACK, Joseph 291
THIEL, John 301
THOMAS, E C 181 Elias 192
  George 260 263 Harry 266
  Jonathan 187 Sherman 240
  Wm G 133

THOMPSON, Charles 282 Hugh 302
    Hugh W 270 Irene 169 Joseph 208
    209 Wm 241
THORNBERRY, Leander 245
THURBER, D A 261
THWAIT, R G 28
THWAITEK, Wtadystow 284
THWAITS, 19 R G 18
THWAITS' ACCOUNT OF
    MASSACRE, 28
TICICH, Anthony Frank 283
TIMBLIN, Louis Mcfarland 289
TIMMONS, Cecil 295
TIRITILLA, Antonio 287
TKACH, Joseph 278
TOCHILENKOW, Carl 284
TODD, Ruth 169 Vere R 280
TOMILSON, James 78 Joseph 78
    Joseph Sr 78 Samuel 78
TOMLINSON, 11 12 27 Alfred 262
    Elizabeth 10 95 97 Hager 226 260
    263 James 9 11 25 90 91 92 John
    G 264 Joseph 9 10 11 15 25 44 83
    90 91 92 95 96 223 306 307 310
    Joseph Jr 10 Joseph Sr 10 Mr 10
    46 77 96 Mrs 96 306 Mrs
    Elizabeth 87 Rebecca 77 78
    Robert 126 Samuel 9 11 17 25 90
    91 Simeon 262 263 W H 272
    William 260 263
TOMLINSON'S CABIN FORTIFIED,
    10
TONER, Charles J 269
TRACY, David 208 E M C 172
    Edward 147
TRAINER, Thos H 181
TRAVIS, Ethel 172 Jackson 126 154
    James Wesley 270 Mrs J W 297
TREADWAY, Wm M 203
TRENTER, John 226
TRIAN, Charles 258
TRIBETT, Earl 272 291
TROUT, Joseph H 218
TRUAX, John Francis 280
TRUEMAN, Thomas J 263
TRUMAN, Elias 232 James M 233
    Robert T 233 Thomas C 287

TRUMP, Earl Mcclelland 287
TUCKER, Samuel 272 290
TURNER, A 304 Alfred 146 183
    Charles 142 Dess 295 J M 143
    John M 120 121 122 125 127 132
    137 181 John S 130 288 Joseph
    120 125 127 138 176 177 Miss
    Lou 296 Samuel 241 Thomas M
    227 228
TURNEY, John 219
TURVEY, Frank 292 Frank H 285
TUSH, 36 Family Murder of 35
    George 35 Mrs 35
TUSIN, Marko 274
TUTTLE, Joel 249
TYSON, David Willis 271
ULLUM, Alfred 249 S P 303 Stephen
    218
UNDER The Second Constitution 145
    155
UNDER The First Constitution 118
UNDERDONK, Jacob 274
UNDERWOOD, Isaac 188
VAJVZEK, John 270
VALIRAKIS, Nick 277
VANBRUGH, Sheldon R 288
VANCE, G W 131
VANDERHOOF, Cornelius 210 214
VANDEVENDEN, Nicholas 188
VANDINE, Chester 269 290 Okley
    Ray 284
VANDYNE, Charles Foster 283
    Clarence W 288 Myrtle 297
VANO, Benedict 270
VANSCYOC, James 187 John 188
    Joshua 232 Wm 117
VANSYOC, Joseph 275 Leslie 276
    William 109
VARLAS, George 283
VARLEY, Robert M 258 William 254
    Wm 126 143 153
VARLIS, George 290
VARNER, Mildred 171
VAUGHN, Eli 140 250
VENAMAN, James 143
VENGDINSKI, Konstanz 274
VENLJARICH, John 274

VENUS, David 178 Joseph 134
    Joseph Allen 245 Samuel 109 116
    Samuel V 262 William 208
VERDERBRUGGEN, Joe 303
VERNON, John W 142
VICK, Harry Wilbur 276
VICKERS, Andrew 246
VIGNDICIK, Nick 274
VILLARS, James 215
VILLERS, Albert 218 Charles Otto
    287
VINCENT, Amos B 133 John 29 Wm
    H 218
VINEY, Bartholomew 29
VIRGIN, J M 269 Thomas James 287
VOIGHT, Edward 279
VOITEL, Louis R 284
VOITLE, Joe F 300
VOKOVICH, Joseph 283
VOLTZ, James Wm 278
VONPHILIP, Albert C 287 Bertha 169
VOORHIES, Silvia 287
VORDERBRUEGGEN, Antoine 296
    John 275 Mrs Joseph 297
VUCELICH, Michael 291
WABLE, John W 134
WADE, A L 157 Charles 286 Joseph
    169 Shirley Eggleston 276 Wm W
    266
WAGNER, Chas 280 W F 304
WALEN, Chester Clyde 278
WALK, Emil George 274
WALLACE, Henry 233 Henry C 228
    Ida 173 Isaiah 250 Joseph 120 129
    232 W C 173 William C 278 Wm
    F 232
WALTERS, Edna M 169 Malen
    Laurel 286
WALTON, Emma L 296 George 270
    George Earl 270 H W 300 Hiram
    210 214 Mrs J G 296 S A 294
    Sam'l W G 269 Wm F 270
WAR PATHS, 80
WARD, Daniel 188 Eugene A 279
    John 109 116 Wesley Harrison
    289 William 96
WARNER, Louis 275 William 283

WARSINSKI, Albert 281
WASHINGTON, Col 91 Gen 13 92 93
    94 Geo 95 George Letter To Col
    Mclean 94
WASMUTH, George P 299 James P
    276 Pearl 303
WATKINS, Albert H 270 Charles A
    288 Curtis Clay 287 Daniel 220
WATSON, 35 Wilber 301 William
    188 284 Wm J 272
WAYMAN, Carl Covert 279 J C 183 J
    F 172 Jno P 146 John 188 John P
    182 Vincent John 281 Zachariah
    109
WAYNE, Bessie 169 Donald L 286 E
    C 299 Gen 79 84 Sarah E 297
WAYT, Allen N 238 Eliza C 295
    Joseph 131 261 Mrs W B 297
    Reuben 201 Thomas 206 W B 169
    W D 183
WEATHER RECORD, 314
WEAVER, Chas H 292 Edward E 279
    George Sparry 283 Mary Etta 294
    296 303 Mrs V A 296 Robert
    Vinton 281 V A 294 302
WEBB, William 280
WEEKLEY, D Violet 170 William
    Nelson 278
WEEKLY, James 188 Louis Edwin
    289 Mrs J M 297 W P 172
WELCH, J Sherman 158 186 J W 170
    Robert 129 Thomas 285 Thomas
    D 134 Thos D 245
WELLING, Edward 196 Henry 254
    Henry W 142 James Alfred 281
WELLMAN, Carl Austin 286 Hugh
    Barger 288 J W 299 Mrs S M 297
    Paul Revere 288 Samuel 146
WELLS, C P 114 Charles P 111
    Daniel 187
    David 116 138 140 246
    Ephraim Owen 265
    Stewart 262
    Vane Constant 271
WELSCH, Sherman 286
WENDT, Harry August 284
    John 301

WEST, Charles Edgar 276 Edward 281 291 Everett William 287 I 139 Isaac 140 253 John B 114 John C 210 Mamie Wade 172 Sedry Earl 284
WESTBROOK, Samuel 188
WESTFALL, John 196 199
WETZAL, Martin 47
WETZEL, 9 36 49 57 59 60 68 69 72 73 Christina 48 Family 47 George 48 49 82 George Death of 48 Jacob 36 48 49 50 68 Jacob & Simon Kenton Attack A Camp & Kill Four Indians 68 Jacob Kills A Noted Indian Chief 68 John 8 9 47 48 49 64 66 67 74 77 82 John & Veach Dickerson Go In Quest of A Prisoner 67 John Captured By Indians 64 John Captures Indian Prisoner 67 John Compelled To Kill Indian Prisoner 67 John Death of 48 John Goes With A Party In Pursuit of Stolen Horses 66 John Party Attacked By Indians & Several Killed 66 John Recaptures Horses & Starts Home 66 John Rescued At The Mouth of Big Grave Creek 65 John Sr 48 John T 48 210 Lewis 48 49 50 51 52 53 54 55 56 58 61 Lewis And A Young Man Pursue Murderers And Rescue Girl 58 Lewis And Veach Dickerson Shoot At An Indian 56 Lewis Arrested At Maysville Ky 58 Lewis Arrested for Killing An Indian 56 Lewis Attack Party And Kill All The Murderers 60 Lewis Captured By Indians 49 Lewis Encounters Indians And Kills Three 51 Lewis Escapes From A Cabin And Kills An Indian 61 Lewis Escapes From Fort Harmer 56 Lewis Goes With A Party In Quest of Scalps 53 Lewis Joins A Party In Pursuit of Indians 50 Lewis Kills A Red Gobbler Near Wheeling 61

WETZEL (continued) Lewis Party Finds Indians But Returns 54 Lewis Remains And Gets A Scalp 54 Lewis Takes A Fall Hunt And Kills An Indian 54 Louis 54 Martin 21 25 47 48 49 62 63 64 Martin Captured By Indians 62 Martin Goes With Three Indians On A Fall Hunt 63 Martin Kills All Three Indians And Escapes 63 Miss 64 Mrs 49 Susan 48
WHEAT, Betsey 19
WHELAN, James A 300
WHERRY, John 121
WHETZAL, James 237 Martin 229
WHETZEL, Louis C 281
WHIPKEY, 198 Alexander 131 192 194 Alexander Jr 197 Charles 288 Eli 196 199 Everett 278 Freeman 210 Jacob 197 John 206 Josiah 205
WHITE, Alexander 233 Alpha O 220 Charles 140 250 David C 192 Edward 198 200 245 George Raymond 280 H S 146 182 183 Jacob 188 John 274 John W 192 Joseph 117 M Z 311 Milton B 238 Mrs Spencer 296 Pewgrine 187 Richmond Lee 272 Vachel M 196 William W 276 Wm 126 154 Zachariah A 189
WHITELAW, Reed South 273
WHITELY, Albert H 210
WHITESIDE, Lester T 272
WHITKANAC, John 188
WHITLATCH, Clarence B 284 Clinton 274 Frank 276 287 George 140 253 287 George L 250 J V 270 Jacob 130 Jesse B 222 John W 281 Noah 223
WHITLEY, Leonard 302
WHITNEY, Ruth 173
WHITTAKER, Alexander Q 137
WHITTINGHAM, Harley Otto 287 James 237
WHORTON, Elbert 281 290 John 241

WHYPAMABI, Daxutres 278
WIATT, Gilbert W 278
WIBLIN, Joe S 275 290
WICHTERSON, Jacob 172
WICK, John James 272 Matthew P 277
WIDOWS, George W 131
WIEDEBUSCH, August 265
WILBER, Charles 141
WILEY, Sadie 169
WILHELM, Archie R 270 Jesse 273
WILKINSON, E 302 James M 129 131 264 James R 290 Jas R 272
WILLARD, Henry 192 Peter E 142 Porter 254 T E 301
WILLIAMS, 77 Andrew J 192 C M 121 C W 226 D F 172 Edward 142 253 Frank 302 George 279 Grafton E 284 Isaac 10 11 65 75 76 78 John M 290 John Maywood 278 291 Marion 237 Mr 79 Mrs 10 75 79 80 Peter 206 Price 271 Ralph Caldwell 287 Rebecca 77 78 Robert T 270 S H 237 Thomas 261 263 Thomas H 135 W H 237 Wesley 237 William 117
WILLIAMSON, 34 C D 268 271 302 F L 242 Frank 258 Franklin W 134 Thos H 245
WILLIS, Jesse 275
WILLISON, Amos 250
WILSON, A W 126 Amos 140 Arleigh O 280 C H 267 C J 169 Chas Conn 274 Daniel 278 Daniel L 267 David 29 30 208 Ellen 297 Ensign 29 Ephraim 262 George D 200 George W 206 Harry W 270 I B 299 James 192 232 John 29 114 208 304 John E 300 Joseph 112 121 Joseph G 233 Joseph H 135 245 L G 169 Lawrence 279 O P 299 Oscar 299 Samuel 121 232 Samuel B 275 Samuel H 232 Samuel W 140 250 Samuel W Jr 250 Stanley B 267 Stanley Bruce 271 Thomas J 282 Thomas Samuel 277 Thos G 272

WILSON (continued) Walter E 287 Wm A 271 Wm D 200 Wylie 275
WILSON, Report of 29
WINESBERRY, Benj 142
WINESBURG, Barney 253
WINGROVE, John 131
WINSEL, James L 226
WINTER, Albert S 158 185 Charles Schrader 275
WINTERS, Alonzo 239 Harvey 239 Isaac 239 241 J W 127 154 John 119 120 127 188 Myrtle 273
WIRT, W M 156 158 172 184
WISEMAN, Isaac 57
WISENBALER, Earl 286 George William 281
WITHERS, 18 19
WODISKE, William 274 291
WOLFE, George W 142 James H 301 John 140 218 250
WOMEN RENDER SERVICE IN THE DEFENSE, 31
WOOD, A 108 Asa 141 250 Asa T 269 Leah 169 Newton 218 Oakley Lemuel 279 Sanford 141 251 William 218
WOODBURN, Alexander G 198 200 Charles D 140 250 Ethel 296 Grace 296 Mildred 171 William 109 110 Winford 274
WOODEN CANNON, 33
WOODRUFF, Dorsey 285 John L 284 Ralph 268 271 S H 294 Sarah Margaret 296
WOODRUG, R L 271
WOODS, James 197 John 210 Joseph D 283 Mrs J L 297 Preston H 192 Robert 111
WOODWARD, Roy 269
WOODY, Amy 171
WORK, Alfred 192
WORKMAN, Benj M 238 Charles H V 287 Daniel 241 Riley 300

WORLD WAR, 267 Aero Sector
Signal Service 272 Aid In War
Funds 293 Artillery 269 Captured
By Germans 292 Casualty List
290 Coast Artillery 271 Coast
Artillery Corps 271 Died In Camp
292 Died of Wounds 290
Engineers 272 Field Artillery 270
General Pershing Club 300
Infantry 268 Killed By Accident
290 Killed In Action 290 List of
Commissioned Officers 267 List
of Volunteers 268 Lost At Sea 292
Marines 270 Medical Department
271 Men Entrained for Baltimore
Dental College Oct 21 1918 289
Men Entrained for Bethany
College Oct 10 1918 289 Men
Entrained for Bethany College Oct
15 1918 289 Men Entrained for
Camp American University Feb 10
1918 277 Men Entrained for Camp
Custer Sept 1 1918 286 Men
Entrained for Camp Devens Oct 17
1917 276 Men Entrained for Camp
Dix Apr 16 1918 279 Men
Entrained for Camp Dix Mar 28
1918 278 Men Entrained for Camp
Dix May 6 1918 279 Men
Entrained for Camp Dodge Apr 29
1918 279 Men Entrained for Camp
Dodge Jan 22 1918 277 Men
Entrained for Camp Forest July 29
1918 285 Men Entrained for
Camp Gordon May 29 1918 282
Men Entrained for Camp Grant
June 3 1918 282 Men Entrained
for Camp Green Aug 30 1918 286
Men Entrained for Camp Greenleaf
Aug 29 1918 286 Men
Entrained for Camp Greenleaf Feb
25 1918 277 Men Entrained for
Camp Greenleaf June 25 1918 282
Men Entrained for Camp Greenleaf
June 6 1918 282 Men Entrained
for Camp Greenleaf Mar 10 1918
277

WORLD WAR (continued)
Men Entrained for Camp Greenleaf
Mar 13 1918 277 Men Entrained
for Camp Humphrys May 28 1918
282 Men Entrained for Camp
Humphrys Oct 15 1918 289 Men
Entrained for Camp Humphrys
Sept 10 1918 288 Men Entrained
for Camp Humphrys Sept 6 1918
287 Men Entrained for Camp
Jackson May 28 1918 282 Men
Entrained for Camp Kelley Field
Apr 1 1918 278 Men Entrained for
Camp Kelley Field Feb 25 1918
277 Men Entrained for Camp
Kelley Field Mar 25 1918 278
Men Entrained for Camp Kelley
Field Mar 9 1918 277 Men
Entrained for Camp Lee Apr 2
1918 278 Men Entrained for Camp
Lee Apr 4 1918 279 Men
Entrained for Camp Lee Apr 7
1918 279 Men Entrained for Camp
Lee Aug 29 1918 285 Men
Entrained for Camp Lee June 26
1918 283 Men Entrained for Camp
Lee May 26 1918 280 Men
Entrained for Camp Lee Oct 27
1917 276 Men Entrained for Camp
Lee Oct 4 1917 275 Men
Entrained for Camp Lee Sept 10
1917 273 Men Entrained for Camp
Lee Sept 13 1918 288 Men
Entrained for Camp Lee Sept 20
1917 274 Men Entrained for Camp
Lee Sept 4 1918 286 Men
Entrained for Camp Lee Sept 5
1917 273 Men Entrained for Camp
Lee Sept 6 1917 273 Men
Entrained for Camp Lee Sept 7
1917 273 Men Entrained for Camp
Lee Sept 8 1917 273 Men
Entrained for Camp Lewis June 17
1918 282 Men Entrained for Camp
Meade Apr 26 1918 278 Men
Entrained for Camp Meade July 26
1918 283

WORLD WAR (continued)
Men Entrained for Camp Meade May 20 1918 280 Men Entrained for Camp Sevier May 17 1918 279 Men Entrained for Camp Sherman July 26 1918 283 Men Entrained for Camp Sherman May 24 1918 280 Men Entrained for Camp Sherman Oct 11 1917 276 Men Entrained for Camp Sherman Oct 23 1918 289 Men Entrained for Camp Sherman Sept 15 1918 288 Men Entrained for Camp Sherman Sept 4 1918 286 Men Entrained for Camp Shermen Dec 5 1917 276 Men Entrained for Camp Taylor Oct 23 1918 289 Men Entrained for Camp Taylor Sept 2 1918 286 Men Entrained for Camp Vancouver Barracks June 21 1918 282 Men Entrained for Camp Wadsworth May 22 1918 278 Men Entrained for Camp Walter Reed Hosp June 19 1918 282 Men Entrained for Camp Zac Taylor May 29 1918 282 Men Entrained for Columbus Barracks Aug 17 1918 285 Men Entrained for Columbus Barracks June 13 1918 282 Men Entrained for Columbus Barracks May 23 1918 280 Men Entrained for Columbus Barracks May 29 1918 282 Men Entrained for Columbus Barracks Oct 1 1918 288 Men Entrained for Fort Benjamin Harrison May 17 1918 280 Men Entrained for Fort Levenworth May 8 1918 279 Men Entrained for Fort Oglethorpe Feb 2 1918 277 Men Entrained for Fort Scriven Dec 20 1917 276 Men Entrained for Fort Scriven Jan 25 1918 277 Men Entrained for Fort Thomas May 13 1918 279 Men Entrained for Marietta College Oct 11 1918 289

WORLD WAR (continued)
Men Entrained for Med Supply Camp May 22 1918 280 Men Entrained for Ohio College Surgery Nov 11 1918 290 Men Entrained for Ohio Wesleyan College Oct 5 1918 288 Men Entrained for Ohio Wesleyan College Oct 9 1918 289 Men Entrained for Penn State College Oct 5 1918 289 Men Entrained for Pitt University Oct 1 1918 288 Men Entrained for Richmond Commercial Club Aug 31 1918 286 Men Entrained for Sergt Gen Office Aug 17 1918 285 Men Entrained for U S Marine Surgery Nov 11 1918 290 Men Entrained for University of Akron May 15 1918 279 Men Entrained for University of Pennsylvania Oct 11 1918 289 Men Entrained for University of Wva Aug 15 1918 285 Men Entrained for Vancouver Barracks June 17 1918 282 Men Entrained for Wesleyan College Oct 3 1918 288 Men Entrained for West Virginia University Nov 5 1918 289 Men Entrained for West Virginia University Oct 2 1918 288 Men Entrained for West Virginia University Oct 29 1918 289 Miscellaneous 272 Missing In Action 292 National Guards 270 Navy 269 Officers Training Camp 271 One Thousand Dollar Club 299 Red Cross Nurses 273 Reserve Officers Training Camp 271 Unclassified 272 War Hero Club 293 Women's Saving Stamp Club 294 Wounded 291
WOSICK, Charles 279
WRIGHT, Charles 272 Florence Anna 171 Joseph 135 Josephus 245 Nathan 254 Thadeus 266 W S 237 Wm 130
WUCELICH, John 268 291

WYCHOFF, William 250
WYKART, Nicholas 114 Samuel 120
    130
WYRICK, J W 226
YAHRLING, Chas F A 203
YANNI, Francisco 285
YATES, Henry Robert 284 Pearl R
    292 Pearl Robert 287 Thomas
    Mcland 277 William T 280 291
YEAGER, George 269
YEATER, Archie 169 Chancy L 281
    Chris E 300 Clarence B 288
    Harvey U 271 J W 173 John B 285
    N W 173
YODERS, George 250
YOHO, Bess 297 Bismark C 304 Blair
    302 Cecil May 304 Clem James
    276 Cyrus 303 E C 294 Ella 298
    Elmer Elsworth 287 F C 300 F F
    302 F V 172 Frank Francis 276
    Friend 294 H B 126 Henry 70
    Henry Attacked By Indians 70
    James D 140 250 Jehu 304 Joshua
    Earl 274 Laura L 303 Mrs E C 297
    304 Mrs F L 297 Mrs J H 298 N R
    300 302 Nola 304 Okey Espey
    281 Orion 274 Peter 126 R C 266
    267 Ransel 281 Robert C 185
    Rosco Floyd 275 Samuel 254
    Sidney 268 Sidney F 271 Tola 295

YOHO (continued)
    V C 300 W P 302 William Jacob
    281
YOKUM, Clarence E 270 Thomas L
    270 Thurman 270
YONKINS, Jesse Edgar 275
YOST, Joseph 272 Oscar 277
YOUNG, Catherine 172 Charles A
    286 Clarence R 272 Frank A 280
    Geneva B 169 Guy 271 Guy
    Edwin 277 James 142 John F 183
    John Frederick 281 Nora 171 T E
    294 302 Wm F 142
YOUNKEN, 47 Daniel 265 Samuel F
    226 Thomas 46
YOUST, Jacob 250
YUZAPOS, John Bell 281
ZAMANTASKI, Amanoilis 274
ZANE, 47 49 Andrew 8 17 25 Col 18
    20 31 32 34 Ebenezer 8 9 25 30
    76 Elizabeth 31 33 Jonathan 8 25
    76 Mrs 31 80 Mrs Ebenezer 25 79
    Silas 8 9 25 31 33
ZANE'S CABIN, 31
ZEDIKER, Nicholas 120
ZERRAS, Peter 279
ZIMMERMAN, Carrie 171
ZINK, H J 294 303 Joseph 138 139
    250 Reuben 126 146 154
ZUARANTA, Guiseppe 281

www.ingramcontent.com/pod-product-compliance
Lightning Source LLC
Chambersburg PA
CBHW070717160426
43192CB00009B/1220